KT-489-869

The
ORGANIC
GARDENER'S
Home Reference

◆

A Plant-by-Plant Guide to Growing Fresh, Healthy Food

The

ORGANIC
GARDENER'S
Home Reference

◆

A Plant-by-Plant Guide to Growing Fresh, Healthy Food

Tanya Denckla

HOUGHALL COLLEGE LIBRARY	
CLASS No.	635.0484
ACC No.	96410
ORDER No.	DП3

A Garden Way Publishing Book

STOREY

Storey Communications, Inc.
Schoolhouse Road
Pownal, Vermont 05261

Edited by Deborah Balmuth

Cover photographs (left to right): Courtesy of National Gardening Bureau; © Storey Communications, Inc.;
© Photo/Nats by Betsy Fuchs; © Storey Communications, Inc. by David J. Bausman; © Photo/Nats by Priscilla Connell

Back cover photograph by Cecil Cobb

Cover design by Meredith Maker

Text design and production by Wanda Harper Joyce

Line drawings by Melody Sarecky

Indexed by Northwind Editorial Services

The author gratefully acknowledges permission to reproduce the following copyrighted material:

Adapted passages from *Nut Tree Culture in North America*, edited by Richard A. Jaynes. Copyright 1979 by Northern Nut Growers Association, Inc. Permission granted by Richard A. Jaynes.

"Pear Cold Storage Chart" and adapted passages on grape pruning from *Backyard Fruits and Berries*, by Diane E. Bilderback and Dorothy Hinshaw Patent. Copyright 1984 by Diane E. Bilderback and Dorothy Hinshaw Patent. Permission granted by Rodale Press, Inc: Emmaus, PA, 18098.

Vegetable storage conditions (temperature, humidity, and length of storage) from *Knott's Handbook for Vegetable Growers, 3rd Edition*, by James E. Knott and edited by Oscar Anthony Lorenz and Donald N. Maynard. Copyright 1988 by John Wiley & Sons, Inc. Permission granted by John Wiley & Sons, Inc.

Food storage conditions and times from *The Self-Sufficient Suburban Garden*, by Jeff Ball. Copyright 1985 by Jeff Ball. Permission granted by Jeff Ball.

Excerpts from apple and plum rootstock charts and "Intercropping For Pest Reduction: Successful Scientific Trials," from *Designing and Maintaining Your Edible Landscape Naturally*, by Robert Kourik. Copyright 1986 by Robert Kourik. Permission granted by Robert Kourik.

Copyright © 1994 Tanya Denckla

All rights reserved. No part of this book may be reproduced without written permission from the publisher, except by a reviewer who may quote brief passages or reproduce illustrations in a review with appropriate credits; nor may any part of this book be reproduced, stored in a retrieval system, or transmitted in any form or by any means — electronic, mechanical, photocopying, recording, or other — without written permission from the publisher.

The information in this book is true and complete to the best of our knowledge. All recommendations are made without guarantee on the part of the author or Storey Communications, Inc. The author and publisher disclaim any liability in connection with the use of this information. For additional information, please contact Storey Communications, Inc., Schoolhouse Road, Pownal, Vermont 05261.

Garden Way Publishing was founded in 1973 as part of the Garden Way Incorporated Group of Companies, dedicated to bringing gardening information and equipment to as many people as possible. Today the name "Garden Way Publishing" is licensed to Storey Communications, Inc., in Pownal, Vermont. For a complete list of Garden Way Publishing titles, call 1-800-827-8673. Garden Way Incorporated manufactures products in Troy, New York, under the Troy-Bilt® brand including garden tillers, chipper/shredders, mulching mowers, sicklebar mowers, and tractors. For information on any Garden Way Incorporated product, please call 1-800-345-4454.

Printed in the United States by Book Press
First Printing, December 1993

Library of Congress Cataloging-in-Publication Data

Denckla, Tanya, 1956–
    The organic gardener's home reference : a plant-by-plant guide to growing fresh, healthy food. / Tanya Denckla.
       p. cm.
    Rev. ed. of: Gardening at a glance. c1991.
    "A Garden Way Publishing book."
    Includes bibliographical references and index.
    ISBN 0-88266-840-4 (hc) — ISBN 0-88266-839-0 (pbk)
       1. Vegetable gardening — Handbooks, manuals, etc. 2. Organic gardening — Handbooks, manuals, etc. 3. Herb gardening — Handbooks, manuals, etc. 4. Fruit-culture — Handbooks, manuals, etc. 5. Nuts — Handbooks, manuals, etc.
    I. Denckla, Tanya, 1956– Gardening at a glance. II. Title.
SB324.3.D47   1994
635' .0484 — dc20
                                  93-22835
                                     CIP

Table of Contents

HOUGHALL
COLLEGE
LIBRARY

Acknowledgments

Special Awards

For Making This Book Possible

W. Donner Denckla, for invaluable guidance on major directions, content, presentation, and concepts such as open-field hydroponics and self-sustaining gardens. His unflagging support and forest-from-the-trees perspective kept me going through numerous setbacks, for he deeply believed that the project was useful not only for our own purposes but also helpful to others.

Marlene Taylor, for extensive research assistance, attention to detail, proofreading, copy editing, and marketing. Her continuous technical support and enthusiasm reduced this from a herculean task to a manageable endeavor. I also am indebted to her for conceiving the final title of the first edition of this book, *Gardening at a Glance*.

Jennifer Taylor, for research assistance in updating the book for a second edition. Her careful work through several months in 1992 made it possible for me to give my publisher important revisions to keep the book current.

Special Thanks

For Making This Book More Probable

The following people all generously shared their expertise and experience during their busiest of seasons; their contributions enriched this book immeasurably and helped it grow to maturity:

Doug Britt, president of Ag Life — for reviewing both the insect and disease charts.

John Brittain, president of Nolin River — for numerous helpful suggestions on nut varieties.

Rosalind Creasy, author, edible landscaper, *L.A. Times* syndicated columnist — for a detailed review and helpful contributions to the entire manuscript, as well as for suggestions about layout and regional issues.

Galen Dively, Ph.D., entomologist, University of Maryland — for a detailed review of the macro pest charts, and many valuable contributions.

Frank Gouin, Ph.D., horticulturist, Chairman of the University of Maryland's Department of Horticulture — for reviewing the herb entries, and for kindly arranging review of the vegetable section too.

Patrick J. Hartmann, president of Hartmann's Plantation, Inc. — for suggesting appropriate blueberry cultivars and help with *Phytophthera cinnomomi*.

Richard A. Jaynes, Ph.D., geneticist, president of the Northern Nut Growers Association — for reviewing the nut entries and thoughtful suggestions on nut varieties.

Clay Stark Logan, president of Stark Bro's Nurseries and Orchards, Co., and **Joe Preczewski, Ph.D.,** director of Stark Bro's Field Research and Product Development — for reviewing the fruit entries and suggesting appropriate fruit varieties.

Alan MacNab, Ph.D., plant pathologist, Pennsylvania State University — for valuable contributions to vegetable disease remedies and especially for raising critical issues of presentation.

Charles McClurg, Ph.D., horticulturist, University of Maryland — for reviewing the vegetable entries.

John E. Miller, president of Miller Nurseries — for reviewing the fruit entries and suggesting appropriate fruit varieties.

Tom Mills, president of Indiana Walnut Products — for suggesting nut varieties.

Carl Totemeier, Ph.D., horticulturist, retired vice-president of the New York Botanical Gardens — for a very detailed review and contributions to the entire manuscript.

And many thanks to the following people for their kind support and assistance in various forms:

Jeff Ball, author, communicator, president of New Response, Inc.

Judy Gillan, of The Organic Foods Production Association of North America (OFPANA)

Lewis Hill, author, former owner of Hillcrest Nursery

Richard Packauskas, Ph.D., entomologist, University of Connecticut

Robert D. Raabe, Ph.D., plant pathologist, University of California, Berkeley

Preface

I marvel at how tiny seeds of all kinds germinate — mere potential transformed into dynamic, never quite predictable life. Such has been the history of this compendium.

The beginning seed for this book was planted in metropolitan Washington D.C, where I played at gardening in a tiny backyard. Starting with a few peach and pear trees, I slowly expanded the garden to include some perennial flowers, herbs, and annual vegetables. In those first few years my little retreat thrived and, to my untrained eye, seemed a bucolic environment for unlimited growth. Laissez-faire was my motto. Gardening seemed ever so easy.

It was about year three that the fruit trees signalled a transformation from simple fun to complex war. Peach tree borer, fireblight, Japanese beetles — as each new pest invaded and the trees suffered increasingly more serious damage, I experienced parental panic attack. No mere fungus or insect would harm *my* plants. To my partner Donner's horror, I pulled out the "big gun" insecticides, fungicides — anything with a scientific name on the label. And I sprayed everything, everywhere, sprayed mercilessly. I had entered full battle mode, re-enacting the ancient war of Man versus Nature. Control would be established.

Needless to say, I might have won the skirmish that summer, but the war was already lost. The garden ecosystem, frail and imbalanced from a lack of proper nurturing for sustained growth, was further weakened not strengthened, by my panic spraying. As a natural consequence, pests renewed their attack the next year, with increased strength and a vengeance. Two seasons later, with regretful hindsight, to cleanse the garden of its continued abcess and to end the futile struggle, I cut the fruit trees to the ground.

Never again did I spray wholesale. From Donner, a physician who ardently believes in a *systems* approach to all living things, I gained understanding and respect for the delicate ecosystem in a garden. I learned the value of spot spraying. Reading more, I learned to avoid high N, P, and K fertilizers that can kill earthworms and other beneficial garden helpers. Spiders, once a sure way to make me shriek, became a welcome sight. At heart, I learned an *attitude* that, if nothing else, transformed angry garden warrior into neophyte garden steward.

Real strong on attitude. However, still real weak on knowledge. At this stage, some friends and I were ready to buy a country property where we hoped to build a model self-sufficient farm. To divide labor, we decided I would plan the food and flower gardens. With renewed gusto, I delved into accumulating heaps of garden magazines and books. Months of reading, however, resulted in frustrations and feeling so overwhelmed that I was almost ready to quit before a single seed had been planted. Gardening, surely, could not be so complicated. Why was a clear picture of, say, *tomato* so hard to achieve? One book might be good on tomato pests, but lack information on planting times or varieties. Another might have a lot of information on tomato, but scatter it through various charts and sections, causing page-flipping fingeritis and more frustration — not to mention the confusion brought on when two books gave conflicting information. I felt I would never be able to *really* plan a garden.

As a last ditch attempt to rationalize what I was reading, and to avoid twenty books strewn over the floor to find one answer, I started to centralize information on my home computer. Slowly, a database took shape. Someone noted it was becoming almost, well, a *book*. And much later — a full four years of research and compilation later — someone asked for a copy of the *book* when it was done.

Book? Another seed began to germinate. By now my small Washington garden had recuperated from the earlier pharmaceutical rampage. Though it wasn't a great showpiece, it was thriving from a minimalistic and organic approach. The farm garden had been put on hold as terra-forming and massive building commenced. A little head scratching led to some research into publishing, consultation with expert growers, and hours of discussion with farm cohorts — all eventually led me to take a huge gulp of air and plunge into the ocean of self-publishing.

And what a wonderful swim it has been! Reviews streaming in, letters from grateful gardeners, and orders more numerous than I could have imagined for such an ugly-duckling reference book. Most rewarding has been the thanks from readers. From small backyard gardeners to larger market gardeners, you have thanked me for creating a sourcebook that helps you do what you love to do, better and quicker. What a satisfying feeling, to know the book accomplishes what was intended — to make gardening a little easier and more fun.

Perhaps the final thrill to this adventure has been Storey Communication's desire to publish it. The offer came at a good time when I wanted to move on to other projects. I couldn't have asked for a better shepherd for this project.

The Natural Gardener's Companion was first published under the title *Gardening at a Glance*, under the imprint "Wooden Angel Publishing." Many readers have asked, "From whence the name Wooden Angel Publishing?" Our country farm has a most bizarre shape that one day, while examining an aerial view and plat, evoked for Donner the image of a Christmas "wooden angel" ornament. The shape is simple: head, wing curved back toward the sky, long body, and skirt slightly curving outward. Wooden Angel stuck as the farm's name, and it seemed only fitting to name the publishing business after its inspiration.

Now a city woman turned country "girl," I enjoy gardening in Virginia's Shenandoah Valley. Close by, in West Virginia, the ever more beautiful Wooden Angel Farm is continually developing and evolving. In my own little backyard plots, I gain a little more expertise and experiment with a few more unusual edible plants every year. I annually add notes in the columns of this book, and every year it becomes a shade more brown from garden soil. Since publishing the book, I have expanded my work with environmental causes to co-found and become director of a nonprofit citywide beautification organization. I've also become an active mediator and facilitator and hope, someday, to use these skills in the environmental arena.

In the first edition, I assumed and mistakenly stated that this is not a primary text. Since then, beginners have used this book with no other helping text to start their first garden. It is also being used as a text by the Oglalla Lakota College for courses in organic gardening. So use this resource as you see fit, whether you are a beginner or a professional. Most important, I hope this reference helps you *read less and plant more seeds!* To paraphrase a special film, *plant it and you will grow.*

With peace and humor,

Tanya Denckla
Harrisonburg, Virginia
April 1993

Garden Stewardship

An organic garden is not a machine. It is a living system of balanced forces between, for example, predator and prey, and these forces are always in flux. Soil composition, air quality, water, birds, bugs, weeds — these are just a few of the forces that determine the nature and health of your garden. Your role as garden steward is to *encourage* the balance in your favor, not to take over nature's role in the name of achieving perfection.

Efforts to control or impose a balance for picture-perfect produce can eventually backfire. Many growers have aimed for this perfection because consumers preferred and then demanded unblemished produce. A common result is that the grower's land may not have pests, but it also may not have earthworms in the soil, birds in the fields, or beneficial predatory insects. This may seem benign, but is not. Many of the practices used to obtain high yields of unblemished produce, for a variety of complex reasons, eventually promote the loss of topsoil, loss of water penetration, and loss of biologically available nutrients. Thus the soil depends more and more on human-provided nutrients.

Our desire for perfect produce, among other factors, and the associated agricultural practices of this century have led to unprecedented conditions that might be called *open-field hydroponics.* Hydroponics is a method for growing crops in greenhouses. It mechanically delivers to plants every macro- and micronutrient. Hydroponic plants grow in various inert materials, from gravel to sand, that can structurally support plant and root growth. The term, open-field hydroponics, indicates a similar situation in fields where the soil is increasingly inert and provides structural support but contributes little nutritionally to plant growth.

Many small and large-scale growers are alarmed by soil-depletion and related trends, for both ecological and economical reasons. Many have adopted *sustainable agriculture* as a goal. Specific definitions of sustainable agriculture may differ, but it generally refers to practices that are viable over long periods of time, both environmentally and economically. Sustainable agriculture strives, for example, for soil that can produce crops reliably without nutrient depletion and with minimal human amendments. Sustainable agriculture is a philosophical shift for the gardener away from control to cooperation, from master to steward.

> ### ANNALS OF PEST CONTROL
> - Percentage increase of U.S. pesticide use since 1940: 3,000
> - Percentage increase of potency of U.S. pesticides since 1940: 1,000
> - Percentage of U.S. crops lost to insects in 1940: 31
> - Percentage of U.S. crops lost to insects today: 37
> - Percentage decline in pesticide use in Sweden between 1985 and 1990: 50
> - Percentage decline in crop yields in Sweden between 1985 and 1990: 0
>
> (from *Greenpeace*, Jul/Aug 1991)

The role of backyard steward is not hard to achieve, especially if adopted at the outset. One of its most important precepts is, *feed the soil, not the plants.* The role is perhaps most demanding during the planning phase, when you make crucial decisions about where to put your garden, what varieties to plant, when and where to plant them, how to feed the soil, where to put the compost pile (or have one at all), what kind of mulch to use, and — perhaps most important — how perfect you wish your produce to appear.

It is these decisions that will help you avoid the quick chemical fix. Some farmers have actually likened chemical sprays and fertilizers to cocaine: once started, an addictive cycle begins that is difficult to stop. The quick "fix" can take a long time to unfix. Some trials in Israel and elsewhere indicate that farms transitioning away from chemical inputs initially obtain lower yields, for a period of 3 to 5 years, following which yields increase to match and then sometimes exceed those obtained with chemicals. This is a good reminder of the long-term effects of chemical inputs and the need to maintain a long-term perspective on your garden health.

As steward, you may decide to avoid even the so-called organic sprays such as copper-based fungicides because they can sometimes kill the garden's best friend, earthworms. On the other hand, your goals may dictate using some sprays for limited and highly targeted purposes. The issue is to define your own goals in advance and the reasons for them, and then stick to them. In the absence of such goals, the temptation to zap this or that pest during the growing season may become habitual.

The Self-Sustaining Garden

Another desirable goal beyond stewardship for the backyard gardener is a self-sustaining garden. A self-sustaining garden supplies all of its own essential nutrients for balanced growth, from organic matter for compost to micronutrients for healthy plants. It doesn't require importation of beneficial insects, for example, because they are already there. It doesn't require the application of lime to buffer the effects of acid soil, because earthworms and compost do the buffering for you. A self-sustaining garden is, in many ways, the extreme opposite of open-field hydroponics: a diametrically opposed approach with diametrically opposed results. The former has been effective without any help from humans for millions of years, and the latter has already displayed severe limitations within 40 years.

As steward of a self-sustaining garden, your first job is to recognize that the forces in your garden will never be in "perfect" balance. There will always be some plant damage. The plants in your garden do not come with unconditional guarantees because they do not come out of a factory. Your second job is patience. It usually takes several years to establish an ecosystem that operates in your favor — an ecosystem with earthworms, insect-eating birds, beneficial predatory insects, soil with organic matter sufficient to both drain well and retain water to prevent runoff, and soil nutrient levels that support healthy plant growth.

The advantage of a self-sustaining garden is that it requires the least amount of money and time in the long run. You may need to invest in a first colony of earthworms (if there is none already there), to build or buy bird houses, to buy compost and organic matter (before your garden produces it for you), and perhaps even to buy irrigation soaker hoses and row cover material. But these investments should pay you back many times over in several years with a healthy garden that doesn't require lots of imported materials or time-consuming pest controls.

Important Friends

Earthworms are the gardener's best friend. Through both their tunneling and nitrogen-rich castings (excrement) they perform all the following jobs for you — free of charge!
Earthworms:

- Aerate the soil, improving oxygen availability to plant roots
- Improve water retention capacity, decreasing your need to water
- Keep the soil loose and friable, improving plant root capacity for growth
- Raise important minerals from the subsoil to the topsoil where plants can use them
- Counteract leaching out of nutrients by improvement of water retention
- Break up hardpan soils, which are inhospitable to plant growth
- Homogenize soil elements so they're more evenly available to plants
- Create fertile channels for plant roots
- Liberate essential nutrients into a form that is soluble and available to plants
- Neutralize soils that are too acid or too alkaline for healthy plant growth
- Balance out organic matter in the soil, so you needn't worry about exceeding the 5 to 8 percent optimal level
- Enhance the soil's environment for growing healthy self-sustaining plants

Take the following steps to protect earthworms.

- Till minimally, because tilling can disturb and kill earthworms and other soil microorganisms through mechanical abrasion, drying out, and disruption of their environment.

- When you do till, keep it shallow for the reasons above. An optimal tilling depth is 3 inches. To expose the eggs and cocoons of some insects to hungry birds, you may need to till up to 6 inches. Generally, unless you are creating a first year bed and need to rototill up to 12 or 14 inches, you should never till deeper than 6 inches.

- Avoid heavy doses of chemical fertilizers because these can harm soil microorganisms and decrease earthworm activity. Excessive nitrogen fertilizer not only harms the soil, whatever its source, but also has been shown by the USDA to cut the vitamin C content in some green vegetables. Use compost instead to provide a slow release food to the soil and plants.

- Avoid uncomposted manure of any kind because it contains disease pathogens and seeds. If you must use manure, make sure it has been composted up to 160°F.

- Water regularly, and avoid excesses. Flooding or overwatering, and drought or drying out of the soil can kill earthworms as well as soil microorganisms.

Compost is another major player in the self-sustaining garden. Compost, essentially, is any organic material, including manure, that has decayed into a simpler form by the action of anaerobic or aerobic bacteria, depending on the composting method. *Humus* is any partially decomposed organic material, vegetable or animal, that is used to improve soil quality by mixing it into the soil. *Mulch* is any material used to cover the soil, whether nutrient-poor such as newspaper, nutrient-neutral such as plastic, or nutrient-rich such as compost.

Compost can be used wherever humus or mulch is recommended. The process of composting reduces the original bulk of the organic material by one-fourth to one-tenth. So, where a thick mulch is desired, you may prefer uncomposted material such as straw or chopped leaves. On the other hand, if you have access to large amounts of compost, it is a highly beneficial mulch because it also feeds the soil. Compost does the following:

- Feeds the soil and its creatures gently, unlike chemical fertilizers that can kill earthworms and other beneficial organisms

- Lasts a long time because it releases nutrients slowly in a readily available form, unlike chemical fertilizers that provide a quick boost and then peter out

- Improves soil drainage by adding porous organic matter (humus)

- Improves water retention, again by the addition of organic matter (humus)

- Provides food that usually has a neutral pH (unlike some chemical fertilizers), and also buffers the soil against rapid pH changes

- Builds organic matter in the soil, which improves oxygen diffusion

- Feeds the earthworms

- Doesn't depend on chemical manufacturers and thus doesn't contribute to any form of environmental pollution or depletion of natural resources

- Is easy to make in any home garden or farm

Compost is a multipurpose tool. Some people apply large quantities to their garden, but a healthy minimum is to spread 1 inch of compost through your garden every year in the spring before planting. It's helpful to apply another layer during the growing season. You can use compost as:

- Fertilizer, before planting, at planting, after planting, and in the fall after harvest

- Mulch, to help retain soil moisture, to keep summer soil cool, to keep winter soil warm, to smother weeds, and in some cases to discourage pests

- Side-Dressing, during the growing season as an extra food-boost to the plant

Compost can be bought commercially (many of the suppliers listed in Appendix C offer it). It is also easy to make. Compost is an ideal way to recycle many different household items such as kitchen waste, newspaper, typing paper (no gloss, no colors other than black), paper napkins, unwaxed cardboard, sawdust, or other carbon-rich materials.

There are many different ways to compost, from production of 50 pounds in the backyard to thousands of tons on a commercial scale. It can be made in dug holes or in windrows, in silos or in barrels, in layers on top of the ground or in huge concrete vats. Because there are so many different methods and possible ingredients, a full discussion of composting is beyond the scope of this book.

Understanding that bacteria are living organisms that chemically "chew up" the organic material in a compost pile will help you identify the optimal conditions for compost. Aerobic (oxygen-requiring) bacteria work faster, are usually less smelly, and generate higher temperatures in the compost pile that can help kill certain disease pathogens. To favor these bacteria, you must either

BASIC COMPOSTING PRINCIPLES

Size

■ For the most rapid composting on a small scale, aim to build a pile at least 3' x 3' x 3'

Materials

■ Combine roughly equal parts of dry plant material and green plant material to achieve the desired carbon-to-nitrogen ratio of 30:1

   Green plant material can include grass clippings, old flowers, weeds, fresh vegetable, and fruit kitchen wastes. Leafy materials that were cut green and allowed to dry are still considered green.

   Dried plant material can include autumn leaves, straw, dried and cut-up woody material, sawdust, and shredded white paper, newspaper, paper bags, cardboard boxes and cartons. Straw is the hollow dried stems of grain-producing plants, whereas hay ("green" material) is the entire plant (stem and leaves) and is therefore much higher in nitrogen. Some studies show birch and blackthorn (Prunus spinosa) leaves added to compost help restore exhausted soil.

   Do not include carnivorous animal manure, wood ashes, charcoal, animal meat, soils with a basic pH (such as those in California), and diseased plants.

■ Use a wide variety of materials, if possible, because this provides a better balance of pH, nutrients, and microbial organisms

■ Do not use bug-infested or diseased plants

■ Shred or cut material (including kitchen waste), when possible, before adding it to the pile; the smaller particles decompose faster, but having some larger materials helps improve aeration

■ For the most rapid results, do not add material to the heap once it has started composting

Care

■ Cover your pile with a tarp, black plastic, or a lid of some kind; sunlight kills the bacteria that do the composting work, so a pile exposed to sunlight will not compost well in the outer layers.

■ Water your pile regularly to keep it evenly moist at about the 50 percent moisture level, so it has the consistency of a damp sponge, moist but not soggy. A dry pile will not compost at all, while an over-watered or soggy pile will simply rot. One option is to uncover the pile during rain and recover it promptly to trap the moisture.

■ You may want to add commercially available composting activator, a fine powder that contains helpful bacteria to speed along decomposition. Much like using a sourdough starter mix instead of trusting in the presence of sufficient yeast organisms in the air, the composting activator is not necessary but can be used to speed results.

■ Turn your pile regularly to aerate and provide sufficient oxygen to the bacteria, every two to seven days. Backyard piles often fail because oxygen cannot penetrate through the pile. It is possible to overventilate, but this problem would generally occur only when the pile is ventilated through the sides and bottom and is also turned on something like a daily basis. Some sources warn that turning piles reduces nitrogen levels in the final product, another reason to avoid zealous turning.

turn the pile regularly, somehow introduce oxygen into the pile (such as with perforated pipes), or make the pile small enough so that oxygen can readily diffuse into the pile. In contrast, anaerobic bacteria do not require oxygen to work, take longer to accomplish the job, and do not generate high temperatures. Earthworms in an anaerobic compost pile will encourage some aerobic activity and will therefore expedite the composting process. Their castings will also make it a richer source of nutrients. Aerobic methods can produce compost in as little as 14 days, but the pile needs to be built all at once. Anaerobic methods may take up to 1 year to produce compost, but the pile can be built slowly over the summer.

Both aerobic and anaerobic composting methods require moisture, since dry bacteria are "dead" bacteria. Both also need a large excess of carbon compared to nitrogen, usually a ratio of 30:1. In the absence of a large excess of carbonaceous material, bacteria digest their meal in a malodorous way, much like people eating beans. A compost pile that smells is usually working anaerobically and either needs more carbon material, needs to be turned, or both.

Certain materials are to be avoided. Under most circumstances, extremely high sources of nitrogen (for example, animal meat and carnivorous animal manure) not only give your pile indigestion, produce bacterial flatulence, and attract nuisance insects, but more important can contain disease pathogens. Diseased plant materials should also be avoided. Destroy diseased plant material by burial in an area away from your garden or by burning, if permitted. Although some diseases can be destroyed by the high temperatures generated in aerobic composting, most backyard gardeners cannot reliably depend on this result. The hottest temperatures occur at the center of the compost pile, so unless the pile is turned adequately and evenly mixed, certain parts of the pile may never reach the temperatures needed to destroy the disease pathogens. For a fuller discussion of composting, please consult sources in the Bibliography such as Stu Campbell's, *Let It Rot!*

Birds and bats that eat insects are other key aspects of a self-sustaining garden. They help keep the garden clean of flying and crawling insects, and some even eat grubs in the ground. The author and expert gardener Jeff Ball has written that insect damage in his garden virtually disappeared after putting up bird houses that attracted insect-eaters. What more needs to be said?

Beneficial insect-eating birds include bluebirds, downy woodpeckers, barn swallows, purple martins, sparrows, blackbirds, phoebes, Baltimore orioles, chickadees, juncos, purple finches, brown thrashers, warblers, chickens, ducks, and geese. Swallow-family birds, such as the purple martin, are often considered the most desirable insect-eaters. Purple martin "hotel" houses are expensive but well worth the initial investment because these birds eat prodigious amounts of above-ground insects and, although they migrate in the fall, become residents that return in the spring. Chickens, on the other hand, are always available in the fall and eat insects in, on, and above the soil. They're one of the most thorough garden cleaners to keep. If you do keep fowl, only allow them in the garden before planting, after plants have grown to maturity, and after harvest; do not allow them in the garden when seedlings are predominant. Bats are not at all the blood-sucking horrors legend would make of them. They have a voracious appetite for the insects they eat at night, and their houses are simple structures that are becoming widely available. Plants that attract birds include shrubs and trees with fruits such as hackberry, elderberry, mulberry, Japanese berry, and viburnum.

Bees, Wasps and Other Beneficial Insects are vital garden friends. Bees are nature's best pollinator, making possible the fruits and vegetables we all enjoy. Wasps, like other beneficial insects, not only prey on various destructive insects but also parasitize eggs, larvae, and adult insects. To attract wasps and other beneficial insects you can plant companion herbs (especially *Umbelliferae* herbs), flowers, and clovers around the edge of your garden.

Planning and Maintenance

To be self-sustaining, your garden should be able to defend itself from severe damage from most pests most of the time. Such natural defense is promoted by four major factors: sun, water, soil, and air circulation. All of these factors are interactive; each is necessary but not sufficient alone.

Start with location. Choose a sunny spot, preferably one with morning and afternoon sun. In humid, moist, or rainy regions where fungus can be expected, morning sun is especially important to dry the dew as quickly as possible. Try to locate the garden where it will get good air circulation; avoid low areas susceptible to pockets of fog and high locations with exposure to harsh winds.

If your soil is clay or sandy, mix in peat humus to improve drainage and water retention. Whatever the condition of your soil, you should consider building **raised beds**. Although they require an initial investment of time and sometimes of money, they will pay you back in many different ways over the years. Raised beds are a big step toward attaining the self-sustaining garden. Raised beds:

- Minimize soil compaction, because you never walk on the growing medium

- Have better oxygen availability to plant roots, because there is little soil compaction

- Drain better, because there is little soil compaction

- Retain water better, because there is little soil compaction

- Are easier to plant, weed, and maintain, because there is no soil compaction

- Have greater yields because of better penetration of air, water, and sunlight and also higher germination rates for early plantings

- Allow earlier and later planting as they warm up earlier in spring and hold heat longer in fall

- Allow greater root development, because of low soil compaction, good drainage, and oxygen diffusion

- Save space, since plants can be spaced closer together because you don't need room to walk around them

There are several different types of raised beds, and different ways of preparing them, some of which do not involve double-digging. Raised beds can have rounded tops, flat tops, rounded sides, or straight sides. A good discussion of raised beds and how to build them can be found in *High Yield Gardening* by Marjorie Hunt and Brenda Bortz (see Bibliography). Our preferred method is to build a contained raised bed 12 to 16 inches high, which allows you to sit on the edge while weeding or planting. An ideal size for a raised bed is 4 feet by 12 feet. This size lets you reach easily into the center of the bed without stepping onto the soil or stretching your arms too far.

You can build contained raised beds with a variety of nontoxic substances, such as stone, brick, concrete blocks, or untreated wood that is naturally rot-resistant such as cedar, cypress, or locust. In a food garden you should not use any treated lumber, whether or not "EPA-approved," such as lumber treated with chromated copper arsenate (CCA), creosote, or pentachlorophenol. Pressure-treated lumber is soaked with the preservative CCA. In fact, since 1984 the EPA has directed that all treated wood products should not be used anywhere they come into contact with food, animal feed, or direct or indirect contact with drinking water.

Nontoxic Preservative for Untreated Wood

If you wish to preserve untreated wood for raised beds, decks, picnic tables, or swing sets, the USDA suggests the following nontoxic preservative. Studies show it to be as effective as the highly toxic preservative pentachlorophenol, and it endures for 20 years.

3 cups exterior varnish or 1½ cups boiled linseed oil
1 ounce paraffin wax
Enough solvent (mineral spirits, paint thinner, or turpentine at room temperature) to make a total volume of 1 full gallon

In a double boiler, melt the paraffin (do not heat over direct flame!). Away from the heat vigorously stir the solvent, then slowly pour in the melted paraffin. Add the varnish or linseed oil and continue to stir thoroughly. Apply by dipping the untreated lumber into the mixture for 3 minutes or by applying a heavy coat. The wood can be painted when thoroughly dry.

Research studies on treated wood have found that the chemicals chromium, copper, and arsenic leach out in significant amounts into soil, into food crops, into beehives (where treated wood is now strictly prohibited), and onto hands in "wipe" tests on playground equipment. If you already have used treated lumber, you should create a plastic or other barrier between the lumber and soil. You may also want to test your soil to determine the amount of leachate already present. Toxin testing may be available from Timberleaf Soil Testing Services, 5569 State Street, Albany, OH 45710.

For noncontained raised beds, a quick and easy way to build a raised bed without double digging is to use a tractor outfitted with a 4- or 5-bottom plow and rotary hoe. Plow a row in one direction. Turn around and plow the same row in the other direction, which flips the soil twice and creates a raised bed. Then using a rotary hoe, straddle the bed with the tractor and run the hoe over the bed to break up the surface and create a smooth bed. Presto, a raised bed!

Planning and maintenance are integrally linked with pest control. A detailed discussion of steps to take at the planning stage to aid in pest prevention and in finding remedies is presented in the section in Part 4, pages 152–154.

How to Use the Plant Charts

You can use this handbook in many different ways. Information is organized and cross-referenced for easy retrieval. You will find an overview of each plant under its own entry, and an overview of insects and diseases in the charts beginning on page 163. For all major topics, especially those concerning fruit and nut trees, we cover the basics, but not more. To find sources with more complete discussions of these topics, please see the Bibliography on page 258. Following are explanations of the categories used in the plant entries.

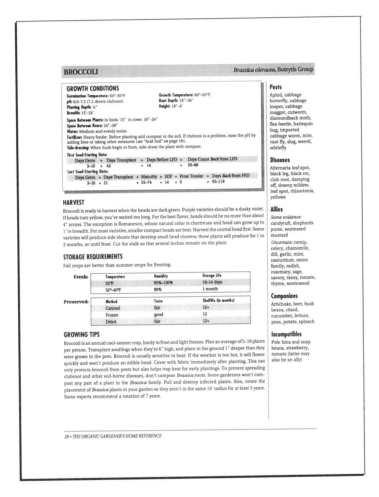

Plant Names. For each plant, we have listed the genus and species, the family name (both in Latin and English), and the common name. We included Latin names to help you problem solve. Because some plants may look so different, it can be useful to know they are members of the same family for planning crop rotations and to be prepared for similar insect and disease problems.

GROWTH CONDITIONS

Germination Temperature. This is optimum soil temperature for seed germination, in Fahrenheit degrees. Seeds germinate at temperatures outside the optimum range noted, but count on longer germination at lower temperatures and, except for extremely high temperatures, shorter times at higher temperatures.

Growth Temperature. This lists the optimum air temperature for plant growth, in Fahrenheit degrees.

pH. On this scale of soil alkalinity/acidity a 7.0 is neutral. Most plants will grow well in a pH range from 6.0 to 7.0. Home test kits are widely available; see Appendix C for a list of suppliers.

Root Depth. Wherever possible, we've given a range of average-to-maximum recorded root depth. Where a range isn't given, we've provided the average. The better worked your soil is, the deeper the roots extend.

Planting Depth: Best planting depth for germination and root lodging.

Soil: The soil type the plant likes best (clay, clay-loam, sand, sandy loam, etc.).

GROWTH CONDITIONS

Germination Temperature: 50°–85°F   **Growth Temperature:** 60°–65°F
pH: 6.0–7.5 (7.2 deters clubroot)   **Root Depth:** 18"–36"
Planting Depth: ¼"   **Height:** 18"–4'
Breadth: 15'–24'

Space Between Plants: in beds: 15"   in rows: 18"–24"
Space Between Rows: 24"–36"
Water: Medium and evenly moist.
Fertilizer: Heavy feeder. Before planting add compost to the soil. If clubroot is a problem, raise the pH by adding lime or taking other measures (*see "Acid Soil" on page 161*).
Side-dressing: When buds begin to form, side-dress the plant with compost.

First Seed-Starting Date:

Days Germ	+	Days Transplant	+	Days Before LFD	=	Days Count *Back* from LFD
3–10	+	42	+	14	=	59–66

Last Seed-Starting Date:

Days Germ	+	Days Transplant	+	Maturity	+	SDF	+	Frost Tender	=	Days *Back* from FFD
3–10	+	21	+	55–74	+	14	+	0	=	93–119

Space Between Plants.

In beds: This is the recommended closest spacing between plants under optimal conditions in French intensive beds, raised beds, biodynamic gardens, and any other garden in which plants are spaced very close together. (Note: If your climate is damp and humid, you probably should use broader spacing to allow for more air circulation and sun penetration, which prevent fungal and other diseases.)

In rows: Recommended spacing to use between plants in conventional rows, not raised beds.

Space Between Rows.

Spacing needed between conventional rows.

Water. This describes the individual plant's watering needs.

Heavy = 1 gallon per square foot, or 1.4"–1.6" per week
Medium = ¾ gallon per square foot, or 1"–1.2" per week
Low = about ½ gallon per square foot, or .8" per week

Mulch. Any material spread to completely cover the soil is considered mulch. It suppresses weed growth, keeps moisture in the soil by reducing evaporation, insulates the ground to keep it warm in winter and cool in summer, and can help prevent the emergence of certain harmful insects. Thick mulch around potatoes, for example, can help deter the Colorado potato beetle. In moister climates, some gardeners have reported using thick mulches of 4" to 8" or more and never having to water or fertilize again. In hot, dry climates, however, mulch should not be so thick because it absorbs rain or irrigation water, preventing water from reaching the soil. Thick mulch can also be counterproductive in areas that experience slug problems. All fruit trees should be mulched with organic matter, ideally compost. Keeping 3" to 12" clear around the trunk to discourage rodents and prevent rot, spread a 3" to 6" deep layer of mulch out to the drip line or 6', whichever is greater.

In spring, lightly hoe the mulch into the ground. Avoid large amounts of hay, which release nitrogen late in the season when tree growth slows. Examples of mulch include compost, straw, chopped leaves, wood chips, cocoa bean shells, pebbles, plastic, and landscape fabric.

Grass clippings, contrary to some wisdom, can be a very effective mulch as long as you do not use grass that has been sprayed with herbicides or pesticides. In fact, grass clippings were shown in experiments at the University of Tennessee to promote an abundance of pest-controlling spiders, an organic gardener's best friend. Grass clippings can sometimes retard germination and emergence, such as with carrots, so it is best to apply after shoots have emerged through the soil.

To attract spiders easily, apply at least a thin layer of mulch before hot summer weather sets in. Spiders in the spring "balloon" through the air on fine silk threads to find hospitable homes for the summer. Mulch offers the cool, damp environment they need to minimize their water loss, and garden pests provide their food. Research has discovered that spiders regularly migrate hundreds of miles. One study found that 65 percent of the spider population originated from far away, rather than from neighboring gardens.

Colored mulch, such as painted plastic, can serve other purposes as well, such as raising yields or deterring specific insects. In South Carolina, red mulch increased yields of cowpeas as much as 12 percent over the yields achieved with white or black mulch. Red is also thought to increase tomato yields, particularly early in the season, but has also been found to attract some pests. Orange mulch repels sweet potato whitefly, but may attract other pests. Studies at the University of Florida have shown that of all the colors, red attracts the most white flies, blue attracts the most aphids and thrips, and white aluminum is the least attractive to all three pests.

Fertilizer. Organic gardeners usually fertilize (often with just compost) twice in one season, once before planting and again in the middle of the growth cycle. See pages 159–160 for different types of organic fertilizers. For fruit trees, appropriate new growth is noted wherever possible because this is one of the easiest ways to determine whether the tree is obtaining proper nourishment — all other factors being equal (e.g., light, soil, moisture, temperature). If tree growth is less than the appropriate range, it may need more nitrogen, again assuming other conditions are favorable. If tree growth is greater than the appropriate range, it may be receiving too much nitrogen.

Side-Dressing. Any addition to the soil — such as fertilizer, compost, or soil amendments — after the plant is already set in the soil is side-dressing. To add, create a narrow furrow 1" to 3" deep at the plant's drip line, or 6" from the plant base (whichever is greater); sprinkle the amendment into the furrow and cover with soil.

Chilling Requirement. This is the number of hours a fruit or nut tree needs below a certain temperature, usually 45°F, before it will blossom. Those trees with lower chilling requirements bloom earlier and, therefore, are more susceptible to late spring frosts.

Site. Avoid planting fruit and nut trees in low pockets or areas where fog and frost may collect. Most fruit trees require full sun. Morning sun is especially important to dry the dew as rapidly as possible, which helps prevent fungus problems. Some fruit trees that are susceptible to late frost damage are better sited on a north-sloping hill, or 12' to 15' away from a north wall, in order to delay budding as long as possible. To avoid nematode and verticillium wilt problems, you might choose a site where grass or cover crops were grown for the previous 2 years.

For Fruits and Nuts Only

Rootstocks. Most fruit and some nut trees sold today are grafted onto a rootstock. Grafting primarily aims to combine the desired fruit variety with a rootstock that controls the ultimate tree size. A more rapid form of propagation than seed-starting, grafting is also beneficial because it hastens the onset of bearing fruit and nuts. Rootstocks are numerous and not easy to sort through because most nursery catalogues and books mention certain characteristics and omit others, making it difficult to get an overview. Your choice of rootstock should depend on such things as ultimate size tree you desire, the natural growing height of the tree variety, soil drainage, soil fertility, and the specific insect and disease problems in your area. When you buy a tree, be sure to find out the rootstock it is attached to, if any, and the rootstock's growing characteristics, as this can affect things such as your tree's ultimate size, how early it bears, and disease resistance. For final decisions on which rootstock is best for your garden, consult reliable nurseries, many of which are listed in Appendix B.

Pruning. Major pruning is almost always done when the tree is dormant. Do **not** prune new transplants until after the first year of growth. Old wisdom prescribed pruning at the time of transplanting to bring the tree's top growth into balance with root growth. Research has shown, however, that such pruning will stunt a tree's growth for years. Summer pruning is usually limited to balanced thinning to ensure high quality fruit.

Pruning should always remove diseased, damaged, dead, and disfigured material. It also is used to increase light penetration and air circulation for better-quality fruit and better disease control. Unless diseased, pruned material can be composted. Diseased material should be destroyed.

The information we've included under pruning is intended primarily as a quick reminder for the experienced gardener. Both a science and an art, pruning is above all a visual experience and, in our opinion, cannot be taught without diagrams or hands-on experience. Consult the Bibliography for books with more extensive directions on pruning, such as Lewis Hill's, *Pruning Simplified*.

For Vegetables and Herbs Only

Seed-Starting Dates. Most catalogues and books suggest specific seed-starting dates (e.g., mid-May) based on a national average. Some may even break down starting dates by zone. Such dates, however, are not necessarily the best for you and your backyard, because your microclimate may differ significantly from these average temperatures. The equations we list give you the power to figure seed-starting dates for your own garden, whether in Alaska or Florida, no matter how idiosyncratic your microclimate. They also give you the flexibility to plant varieties of the same vegetable with differing maturation times. Overall, these computations should provide a higher level of confidence that each seed started will grow safely to maturity. For each part of the equation, substitute your own numbers after you've done several trials.

Days Germ(inate): The average number of days for the seed to germinate, which is when green shoots emerge through the soil.

Days Transplant: The average number of days after germination that the plant needs to grow inside until it is transplanted outside. (Note: This number *includes* the 4–7 days that may be needed for hardening off.)

LFD: Last Frost Date in the spring, an average date available from your local extension agent. If possible, keep your own records to figure your own average LFD.

Days Before (After) LFD: The average number of days before (or after) the Last Frost Date that the plant can tolerate living in outdoor soil. Use this number to determine the approximate dates you should transplant the seedling outside. This number also gives you a more precise measurement of the plant's frost hardiness. As different sources suggest different setting-out dates, we've given the widest possible range.

Maturity: The average number of days for the plant to reach horticultural maturity for harvest. For plants that are transplanted, the days to maturity are *in addition* to the germination days and days to transplant. So if you don't want to start your seeds inside and, instead, direct-sow outside, figure the total days to horticultural maturity by *adding in* the Days Germinate and Days Transplant.

SDF: Short Day Factor for late summer or fall plantings. Horticultural maturity times noted in seed catalogues assume long days and warm temperatures. For late-summer or fall plantings of many vegetable species you need to adjust horticultural maturity times by 2 weeks to accommodate shorter and cooler days. Some species, like the radish, require short days to form and thus don't need such adjustments. Wherever possible, we've noted which species require this Short Day Factor adjustment.

Frost Tender: An additional 2-week adjustment for frost-tender vegetables, which need to mature at least 2 weeks before frost in order to produce a full harvest.

FFD: First Frost Date in the fall, an average date available from your local extension agent. If possible, keep records to figure your own average FFD.

HARVEST

How and when to harvest. Special tips on how to recognize that the vegetable is ready for harvest. Special preparations or directions for curing the vegetable before eating or storing.

For those of you concerned about nitrate levels in your vegetables, studies show levels can be reduced by the way you harvest. The morning of harvest, break up the soil around the vegetables with a long pitchfork, or use some other mechanism to sever most of the roots. This stops nitrogen uptake. Crops should then be harvested late in the day when nitrate levels are at their lowest.

STORAGE REQUIREMENTS

Special tips on the best ways to store the edible harvest.

Fresh: How long fresh harvest will keep, at optimum storage temperature and humidity.

Preserved: The number of months the harvest will keep by specific preservation methods.

Parts of the storage information we include are reprinted from *Knott's Handbook For Vegetable Growers, 3rd Edition*, edited by Oscar Lorenz and Donald Maynard, and from Jeff Ball's *The Self-Sufficient Suburban Garden*. Many thanks to them both. See the Bibliography for complete references.

GROWING TIPS

Is the plant a cool- or warm-season crop? How frost hardy is it? How much should you plant per person? Also look here for special tips on starting seeds, planting, spacing, and background information on the plant.

Pests; Diseases. No matter how many of these are listed, you probably won't see more than a few in your garden. The diseases listed are primarily for your easy reference to textbooks. The diseases listed in each entry are limited to those which are promoted by an insect vector, are highly infectious, or for which there are remedies over and above the preventive measures described on pages 152–157. All of the diseases and animal pests are described in more detail in the charts in Part 4.

Allies. Allies are alleged to actively repel insects, or to enhance growth or flavor of the target plant. Part 5 offers important caveats on allies, and a listing of each one's reputed function, which may be helpful in determining if it would be useful in your garden.

Some evidence: Allies whose effects have been tested in field trials. If the source and location of the field test is unknown, the claim is listed as Uncertain. This is important because an ally tested in the tropics may not work in northern Maine. Further, we believe it is important to list sources because we understand that claims may be made and propagated by well-meaning but misinformed or untrained individuals.

Uncertain: Claims of allies' effects that have not been scientifically tested in field trials, but are usually based on tradition, folklore, and anecdotes. Presumably, for most of these, positive correlations have been noted for the information to be passed down through generations. Observations made at an unknown place and time, however, are a long way from hard evidence. If you decide to act on this information, be aware that it falls under the rubric of experimentation.

Companions. Companions are alleged to share space and growing habits well, but do not necessarily play an active role in insect protection or growth. Again, use your own garden as a test bed. Some of these companions may work well, others not at all, or one may prove to be a true ally by providing insect protection.

> ### IMPORTANT NOTE ON ALLIES, COMPANIONS, AND INCOMPATIBLES
>
> For planning purposes, all allies, companions, and incompatibles are cross-referenced. If a source says that squash hinders potato growth, that does not necessarily mean potatoes hinder squash growth. Nevertheless, we decided that if one plant is alleged to harm the growth of another, they should be considered incompatible to each other. So, squash is listed as an incompatible in the potato entry, and vice-versa. The same practice applies to companions and allies.

Incompatibles. Incompatibles are alleged to play an actively negative role in each other's growth by diminishing vigor or flavor, increasing the risk of insect or disease invasion, or decreasing yields. Although these claims may not be proven any more than those pertaining to companions or allies, we feel it may be safer to avoid placing alleged incompatibles near one another.

Varieties. Recommended varieties have been selected by the following criteria: (1) disease resistance; (2) ease of growing in organic gardens; (3) good flavor; (4) good storage qualities; (5) special height, size, or habit; (6) high yields; (7) self-pollination (fruits); (8) open-pollinated types for seed savers (vegetables); (9) ease of harvest, including factors such as size, bruising, or peeling; (10) heirloom varieties grown years ago but not often found at local nurseries; (11) unusual color or ornamental qualities; and (12) hybrids with good yield potential. Vegetable and herb varieties are ordered alphabetically. Fruits are ordered by fruit maturation (ripening, not flowering). For vegetables, days to maturation (e.g., 51 days) can refer to either the time from seeding to harvest or the time from transplanting to harvest, depending on which catalog is used as a source. Maturation time varies greatly by region, climate, soil conditions, annual rainfall, or a host of other variables. So, be sure to use the days to maturation only as a relative, not absolute, number with which to compare different varieties.

The success of a particular variety in your garden cannot be predicted. In addition, varietal characteristics may differ depending on which company you order from, especially with heirloom and open-pollinated types. Obviously, the ultimate test of a variety is to actually try growing it in your garden. The space left for "Notes" is a good place to record your results.

Additional Planting Information — Fruits and Nuts

Planting Time. Always plant when the fruit tree, bush, cane, or vine is dormant and the ground is workable. In climates with milder winters, you can plant in late fall. Where there are cold winters, plant in early spring. One evolving rule of thumb is that you can plant in the fall in zones 5 and below, and should plant in the spring in zones 4 and above. However, Windmill Point Farm & Nursery in zone 4 in Québec, Canada, still recommends fall planting. There are many advantages to fall planting, but if you're at all uncertain about your microclimate, you might wait until spring.

Tree Planting Preparation. Prepare a hole that is 3 to 5 times greater in diameter than the root ball. The hole should be no deeper than the depth of the root system, or 10 percent shallower than the root ball. Recent studies indicate that it is more important for fruit trees to be given a wide planting hole, as opposed to older wisdom that they need the depth, because of their tendency to grow shallow roots. Add humus and compost to improve drainage. Install around the trunk a ¼" to ½" hardware cloth barrier that extends 4" below ground to deter gophers and other rodents, and that rises 18" to 24" above ground to prevent rabbit damage (especially in winter months). For trees on dwarf rootstock characterized by poor anchorage, nestle in a 4' to 6' stake before filling the hole. Form a small trench, mounding up the sides of the trench, about 18" away from the trunk. Fill the trench to the top with water. This drenching helps to eliminate soil air pockets, which are not good for roots. Wrap the bark with a spiral white plastic tree guard to protect it from mice, rodents, and other pests. If you use a wire tree guard, whitewash the trunk first while it is still dormant with a commercial whitewash or interior white latex (never oil-based) paint.

PART 1

Vegetables

GROWTH CONDITIONS

Germination Temperature: 60°–70°F
pH: 6.5
Planting Depth: Set buds just above the soil surface
Breadth: 3'–6'

Growth Temperature: 60°–65°F
Root Depth: More than 4'
Height: 3'–6'
Site: Sunny and sheltered.

Space Between Plants: in beds: 2'–3' in rows: 4'–6'
Space Between Rows: 6'–8'
Water: Heavy.
Mulch: Apply over winter, and when plants are 6"–8" high.
Fertilizer: Heavy feeder; lots of well-rotted manure or compost.
Side-dressing: Every 3–4 weeks.
Propagation: Seed or suckers. To propagate by sucker, use a trowel to slice 10"-tall suckers off the parent plant, each with a section of root. In warm climates, plant the suckers in a 4" hole. In cold climates, plant the suckers in a pot to overwinter indoors.

First Seed-Starting Date: Start 6 weeks before the LFD in 4" deep pots in an area where the temperature is about 65°F. When germinated, put in full sun where the temperature is about 55°F. Transplant when four true leaves have appeared.

Pests

Aphid, plume moth, slug

Diseases

Curly dwarf (virus), southern blight, verticillium wilt

Allies

None

Companions

Brassicas

Incompatibles

None

HARVEST

When heads are still closed, about the size of an orange, and while the stem 2" below the bud is still supple, cut off the head with 1"–2" of stem. Heads that have already opened are tough. Always harvest the central bud first. After harvest, cut the stems to the ground, or 12" above the ground to encourage side shoots. Side shoots produce buds smaller than the first central bud.

STORAGE REQUIREMENTS

Keep in a paper bag to increase humidity. Some say artichokes can be kept for up to 1 month in the refrigerator.

Fresh:

Temperature	Humidity	Storage Life
32°F	95%–100%	2–3 weeks

Preserved:

Method	Taste	Shelflife (in months)
Canned Hearts	good	12+
Frozen Hearts	good	4+
Dried	N/A	N/A

GROWING TIPS

Globe Artichoke is a cool-season crop, tender to frost and light freezes. Plan an average of 3 plants per person. In warm climates with mild winters, artichoke is grown as a perennial, in cold climates as an annual. Before planting, add plenty of compost or rotted manure to the soil and again when the plants are 6"–8" high. In cold climates, plant artichokes in large containers to keep the roots alive through winter. In warm climates cut the plants to the ground in the fall. In cooler areas, to prepare for winter either cut the plants to the ground and bring containers indoors, or cut them to 15"–20" above the ground, bend the stalks over, mulch heavily with leaves, and cover with a rain-proof tarp or basket. Some gardeners recommend removing side shoots during the growing season. This increases the size of the central head, but reduces the overall yield. One Oregon gardener harvested almost 30 heads from just the side shoots of one plant. If the bud is not harvested for your table, it will blossom into beautiful purple-blue flowers that can be cut for arrangements.

SELECTED VARIETIES

Greenhouse

None

Outdoor

Grand Beurre Produces early enough to bear as an annual in cold climates; not available in the United States

Green Globe Excellent flavor; does well in long growing seasons, mild winters and damp climates (Burpee, Fowler, Park, Seeds Blum)

Purple Variety Pretty violet color (write to Cook's and Shepherd's — seeds may be occasionally available, although not necessarily listed in catalogs)

Notes

_____

_____

_____

_____

_____

_____

_____

_____

_____

_____

_____

_____

_____

_____

_____

GROWTH CONDITIONS

Germination Temperature: 60°–85°F
pH: 6.0–8.0
Planting Depth: 8"–10" (*see* Growing Tips)
Breadth: 2'–4' (fern growth, depending on soil and climate)
Space Between Plants: in beds: 12" in rows: 15"–18"
Space Between Rows: 3'–4'
Water: Heavy.
Mulch: Use straw or light material over the winter and remove it in spring. Use compost during growing season.
Fertilizer: Heavy feeder; apply compost in autumn to first year beds, and in spring after harvest to established beds. Apply fish emulsion twice yearly. Beds may need P and K before planting, and N after planting.
Average Bearing Age: 3 years from seeds, 2 years from crowns.

Growth Temperature: 60°–70°F
Root Depth: More than 4'
Height: 3'–8' (fern growth, depending on soil and climate)
Best Planting Time: Early spring

Pests

Aphids, asparagus beetle (early May), cucumber beetle, garden centipede, gopher, Japanese beetle, mite, slug, snail, spotted asparagus beetle

Diseases

Asparagus rust, fusarium wilt

Allies

Uncertain: basil, goldenrod, nasturtium, parsley, pot marigold, tomato

Incompatibles

Onion family, weeds (during first 6 weeks of asparagus growth)

HARVEST

When spears are ⅜" thick and 6"–8" high, cut spears ½" below the soil surface to lessen the chance of disease and pest infestation. Heads should be tight and spears brittle. Stop harvesting when stalks are less than ⅜" thick. When grown from roots, do not harvest the first year. Let the plants go to foliage, and when they brown in the fall, cut them to ground level. The second year, harvest spears for about 4 weeks. In following years, the harvest will last 8–10 weeks.

STORAGE REQUIREMENTS

Wrap spears in moist towels or stand upright in a glass of water, then refrigerate in plastic bags. Blanch asparagus before you freeze it.

Fresh:	Temperature	Humidity	Storage Life
	32°–35°F	95%–100%	2–3 weeks

Preserved:	Method	Taste	Shelflife (in months)
	Canned	good	12+
	Frozen	excellent	12
	Dried	fair	12+

GROWING TIPS

Asparagus is a perennial, early spring crop. Plan an average of 10 plants per person. Plant in a sunny spot protected from the wind and, because asparagus roots often extend both downward and outward 5'–6', plant in deeply rototilled soil that has incorporated green manure and compost. Traditionally, roots are planted in furrows 8"–10" deep and 10" wide. Spread the roots, cover the crowns with 2"–3" of sifted compost humus, and water well. As the plant grows through the summer, add more soil, but do not cover the tip. If you prefer to plant individually, dig holes 8"–10" deep and 5" in diameter, then proceed with the same method for furrow planting. Every spring, asparagus rows should be "ridged" by drawing up several inches of topsoil or, better, newly applied compost. This counters the crown's tendency to get too close to the surface. After harvest, sow a cover crop of cowpeas or other legume between the asparagus rows, which discourages weeds and add to the organic matter when dug under. University of Minnesota trials have shown that fall plantings of 9- to 11-week-old seedlings equal or exceed the growth of spring transplants. Carl Cantaluppi of the University of Illinois confirmed in 1988 that you can increase yields by up to 40 percent by planting crowns at a depth of 5"–6", rather than at 10"–12". He also claims that asparagus is not a heavy nitrogen feeder because the ferns return most of the nitrogen to the soil. Decide for yourself.

SELECTED VARIETIES

Greenhouse

None

Outdoor

Connover's Colossal Open-pollinated; good for general use and raising from seeds (Bountiful Gardens)

Jersey Giant One of the new all-male varieties (meaning it produces more harvest); vigorous, with very high yields; resists rust; tolerates fusarium crown and root rot; adapted to a wide variety of climates from New England across to Washington and south to the Carolinas (Burpee, May, Nourse, Park)

Mary Washington Heirloom; good flavor; rust resistant (widely available)

Rutgers SYN-4-56 Hybrid; offspring of Jersey Giant; high yields; resists rust; tolerates fusarium. Some female plants but most are male (Nourse Farms)

UC 157 A new hybrid developed by the University of California for the West Coast and the South; good flavor and quality (Burpee)

Waltham Hybrid; uniform spear size; heavy producer; rust resistant (widely available)

Notes

GROWTH CONDITIONS

Germination Temperature: 60°–85°F
pH: 6.2–7.5
Planting Depth: 1"
Breadth: 4"–8"

Growth Temperature: 60°–75°F
Root Depth: 36"–48"
Height: 10"–24"

Space Between Plants: 2"–6"
Space Between Rows: 12"–30"/ 8" on center in raised beds
Water: Average and constant.
Fertilizer: Light feeder. Because bean plants fix N when inoculated properly, they should require low N. After the plant flowers apply fertilizer low in N, medium P and K. Avoid low K at all times.

First Seed-Starting Date: Transplant or direct sow when soil temperature is 60°F.

Days Germ	+	Days Transplant	-	Days After LFD	=	Days Count *Back* from LFD
4–10	+	21–28	-	0–10	=	25–28

Last Seed-Starting Date:

Days Germ	+	Days Transplant	+	Maturity	+	SDF	+	Frost Tender	=	Days *Back* from FFD
4–10	+	0 (direct)	+	98–125	+	14	+	14			=	130–163

HARVEST

Wait until the plant's leaves have fallen in autumn to pick dry pods or to pull the entire plant. Harvest before the first frost. Soybeans and limas, however, should be picked when any split pods are spotted since beans often drop from the shells as they dry. Cure for several weeks in a well-ventilated area, piling them on screens or slatted shelves. Beans are dry and ready to thresh when they don't dent when bitten. Four methods of threshing:

1. Thrash the plant back and forth on the inside of a clean trashcan

2. Place the plant in a large burlap bag with a hole in the corner and flail

3. Put plants in a cone-shaped bag, tie the bottom, walk or jump on the bag

4. Put the beans into a bag with a hole in the bottom (tied closed); hang from a tree and beat well, then untie the hole and, with the help of a good wind, the chaff will blow away and the beans will fall into a container placed below.

Professional threshers are available from Peaceful Valley Farm Supply.

STORAGE REQUIREMENTS

Remove all bad beans. Place on shallow trays and heat at 170°–180°F for 10–15 minutes. Cool. Store in a cool, dry area in tight jars. To avoid weevil damage *see* **Pest Chart** on page 183.

GROWING TIPS

Beans are a warm-season crop, tender to light frosts and freezes. Plan an average of 10–20 plants per person. Cold, wet weather fosters disease; to prevent disease, do not: sow or transplant too early, touch the plants when wet, or touch healthy plants after working with diseased ones. Most dried beans, whether bush or semivining, require long growing seasons. To direct sow them, try layering grass mulch 4"–6" deep on the bed in fall. This will decompose down to about 2" by spring, keep the soil warm 6" deep, and won't pull nitrogen out of the soil, allowing you to plant earlier in the spring. *See* **Snap Beans** (page 24) for comments on presoaking and inoculation. Dried beans are very high in protein. Like other legumes, soybeans and cowpeas are excellent green manure crops that enrich the soil with organic matter and nitrogen.

Pests

Aphid, bean leaf beetle, beet and potato leafhopper, cabbage looper, corn earworm, cucumber beetle, cutworm, flea beetle, garden webworm, Japanese beetle, leaf-footed bug, leafminer, Mexican bean beetle, mite, root knot nematode, seedcorn maggot, slug, tarnished plant bug, thrips, webworm, weevil, whitefly, wireworm

Diseases

Anthracnose, bacterial blight and wilt, bean mosaic, common mosaic, curly top, damping off, powdery mildew, rust, southern blight, white mold, yellow mosaic. Burn diseased plants (where allowed).

Allies

Some evidence: goosegrass, red sprangletop, sorghum mulch (for cowpeas)
Uncertain: catnip, celery, corn, golden-rod, marigold, nasturtium, oregano, potato, rosemary, savory

Companions

Beet, cabbage, carrot, celery, corn, cucumber, eggplant, peas, potato, radish, strawberry

Incompatibles

Fennel, garlic, gladiolus, onion family

SELECTED VARIETIES

All varieties listed are open-pollinated

Greenhouse

Butterbean Short-season and bush plants

Outdoor

Aprovecho Select Fava Bush; large seeds; sweet flavor; good fresh or dry; hardy to below 20°F; matures 2–3 weeks before pole beans; good in maritime Northwest and East Coast (Abundant Life)

Black Coco Bush; milder black bean; buttery flavor; good fresh or dried (Territorial)

Black Valentine 50 days; bush, tall spreading plant; heirloom; meaty black bean; enjoyable flavor (Abundant Life, Seeds Blum, Southern Exposure, Southwest)

Borlotto 68 days; beautiful bush plant with speckled rosy red and cream pods; delicious fresh or dried; an Italian heirloom rarely seen in markets (Shepherd's)

Butterbeans or Green Vegetable Soybean (Glycine max) 88 days; very digestible; good fresh or frozen; stocky and highly branched plants (Garden City, Johnny's, Southern Exposure)

Buttergreen 45 days; bush; very short season; good dried or young as snap beans; resists bean mosaic; mellow flavor; introduced in 1989 (Burpee)

Chickpea or Garbanzo 100 days; bush; usually only one seed per pod (Burpee); **Desi** Bush; small seeds native to India; better for home garden than large white commercial type; for interior Northwest and short-season dry areas, not good for coastal fog areas (Abundant Life); **Kabuli Black** 95 days; black-seeded (Ethiopian origin); small seeds; better for home garden than large white commercial type (Garden City); **Dolores de Hidalgo** Prolific in low desert winters; produces small beans; suitable for high and low desert (Native Seed)

Cowpea (Blackeyed or Southern pea) — Calico Crowder 79 days; very flavorful; tan with maroon splashes; good for southern and warm coastal areas (Southern Exposure); **Queen Ann** 68 days; compact 26" plants with no runners; no significant insects or diseases in Rodale trials *(Organic Gardening,* 2/89); high and reliable yields; good fresh, fried, frozen or canned (Southern Exposure);

Pima Bajo Excellent green or dried; suitable for low desert planting (Native Seed)

Fava (Tarahumara Habas) Frost hardy; suitable for high and low desert (Native Seed)

French Horticultural 66 days; bush produces some runners; 6"–8" pods; good fresh, dried, or frozen (Harris, Stokes)

Jacob's Cattle or Trout 85–95 days; bush 24" tall; short-season baked bean type; a beautiful white with splashes of maroon; very tasty and meaty; good fresh or dry; an heirloom favorite in Vermont and Maine (Abundant Life, Garden City, Johnny's, Seeds Blum)

Pinto 85 days; bush 14"; short half-runner plant; beans are tan with brown speckles; susceptible to mosaic damage in Rodale trials *(Organic Gardening,* 2/89); medium-to-high yields (Abundant Life, Burpee, Field's, Johnny's, Park); **San Juan Pinto** Suitable for high desert planting (Native Seed)

Red Kidney 95 days; bush 16"–22"; some mosaic and Japanese beetle damage in Rodale trials *(Organic Gardening,* 2/89); bush 16"; high yields (widely available)

Santa Maria Pinquito 120 days

Soldier Heirloom; kidney-shaped white bean with yellow-brown eye; very rich and meaty flavor (Blum, Territorial)

Vermont Cranberry Bush; beautiful with swirls of red on a cream background (Cook's)

Notes

GROWTH CONDITIONS

Germination Temperature: 65°–85°F
pH: 6.0–7.0
Planting Depth: 1½" to 2"
Breadth: Pole: 6"–8" Bush: 4"–8"

Growth Temperature: 60°–70°F
Root Depth: 36"–48"
Height: Pole: 8'–15' Bush: 10"–18"

Space Between Plants: in beds: Pole — 6" Bush — 4"–6"
    in rows: pole — 10"–18" bush — 6"–8"
Space Between Rows: 36"–48"
Water: Average and constant.
Fertilizer: Light feeder. Beans fix N when inoculated properly, so most need low N; medium P and K.
Side-dressing: 4 weeks after planting apply a balanced or low N fertilizer, or compost.
Support Structures: Use a 6' post, A-frame, teepee (3 poles tied at the top), or trellis for pole beans.

First Seed-Starting Date:

Days Germ	+	Days Transplant	-	Days After LFD	=	Days Count *Back* from LFD
7–18	+	21–35	-	14–28	=	14-25

Last Seed-Starting Date:

Days Germ	+	Days Transplant	+	Maturity	+	SDF	+	Frost Tender	=	Days *Back* from FFD
7–18	+	0	+	60–80	+	14	+	14	=	95–126

HARVEST

For the best fresh flavor, pick beans when young. To encourage the plant to set more beans, pick when beans are bulging through pods. For dried beans, wait until pods turn brown or leaves drop in the fall. Pick pods and cure for several weeks in a well-ventilated area, piling them on screens or slatted shelves. Beans are dry and ready to thresh when they don't dent when bitten. *See* **Dried Shell Beans** (page 20) for threshing methods.

STORAGE REQUIREMENTS

Blanch before freezing. Store dried beans in jars in a cool, dry place.

Fresh:

Temperature	Humidity	Storage Life
37°–41°F	95%	5–7 days

Preserved:

Method	Taste	Shelflife (in months)
Canned	fair	12+
Frozen	excellent	12
Dried	excellent	12+

GROWING TIPS

Lima beans are a warm-season crop, very tender to frost and light freezes. Plan an average of 10–20 plants per person. For every 2 pounds of filled pods you should get 1 pound of shelled beans. Limas are more sensitive to cold soil and calcium deficiency than snap beans. Limas don't like transplanting, so it's often recommended to sow them directly in the beds; however, seeds will not germinate if the soil isn't warm enough. *See* **Snap Beans** (page 24) for comments about presoaking, inoculation, and cold, wet weather. For direct sowing, plant 5–6 seeds in a hill and thin to 3"–4". Bush beans usually mature more quickly than pole beans and are determinate with one clean harvest. Pole limas generally have better flavor and are indeterminate with a continuous harvest, but they require a trellis and some extra effort. Bush limas don't do well in wet weather; they develop an unpleasant earthy taste where pods touch the ground. Corn plants can provide a substitute support for nonrampant pole beans; plant the beans between 6"–8" tall corn plants, that are not too densely planted.

Pests

Aphid, bean leaf beetle, beet and potato leafhopper, cabbage looper, corn earworm, cucumber beetle, cutworm, flea beetle, garden webworm, Japanese beetle, leaf-footed bug, leafminer, Mexican bean beetle, mite, root knot nematodes, seedcorn maggot, slug, tarnished plant bug, thrips, webworm, weevil, whitefly, wireworm

Diseases

Anthracnose, bacterial blight and wilt, bean mosaic, common mosaic, curly top, damping off, powdery mildew, rust, southern blight, white mold, yellow mosaic (If legal, burn diseased plants.)

Allies

Some evidence: goosegrass, red sprangletop

Uncertain: catnip, celery, corn, marigold, nasturtium, oregano, potato, savory, rosemary

Companions

Carrot, corn, cucumber, eggplant, lettuce, peas, radish

Bush only: beet, all *Brassicas,* strawberry

Incompatibles

Fennel, garlic, onion family

Pole only: beet, all *Brassicas,* kohlrabi, sunflower

SELECTED VARIETIES

All varieties listed are open-pollinated

Greenhouse

Fordhook 242, Henderson Bush, King of the Garden *(see* below)

Outdoor

Pole.

Christmas or Speckled Calico, Giant Florida 85 days; rich "butter bean," nutty flavor; large beautiful red-speckled beans (Blum, Field's, Park, Southern Exposure)
Hopi White, gray, yellow and red types; native to the Southwest; suitable for high and low desert (Native Seed)
Hyacinth Introduced in 1989; baby white limas; some drought tolerance (Park)
King of the Garden 100 days; early, 5" pods; heirloom; high yields, good fresh or dried (Park, Seeds Blum, Southern Exposure)
Prizetaker 90 days; very large bean of good quality (Burpee)

Bush.

Baby Fordhook 70 days; 14" bush; thick seeded; small lima; high quality (Burpee)
Fordhook 242 75 days; AAS winner; heat resistant; upright; early butterbean; good fresh, canned, or frozen (Gurney's, Field's, Park, Seeds Blum, Stokes)
Henderson Bush 65 days; baby white (when dried); flat pods; withstands hot weather; good canned or frozen; good in all climates (Burpee, Field's, Seeds Blum)

Notes

GROWTH CONDITIONS

Germination Temperature: 60°–85°F
pH: 6.2–7.5
Planting Depth: 1" spring; 2" fall
Breadth: Pole: 6"–8" Bush: 4"–8"

Growth Temperature: 60°–70°F
Root Depth: 36"–48"
Height: Pole: 8'–15' Bush: 10"–24"
Soil: Loam

Space Between Plants: in beds: Pole — 6" Bush — 2"–4"
  in rows: Pole — 12" Bush — 4"–6"
Space Between Rows: (pole or bush) 18"–36"
Water: Low until the plant flowers, then average.
Fertilizer: Because bean plants fix N when inoculated properly, they should require low N; after it flowers, apply light N; avoid low K.
Support Structures: Use 6' posts, A-frame, teepee, or trellis to support pole beans.

First Seed-Starting Date:

Days Germ	+	Days Transplant	-	Days After LFD	=	Days Count *Back* from LFD
4–10	+	21–28	-	7–14	=	18-24

Last Seed-Starting Date:

Days Germ	+	Days Transplant	+	Maturity	+	SDF	+	Frost Tender	=	Days *Back* from FFD
4–10	+	0 (direct)	+	48–95	+	14	+	14	=	80–133

HARVEST

For best flavor, pick early in the morning, after leaves are dry. Harvest before seeds bulge, when beans snap off the plant and snap in half cleanly. Continual harvest is essential for prolonged bean production. **Bush, snap:** Pick when ¼"–⅜" diameter. **Filet:** Pick daily and, for peak flavor, when no larger than ⅛" diameter, regardless of length.

STORAGE REQUIREMENTS

Blanch before freezing.

Fresh:

Temperature	Humidity	Storage Life
40°–45°F	95%	7–10 days

Preserved:

Method	Taste	Shelflife (in months)
Canned	fair	12+
Frozen	excellent	12
Dried	excellent	24

GROWING TIPS

Beans are a warm-season crop, tender to light frosts and freezes. Plan an average of 10–20 plants per person. Bush beans are usually determinate with one clean harvest, so plant every 10 days for continuous harvest. Pole beans are usually indeterminate with a continuous harvest for 6–8 weeks if kept picked, so only one planting is necessary. Bean roots don't tolerate disturbance so handle seedlings minimally. Plant outside at the same depth they grew in the pot.

For pole beans, pinch off growing tips when plants reach the top of their support system. Some gardeners recommend presoaking the seeds, but research indicates that presoaked seeds absorb water too quickly, causing the outer coats to spill out essential nutrients, which encourages damping-off seed rot. Yields can increase 50–100 percent by inoculating with Rhizobia bacteria. To inoculate, simply roll seeds in the powder. Cold, wet weather fosters disease, so don't sow or transplant too early, touch plants when wet, or touch healthy plants after working with diseased ones. For a substitute support, plant nonrampant pole beans between corn that isn't too densely planted, when the corn is 6"–8" tall.

Pests

Same as Lima Beans, with the addition of the European corn borer

Diseases

Anthracnose, bacterial blight and wilt, bean and common mosaic, curly top, damping off, powdery mildew, rust, southern blight, white mold, yellow mosaic. If legal, burn diseased plants.

Allies

Some evidence: goosegrass, red sprangletop

Uncertain: catnip, celery, corn, marigold, nasturtium, oregano, potato, rosemary, savory

Companions

Both pole and bush: carrot, chard, corn (corn rows can be wind breakers for dwarf beans), cucumber, eggplant, peas, radish, strawberry

Bush only: beet, all *Brassicas*

Incompatibles

Both pole and bush: basil, fennel, garlic, gladiolus, onion family

Pole only: beet, all *Brassicas*, sunflower

SELECTED VARIETIES

All varieties listed are open-pollinated

Greenhouse

Tendercrop, Topcrop *(see* below).

Outdoor

Bush Snap.

Blue Lake 274 55 days; 16" semi-erect plant; 6" pods; white seeds; mature all at once; long season; high yields; good fresh or frozen; resists bean mosaic (Garden City, Gurney's, Park, William Dam)

Pencil Pod Black Wax 52 days; 15" plant; heirloom; stringless, tough yellow skins with black bean; fullest rich black bean flavor when mature; early and extended producer; good fresh or canned (Jung, Gurney's, Blum, Southern Exposure, William Dam)

Romano or Roma 50–60 days; 2' plant; long, flat, stringless Italian bean; mosaic resistant; good snap or dried, canned, or frozen; also available as pole (widely available)

Royal Burgundy 51 days; unusual purple flowers and pods; beans turn green when cooked; tolerates cold soil (widely available)

Tendercrop 53 days; reliable in poor weather; high yields; dark green, slender bean; thick clusters off the ground; resists mosaic, powdery mildew and pod mottle virus; good for canning (Gurney's, Field's, Nichols, Park)

Topcrop 49 days; AAS winner; stringless, slender, meaty bean; mosaic resistant; hardy (Burpee, Gurney's, Field's, William Dam)

Pole Snap.

Blue Lake 62 days; 8'; 6" pods; stringless; excellent flavor; white seeds also good as shell beans; very sweet and tender (widely available)

Kentucky Wonder 65 days; 9" stringless pod; heirloom; very popular; good flavor; resists rust; also available as bush (widely available)

Wren's Egg 65 days; pretty streaked pods; large shelling beans (Blum)

Pole Runner. These are perennial in warm climates; dig up bulbous root and replant in spring.

Scarlet Runner *(P. coccinus)* 70 days for fresh beans; 115 days for shell beans; vine to 10'; pretty ornamental red flowers are edible; 8" pods; good soup bean; tolerates cool weather; pods won't set in hot weather (widely available)

Scarlet Runner *(Tarahumare Tecomari)* Red flowering variety that produces purple, lavender, black, and mottled beans; suitable for high desert (over 4,000 ft) (Native Seed)

Filet (pencil-thin).

Aramis 65 days; bush; best taste raw and cooked in Rodale trials *(Organic Gardening,* 4/88); disease resistant; very uniform high yields; stringless (Garden City, William Dam)

Camile Most productive in Rodale trials *(Organic Gardening,* 4/88); disease resistant; good sweet flavor; best lightly steamed (Cook's, Horticultural Products)

Finaud Small 6" bush; a true filet that doesn't need to be picked every day; introduced in 1988 (Cook's)

Fin de Bagnols Very slender pods; early; uniform; tender; sweet, delicate flavor; grow like bush beans (Cook's)

Flageolet. These rich, meaty shelling beans are often eaten fresh like limas.

Chevrier A delicacy when eaten fresh, flageolet are also grown as shell beans for drying; pick when seeds are ½" in the shell (Cook's)

Notes

GROWTH CONDITIONS

Germination Temperature: 50°–85°F
pH: 5.8–7.0 (5.3 for scab)
Planting Depth: ¼"
Breadth: 4"–8"

Growth Temperature: 60°–65°F
Root Depth: 24"–10'
Height: 12"

Space Between Plants: in beds: 3"–4" in rows: 6"
Space Between Rows: 18"–24"
Water: Average and evenly moist.
Fertilizer: Heavy feeder. Needs high P; avoid high N; good tops may mean the roots are poorly developed and the plant is getting too much N.
Side-dressing: Every 2 weeks provide a light and balanced feeding; when tops are 4"–5" use low N.

First Seed-Starting Date:

Days Germ	+	Days Transplant	+	Days Before LFD	=	Days Count *Back* from LFD
5–10	+	0 (direct)	+	9–18	=	14–28 days

Last Seed-Starting Date:

Days Germ	+	Days Transplant	+	Maturity	+	SDF	+	Frost Tender	=	Days *Back* from FFD
5–10	+	0 (sow direct)	+	55–80	+	14	+	0	=	74–104

HARVEST

In late June, or before the hot season enters its prime, scrape some soil away from the beets to check their size. Pull or dig when the beets are 1"–2" across. They can become tough and woody-flavored when allowed to grow much larger, depending on the variety.

STORAGE REQUIREMENTS

Remove all top greens, leaving about 1" of stem with the beet. Do not wash. Pack beets in straw or moist sand. Beets can also be left in ground and dug up from under the snow.

Fresh:

Temperature	Humidity	Storage Life
32°F	98%–100%	4–7 months topped; 10–14 days bunched

Preserved:

Method	Taste	Shelflife (in months)
Canned	good	12+
Frozen	fair	8
Dried	fair	12+

GROWING TIPS

Beets are an annual cool-season crop, half-hardy to frost and light freezes. Plan an average of 10–20 plants per person. Most beet cultivars are open-pollinated and multigerm, where one seed yields a clump of 4–5 plants that need to be thinned. These multigerm seeds, also known as "seed balls," germinate better if soaked an hour before planting. There are three main types of eating beets: Long (Cylindra), Medium (Semiglobe), and Short (Globe). Cylindra types mature slowly and, because they grow as long as 8", require deep soil. They can also be a good organic matter crop. For all types, look for cultivars resistant to bolting as well as to downy mildew. Yellow and white beets are sweeter than red varieties. Newer hybrids are usually sweeter than older varieties and offer more green leaves. Most beets contain 5–8 percent sugar while the newer hybrids such as Big Red run 12–14 percent. Hybrids tend to mature 7 to 14 days earlier, are more upright, and tend to have higher yields. Like kale and some other vegetables, most beets in hot weather get tough, woody, and develop an "off" flavor. An exception, according to some, is Detroit Crimson Globe. If your summers are hot, generally choose a variety that matures in 45 to 60 days. In greenhouses, beets are often grown for their greens only.

Pests

Mostly pest free; occasional beet leafhopper, carrot weevil, ear wig (seedlings), garden webworm, leafminer, mite, spinach flea beetle, whitefly, wireworm

Diseases

Mostly disease free; occasional cercospora, downy mildew, leaf spot, rust, scab

Allies

Uncertain: garlic, onion family

Companions

All *Brassicas*, bush beans, head lettuce

Incompatibles

Field mustard, all pole beans

SELECTED VARIETIES

Greenhouse

Greenhouse beets are usually grown for their greens.
Detroit Dark Red, Green Top Bunching, Lutz Green Leaf *(see* below).

Outdoor

Albino White 50 days; unusual white beet won't "bleed"; mild, sweet (Blum, Cook's, Field's, Stokes)

Burpee's Golden or Golden 50–55 days; beautiful yellow color; won't bleed into other foods; holds its flavor well into the growing season and when allowed to grow large, both root and greens are tasty; a poor germinator that requires more thick sowing (widely available)

Chioggia 50 days; open-pollinated; gourmet red and white striped beet; try the Improved variety (Cook's, Johnny's, Seeds Blum, Shepherd's)

Crosby's Egyptian 60 days; open-pollinated; heirloom; flattened shape; sweet and rich; one of the best in Harrowsmith 1988 trials *(Harrowsmith,* 1/89) (Southern Exposure, Seeds Blum)

Cylindra 60 days; up to 8" (like carrot); needs deep soil (widely available)

Detroit Dark Red 60 days; most widely sold beet; reliable; high-quality (widely available)

Green Top Bunching 65 days; roots and greens retain color in cooler weather (Stokes)

Kleine Bol 50 days; a true baby beet that grows fast (Shepherds)

Lutz Green Leaf 70 days; open-pollinated; good yields; improves in storage and stays tender; high in vitamins A and C; one of best in Harrowsmith 1988 trials *(Harrowsmith,* 1/89) (Abundant Life, Burpee, Cook's, Southern Exposure, Park)

Red Ace 52 days; hybrid; midseason; milder than "Detroit Dark Red"; sweet and rich; stays tender when older; one of best in Harrowsmith 1988 trials *(Harrowsmith,* 1/89) (widely available)

Swiss Chard *(B. vulgaris var. cicla).* Closely related to the beet, chard is grown for its greens which taste like spinach. Rich with vitamin C, calcium, and iron, the leaves can be used fresh in salads, or cooked in stir-fry dishes, quiche, or even stuffing. The stalks can be cooked with the leaves, or separately, like asparagus. Chard can be grown year-round in zones 9 and 10, and as an annual elsewhere. Harvest outer leaves, or cut to a few inches above the ground and new leaves will grow. It can withstand fall frosts of 15°–20°F.

Fordhook Giant 60 days; easy-to-grow; large dark green, crinkled leaves; yields well even in hot weather (Burpee, Harris, Johnny's, Stokes, Territorial)

Large White Ribbed 60 days; smooth and tender leaves with white ribs (Blum, Harris)

Lucillus 60 days; extremely heat tolerant and non-bolting (Field's, Gurney's, Jung, Park, Southern Exposure)

Ruby or Rhubarb 60 days; a beautiful red-stalked plant; pretty in the garden among flowers or vegetables; some of the color bleeds in cooking; excellent flavor (widely available)

Notes

GROWTH CONDITIONS

Germination Temperature: 50°–85°F
pH: 6.0–7.5 (7.2 deters clubroot)
Planting Depth: ¼"
Breadth: 15'–24'

Growth Temperature: 60°–65°F
Root Depth: 18"–36"
Height: 18"–4'

Space Between Plants: in beds: 15" in rows: 18"–24"
Space Between Rows: 24"–36"
Water: Medium and evenly moist.
Fertilizer: Heavy feeder. Before planting add compost to the soil. If clubroot is a problem, raise the pH by adding lime or taking other measures (*see "Acid Soil" on* page 161).
Side-dressing: When buds begin to form, side-dress the plant with compost.

First Seed-Starting Date:

Days Germ	+	Days Transplant	+	Days Before LFD	=	Days Count *Back* from LFD
3–10	+	42	+	14	=	59–66

Last Seed-Starting Date:

Days Germ	+	Days Transplant	+	Maturity	+	SDF	+	Frost Tender	=	Days *Back* from FFD
3–10	+	21	+	55–74	+	14	+	0	=	93–119

HARVEST

Broccoli is ready to harvest when the heads are dark green. Purple varieties should be a dusky violet. If heads turn yellow, you've waited too long. For the best flavor, heads should be no more than about 4" across. The exception is Romanesco, whose natural color is chartreuse and head can grow up to 1' in breadth. For most varieties, smaller compact heads are best. Harvest the central head first. Some varieties will produce side shoots that develop small head clusters; these plants will produce for 1 to 2 months, or until frost. Cut the stalk so that several inches remain on the plant.

STORAGE REQUIREMENTS

Fall crops are better than summer crops for freezing.

Fresh:

Temperature	Humidity	Storage Life
32°F	95%–100%	10–14 days
32°–40°F	80%	1 month

Preserved:

Method	Taste	Shelflife (in months)
Canned	fair	12+
Frozen	good	12
Dried	fair	12+

GROWING TIPS

Broccoli is an annual cool-season crop, hardy to frost and light freezes. Plan an average of 5–10 plants per person. Transplant seedlings when they're 6" high, and place in the ground 1" deeper than they were grown in the pots. Broccoli is usually sensitive to heat. If the weather is too hot, it will flower quickly and won't produce an edible head. Cover with fabric immediately after planting. This not only protects broccoli from pests but also helps trap heat for early plantings. To prevent spreading clubroot and other soil-borne diseases, don't compost *Brassica* roots. Some gardeners won't compost any part of a plant in the *Brassica* family. Pull and destroy infected plants. Also, rotate the placement of *Brassica* plants in your garden so they aren't in the same 10' radius for at least 3 years. Some experts recommend a rotation of 7 years.

Pests

Aphid, cabbage butterfly, cabbage looper, cabbage maggot, cutworm, diamondback moth, flea beetle, harlequin bug, imported cabbage worm, mite, root fly, slug, weevil, whitefly

Diseases

Alternaria leaf spot, black leg, black rot, club root, damping off, downy mildew, leaf spot, rhizoctonia, yellows

Allies

Some evidence: candytuft, shepherds purse, wormseed mustard

Uncertain: catnip, celery, chamomile, dill, garlic, mint, nasturtium, onion family, radish, rosemary, sage, savory, tansy, tomato, thyme, wormwood

Companions

Artichoke, beet, bush beans, chard, cucumber, lettuce, peas, potato, spinach

Incompatibles

Pole lima and snap beans, strawberry, tomato (latter may also be an ally)

SELECTED VARIETIES

Greenhouse

DeCicco, Green Comet, Italian Green Sprouting, Spartan Early (*see* below).

Outdoor

DeCicco 65 days; open-pollinated; old Italian variety; small heads; long harvest with side-shoots (Garden City, Hi Altitude, Johnny's, Southern Exposure, William Dam)

Green Comet 55 days; hybrid; extra large and tight heads; heat and disease resistant (Burpee, Gurney's, Park, William Dam)

Green Goliath 55 days; open-pollinated; high yields; early and extended harvest; many side shoots; good for freezing (Burpee, Jung, William Dam)

Green Valiant 66 days; hybrid; large heads; good for intensive planting; good for fall planting; frost resistant; dense heads and heavy stalks; develops side shoots (Johnny's, Territorial)

Italian Green Sprouting (aka: Calabrese) 65–80 days; open-pollinated; forms many sideshoots after central harvest; prolific (Abundant Life, Cook's, Nichols, Seeds Blum, Stokes)

Mercedes 58 days; hybrid; introduced in 1990, reliable for fall planting and harvest before winter; matures in 2 months from seed (Shepherd's)

Premium Crop 60–80 days; hybrid; large heads; good for summer and fall crops; uniform; compact; holds firmness well (widely available)

Purple Sprouting 220 days (from seed); open-pollinated; one of oldest heirlooms (pre-1835); profusion of tender, very sweet shoots; hardy to -10°F; in some areas must overwinter before it flowers in the spring (Abundant Life, Bountiful Gardens, Cook's, Territorial)

Rapini or Broccoli Raab or Ruvo Kale *(B. rapa ruvo)* 60 days; not a true broccoli; Italian specialty item; doesn't develop real heads; grown for leaves, ribs, and flower buds. Sow very early spring with radishes, or in fall. Sauté with garlic and olive oil, or use like kale (Nichols)

Romanesco Unusual yellow color; open-pollinated; spiraling large head; needs a long season so start seeds early; also needs extra feeding; different strains have different maturation times for short or long seasons: make sure to order a strain that will do well in your area (Bountiful Gardens–for Northern climates, Burpee–75 days, Gurney's–105 days, Johnny's–75 days for cultivar "Minaret," Shepherd's–100 days)

Silvia Developed in 1989; more resistant to powdery mildew than most (Letherman's)

Spartan Early 47–76 days; open-pollinated; extra early; good-sized, solid center heads; doesn't go to seed; good flavor (Field's, Seeds Blum, Southern Exposure, Stokes)

Waltham 29 74 days; open-pollinated; for early fall planting; will mature in cold weather; long harvest; good for freezing (Abundant Life, Seeds Blum, Southern Exposure)

Notes

GROWTH CONDITIONS

Germination Temperature: 50°–80°F
pH: 6.0–7.5
Planting Depth: ¼"
Breadth: 24"

Growth Temperature: 60°–65°F
Root Depth: 18"–36"
Height: 24"–48"

Space Between Plants: in beds: 16"–18" in rows: 18"–24"
Space Between Rows: 24"–40"
Water: Medium and evenly moist.
Fertilizer: Heavy feeder; use compost, or 2–3 bushels of manure per 100 square feet.
Side-dressing: Apply 2 weeks after transplanting, and twice more at monthly intervals.

First Seed-Starting Date:

Days Germ	+	Days Transplant	+	Days Before LFD	=	Days Count *Back* from LFD
3–10	+	28–49	+	14–21	=	45–80

Last Seed-Starting Date:

Days Germ	+	Days Transplant	+	Maturity	+	SDF	+	Frost Tender	=	Days *Back* from FFD
3–10	+	21	+	80–100	+	14	+	0	=	118–145

HARVEST

For the best sprout growth, when a node begins to bulge, remove the leaf below it. Harvest from the bottom of the stalk up. When sprouts are firm and no more than about 1" across, use a sharp knife to cut off the sprouts and remove lower leaves. Leave enough trunk so that new sprouts can grow. As the harvest slows, pinch the top of the plant to direct nutrients to the sprouts. For maximum vitamin C, harvest when the temperature is around freezing. Some say never to harvest unless you've had at least two frosts, since frost improves flavor. It has also been reported that sprouts can be harvested throughout the summer and still be tender if continuously picked when they reach the size of marbles. If you want to harvest all at once instead of continuously, cut or pinch off the stalk top 4–8 weeks before your intended harvest time. After harvest, remove the entire plant from the ground to minimize the chance of disease next season.

STORAGE REQUIREMENTS

Store entire plant in a cool root cellar. Otherwise, leave the stalk in the ground and pick sprouts when ready to eat. Some report harvesting through the snow.

Fresh:	Temperature	Humidity	Storage Life
	32°F	95%–100%	3–5 weeks

Preserved:	Method	Taste	Shelflife (in months)
	Canned	fair	12+
	Frozen	good	12
	Dried	poor	

GROWING TIPS

Brussels sprouts are an annual cool-season crop, hardy to frost and light freezes. Plan an average of 2–8 plants per person. There are two basic types of Brussels sprouts varieties: (1) the dwarf (e.g., "Jade Cross"), which matures early and is winter hardy but more difficult to harvest; and (2) the taller (e.g., "Long Island Improved") which is less hardy but easier to harvest. Brussels sprouts have shallow roots, so as they become top heavy you may need to stake them, particularly if exposed to strong winds. As with other *Brassicas,* Brussels sprouts are susceptible to pests and diseases that must be kept under control early in the season. Row covers are one of the easiest pest controls to use, provided no pest eggs are already present. To prevent spreading soil-borne diseases, don't compost *Brassica* roots. Rotate at least on a 3-year basis, or optimally, on a 7-year basis.

Pests

Aphid, cabbage butterfly, cabbage looper, cabbage maggot, cutworm, flea beetle, harlequin bug, mite, root fly, slug, thrips, weevil, whitefly

Diseases

Black leg, black rot, club root, damping off, leaf spot, rhizoctonia, yellows

Allies

Some evidence: candytuft, clover (white), cover grass, french beans, shepherd's purse, weedy ground cover, wormseed mustard

Uncertain: celery, chamomile, dill, garlic, mint, onion family, radish, rosemary, sage, savory, tansy, tomato, thyme, wormwood

Companions

Artichoke, beet, peas, potato, spinach

Incompatibles

Kohlrabi, all pole beans, strawberry, tomato (Latter may also be an ally)

SELECTED VARIETIES

Greenhouse

Early Dwarf Danish, Jade Cross, Long Island Improved *(see* below).

Outdoor

Early Dwarf Danish 95 days; early; open-pollinated; well suited for short seasons; dwarf habit aids mulching; large sprouts (Abundant Life, Garden City)

Jade Cross 80 days; dwarf hybrid; good for short season; sweet and mild (but can be bitter); heat tolerant (widely available)

Long Island Improved (Catskill) 80 days; excellent standard variety; open-pollinated; tall variety; small globe-shaped heads; tender, delicate flavor; good frozen (Nichols, Stokes)

Oliver Hybrid; earliest variety; easy to grow (Burpee, Harris, Johnny's)

Ormavon 117 days; hybrid; grows sprouts up the stem and "cabbage" greens on top; harvest tender greens after sprouts; interesting dual-purpose item (Thompson & Morgan)

Peer Gynt 140 days; dwarf; long maturation and high quality sprouts (Thompson & Morgan)

Prince Marvel 90 days; tall plant; firm and excellent quality sprouts; tolerates bottom rot; reduced cracking (widely available)

Rubine Red 80 days; open-pollinated; beautiful red; late variety (Cook's, Gurney's, Harris, Nichols, Seeds Blum, William Dam)

Silverstar Hybrid; good flavor; early sprouts; very hardy variety; can overwinter in mild areas or where there is good snow cover (Cook's)

Valiant 110 days; hybrid; 2' plant; cylindrical sprouts; tender and sweet, not bitter; resists rot and cracking; reliable heavy producer (Shepherd's)

Notes

This vegetable is high in calcium and iron, as well as a good source of vitamins A and C.

GROWTH CONDITIONS

Germination Temperature: 45°–95°F
pH: 6.0–7.5 (7.2 deters clubroot)
Planting Depth: ¼"–½"
Breadth: 24"–40"

Growth Temperature: 60°–65°F
Root Depth: 12"–5'
Height: 12"–15"

Space Between Plants: in beds: 15" in rows: 18"
Space Between Rows: 24"–30"
Water: Heavy early and medium late in the season.
Fertilizer: Heavy feeder; high N and K; may need to add lime to raise the pH to deter clubroot.
Side-dressing: Every 2 weeks.

First Seed-Starting Date:

Days Germ	+	Days Transplant	+	Days Before LFD	=	Days Count *Back* from LFD
7–12	+	42	+	14–21	=	63–75

Last Seed-Starting Date:

Days Germ	+	Days Transplant	+	Maturity	+	SDF	+	Frost Tender	=	Days *Back* from FFD
4	+	21	+	65–95	+	14	+	0	=	104–130

HARVEST

For eating fresh, cut the head at ground level as soon as it feels solid. Smaller heads may grow from the remaining leaves and stems. For the best storage heads, pick when still firm and solid and before the top leaves lose green color. Pull the entire plant and roots from the ground. If left too long in the ground, the cabbage core becomes fibrous and tough, and the head may split.

STORAGE REQUIREMENTS

Some recommend curing heads in the sun for a few days before storing for long periods. Such curing requires covering at night. Because of the strong odors emitted, store in either a well-ventilated place or a separate room reserved for *Brassicas*. To store, trim off all loose outer leaves. Hang by its roots, or wrap individually in paper, or layer in straw in an airy bin, or place several inches apart on shelves.

Fresh:	Temperature	Humidity	Storage Life
	32°–40°F	80%–90%	about 4 months

Preserved:	Method	Taste	Shelflife (in months)
	Canned	poor	
	Frozen	good	8
	Dried	fair	12+

GROWING TIPS

Cabbage is an annual cool-season crop, hardy to frost and light freezes. Plan an average of 3–5 plants per person. Young plants may bolt if grown at 50°F for a long time; mature plants of late varieties improve flavor in cold weather. A smaller cabbage head has better flavor and can stay in the field longer without splitting. To keep them small, plant close together or, when the head is almost full, give the plant a sharp twist to sever feeder roots. After harvest, continued growth causes cabbage to need additional food reserves. Rapid growers keep poorly as they use up their food reserves faster. Early varieties are generally the smallest, juiciest, and tenderest, but they store poorly and split easily. Midseason varieties keep better in the field. Late varieties, best for sauerkraut, provide the largest and longest-keeping heads. Yellow varieties tend to be hotter than white. To prevent spreading soil-borne diseases, don't compost any *Brassica* roots; pull and destroy infected plants. Also, rotate these plants on at least a 3-year basis, or optimally on a 7-year basis.

Pests

Aphids, cabbage butterfly, cabbage looper, cabbage maggot, cabbage-worm, cutworm, diamond-back moth, flea beetle, green worm, harlequin bug, leafminer, mite, mole, seedcorn maggot, root fly, slug, stink bug, weevil

Diseases

Black leg, black rot, club root, damping off, fusarium wilt, leaf spot, pink rot, rhizoctonia, yellows

Allies

Some evidence: candytuft, clover (red and white), shepherd's purse, wormseed mustard

Uncertain: celery, chamomile, dill, garlic, hyssop, mint, nasturtium, onion family, radish, rosemary, sage, savory, tomato, tansy, thyme, southern-wood, wormwood

Companions

Artichoke, beet, bush beans, cucumber, lettuce, peas, potato, spinach

Incompatibles

All pole beans, basil, strawberry, tomato (*Note:* latter might also be an ally)

SELECTED VARIETIES

Greenhouse

All **Chinese cabbages, Market Prize** (*see* below).

Outdoor

Red.
Pierette Hybrid; midseason; large, round heads; tolerates splitting (Stokes)
Red Danish Open-pollinated; resists thrips, cabbage looper, and moths (Stokes)
Ruby Ball Hybrid; early; red leaves retain color in cooking (Harris, Territorial)

White.
Danish Ballhead 100 days; open-pollinated; late keeper; good for kraut; resists thrips; sweet flavor; resists cracking; keeps through winter (widely available)
Early Jersey Wakefield 63 days; open-pollinated; heirloom; space-saving pointed heads; good flavor; reliable; well-adapted to different soils; resists yellows (widely available)
Grenadier 65 days; 2-pound heads; hybrid; excellent fresh eating; tender; juicy; resists cracking and long holding qualities; prefers cool weather; doesn't tolerate yellows (Shepherd's, Stokes)
Lariat 125 days (from seed); 5–8 pound heads; open-pollinated; very late season; best long-term keeper; still high quality after several months storage (Johnny's)
Market Prize 76 days; hybrid; blue-green; good yields under a wide variety of conditions; good holding quality; resists yellows and splitting (Harris)
Perfect Ball 87 days; hybrid; midseason; sweetest and smallest core of midseasons; resists yellows; good holding quality in field; large wrapping leaves (Johnny's)
Prime Time 76 days; hybrid; midseason; especially good for salads if picked early as a loose, round head (Stokes)
Multikeeper 86 days; hybrid; late season; tolerates yellows and black rot (Stokes)
Savoy Ace 85 days; AAS winner; resists heat and frost; holds well for long harvest; resists yellows and insects (widely available)
Savoy King 90 days; very dark green, crinkled (savoyed) leaves; high in vitamin A; semiflat heads resists yellows and insects (widely available)
Stonehead 67 days; AAS winner; hybrid; early; popular for firm, solid interior; resists cracking; resists yellows; good for small areas (widely available)

Chinese. Good in soups, stir-fries, or salads
Jade Pagoda (Michihi type) 68 days; hybrid; tall cylinder shape; thick, leafy, and savoyed; mild; sweet; vigorous; high yields; easy to grow; resists bolting (Harris, Park, Stokes)
Nagoda 50 days; tolerates heat and cold; standard in stores (Johnny's)
Joi Choi 45 days; hybrid between Pak Choi and Lei Choi; slow bolting; stands warm weather; excellent flavor (Harris, Park, Stokes)

Notes

GROWTH CONDITIONS

Germination Temperature: 45°–85°F
pH: 5.5–6.5
Planting Depth: ¼"–½"
Breadth: 12"–24"

Growth Temperature: 60°–65°F
Root Depth: 24"–7'
Height: 12"

Space Between Plants: in beds: 2"–3" in rows: 6"
Space Between Rows: 16"–30"
Water: Medium.
Fertilizer: Light feeder; too much top growth may mean too much N.
Side-dressing: Apply 3 weeks after germination, and again when 6"–8" high.

First Seed-Starting Date:

Days Germ	+	Days Transplant	+	Days Before LFD	=	Days Count *Back* from LFD
6–14	+	0	+	8–14	=	14–28

Last Seed-Starting Date:

Days Germ	+	Days Transplant	+	Maturity	+	SDF	+	Frost Tender	=	Days *Back* from FFD
6–14	+	0	+	65–70	+	14	+	0	=	85–98

HARVEST

Gently pull the roots out by their green tops. For most newer varieties, don't let carrots grow fatter than 1½" across or they'll become woody. Some older varieties can still be succulent and delicious when large.

STORAGE REQUIREMENTS

Remove the green tops, but do not wash the carrot before storing. Store in sawdust or sand in containers.

Fresh:

Temperature	Humidity	Storage Life
32°F	90%–95%	4–5 months
35°F	95%–100%	7–9 months

Preserved:

Method	Taste	Shelflife (in months)
Canned	fair	12+
Frozen	good	8
Dried	fair	12+

GROWING TIPS

Carrots are an annual cool-season crop, half-hardy to frost and light freezes. Plan an average of 10–40 plants per person. One way to break the soil crust for carrot seeds is to plant a few fast-germinating radish seeds in the carrot bed. Carrots produce best in friable soil, so dig well before planting or grow smaller carrots that don't need deep soil. Sow seeds evenly in a very shallow furrow, about ¼" deep, and keep seeds moist so they will germinate. When the first leaves emerge, thin to 1" apart; when true leaves emerge, thin to 3" apart. If you delay the final thinning a bit, you can use the removed roots as baby carrots. The darkest and greenest tops indicate the largest carrots. To prevent greening at the shoulders, hill dirt up around the greens. The sweetest and best textured carrots are the Nantes-types, cylindrical and blunt-tipped. The long and tapered characteristics are typical of Imperator varieties. Nantes-types absorb more water and therefore have less dry matter, making them more succulent and crisp. They are also lower than other types in terpenoids, which cause a soapy turpentine-like taste; the amount of terpenoids depends entirely on variety, not on the soil. Terpenoids break down in cooking so that carrots taste sweeter when cooked. Nantes now describes any carrot with the above traits, not true lineage to the French region where the type originated.

Pests

Carrot rust fly, carrot weevil, cutworm, flea beetle, leafhopper, nematode, snail, slug, parsleyworm, weevil, wireworm

Diseases

Alternaria leaf spot, cercospora, damping off, leaf blight, soft rot, yellows

Allies

Some evidence: onion family

Uncertain: black salsify, chives, coriander, flax, lettuce, pea, penny-royal, radish, rosemary, sage, wormwood

Companions

All beans, leek, pepper, tomato

Incompatibles

Celery, dill (retards growth)

SELECTED VARIETIES

Greenhouse

Early Scarlet Horn, Planet, Caramba, or other shorter carrots (*see* below).

Outdoor

A-Plus 71 days; hybrid; rich in vitamin A; Nantes-type (widely available)

Caramba 75 days; Dutch; open-pollinated; grow for "mini" or regular size; crispy; makes sweet juice (Shepherd's, Territorial)

Danvers Half Long 75 days; open-pollinated; good keeper in underground storage; adapted to many soil types (Burpee, Garden City, Fields, Gurney's, Southern Exposure, William Dam)

Early Scarlet Horn open-pollinated; heirloom "baby" carrot; good for greenhouse forcing and early outdoor planting (Abundant Life)

Ingot 68 days; hybrid; Nantes-type; high flavor and texture rating by Rodale (Johnny's, Stokes)

Lindoro 63 days; hybrid; Nantes-type; high flavor and texture rating by Rodale (Park)

Mokum Hybrid; good for early spring crop under row covers (Cook's)

Nantes Half Long (aka: Coreless and Scarlet Nantes) 70 days; open-pollinated; sweet and tender eating carrot; coreless; standard home gardener variety (widely available)

Nantes Tip Top 73 days; Dutch; excellent eating quality; for wide range of soils (Shepherd's)

Napoli 58 days; hybrid; introduced in 1989; tender; sweet; early; blight-tolerant (Johnny's)

Planet 68 days; French; open-pollinated; a small round baby carrot of deep orange/red color; doesn't need deep soil (Shepherd's, Stokes)

Royal Chantenay 70 days; excellent for heavy, clay, or shallow soils; popular (widely available)

Touchon 75 days; French; open-pollinated; Nantes-type; fine texture; sweet; flavor suffers in hot summers; good for juicing (Abundant Life, Blum, Cook's, Nichols, Stokes)

White Belgium 75 days; unusual white all the way through; taste may get too strong in hot summers (Nichols)

Notes

GROWTH CONDITIONS

Germination Temperature: 45°–85°F
pH: 6.0–7.5
Planting Depth: ¼"– ½"
Breadth: 2' to 2½'

Growth Temperature: 60°–70°F day, 50°–60°F night
Root Depth: 18"–4'
Height: 18"–24"

Space Between Plants: in beds: 12"–15" in rows: 18"
Space Between Rows: 24"–46"
Water: Medium; critical early in season and during warm weather.
Fertilizer: Heavy feeder; needs high N and K.
Side-dressing: Every 3–4 weeks.

First Seed-Starting Date: If covered, transplants can be set out almost 4 weeks earlier (*see* below).

Days Germ	+	Days Transplant	-	Days After LFD	=	Days Count *Back* from LFD
4–10	+	35–49	-	14 (no cover)	=	25–45 (uncovered at transplanting)
4–10	+	35–49	+	14 (covered)	=	53–73 (covered once transplanted)

Last Seed-Starting Date:

Days Germ	+	Days Transplant	+	Maturity	+	SDF	+	Frost Tender	=	Days *Back* from FFD
4–10	+	21	+	50–95	+	14	+	N/A	=	89–140

HARVEST

When heads are 8"–10" in diameter, harvest by pulling the entire plant from the soil. Cauliflower heads deteriorate quickly, so check periodically and harvest when ready.

STORAGE REQUIREMENTS

Wrap individual plants, head and roots, in plastic. Store in a root cellar or cool place.

Fresh:

Temperature	Humidity	Storage Life
32°F	95%–98%	3–4 weeks

Preserved:

Method	Taste	Shelflife (in months)
Frozen	good	12
Pickled	good	12

GROWING TIPS

Cauliflower is an annual cool-season crop, half-hardy to frost and light freezes. Plan an average of 3–5 plants per person. Cauliflower can be difficult to grow as a spring crop because it bolts in the heat. While it is the most sensitive of all *Brassicas* to frost, it is generally easier to grow as a fall crop. Note on the seed-starting dates that cauliflower shouldn't be transplanted outdoors until all danger of frost is past, unless covered. It also needs to mature before hot summer arrives. A compromise might be to choose an intermediate starting date and cover the plants when set out to protect from cold. Purple cauliflower is an easier crop because it's more pest resistant and hardier than white varieties. Early in the season it looks and tastes more like broccoli, but after a cold snap, its flavor is more like cauliflower. Depending on your area, cauliflower might be better grown as a fall crop to reduce the threat of insect damage and bolting.

Plant transplants 1" deeper than they were grown in starting pots, and cover with netting to protect from pests. Spacing between plants determines head size: the closer together, the smaller the head. When heads start forming, prevent yellowing by tying several upright leaves loosely together with string, covering the rest of the head from sun. To prevent spreading clubroot and other soilborne diseases, don't compost any *Brassica* roots. Pull and destroy all infected plants. Also, rotate *Brassica* plants on at least a 3-year basis, or optimally on a 7-year basis.

Pests

Aphid, cabbage butterfly, looper and maggot, cutworm, diamondback moth, harlequin bug, mite, root fly, root maggot, slug, snail, striped flea beetle, weevil

Diseases

Black leg, black rot, clubroot, damping off, downy mildew, leaf spot, rhizoctonia, seed rot, yellows (*Note:* Hollow stems have been found by two British horticulturists to be caused by large head size not boron deficiency, as commonly believed.)

Allies

Some evidence: candytuft, corn spurry (spergula arvensis), lamb's quarters, shepherd's purse, tomato, white or red clover, wormseed mustard

Uncertain: chamomile, celery, dill, mint, nasturtium, onion, rosemary, sage, savory, thyme, wormwood

Companions

Artichoke, aromatic plants, beet, bush beans, garlic, lettuce, peas, potato, spinach

Incompatibles

Pole bean, strawberry, tomato (latter also might be an ally)

SELECTED VARIETIES

Greenhouse

Extra Early Snowball, Purple Head, Snow Crown, Snow King (*see* below).

Outdoor

Early Purple Sicilian Open-pollinated; purple heads, like purple broccoli (Abundant Life)

Extra Early Snowball 50 days; open-pollinated; early variety; pest resistant; resists yellows (Seeds Blum, Southern Exposure, Stokes)

Purple Head 80–85 days; open-pollinated; easier to grow than white types; turns green when cooked (Burpee, William Dam)

Snow Crown 50–53 days; hybrid; AAS winner; early and reliable producer; vigorous; tolerates adverse weather (Burpee, Harris, Jung, Stokes, Territorial, William Dam)

Snow King Hybrid 50 days; AAS winner; very early; excellent flavor (Gurney's, Field's, Park, Thompson & Morgan, William Dam)

White Sails 68 days; hybrid; good for fall planting; leaves self-wrap to protect inner curds; deep large heads (Southern Exposure, Stokes)

Violet Queen 54 days; hybrid; earliest purple; considered by some as best purple variety; easy to grow; uniform (Cook's, Harris, Johnny's)

Notes

GROWTH CONDITIONS

Germination Temperature: 70°F
pH: 6.0–6.5
Planting Depth: ⅛"
Breadth: 12"

Growth Temperature: 60°–65°F
Root Depth: 18"–24"
Height: 12"

Space Between Plants: in beds: 4"–7" in rows: 12"
Space Between Rows: 15"–26"
Water: Heavy, infrequently, but keep evenly moist, especially during hot spells.
Fertilizer: Heavy feeder.

First Seed-Starting Date: Usually 8–12 weeks before last frost.

Days Germ	+	Days Transplant	-	Days After LFD	=	Days Count *Back* from LFD
10–21	+	46–60	-	0–14	=	56–67

Last Seed-Starting Date:

Days Germ	+	Days Transplant	+	Maturity	+	SDF	+	Frost Tender	=	Days *Back* from FFD
10–21	+	50	+	110–120	+	14	+	N/A	=	184–205

HARVEST

After the first fall frost, and when the bulbs are 2"–4", carefully dig or pull out the roots. The larger the root (more than 4"), the more it will be contaminated by involutions of the skin.

STORAGE REQUIREMENTS

Celeriac is best stored fresh. The results of various preservation methods are unknown. Do not wash the root before storing. Rub off side shoots. Store in boxes of moist peat. When covered with a thick mulch, the roots will keep in the ground for about one month beyond the first frost.

Fresh:	Temperature	Humidity	Storage Life
	32°F	97%–99%	6–8 months

GROWING TIPS

Celeriac is a cool-season root crop, half-hardy to frost and light freezes. Plan an average of 1–5 plants per person. It is a pest-, disease- and problem-free biennial vegetable that is usually grown as an annual. In zones 5 and northward, this root can be overwintered in the ground if mulched heavily with straw to prevent frost penetration. Sow seeds thickly in pots indoors. Thin seedlings to one per pot. Set out when 2 to 2½" tall. Remove side-shoots from the base of the plant. When transplanting, keep as much as possible of the original potting soil around the root. After setting in the roots, reach under and gently squeeze the soil around the roots to eliminate air gaps. Too much oxygen exposure during transplanting will cause them to dry out and die. Root quality drops when watered regularly, so water deeply and less frequently. To achieve the deep fertile soil needed for celeriac, try adding 1 bushel of well-rotted manure for 20' of row, and spading it in 8"–10" deep. Celeriac has been enjoyed in Europe for ages and only recently has begun to make a showing in the United States. It is an unsightly root that tends to develop involutions filled with dirt, which cause wastage in food preparation. With a delicious, delicate flavor similar to that of celery heart, celeriac is worth the effort of cutting off all of the skin and the involutions with dirt. It can be boiled and added to potatoes, or eaten raw as an addition to salads. We cut it into thin strips, blanch and tenderize it for 30 minutes by adding lemon juice and a little salt, then toss and serve it with a remoulade sauce.

Pests

Aphid, celeryworm, slug, weevil, wireworm

Diseases

Septoria leaf spot

Allies

None

Companions

Squash, tomato

Incompatibles

None

SELECTED VARIETIES

Greenhouse

Celeriac, as a root vegetable, doesn't grow well in the greenhouse.

Outdoor

Alabaster 120 days; open-pollinated; large thick roots (Burpee)
Large Smooth Prague 110 days; open-pollinated (Jung, Seeds Blum, Stokes, William Dam)
Jose or **Brilliant** 110 days; open-pollinated; resists pithiness and hollow heart; relatively smooth; good taste (Cook's, Johnny's)

Notes

GROWTH CONDITIONS

Germination Temperature: 60°–70°F
pH: 6.0–7.0
Planting Depth: ¼"–½"
Breadth: 8"–12"
Space Between Plants: in beds: 6"–8" in rows: 8"–12"
Space Between Rows: 18"–36"
Water: Heavy.
Fertilizer: Heavy feeder; 2–3 weeks before planting, apply compost worked 12" into soil.
Side-dressing: Apply every 2 weeks, especially 3 weeks after transplanting; repeat 6 weeks later.

Growth Temperature: 60°–65°F, with nights higher than 40°F
Root Depth: Shallow, upper 6"–12"
Height: 15"–18"

First Seed-Starting Date:

Days Germ	+	Days Transplant	-	Days After LFD	=	Days Count *Back* from LFD
5–7	+	70–84	-	14–21	=	61–70

Last Seed-Starting Date:

Days Germ	+	Days Transplant	+	Maturity	+	SDF	+	Frost Tender	=	Days *Back* from FFD
6	+	30	+	90–135	+	14	+	0	=	140–185

HARVEST

Harvest self-blanching celery before the first frost. Harvest blanched varieties after the first frost. Dig out each plant whenever needed.

STORAGE REQUIREMENTS

Celery is best stored at cold temperatures in a perforated plastic bag. To refresh wilted stalks, simply place them in a tall glass of cold water.

Fresh:

Temperature	Humidity	Storage Life
32°F	98%–100%	2–3 months
32°F	80%–90%	4–5 weeks

Preserved:

Method	Taste	Shelflife (in months)
Canned	fair	12+
Frozen	good	5
Dried	good	12+

GROWING TIPS

Celery is a cool-season crop, half-hardy to frost and light freezes. Plan an average of 3–8 plants per person. Soak seeds overnight to help germination. The seedlings need to be transplanted at least once before setting outside. Transplant outside when seedlings are 4"–6" tall and night temperatures don't fall below 40°F. Water plants before they are transplanted. There are two basic types of celery: blanching and self-blanching.

Self-blanching varieties are much easier to grow, as they can be grown in flat soil without trenches. Their harvest, however, is earlier and more limited. For celery that needs blanching, (1) plant in the center of 18"-wide trenches, (2) remove suckers in midseason and wrap stalk bunches with brown paper, newspaper, or cardboard to prevent soil from getting between the stalks, (3) 2 months before harvest fill the trench with soil up to the bottom of the leaves, and (4) keep mounding soil around the base of the plant every 3 weeks. Make sure the mound is sloped to help drainage.

Pests

Aphid, cabbage looper, carrot rust fly, carrot weevil, celery leaftier, flea beetle, earwig, leafhopper, mite, nematode, parsleyworm, slug, tarnished plant bug, weevil, wireworm

Diseases

Black heart, celery mosaic, damping off, early and late blight, fusarium, pink rot, yellows

Allies

Uncertain: black salsify, cabbage, chive, coriander, garlic, nasturtium, pennyroyal

Companions

All beans, all *Brassicas*, celery, spinach, squash, tomato

Other Benefits

Cucumbers provide shade and moisture to other plants such as celery

Incompatibles

Carrot, parsnip

SELECTED VARIETIES

All varieties listed are open-pollinated

Greenhouse

Try the self-blanching varieties.

Outdoor

Blanching.

Fordhook Stocky; early; 15"–18"; good keeper; silvery white after blanching (Seeds Blum)

Red Unusual red-bronze stalks; stay red when cooked; hardier than green varieties (Blum)

Summit 100 days; very dark green; tolerates fusarium wilt; compact; 10" (Stokes)

Tall Utah 52-70R Improved 98 days; long, dark green, thick stalks; high yields; resists boron deficiency; high quality (Abundant Life, Burpee, Garden City, Jung, Park, Stokes)

Tendercrisp 105 days; early; high yields; more upright than most; Pascal type; ribless; pale green stalks (Field's, Stokes)

Ventura 100 days; tall Utah type; some tolerance of fusarium wilt (Johnny's, Stokes)

Self-Blanching.

Golden Self-Blanching 115 days; heirloom; early; crispy; delicate flavor; dwarf (Seeds Blum)

Seasoning or Cutting Celery. This has the same general culture as celery, but is generally grown only for its leaves. It is easier to grow than other celery due to fewer pest and disease problems, and minimal requirements for water and feeding. Cutting celery also can be harvested over a longer period of time.

Leaf Celery Pungent seasoning; excellent as dried flavoring (Seeds Blum)

Amsterdam Fine Seasoning Celery 12"–18" tall; leaves like a shiny flat-leafed parsley; easy to dry and retains flavor well (Shepherd's)

Notes

GROWTH CONDITIONS

Germination Temperature: 60°–95°F
pH: 5.5–7.0
Planting Depth: 1"–2" sh² types, ½ "
Breadth: 18"–4'

Growth Temperature: 60°–75°F
Root Depth: 18"–6'
Height: 7'–8' (but some flour and field corns grow much higher)

Space Between Plants: in beds: 8"–12" in rows: 18"
Space Between Rows: 30"–42"
Water: Medium; provide more when the stalks flowers.
Fertilizer: Heavy feeder; apply manure in the fall, or compost a few weeks before planting.
Side-dressing: Apply every 2 weeks, and additionally when stalks are 8"–10" and knee high.

First Seed-Starting Date: Sow every 10–14 days for continuous harvest.

Days Germ	+	Days Transplant	-	Days After LFD	=	Days Count *Back* from LFD
4–21	+	0 (direct)	-	0–10	=	4–11

Last Seed-Starting Date:

Days Germ	+	Days Transplant	+	Maturity	+	SDF	+	Frost Tender	=	Days *Back* from FFD
4	+	0		+ 65–95	+	14	+	14		= 97–127

HARVEST

Sweet Corn: About 18 days after silks appear, when they're dark and dry, make a small slit in the husk (don't pull the silks down), and pierce the kernel with a fingernail. If the liquid is (1) clear, wait a few days, (2) milky, pick and eat, or (3) pasty, the ear is past its prime and is best for canning. **Popcorn (var. *praecox*):** Pick when the husks are brown and partly dried. Finish drying corn on the husks. A solar drier is the most rapid method, drying the corn in about 5 days. The kernels are ready for storage if they fall off easily when rubbed by a thumb or twisted. Before using, store in bags or jars to even out the moisture content. The ultimate test, of course, is to pop them.

STORAGE REQUIREMENTS

Corn is best eaten immediately. Some gardeners won't even go out to pick ears until the cooking water is already boiling.

Fresh:

Temperature	Humidity	Storage Life
40°–45°F	80%–95%	4–10 days

Preserved:

Method	Taste	Shelflife (in months)
Canned	excellent	12+
Frozen	good	8
Dried	good	12+

GROWING TIPS

Corn is a warm-season crop, tender to frost and light freezes. Plan an average of 12–40 plants per person, depending on your needs. For good pollination and full ears, plant in blocks of at least 4–6 rows and about 15" on center. If birds are a problem in your garden, stealing seeds or eating seedlings, cover your corn patch with a floating row cover immediately after planting seeds. Corn easily cross-pollinates, so isolate popcorn and field corn from sweet corn by at least 50'–100', or plant varieties that have different pollination times, which is when tassels appear. For seed saving, isolate corns by 1000' for absolute purity. Once pollinated, corn matures rapidly, usually 15–20 days after the first silks appear. Corn has shallow roots, so mulch heavily and avoid cultivating deeper than 1½". In small patches, don't remove suckers; they may bear corn if well side-dressed. Once harvested, cut stalks and till under or compost immediately. White and yellow corn vary in nutrition; white corn contains twice as much potassium, and yellow corn contains about 60 percent more sodium.

Pests

Aphid, birds, corn borer, earworm, maggot and root-worm, cucumber beetle, cutworm, earwig, flea beetle, garden webworm, Japanese beetle, June beetle, leafhopper, sap beetle, seedcorn maggot, thrips, webworm, white grub, wireworm

Diseases

Bacterial wilt, mosaic viruses, rust, smut, southern corn leaf blight, Stewart's wilt

Allies

Some evidence: all beans, chickweed, clover, giant ragweed, peanut, pigweed, shepherd's purse, soybean, sweet potato

Uncertain: alfalfa, goldenrod, odorless marigold, white geranium, peas, potato

Companions

Cucumber, melon, pumpkin, and squash

Incompatibles

Tomato (attacked by some similar insects)

SELECTED VARIETIES

Outdoor

Flour Varieties. These have soft starch, are easiest to grind, and make flour not meal.
Hopi Blue OP; HL; drought tolerant; vigorous; colors vary from black to purple; makes pretty blue flour (Abundant Life, Native Seed: Their strain good for high and low desert) *Note:* most other sources of Hopi Blue are flint varieties
White Posole OP; makes white flour (Plants of the Southwest)

Dent or Field Varieties. These have hard starch on the side and soft starch on the top of the kernel, are easier to grind than flint types, and are good for fresh eating, roasting, and grinding. Versatile.
Beasley's Red Dent 105 days; 9'; OP; HL; high blight and drought resistance; red kernels (Southern Exposure)
Bloody Butcher 110–120 days; 10'–12'; OP; pretty red kernels sometimes interspersed with other colors (Seeds Blum, Southern Exposure)
Mayo Batchi 90 days; OP; HL; short flat ears; staple of region; for low desert (Native Seed)
Northstine Dent 105 days; 7'; OP; HL; excellent for cornmeal and cereal; yellow; good for short seasons; high quality (Johnny's)
Reids Yellow Dent 85–110 days; 7'; OP; HL; very hardy; good in Southern heat; high yields; good for tortillas, meal, and hominy (Field's, Southern Exposure)

Flint Varieties. These have very hard starch and make cornmeal. Generally have good insect resistance and store well.
Hispanic Pueblo Red OP; HL; orange; red and maroon kernels; long ears; for high and low desert (Native Seed)
Longfellow 117 days; OP; orange kernels; makes a sweet cornbread; good in Northern gardens (Johnny's)

Sweet Varieties. Supersweet corn has the Shrunken-2 (sh_2) gene which causes shriveled seeds with weak seed coats, resulting in poor germination. Supersweets are often twice as sweet as "eh" types. They develop a watery texture when frozen. Sugar Enhanced corn has the "se" gene which causes higher sugar levels than "eh" types and also longer retention of sugar and tenderness, for up to 10–14 days. Everlasting Heritage corn has the "eh" gene designed for sweetness and texture.
Country Gentleman or Shoepeg 96 days; OP; HL; white; tender; resists drought and wilt; kernels are not in rows (widely available)
Florida Staysweet 87 days; supersweet; yellow; great flavor and yields; tight husks (Johnny's)
Hopi Early Cold tolerant; short-season crop; plant in early spring; small ears; for high and low desert (Native Seeds)
Honey and Cream 78 days; "eh"; white and yellow; tight husks (Burpee, Gurney's, Shepherd's)
Illini Gold 80 days; supersweet; yellow; excellent in trials (Jung, Park)
Improved Golden Bantam 82 days; OP; yellow; midseason; flavorful; performed well in *Harrowsmith* 1988 trials (Abundant Life, Nichols)
Iochief 86 days; AAS winner; 7½'; hybrid; yellow; top rated by *Organic Gardening* readers for reliability, productivity, drought tolerance, and taste (Gurney's, Field's)
Kandy Korn 84 days; "eh"; yellow; good flavor; doesn't require isolation; stays sweet several days after harvest; pretty purplish stalks and husks (widely available)
Polar Vee 53 days; yellow; produces well in cool regions (Field's, Gurney's, Stokes)
Silver Queen 92 days; standard hybrid; white; late season; top rated for flavor, productivity, drought tolerance, and disease resistance; tolerates Stewart's wilt and leaf blight (widely available)

Popcorn. These have the hardest starch of all corns.
Strawberry 105 days; 4'; HL; OP; stalks bear several ears; red kernels (widely available)
Tom Thumb 85 days; dwarf 3½'; yellow; can grow closely spaced (Johnny's)
White Cloud 95 days; hybrid; not heavy producer but one of best for popping (Stokes)

KEY

OP = Open-pollinated
HL = Heirloom

Notes

Studies show hybrid varieties to have greater ear and kernel growth rates, bigger kernel size, a longer period of kernel-filling, as well as greater redistribution of stalk-stored food to the kernel.

GROWTH CONDITIONS

Germination Temperature: 60°–95°F
pH: 5.5–7.0
Planting Depth: ½"–1"
Breadth: trellis: 12"–15" on ground: 12–20 square feet

Growth Temperature: 65°–75°F
Root Depth: 12", tap root to 2'–3'
Height: 6'

Space Between Plants: in beds: 12" in rows: 24"–48"
Space Between Rows: 4'
Water: Heavy during fruiting; all other times average and evenly moist. Deep watering.
Fertilizer: Heavy feeder; before planting apply compost.
Side-dressing: Every 2–3 weeks.
Support Structures: Use a 6' post, A-frame, teepee (three poles tied together at the top), or a trellis.

First Seed-Starting Date:

Days Germ	+	Days Transplant	-	Days After LFD	=	Days Count *Back* from LFD
6–10	+	28	-	14–21	=	17–21

Last Seed-Starting Date:

Days Germ	+	Days Transplant	+	Maturity	+	SDF	+	Frost Tender	=	Days *Back* from FFD
6–10	+	28	+	22–52	+	14	+	14	=	84–118

HARVEST

When the fruit is slightly immature, before seed coats become hard, pick with 1" of stem to minimize water loss. In warm weather, all cucumber plant types should be picked daily. Always pick open-pollinated varieties underripe. Harvest pickling cucumbers at 2"–6", and slicing cucumbers at 6"–10".

STORAGE REQUIREMENTS

Keep the short piece of stem on each fruit during storage.

Fresh:

Temperature	Humidity	Storage Life
45°–55°F	85%–95%	10–14 days

Preserved:

Method	Taste	Shelflife (in months)
Canned	good (as pickles)	12+
Frozen	poor	
Dried	poor	

GROWING TIPS

Cucumbers are a warm-season crop, very tender to frost and light freezing. Plan an average of 3–5 plants per person, depending on your pickling needs. In warm climates, some recommend planting cucumbers in hills spaced 3'–5' apart, with 6–8 seeds per hill. In cooler climates, transplant seedlings on a cloudy day or in the afternoon to minimize transplanting shock. Allow the main stem to grow as high as possible by pinching back some of the lateral shoots and letting others grow into branches. By picking the fruit early you won't have to support heavy fruit or risk arresting plant production.

Variety information: Most cucumbers are monoecious, which produce both male and female (fruit-bearing) flowers. Gynoecious types bear only female flowers, therefore a few male-flowering pollinators are included in the seed packets. Both require pollination by bees. Parthenocarpic types produce few if any seeds and require no pollination, so they can be grown to maturity under row covers. Bitterfree are resistant to damage from cucumber beetles. Dwarfs are good candidates for intercropping with tomatoes and peppers, but they must have a constant water supply. All types must also be picked daily in warm weather.

Pests

Aphid, cucumber beetle, cutworm (seedlings), flea beetle, garden centipede, mite, slug, snail, squash bug, squash vine borer

Diseases

Alternaria leaf spot, anthracnose, bacterial wilt, belly rot, cottony leak, cucumber wilt, downy mildew, leaf spot, mosaic, pickleworm, powdery mildew, root-knot, scab

Allies

Some evidence: broccoli, corn

Uncertain: catnip, goldenrod, marigold, nasturtium, onion, oregano, radish, rue, tansy

Companions

All beans, cabbage, eggplant, kale, melon, peas, sunflower, tomato

Other

Radish can be used as a trap plant; celery is companion plant under the "cuke's" A-frame

Incompatibles

Anise, basil, marjoram, potato, quack grass, rosemary, sage, summer savory, strong herbs

SELECTED VARIETIES

Greenhouse

Bush Champion, Gourmet #2, Pot Luck, Salad Bush, Salty, Spacemaster, Sweet Success (*see* below). *See* Stokes and Thompson & Morgan catalogs for other varieties specifically for the greenhouse.

KEY

CMV = Cucumber Mosaic Virus
DM = Downy Mildew
PM = Powdery Mildew

Outdoor

Notes

Salad/Slicing.

Bush Champion 55 days; short compact vines; 9"–11" fruit; long-season producer in all weather conditions; good for containers and greenhouse (Burpee, Thompson & Morgan)

Gourmet #2 60 days; gynoecious greenhouse type; 14"–16" long; crisp; sweet; tolerates scab and leaf spot (Nichols)

Green Knight Hybrid 60 days; burpless; heat-resistant; vigorous; thin-skinned (Burpee)

Marketmore 80 68 days; bred for resistance to CMV, DM, PM, and scab; straight slicer; bitterfree (widely available)

Pot Luck 45 days; hybrid; developed for small spaces; 18" long vine; 6"–8" fruit; space these 8"–12" in rows (Jung)

Salad Bush 57 days; AAS winner; resists PM, DM, CMV, leaf spot, and scab; small 24" vines; 8" fruit; monoecious (widely available)

Surecrop 60 days; hybrid; AAS winner; early; 8" long; weather resistant; high yields; good taste (Gurney's, Field's, Jung)

Sweet Success 58 days; hybrid; AAS winner; early; 12"–14"; burpless; CMV; resists scab and leafspot; parthenocarpic; provides seedless fruit (widely available)

Spacemaster 60 days; open-pollinated; best dwarf; CMV; resists scab; 7½"; white spine; plant early (widely available)

Picklers.

Edmonson Open-pollinated; heat and disease resistant (Seeds Blum)

Pickalot 54 days; hybrid; introduced in 1989; bush; PM; gynoecious; continuous bearer (Burpee)

Salty 53 days; hybrid; tolerates CMV, PM, and DM; crispy; a white spine gynoecious (Stokes)

Novelties.

Armenian Long (aka: Yard Long) 65 days; open-pollinated; long; good slicer; mild; sweet; bitterfree (Abundant Life, Burpee, Nichols, Seeds Blum, Shepherd's)

China 75 days; open-pollinated; oriental type; 12"–15"; tolerates CMV; crisp; firm; mild; weather tolerant (Stokes)

Crystal Apple 65 days; open-pollinated; non-bitter skins; good slicing and pickling; 2"–3" globes; creamy white skin and spine (Bountiful Gardens, Thompson & Morgan)

Lemon 60 days; open-pollinated; sweet; size and color of lemon (widely available)

White Wonder 58 days; open-pollinated; early bearing; all white; heirloom; high yields; crisp; resists Fusarium Wilt (Garden City, Seeds Blum)

GROWTH CONDITIONS

Germination Temperature: 75°–90°F
pH: 5.5–6.5
Planting Depth: ¼"
Breadth: 3'–4'

Growth Temperature: 70°–85°F
Root Depth: 4'–7'
Height: 24"–30"

Space Between Plants: in beds: 18" in rows: 18"–30"
Space Between Rows: 24"–48"
Water: Heavy.
Fertilizer: Heavy feeder; apply manure water or tea every 2 weeks.
Side-dressing: Apply after the first fruit appears.

First Seed-Starting Date:

Days Germ	+	Days Transplant	-	Days After LFD	=	Days Count *Back* from LFD
5–13	+	42–56	-	14–28	=	33–55

Last Seed-Starting Date:

Days Germ	+	Days Transplant	+	Maturity	+	SDF	+	Frost Tender	=	Days *Back* from FFD
5–13	+	42–56	+	50–80	+	14	+	14	=	125–177

HARVEST

Pick when the fruit is no more than 3"–5" long or 4" in diameter, and before the skin loses its lustre. Cut the fruit with small amount of stem. Fruit seeds should be light-colored. Brown seeds indicate the fruit has ripened too long. Eggplant vines are spiny, so be careful to avoid pricking yourself.

STORAGE REQUIREMENTS

Keep a small piece of stem on the eggplant during storage, so the skin isn't pierced. Eggplant is best used fresh.

Fresh:

Temperature	Humidity	Storage Life
46°–54°F	90%–95%	1 week
32°–40°F	80%–90%	6 months

Preserved:

Method	Taste	Shelflife (in months)
Canned	fair	12+
Frozen	fair	8
Dried	fair	12+

GROWING TIPS

Eggplant is a warm-season crop, tender to frost and light freezes. Plan an average of 2 plants per three people. All parts of the plant except the fruit are poisonous. For indoor seed starting in flats, block out the plants once the seedlings are well-established, by running a knife through the soil midway between the plants, cutting the roots, and leaving each plant with its own soil block. If you start seeds in individual pots this procedure is unnecessary. Make sure outdoor soil temperature is at least 55°–60°F before transplanting; otherwise they become stunted, turn yellow, and are slow to bear. As frost approaches, pinch back new blossoms so that plant nutrients are channeled into the remaining fruits. Eggplant is a versatile fruit often used in Italian dishes such as ratatouille, caponata, and lasagna. Its virtue is that it easily absorbs the flavors of whatever sauce it is cooked in, from herbal tomato sauces to Chinese Szechuan.

Pests

Aphid, Colorado potato beetle, cucumber beetle, cutworm, flea beetle, harlequin bug, lace bug, leafhopper, mite, nematode, tomato hornworm, whitefly

Diseases

Anthracnose, bacterial wilt, botrytis fruit rot, phomopsis blight, tobacco mosaic, verticillium wilt

Allies

Some evidence: none

Uncertain: coriander, goldenrod, green beans, marigold, potato

Companions

All beans, pepper

Other Benefits

Potato can also be used as a trap plant for pests

Incompatibles

None

SELECTED VARIETIES

Greenhouse

Black Beauty, Ichiban, Jersey King (*see* below).

Outdoor

Agora 68 days; improved variation of "Dusky" (*see* below) (Shepherd's)

Black Beauty 73–80 days; open-pollinated; almost round fruit; heavy yields; reliable; a common standard-size fruit (widely available)

Burpee Hybrid 70 days; drought resistant; tall; semi-spreading; vigorous (Burpee)

Dusky 60 days; popular early variety; pear-shaped; glossy; tolerates tobacco mosaic virus; good for Northern gardens (widely available)

Early Long Purple Open-pollinated; very early; a smaller variety for smaller growing areas; heirloom; slender 12" fruit (Seeds Blum)

Florida Market 85 days; open-pollinated; resists phomopsis; good for Southern growing (Blum)

Ghostbuster 80 days; open-pollinated; introduced in 1989; sweet; excellent for cooking (Harris)

Ichiban 61 days; open-pollinated; slender 12" fruit; 36" plants (Gurney's, Park); an improved variation on this is "Tycoon" (Nichols)

Jersey King 73 days; hybrid; dark purple; very long 10" fruit (Stokes)

Little Fingers 68 days; long and very slim, oriental-type fruit; easier to pick because spineless (Harris, Shepherd's)

Orient Express 58 days; hybrid; slender 8"–10" fruit; excellent early yields; sets fruit in cool weather; also tolerates heat (Johnny's)

Rosa Bianca Open-pollinated; unusual beautiful bright lavender color; high yields; vigorous; mild flavor (Seeds Blum, Shepherd's)

Violette di Firenze Open-pollinated; oblong-round fruit are rich lavender; beautiful (Cook's)

White Egg Unusual shiny white-skinned fruit; top quality (Seeds Blum)

Notes

GROWTH CONDITIONS

Germination Temperature: 45°–95°F
pH: 6.0–7.0
Planting Depth: ½"
Breadth: 8"–12"

Growth Temperature: 60°–65°F
Root Depth: 6"–12"
Height 12"–18"

Space Between Plants: in beds: 15"–18" in rows: 18"–24"
Space Between Rows: 24"–46"
Water: Heavy.
Fertilizer: Heavy feeder; use compost.
Side-dressing: Apply when plants are about one-third grown.

First Seed-Starting Date:

Days Germ	+	Days Transplant	+	Days Before LFD	=	Days Count *Back* from LFD
3–10	+	35–70	+	14–28	=	52–108

Last Seed-Starting Date:

Days Germ	+	Days Transplant	+	Maturity	+	SDF	+	Frost Tender	=	Days *Back* from FFD
3–10	+	21	+	56–63	+	14	+	N/A	=	94–108

HARVEST

Harvest younger leaves from the middle and work your way up the stalk as it grows. Keep some of the leaves on the bottom to feed growth at the top. You can also harvest the plant all at once by cutting its stem near the bottom.

STORAGE REQUIREMENTS

For fresh storage, don't wash the leaves. For drying, cut the leaves into strips and steam for 2–5 minutes. Spread on trays no more than ½" thick, and dry. If using an oven set the temperature below 145°F; check and turn every hour.

Fresh:

Temperature	Humidity	Storage Life
32°F	95%–100%	2–3 weeks
32°–40°F	80%–90%	10 months (only fair taste)

Preserved:

Method	Taste	Shelflife (in months)
Canned	good	12+
Frozen	good	12
Dried	fair	12+

GROWING TIPS

Kale is a cool-season crop, hardy to frost and light freezes. Plan an average of 4 plants per person. Kale's flavor is reputed to improve and sweeten with frost. An easy vegetable to grow, it is generally more disease and pest resistant than other *Brassicas*, although it can occasionally experience similar problems. Kale also uses less space than other *Brassicas*. Use it as a spinach substitute in a wide variety of dishes. Kale maintains body and crunch much better than spinach and so can be used in dishes where spinach might not be suitable; it's especially delicious in stir-fry dishes. Author and edible landscaper Rosalind Creasy recommends cooking kale over high heat to bring out the best flavor and prevent bitterness. Creasy also noted that "many specialty growers are planting kale in wide beds only ½" to 12" apart and harvesting kale small as salad greens." In England, close plantings of kale have been shown to prevent aphid infestations through visual masking. Although kale is usually disease- and pest-free, some gardeners won't compost any *Brassica* roots to prevent spreading clubroot and other soil-borne diseases. Pull and destroy plants. Kale is not as likely as other *Brassicas* to suffer from clubroot, but if you experience problems, be sure to rotate plantings so they're not in the same 10' radius for at least 3 years, optimally for 7 years.

Pests

Aphid, cabbage maggot, cabbage looper, celery leaftier, club root, diamond-back moth, flea beetle, harlequin bug, imported cabbage worm, Mexican bean beetle, mites, thrips, weevil

Diseases

Alternaria leaf spot, black leg

Allies

Uncertain: chamomile, dill, garlic, mint, nasturtium, rosemary, sage, tansy, tomato

Companions

Artichoke, beet, bush bean, celery, cucumber, lettuce, onion, peas, potato, spinach

Incompatibles

Pole beans, strawberry, tomato (latter may also be an ally; *see* **Ally Chart** on page 238.)

SELECTED VARIETIES

Greenhouse
All varieties. You can also try bringing plants inside after the first light frost.

Outdoor
Dwarf Blue Curled Vates (a.k.a. Vates Dwarf Blue Curled Scotch) 55 days; open-pollinated; very hardy; compact; lasts nearly all winter (widely available)

Ornamentals Frost is needed to bring out the spectacular colors of ornamentals (widely available)

Ragged Jack Unusual beautiful red oak-type leaves; open-pollinated; heirloom; maintains quality in heat; also good as baby kale (Blum)

Red Russian 65 days; American heirloom; beautiful, red, 2'–3' leaves in cold weather (leaves are blue-green in warm weather); sweet even in warm weather (Nichols, Shepherd's)

Verdura 60 days; Dutch; very sweet; compact; extended harvest in cold weather (Shepherd's)

Notes

GROWTH CONDITIONS

Germination Temperature: 40°–80°F
pH: 6.0–7.5
Planting Depth: ¼"–½"
Breadth: 6"–12"

Growth Temperature: 60°–65°F
Root Depth: 18"–36", with a taproot to 5'
Height: 6"–12"

Space Between Plants: in beds: Head: 10"–12" Leaf: 6"–8" Romaine: 10" in rows: 12"–14"
Space Between Rows: 14"
Water: Low to medium; heavy in arid climates; water early in the morning to minimize diseases.
Fertilizer: Heavy feeder.
Side-dressing: Every 2 weeks, apply balanced fertilizer or foliar spray.

First Seed-Starting Date:

Days Germ	+	Days Transplant	+	Days Before LFD	=	Days Count *Back* from LFD
4–10	+	14 (leaf and head)	+	7–28	=	25–46

Last Seed-Starting Date:

Days Germ	+	Days Transplant	+	Maturity	+	SDF	+	Frost Tender	=	Days *Back* fr. FFD
4	+	14	+	60–95	+	14	+	0	=	92–127 (head)
4	+	14	+	45–65	+	14	+	0	=	77–97 (leaf)
4	+	14	+	55–80	+	14	+	0	=	87–112 (romaine)

HARVEST

For leaf lettuce, start picking the leaves when there are at least 5–6 mature leaves of usable size. Usable size means about 2" long for baby lettuce and 5"–6" long for more mature lettuce. Keep picking until a seed stalk appears or the leaves become bitter. For head lettuce, when the head feels firm and mature simply cut it off at the soil surface. Harvest all lettuce in early morning for the maximum carotene and best taste. Refrigerate immediately.

STORAGE REQUIREMENTS

Lettuce doesn't store well for long periods and is best eaten fresh.

Fresh:

Temperature	Humidity	Storage Life
32°–40°F	80%–90%	1 month
32°F	98%–100%	2–3 weeks

GROWING TIPS

Lettuce is a cool-season crop, half-hardy to frost and light freezes. Plan an average of 10–12 plants per person. Closer spacing results in smaller heads, which may be preferable for small families. Specialty growers are spacing lettuce very close for selling baby lettuces, a rapidly growing produce market.

There are two basic categories of lettuce, heading and nonheading. Head lettuces include crisphead (e.g., iceberg) and butterhead (e.g., bibb and Boston). Nonhead lettuces include leaf and romaine (also known as cos). For head lettuce, one source suggests that you strip transplants of outer leaves to help the inner leaves "head up" better. This is not tested, so treat it as experimental. Head lettuces tend to be milder in flavor but are harder to grow. Lettuce doesn't do well in very acidic soils, and some say the pH shouldn't be lower than 6.5. During hot weather, sow lettuce in partial shade, as it doesn't do well in the heat, and use heat resistant varieties.

Pests

Aphid, beet leafhopper, cabbage looper, cutworm, earwig, flea beetle, garden centipede, leafminer, millipede, slug, snail

Diseases

Bacterial soft rot, botrytis rot, damping off, downy mildew, fusarium wilt, lettuce drop, mosaic, pink rot, powdery mildew, tipburn

Allies

Uncertain: chive, garlic, radish

Companions

Beet (to head lettuce), all *Brassicas* (except broccoli, *see* Incompatibles below), carrot, cucumber, onion family, pole lima bean, strawberry

Incompatibles

None; some studies have shown lettuce to be sensitive to plant residues of broccoli, broad bean, vetch, wheat, rye, and barley

SELECTED VARIETIES

All varieties listed are open-pollinated

Greenhouse

Arctic King, Bibb, North Pole, Parris Cos, Tom Thumb *(see* below). *See* also Cook's and Johnny's for special greenhouse varieties.

Outdoor

Head lettuce (Butterhead and Iceberg types). *Note:* Butterheads are more resistant to leaf aphids, according to Dutch scientists.

Arctic King 80 days; for fall and winter only; butterhead; "cut and come again" lettuce; tasty crinkled leaves (Cook's, Thompson & Morgan)

Au-Isbell Developed at Auburn University; apparently not bothered by insects or rabbits; a spring crop reseeds itself for fall crop, a fall crop reseeds for spring crop; nonbitter; heirloom. Look for it in future years.

Bibb or Limestone 55 days; early spring; favored for its delicacy (Cook's, Nichols, Park)

Buttercrunch 50 days; matures midsummer; bibb; favorite with home gardeners; slow-bolting; tolerates heat; very tender (widely available)

Continuity 70 days; summer bibb; similar to **Four Seasons** but stands longer in dry summer weather (Cook's, Territorial)

Four Seasons (Merveille des Quatre Saisons) 60 days; spring bibb; also for late summer and fall; beautiful red outer leaves; pink and cream interior (Blum, Cook's, Shepherd's)

Ithaca 72 days; spring iceberg; popular; reliable; only iceberg good in Northeast; also good in warm climates; resists tip burn in hot weather; flood to avoid "slime" (Cook's, Dam, Field's, Garden City, Harris)

North Pole 50 days; for fall and winter; butterhead; high cold resistance (Cook's, Nichols)

Red Riding Hood Summer; pretty red butterhead; tolerates heat; resists bolting (Cook's)

Sangria Developed in 1990; beautiful butterhead; resists bolting; superior flavor (Johnny's)

Tom Thumb 65 days; spring; tiny solid butterhead; good for containers (widely available)

Valprize Developed in 1989; butterhead; nonbitter; resists bolting and downy mildew (Jung)

Nonheading, Loose Leaf, or Cutting Lettuce (Romaine, Cos and other types).

Green Ice 45 days; spring; very sweet; very crinkled leaves; slow to bolt (Burpee, Park)

Little Gem or Sugar Cos 60 days for baby heads; 80 days to maturity; romaine summer; 5"–6"; troublefree (Burpee, Cook's, Shepherd's, Territorial, Thompson & Morgan)

Lolla Rossa 56 days; spring; beautiful crinkly leaves with red margins; mild; keep cut to avoid bolting and bitterness (widely available)

Parris Island Cos 68–76 days; all seasons; romaine; mild sweet flavor; slow bolting; 8"–10" heads; resists tip burn and mosaic; vigorous (Burpee, Garden City, Harris, Johnny's, Stokes)

Red Sails 45–50 days; spring; AAS winner; dark red leaf lettuce; resists bolting; little bitterness; fast growing; easy to grow (widely available)

Victoria 52 days; best for summer but also good for spring and fall; developed in 1989; very crisp; sweet and juicy; heat tolerant; resists bolting and bottom rot; sweet (Johnny's)

Winter Density 60 days; winter or year-round in mild climates; romaine like a tall buttercrunch (Cook's, Johnny's, Seeds Blum)

Notes

GROWTH CONDITIONS

Germination Temperature: 75°–95°F
pH: 6.0–6.5
Planting Depth: ½"
Breadth: Bush: 36"–48" Vine: 30–40 square feet on ground

Growth Temperature: 65°–75°F
Root Depth: Shallow, some to 4'
Height: 24"

Space Between Plants: in beds: 2' in rows: 4'–8'
Space Between Rows: 5'–7'
Water: Medium. Apply in deep watering; withhold water when fruits begin to ripen.
Fertilizer: Heavy feeder; before planting, work in compost or rotted manure.
Side-dressing: Apply balanced fertilizer or compost when vines are 12"–18" long and again when fruits form.
Support Structures: Use an A-frame or trellis to grow vines vertically.

First Seed-Starting Date:

Days Germ	+	Days Transplant	-	Days After LFD	=	Days Count *Back* from LFD
4–10	+	21–28	-	14–21	=	18

Last Seed-Starting Date:

Days Germ	+	Days Transplant	+	Maturity	+	SDF	+	Frost Tender	=	Days *Back* from FFD
4	+	21	+	59–91	+	14	+	14	=	112–151

HARVEST

Melon is ready for harvest as soon as it is at "full slip," the ends are soft, (i.e., separate easily from the stem), a crack develops around the stem, and it smells "musky." The skin netting should be cord-like, grayish, and prominent. Winter melons don't "slip" but should be soft. Dip muskmelons in hot water (136°–140°F) for three minutes to prevent surface mold and decay during storage. Store in polyethylene bags to reduce water losses and associated softening of the flesh.

STORAGE REQUIREMENTS

Store fruits in a cool area.

Fresh:

Temperature	Humidity	Storage Life
35°–55°F	80%–90%	about 1 month

Preserved:

Method	Taste	Shelflife (in months)
Frozen	good	3

GROWING TIPS

Melons are a warm-season crop, very tender to frost and light freezes. Plan an average of 2–6 plants per person. Muskmelons *(Reticulatus* group) are often called cantaloupes, but they're not the same botanical variety. True cantaloupes are rarely grown in North America. Winter melons *(Inodorus* group) include honeydew and casaba. Like all *Cucurbits,* melons need bees for pollination. Melons can be sown directly outside, but some gardeners report better germination with pre-sprouted seeds. If you start indoors, use individual cells or peat pots, not flats, as the roots are too succulent to divide. When you direct sow, plant 4–5 seeds in a hill and then thin to appropriate spacing, depending on whether you train them on a trellis or let them spread on the ground. For either direct sowing or transplants, cover seedlings with cloches or hot caps to protect from frost, speed growth, and keep out pests. To encourage side shoots, when seedlings have three leaves pinch out the growing end. When new side shoots have three leaves pinch out the central growing area again. When fruits begin to form, pinch back the vine to two leaves beyond the fruit. Make sure fruits on a trellis are supported by netting or pantyhose, and fruits on ground vines are lifted off the ground by empty pots to prevent disease and encourage ripening. Troughs near the plants can be flooded for effective watering. Melon rinds are good for compost; they decompose rapidly and are high in P and K.

Pests

Aphid, cucumber beetle, cutworm, flea beetle, mite, pickleworm, slug, snail, squash bug and vine borer, whitefly

Diseases

Alternaria leaf spot, anthracnose, bacterial wilt, cucumber wilt, curly top, downy mildew, fusarium wilt, mosaic, powdery mildew, scab

Allies

Uncertain: chamomile, corn, goldenrod, nasturtium, onion, savory

Companions

Radish, squash, pumpkin

Other

Morning glories, radish and zucchini are succession trap plants for cucumber beetles

Incompatibles

None

SELECTED VARIETIES

Greenhouse

Minnesota Midget (*see* below).

KEY

OP = Open-pollinated
HL = Heirloom

Outdoor

Muskmelon and "Cantaloupe."

Ambrosia Hybrid Very popular; juicy; sweet; firm salmon flesh; some resistance to downy and powdery mildews (Burpee, Park, Stokes)

Canada Gem Hybrid Developed in 1989; tolerates downy and powdery mildews and fusarium wilt; good flavor; deep orange flesh (Stokes)

Chaca Hybrid 68 days; gourmet French Charantais type; salmon flesh; resists powdery mildew and fusarium wilt; high yields (Nichols)

Edisto 47 88 days; OP; excellent disease resistance; said to exceed disease resistance of many hybrids; resists or tolerates alternaria leaf spot, powdery mildew, and downy mildew (Southern Exposure)

Golden Golpher OP; resists fusarium wilt; orange flesh (Seeds Blum)

Goldstar Hybrid 87 days; early and long bearing; deep orange flesh; high yields; excellent quality; a standard for mid-Atlantic states (Harris)

Green Nutmeg (or Extra Early Nutmeg) 84 days; OP; HL; green flesh with salmon center; small fruits; unusual (Abundant Life, Seeds Blum, Southern Exposure)

Honeyloupe 75 days; unusual cross of honeydew and cantaloupe; skin is smooth and creamy white, interior is salmon; resists verticillium wilt (Stokes)

Jenny Lind OP; HL; green flesh; excellent flavor; rediscovered and offered in 1987 (Abundant Life, Burpee, Seeds Blum, Thompson & Morgan)

Minnesota Midget OP; uses only 3' of space; earliest maturing melon; 4" fruit; orange flesh; sweet; spicy (Garden City, Gurney's, Seeds Blum, Thompson & Morgan)

Old Time Tennessee 100 days; OP; HL; elliptical fruit 12"–16" long; flavor is outstanding if picked at peak; salmon flesh (Southern Exposure)

Honeydew (C. melo, Inodorous Group).

Hybrid Milky Way 80 days; early enough for the North; pale green; resists wilt (Gurney's)

Kazakh OP; early; bright yellow when ripe; white flesh; not good keeper (Abundant Life)

Limelight Hybrid 96 days; big melons; juicy; green flesh; fairly early (Burpee)

San Juan Compact vines; desert hardy; delicious; prolific; for low and high desert (Native Seeds)

Venus Hybrid 88 days; green flesh; medium fruit; very juicy; sweet; aromatic (Burpee)

Crenshaw.

Crenshaw OP; very sweet; perishable; needs a long season (Seeds Blum)

Early Crenshaw Hybrid 90 days; early enough to be grown in the North; very sweet; yellow-green flesh; each up to 12–14 pounds (Burpee)

Watermelon (*Citrullus lanatus*). These require more space, usually 8'x8' minimum. They should be harvested when tendrils shrivel and brown, the bottom turns green, and the skin hardens.

Charleston Gray 85 days; OP; resists fusarium wilt, anthracnose, and sunburn; red and crisp flesh; 24" long; 28–35 pounds; good in the North or South (Blum, Burpee, Gurney's)

Sugar Baby 75 days; OP; very popular; one of the easiest watermelons to grow; small and sweet; 8" diameter; thin and hard rinds; 8–12 pounds (widely available)

Sugar Baby Bush 80–85 days; space-saver; bush-type vines grow to 3½'; bears 2 oval-round fruits; 8"–10"; 8–12 pounds (Burpee, Gurney's) *Also see* Park's disease-resistant **Bush Baby II**

Yellow Doll or Yellow Baby Hybrid 65–70 days; AAS winner; one of earliest watermelons; juicy yellow flesh; sweet; 7" diameter; grows to 10 pounds (Burpee, Fields, Harris, Jung, Shepherd's)

Notes

GROWTH CONDITIONS

Germination Temperature: 50°–95°F
pH: 6.0–7.5 (Multiplier types: 6.5–7.0)
Planting Depth: ½" Sets: 1"
Breadth: 6"–18"

Growth Temperature: 55°–75°F
Root Depth: 18"–3'
Height 15"–36"

Space Between Plants: To grow scallions: 1" To grow bulbs: 3"
Water: Medium; dry soil will cause the onion to form two bulbs instead of one; don't water one week before harvest.
Fertilizer: Light feeder; use compost.

First Seed-Starting Date: The average time to maturity is 100–160 days for spring starts. See *Notes*.

Days Germ	+	Days Transplant	+	Days Before LFD	=	Days Count *Back* from LFD
4–10	+	28–42	+	14–40	=	46–92

Pests

Japanese beetle, onion eelworm, onion maggot, slug, thrips, vole (storage), white grub, wireworm. Try radish as trap crop for onion root maggot; when infested, pull and destroy.

Diseases

Botrytis, damping off, downy mildew, pink root, smut, storage rot, sunscald, white rot

Allies

Some evidence: carrot
Uncertain: beet, caraway, chamomile, flax, summer savory

Companions

Lettuce, pepper, spinach, strawberry, tomato

Incompatibles

All beans, asparagus, peas, sage

HARVEST

Wait until tops fall over; pushing them can shorten storage life. When bulbs pull out very easily, rest them on the ground to dry and cure. Treat gently as they bruise easily. Turn once or twice in the next few days; cover if it rains. When completely brown, they're ready for further curing. For regular onions, clip tops 1" from the bulb. Do not clip tops of multipliers or separate bulbs. Spread onions no more than 3" deep on wire screens in a shady, warm, dry, well-ventilated area. Cure for up to 2 months before storing for the winter. The flavor and quality of multipliers keeps improving. After 2 months, check for spoilage and remove bad or marginal onions. Separate multiplier bulbs by cleaning and cutting off dried tops about 1" above the bulbs. Keep the smallest bulbs for spring planting.

STORAGE REQUIREMENTS

Onions sprout in the presence of ethylene gas, so never store with apples, apricots, avocados, bananas, figs, kiwis, melons, peaches, pears, plums, or tomatoes. Eat the largest first — they're most likely to sprout.

Fresh:	Temperature	Humidity	Storage Life
	36°–40°F	65%–70%	1–8 months (dry)

Preserved:	Method	Taste	Shelflife (in months)
	Canned	good	12+
	Frozen	fair	3
	Dried	good	12

GROWING TIPS

Onions are a cool-season crop, hardy to frost and light freezes, although certain varieties are exceptions. Plan an average of 40 plants per person. Onions are actually easy to grow, although the daylight requirements and numerous varieties for flavor and storage can be confusing. To start, the best strategy is to plant sets of a variety known to do well locally about 4 weeks before the last frost date. Onions started from seeds generally grow larger and store longer, while sets are easier and faster to grow but are more subject to bolting and rot. Multiplier onions (*A. aggregatum*) such as shallots and perennial potato onions, reproduce vegetatively and are usually started by sets. Similarly, bunching onions (*A. fistulosum*) such as scallions, Welsh, and Japanese, don't form full bulbs and are usually started by sets. Sets should be started with small bulbs about ⅜"–⅞". Sweet onions are best started from seed, as are the common or regular onion. Sweet onions generally store poorly while pungent varieties store well because of a high content of aromatics which act as preservatives. For an easy perennial onion patch, grow potato onions. Almost a lost variety, with a flavor stronger than shallots, they can substitute for regular onions. Buy them once, plant in the fall or spring, and enjoy harvests for decades. For details, consult catalogs or *see Fine Gardening*, December, 88.

SELECTED VARIETIES

Greenhouse

Any variety.

Outdoor

Long Day (need 15+ daylight hours). Plant these in early spring in Virginia and northward to obtain large bulbs; can plant later in regions south of Virginia.

Early Yellow Globe 102 days; early; high yields; keeps 6–12 months; moderately strong (Abundant Life, Burpee, Dam, Garden City, Johnny's, Southern Exposure)

Red Giant Open-pollinated; mild; semiflat; keeps 6–12 months (Seeds Blum)

Sweet Spanish 110 days; some are hybrid and some open-pollinated; large globe-shaped yellow bulbs; sometimes known as "hamburger onion"; mild; sweet (widely available)

Walla Walla Sweet 125 days spring-seeded; 300 days late-summer seeded and overwintered; open-pollinated; large flattened bulbs; mild; plant in August-September for next summer harvest and sweetest onions; short keeper (widely available)

Intermediate Day (need 12–14 daylight hours). These are best for intermediate latitudes.

Fiesta Hybrid 110 days; firm; yellow; Spanish-type; tangy flesh; high yields; keeps 4–6 months (Park, Shepherd's)

Red Hamburger or Red Mac Large, semiflat bulb; red skin; red and white flesh; best in salads; doesn't store for long periods (Burpee, Gurney's, Park)

Ringmaker Hybrid 108 days; early; large, yellow, Spanish-type; mild; keeps 4–6 months (Johnny's, Stokes)

Ruby Open-pollinated; red; strong flavor; keeps 6–8 months (Cook's, Seeds Blum)

Short Day (12 daylight hours). This is best type for fall planting South of Virginia, and spring or fall planting in mid-Atlantic; not good in North where long days force them to bulb too fast.

Granex Hybrid or Vidalia 170 days; large, flat, yellow bulbs; very mild flesh; especially good for mid-Atlantic and South; good for overwintering in the South (Burpee, Field's, Park, Southern Exposure)

Pearl Onions.

Barletta 70 days; cocktail onions; mild flavor; good in soups and stews; good for continuous harvest throughout summer (Shepherd's, Stokes)

Multiplier (perennial).

These include potato onions, Welsh onions and shallots.

He-shi-ko 70–80 days; Welsh scallion; resists bulbing; good in North and South (Field's, Gurney's, Nichols)

Tohono O'odham (Papago) I'itoi's Good for winter growing in low desert areas and summer growing in cooler regions; multiplier type; has a shallot-like flavor (Native Seeds)

Yellow Potato Onion Open-pollinated; very popular; good drought resistance; resists pink root; good keeping quality; heirloom; flavorful but not too strong (Southern Exposure)

Shallots Open-pollinated; French; red-pink bulbs known for culinary uses; tops can be used for scallions (Gurney's, Johnny's, Southern Exposure, William Dam)

Bunching.

Beltsville Bunching 65 days; stands dry summer heat; best for August harvest crisp and mild (Seeds Blum, Stokes)

Evergreen Hardy White 60 days for scallions; open-pollinated; little or no bulbing; hardiest bunching type can be perennial; protect in severe winters (widely available)

Red Beard 60 days; unusual red stems develop color in cool weather; harvest late summer and early fall (Burpee, Shepherd's)

Onions are usually easier to start from sets, which are planted in spring an average of about 4 weeks before the LFD in order to receive enough daylight growing hours for bulb maturation before harvest in mid- to late-summer. Seeds for summer harvest should be started inside in early spring for the same reason. For small storage onions, seed can be sown outside shortly after the last frost date. For overwinter-ing onions, sow seed in mid-summer to early fall. For more planting advice, *see* specific day require-ments and variety requirements.

GROWTH CONDITIONS

Germination Temperature: 40°–70°F
pH: 6.0–7.5
Planting Depth: 1" Or ½"–¾"
Breadth: 6"–10"

Growth Temperature: 60°–65°F
Root Depth: Shallow to 3'
Height: Garden peas: 21"–4' Snap peas: 4'–6'

Space Between Plants: in beds: 2"–4" in rows: 1"–3"
Space Between Rows: 18"–48"
Water: Low initially; heavy after bloom; shallow watering is said to increase germination.
Fertilizer: Light feeder. When inoculated, peas are N-fixing and need low N. Apply liquid seaweed 2–3 times per season.
Side-dressing: When vines are about 6" tall, apply compost or an amendment high in P and K, and light in N.
Support Structures: A 6' post, A-frame or trellis.

First Seed-Starting Date:
Plant every 10 days in case of poor germination.

Days Germ	+	Days Transplant	+	Days Before LFD	=	Days Count *Back* from LFD
7–14	+	0 (direct)	+	28–42	=	35–56

Last Seed-Starting Date:

Days Germ	+	Days Transplant	+	Maturity	+	SDF	+	Frost Tender	=	Days *Back* from FFD
6	+	0 (direct)	+	50–80	+	14	+	0	=	70–100

HARVEST

When pea pods are plump, crisp, and before they begin to harden or fade in color, harvest them with one clean cut. Sugar snaps are best picked when plump and filled out. Harvest snow peas when the pods are young and peas undeveloped. Pick peas every day for continuous production. Pea shoots, the last 4"–6" of the vine, can also be harvested for stir-fry dishes and salads.

STORAGE REQUIREMENTS

Blanch shelled regular peas and whole snap and snow peas before freezing.

Fresh:

Temperature	Humidity	Storage Life
32°F	95%–98%	1–2 weeks

Preserved:

Method	Taste	Shelflife (in months)
Canned	good	12+
Frozen	excellent	12+
Dried	good	12+

GROWING TIPS

Peas are a cool-season crop, hardy to frost and light freezes. Plan an average of 25–60 plants per person, depending on how much you want to freeze, dry, or can for the winter. Add organic matter to the beds in the fall; in the spring when the soil is thawing, gently rake the soil surface. Gardeners with mild winters can plant peas in both spring and fall. Peas have fragile roots and don't transplant well. While some gardeners recommend presoaking seeds, recent research indicates that presoaked legume seeds absorb water too quickly, split their outer coatings and spill out essential nutrients, which encourages damping off seed rot. Yields can increase 50–100 percent by inoculating with Rhizobia bacteria. Peas can cross-pollinate, so for seed-saving space different varieties at least 150 feet apart. Dwarf varieties don't need a trellis if you plant them close together. Pole and climbing peas produce over a longer period and up to five times more than dwarf bush varieties. If a plant has only a few peas on it, pinch back the growing tip to encourage further fruiting. After the harvest, turn under the plant residues, to improve your soil.

Pests

Most problems affect seedlings: aphid, cabbage looper, cabbage maggot, corn earworm, corn maggot, cucumber beetle, cutworm, garden webworm, pale-striped flea beetle, seed corn maggot, slug, snail, thrips, webworm, weevil, wireworm

Diseases

Bacterial blight, downy mildew, enation mosaic, fusarium wilt, leaf curl, powdery mildew, root rot, seed rot

Allies

Some evidence: tomato

Uncertain: Brassicas, caraway, carrot, chive, goldenrod, mint, turnip

Companions

All beans, coriander, corn, cucumber, radish, spinach

Incompatibles

Garlic, onion, potato

SELECTED VARIETIES

All varieties listed are open-pollinated

Greenhouse

Alaska, Burpee Sweetpod, Dwarf Grey Sugar, Frosty, Green Arrow, Little Marvel, Sugar Rae *(see below).*

Outdoor

Bush Green Peas.

Alaska 55 days; 18"–36" tall; plump; good dried as split peas (Abundant Life, Gurney's, Field's, Seeds Blum)

Corvallis 65 days; 2'–3' semi-bush; good for cool, damp areas, especially in the Northwest; like Little Marvel; resists mosaic and enation mosaic (Nichols)

Frosty 65 days; sturdy 18"–24"; excellent for freezing; high yields (Harris)

Green Arrow 70 days; 28"; resists downy mildew; fusarium wilt; excellent freezing quality; high yields; long pods (widely available)

Laxton's Progress No.9 62 days; 14"–20"; resists fusarium wilt; good flavor and quality (Blum, Gurney's, Field's, Jung, William Dam)

Little Marvel 63 days; 18"; very early; summer; good fresh or frozen (widely available)

Novella 65 days; 18"–24" bush; fewer leaves provides better air circulation and lower disease and insect damage; resists powdery mildew (widely available)

Waverex 65 days; 15" bush needs staking; true French petit pois; good in any cool climate; good frozen (Bountiful, Thompson & Morgan)

Vine Green Peas.

Alderman or Tall Telephone 68 days; 5'–6' tall; extra sweet; high yields and quality; sow in early warm weather; late maturing (Blum, Bountiful, Harris, Gurney's, Stokes, Territorial)

Tarahumara Peas are good fresh or dried; not heat adapted; plant in spring in cool climates; for high desert planting (Native Seed)

Wando 68 days; 30" tall; tolerates heat and drought; good yields; best pea variety for late sowing; good for southern areas (widely available)

Edible Pod Peas (Snow peas).

Burpee Sweetpod (Mammoth Melting Sugar) 68 days; 4' vines; resists wilt; can be trellised inside greenhouse (Burpee)

Dwarf Grey Sugar 65 days; 18" bush; no staking needed; high yields (widely available)

Norli 58 days; 4'–5' vine; very early; sweet; good producer (Shepherd's, William Dam)

Oregon Sugar Pod II 64 days; 28"–6' vines; good fresh or frozen (widely available)

Snap Peas. Introduced in the 1980s, these peas have sweet, edible pods that are excellent raw, cooked, or frozen.

Sugar Bon 56 days; 18"–24" vines; matures 2–3 weeks earlier than Sugar Snap; compact 18" plant; resists powdery mildew and pea leafroll; high yields (Burpee, Field's, Park)

Sugar Mel 68 days; 30" vines; very resistant to heat and powdery mildew (Cook's, Park, Southern Exposure)

Sugar Rae 67 days; dwarf 30" vines; its powdery mildew resistance makes it ideal for the greenhouse (Bountiful Gardens, Southern Exposure)

Sugar Snap 70 days; AAS winner; sweet; good raw any size; resists wilt (widely available)

Notes

GROWTH CONDITIONS

Germination Temperature: 60°–80°F
pH: 5.0–6.0
Planting Depth: 1"–1½"
Breadth: 15"–20"

Growth Temperature: 70°–85°F
Root Depth: Shallow
Height: 12"–18"

Space Between Plants: 3"–6" (in 4" high ridge), thin to 12"
Space Between Rows: 30"–36"
Water: Average. When the plant begins to blossom, stop all watering.
Fertilizer: Add rotted manure in the fall so its decomposition won't affect peanut seeds; at blossom time, add calcium (Calcium Sulfate or limestone); additional Potassium may also be required.

First Seed-Starting Date:

Try presprouting extra-large peanuts, which germinate poorly in wet, cool soil.

Days Germ	+	Days Transplant	+	Days Before LFD	=	Days Count *Back* from LFD
7–14	+	0	+	15–28	=	22–42

Last Seed-Starting Date:

Days Germ	+	Days Transplant	+	Maturity	+	SDF	+	Frost Tender	=	Days *Back* from FFD
7–14	+	0 (direct)	+	110–120	+	14	+	14	=	145–162

HARVEST

As the first frost approaches, when the leaves turn yellow-white, kernels drop, and pod veins darken, dig up the entire plant. In short-season areas, you may delay harvest until after the first few light frosts; although the top growth may be killed, the pods will continue to mature. Shake off all loose dirt. Dry roots in the sun for a few days to facilitate separation of the pods, or hang roots in a dry, airy place. Make sure they're out of reach of small animals.

STORAGE REQUIREMENTS

Spread peanuts on shallow trays or hang the entire plant from rafters in a garage or attic. Cure this way in a warm, dry place for a minimum of 3 weeks and no more than 3 months. Peanuts are best stored shelled, in airtight containers in the refrigerator for short periods, or in the freezer for long periods — they are very susceptible to a fungus that produces a highly toxic substance called aflatoxin. To be safe, don't eat any moldy peanuts. Roast nuts at 300°F for 20 minutes before eating.

Preserved:	Temperature	Humidity	Storage Life
(cured or dried)	32°F	low	12 months

GROWING TIPS

Also known as goober peas and groundnuts, peanuts are a warm-season crop, very tender to frost and light freezes. Plan an average of 10–20 plants per person. Peanuts require full sun and can be grown wherever melon grows, as far north as Canada, although commercial production is generally limited to the South. In short-season areas, you may want to start seeds (which are the nuts) inside. For higher yields, inoculate seeds with special peanut inoculant available from nurseries. Plant nuts that are not split and still have their papery skin. Nuts sprout more easily without their shell but filled shells can be planted. Transplant seedlings outside into soil warmed with plastic, choosing a sheltered, south-facing site. They need loose, enriched, sandy soil. For succession planting, peanuts are good planted after early crops of lettuce or spinach. The plant produces peanuts after the stem blossoms; its lower leaves drop and in their place peduncles grow. The peduncles eventually bend over and root in the nearby soil, where clusters of peanuts then grow. When the plants reach 6", begin to cultivate the rows to control weeds and keep the soil aerated. When about 1' high, hill the plants in the same manner as potatoes, mounding soil high around each plant. Hilling is important to help the peduncle root quickly. Mulch between rows with 8" of grass clippings or straw.

Pests

Weeds are the most significant; otherwise backyard gardeners may experience only occasional corn earworm, cutworm, pale-striped flea beetle, potato leafhopper, spider mite, thrips, and different caterpillars

Diseases

No significant diseases, except occasional leaf spot and Southern blight

Allies

Some evidence: corn

Incompatibles

None

SELECTED VARIETIES

Greenhouse

The smaller dwarf bushes (Spanish) might be grown in a greenhouse.

Outdoor

Peanuts are good container plants.

Mammoth Jumbo 120 days; early ripening; can grow as far north as Wisconsin

Spanish or Early Spanish 100–120 days; dwarf bushes; rich flavor; small kernels; can be grown as far north as Canada; provide light, sandy soil and southern exposure (Burpee, Field's, Gurney's, Jung, Park, Stokes)

Valencia Tennessee Red 120 days; large and sweet kernels; southern warm-season type; can be grown as far north as New York (Park)

Virginia or Jumbo Virginia 120 days; 3½' spreading vines; large kernels; grows in the north and corn belt, too; good rich flavor fresh or in peanut butter (Burpee, Field's, Gurney's, Park)

Notes

Peanut hulls are good for mulching and composting as they're rich in nitrogen. For rotation planning, follow peanuts with nitrogen-loving plants.

GROWTH CONDITIONS

Germination Temperature: 65°–95°F
pH: 5.5–7.0
Planting Depth: ¼"
Breadth: 24"

Growth Temperature: 70°–85°F
Root Depth: 8", some to 4'
Height: 2'–3'

Space Between Plants: in beds: 12" in rows: 12"–24"
Space Between Rows: 18"–36"
Water: Medium-heavy.
Fertilizer: Medium-heavy feeder. High N. Rotted manure or compost. Some soils may need calcium.
Side-dressing: Apply at blossom time and 3 weeks later. Apply liquid seaweed 2–3 times per season. At blossom time, try spraying leaves with a weak epsom salt mixture (1 teaspoon per quart) to promote fruiting.

First Seed-Starting Date:

Days Germ	+	Days Transplant	-	Days After LFD	=	Days Count *Back* from LFD
10–12	+	32–44	-	14–21	=	28–35

Last Seed-Starting Date:

Days Germ	+	Days Transplant	+	Maturity	+	SDF	+	Frost Tender	=	Days *Back* from FFD
6–9	+	21	+	60–90	+	14	+	14	=	115–148

HARVEST

For sweet peppers, pick the first fruit as soon as they're usable in order to hasten growth of others. For storage peppers, cut the fruit with 1" or more of stem. For maximum vitamin C content, wait until peppers have matured to red or yellow colors.

STORAGE REQUIREMENTS

Hot varieties are best stored dried or pickled. Pull the entire plant from the ground and hang it upside down until dried. Alternately, harvest the peppers and string them on a line to dry. For sweet peppers, refrigeration is too cold and encourages decay.

Fresh:

Temperature	Humidity	Storage Life
45°–55°F	90%–95%	2–3 weeks

Preserved:

Method	Taste	Shelflife (in months)
Canned	good	12
Frozen	fair	3
Dried	excellent	12
Pickled	excellent	12+

GROWING TIPS

Peppers are a warm-season crop, very tender to frost and light freezes. Plan an average of 5–6 plants per person. All parts of the plant except the fruit are poisonous. To start indoors use pots at least 1½" wide to minimize transplant shock, make a stockier plant, and encourage earlier production. Growers report the following cold treatment of seedlings significantly improves yields and early growth: (1) when the first leaves appear, lower the soil temperature to 70°F and ensure 16 hours of light with grow lamps; (2) when the first true leaf appears, thin seedlings to 2"–3" apart or transplant into 4" pots; (3) when the third true leaf appears, move the plants to a location with night temperatures of 53°–55°F; keep there for four full weeks; (4) return the seedlings to a location with average temperature of 70°F; (5) transplant into the garden 2–3 weeks after all danger of frost has passed. Soil temperature should be at least 55°–60°F for transplanting, or the plants turn yellow, become stunted, and are slow to bear. Some recommend feeding seedlings weekly with half-strength liquid fertilizer until transplanted. Peppers do better planted close together. Except in the West, where peppers may be mostly pest-free, use row covers immediately because pepper pests will be out. If the temperature rises over 95°F, sprinkle plants with water in the afternoon to try to prevent blossom drop.

Pests

Aphid, Colorado potato beetle, corn borer, corn earworm, cutworm, flea beetle, leafminer, mite, snail, slug, tomato hornworm, weevil

Diseases

Anthracnose, bacterial spot, cercospora, mosaic, soft rot, southern blight, tobacco mosaic

Environmental disorders: blossom end rot, sunscald

Allies

Uncertain: caraway, catnip, nasturtium, tansy

Companions

Basil, carrot, eggplant, onion, parsley, tomato

Incompatibles

Fennel, kohlrabi

SELECTED VARIETIES

Greenhouse

Ace, Anaheim, E. Jalapeno, Hungarian Y.W., Staddon's, S. Cayenne, Thai (*See* below).

Outdoor

Sweet.

Ace Hybrid 50 days; green stuffing pepper; medium thick flesh; short, sturdy plants reliable even in adverse conditions; ripens to red (Burpee, Johnny's)

California Wonder 75 days; open-pollinated; very mild flavor; good stuffing pepper; blocky deep green fruit (widely available)

Golden Bell or Golden Summer Hybrid 70 days; unusual bright yellow when ripe; excellent flavor; open growing habit; good yields (widely available)

Gypsy Hybrid 62 days; AAS winner; early; prolific; thin; yellow-red; mild flavor; good for salads and frying; 3"–4" fruits; resists tobacco mosaic virus (widely available)

Large Sweet Cherry 70 days; open-pollinated; red; small fruit, 1½" across; excellent in salads (Nichols, Seeds Blum, Southern Exposure)

Pepperoncini (Italian) 65 days; open-pollinated; shrubby 3' plant; red pencil-thin fruit; prolific; good fresh or pickled for antipasto (Blum, Nichols, Shepherd's, Stokes)

Staddon's Select 72 days; open-pollinated; early; meaty; prolific even under adverse conditions; resists mosaic; popular in the North (Garden City, Seeds Blum, Stokes)

Sweet Banana or Sweet Hungarian 75 days; open-pollinated; pretty light yellow; slender 6"–8" fruit; thin flesh; good for pickling or salads; high yields; sturdy plants (widely available)

Sweet Pimento 65 days; open-pollinated; heart-shaped peppers; bright red; eat fresh in salads or out of hand, roasted, peeled, or canned (widely available)

Yolo Wonder 76 days; open-pollinated; thick flesh; bell pepper; ripens green to red; resists mosaic; thick foliage protects against sunscald (Bountiful Gardens, Jung, Stokes)

Hot.

Anaheim 74 days; open-pollinated; chili type; relatively mild; 7"–8"; thick flesh; good fresh in salsa and chili rellenos, canned, frozen, or dried; may resist tobacco mosaic virus (Cook's, Garden City, Harris, Nichols, Park, Seeds Blum)

Early Jalapeño 70 days; open-pollinated; very hot Mexican type; compact plant; thick flesh; good fresh and in jelly and as pickles (Garden City, Johnny's, Jung, Shepherd's)

Hot Shot 54 days; open-pollinated; larger jalapeño type; medium hot; earlier than jalapeño and larger 4" fruit; high yields and good quality under both heat and cold stress (Johnny's)

Hungarian Yellow Wax 70 days; open-pollinated; pretty yellow; red when ripe; 6"–7"; strong upright plants; medium hot; considered best hot pepper for cool climates (widely available)

Large Red Cherry 80 days; open-pollinated; red 1¼" hot fruit (Blum, Harris, Nichols)

Sandia 6"–9"; good for rellenos, enchilada sauce, and stews; for low and high desert (Native Seeds)

Serrano 75 days; popular in Southwest; extremely hot (Burpee, Fields, Gurney's, Shepherd's)

Super Cayenne 72 days; 1990 AAS winner; 20" plants; more compact and manageable than other cayennes; hot and spicy pepper (Burpee, Park)

Thai Hot Extremely hot; pretty 8" plant; small 1½" fruit; good for containers (Park)

Novelty.

Ariane 70 days; unusual orange; first sweet orange bell; beautiful; good flavor when green or orange; early; high yields; resists tobacco mosaic virus (Nichols, Shepherd's)

Paprika 80 days; open-pollinated; mildly hot and sweet; thick peppers; open-pollinated; excellent dried and ground (Abundant Life, Nichols, Seeds Blum, Southern Exposure)

Szentese 60 days; open-pollinated; unusual lime yellow ripens to orange; semi-hot; an unusual hot Hungarian type; good for greenhouse production, too (Stokes)

Notes

POTATO

GROWTH CONDITIONS

Germination Temperature: 65°–70°F
pH: 5.0–6.0
Planting Depth: 3"–4"
Breadth: 24"

Growth Temperature: 60°–65°F
Root Depth: 18"–24"
Height: 23"–30"

Space Between Plants: in beds: 9"–12" (seed potatoes) in rows: 10"–12"
Space Between Rows: 24"
Water: Medium; heavy watering when potatoes are forming, from blossom time to harvest.
Fertilizer: Light feeder; apply compost at planting.
Side-dressing: 2–3 weeks after 1st hilling, apply fertilizer 6" away from plant and hill again.

First Seed Potato-Planting Date:
2–4 or 6–8 weeks before LFD. In the South and West potatoes are usually started in February or March and harvested in June and July.

Last Seed Potato-Planting Date:
90–120 days (average days to maturity) before FFD.

HARVEST

For small "new" potatoes, harvest during blossoming; for varieties that don't blossom, harvest about 10 weeks after planting. Harvest regular potatoes when the vines have died back half-way, about 17 weeks after planting. Gently pull or dig out tubers with a garden fork. If not large enough, pack the soil back and try again at 2–3 week intervals. If you have many plants, remove the entire plant when harvesting to make room for another crop. For storage potatoes, dig near the first frost when plant tops have died back. To minimize tuber injury, always dig when the soil is dry.

STORAGE REQUIREMENTS

Spring- or summer-harvested potatoes aren't usually stored, but keep for 4–5 months if cured first at 60°–70°F for at least 4 days and stored at 40°F. Dry fall-harvested potatoes for 1–2 days on the ground, then cure at 50°–60°F and a high relative humidity for 10–14 days. Don't cure potatoes in the sun; they turn green. Once cured, store in total darkness in a single layer. Never layer or pile potatoes more than 6"–8" deep.

Fresh:	Temperature	Humidity	Storage Life
	55°–60°F	90%–95%	5–10 months

Preserved:	Method	Taste	Shelflife (in months)
	Canned	fair	12+
	Frozen	good	8
	Dried	good	12+

GROWING TIPS

Potatoes are a warm-season crop in the North, tender to frost and light freezes, and a cool-season crop in the South and West. Plan an average of 10–30 plants per person. All plant parts except the tubers are poisonous. They require full sun. Most are started from small potato pieces called seed potatoes. Each piece should contain 1–3 "eyes," small indentations that sprout foliage. If desired, you can presprout the eyes by keeping the seed potato at 40°–50°F for 2 weeks before planting to break dormancy. There are two methods of preparing seed potatoes for planting: (1) Cut the potato into 2" pieces 2 days before planting; cure indoors at about 70°F in high humidity to help retain moisture and resist rot. (2) Plant small whole potatoes, which are less apt to rot, have more eyes, and don't need curing prior to planting. Potatoes are very disease-prone, so use only certified disease-free ones. Place in trenches 6" deep by 6" wide, spaced 10"–12" apart; cover with 3"–4" of soil. One week after shoots emerge, mound soil around base, leaving a few inches exposed. This "hilling" prevents greening. Side-dress and "hill" again 2–3 weeks later. Cover plants if a hard frost is expected.

Pests

Aphid, cabbage looper, Colorado potato beetle, corn borer, corn earworm, cucumber beetle, cutworm, earwig, flea beetle, Japanese beetle, June beetle, lace bug, leaf-footed bug, leafhopper, leafminer, nematode, slug, snail, tomato hornworm, white grub, wireworm

Diseases

Black leg, early blight, fusarium wilt, late blight, mosaic, powdery mildew, psyllid yellows, rhizoctonia, ring rot, scab, scurf, verticillium wilt

Environmental disorders: black heart

Allies

Uncertain: all beans, catnip, coriander, "dead" nettle, eggplant, flax, goldenrod, horseradish, onion, nasturtium, tansy

Companions

All *Brassicas*, corn, marigold, pigweed

Incompatibles

Cucumber, pea, pumpkin, squash, spinach, sunflower, tomato, raspberry

SELECTED VARIETIES

Greenhouse

None; potatoes won't grow well in the greenhouse.

Outdoor

White. These are good for a variety of purposes.
Kennebec Late; white; delicious big tubers; thin skin; resists mosaic and blight; reliable high yields; good storage (Burpee, Gurney's, Field's, Jung)
Elba 1987 Cornell release; late; white; resists early and late blight, verticillium wilt and golden nematode; high yields; good boiled or baked (Gurney's)

Russet (brownish skin, white flesh). These are the best baking potatoes.
Butte Baking potato; higher in protein and vitamin C than most (Gurney's, Field's)
Burbank The famous "Idaho potato"; late maturing (Territorial)
White Cobbler Early season; the standard popular white potato; smooth skin; tastes best baked; dependable yields under wide growing conditions; not good for storing (Field's)

Red (red skin and white flesh). Good for boiling.
Red Norland Very early potato; very large tubers; resists scab; one of best flavors; smooth skin (Abundant Life, Gurney's, Field's)
Red Pontiac Early to midseason; tolerates heat for Southern growers; excellent for boiling; stays firm for potato salads (Field's, Gurney's)

Yellow Flesh.
Lady Finger Small 1" wide and 4"–5" long fruits; brown skin and yellow flesh; good for baking; excellent boiled or fried (Gurney)
Ruby Crescent Late season; similar to "Lady Finger" but higher yields; rosy skin with yellow flesh; delicious in potato salads or fried with onions; prized by chefs (Seeds Blum, Shepherd's)
Yukon Gold Round; yellow flesh; all-purpose; good flavor; excellent storage (Abundant Life, Burpee, Garden City, Nichols, Seeds Blum)
Yellow Fingerling Salad potato; yellow flesh; long and slender crescent-shaped tubers (Jung, Seeds Blum)
Yellow Finn Bakes and boils nicely; prized in Europe; natural butter flavor (Shepherd's, Territorial)

Novelty.
All-Blue Good yields; unusual blue flesh all the way through; good baked; boiled; roasted; makes beautiful violet vichyssoise (Field's, Seeds Blum)
Blossom Pretty pink skin and pink flesh; oblong; somewhat flat with tapered ends; plant is also pretty with pink flowers (Seeds Blum)

Notes

Buy only certified disease-free potatoes.

GROWTH CONDITIONS

Germination Temperature: 45°–75°F
pH: 6.0–7.5
Planting Depth: ½"
Breadth: 6"–8"

Growth Temperature: 60°–65°F
Root Depth: 1', tap root to 5'
Height: 4"–6"

Space Between Plants: 2", thin to 6"–12" as leaves touch
Space Between Rows: 12"–14"
Water: Light but evenly moist.
Fertilizer: Heavy feeder; before planting apply compost.
Side-dressing: Apply 4 weeks after planting, and thereafter every 2 weeks.

First Seed-Starting Date:
Sow directly every 10 days, starting 4–6 weeks before last frost.

Days Germ	+	Days Transplant	+	Days Before LFD	=	Days Count *Back* from LFD
7–14	+	28	+	21	=	56–64

Last Seed-Starting Date:
Sow later crops directly, as transplanting encourages bolting.

Days Germ	+	Days Transplant	+	Maturity	+	SDF	+	Frost Tender	=	Days *Back* from FFD
5	+	0	+	40–50	+	14	+	N/A	=	59–69

HARVEST

Cut individual leaves when they're large enough to eat. Continual harvest prevents bolting. When the weather warms, cut the plant to ground level. Its leaves will grow back. For the best nutrition, harvest leaves in the morning.

STORAGE REQUIREMENTS

For freezing and drying, cut the leaves into thick strips. Blanch for 5 minutes before drying, or 2 minutes before freezing. It's best to use only the smallest and most tender leaves for freezing.

Fresh:

Temperature	Humidity	Storage Life
32°F	95%–100%	10–14 days

Preserved:

Method	Taste	Shelflife (in months)
Canned	good	12+
Frozen	good	12
Dried	unknown	

GROWING TIPS

Spinach is a cool-season crop, hardy to light frosts and freezes. Plan an average of 10–20 plants per person. Spinach can be grown as soon as the soil is workable. After thinning to 4"–6", cover the plants with row covers to keep pests away. Fall crops usually taste better and suffer no leafminers or bolting. Also, if you plant a late fall crop and mulch it, a very early crop will come up in the spring. Spinach bolts when there's 14–16 hours of light, regardless of the temperature, although warmer temperatures will cause it to bolt faster. The exceptions are New Zealand and Basella Malabar "spinach," which thrive in warm weather. They aren't true spinach, but when cooked they taste like the real thing. Malabar is also a pretty ornamental vine which is easily grown on arbors where it provides summer shade and a constant supply of summer greens.

Pests

Aphid, beet leafhopper, cabbage looper, cabbageworm, flea beetle, leafminer, slug, snail

Diseases

Curly top (spread by beet leafhopper), damping off, downy mildew, fusarium wilt, leaf spot, spinach blight (caused by cucumber mosaic virus spread by aphids, *see* Mosaic)

Allies

Uncertain: strawberry

Companions

All beans, all *Brassicas*, celery, onion, peas

Incompatibles

Potato

SELECTED VARIETIES

Greenhouse

America, Bloomsdale, Melody *(see* below).

Outdoor

(Note: Savoyed = crinkled leaves)

America 43 days; open-pollinated; AAS winner; milder taste when fresh; excellent taste stir-fried; holds quality long; good for canning; spring or fall crop; dark green crinkled leaves; slow bolting; 40–50 days (Southern Exposure, Stokes)

Bloomsdale Long Standing 48 days; open-pollinated; late spring-early summer crop; best flavor for salads; heavy yields; glossy crinkled leaves; bolt resistant; long harvest; can be overwintered (widely available)

Hybrid No.7 42 days; for early spring plantings, and fall or winter crop; upright; semi-savoy type; resists downy mildew and mosaic; dark green; large crinkled leaves (Nichols, William Dam)

Melody 42 days; hybrid; spring or fall crop; quick growing; 40–50 days; resists downy mildew and mosaic; bred for the home garden; upright; easy harvest of dirt-free leaves; good fresh, frozen, or canned (widely available)

Savoy, Cold-resistant 45 days; open-pollinated; late summer or fall crop; good for overwintering for early spring crop; tolerates heat, cold, and blight; good fresh flavor; well-savoyed (Seeds Blum, Southern Exposure, Stokes)

Tyee 42 days; hybrid; excellent savoy type; upright habit makes easier harvest; tolerates downy mildew; good for spring, summer, and fall crops; very slow to bolt; stands longer than Melody (Johnny's, Southern Exposure)

Wolter 45 days; Dutch hybrid; rapid growing; high yields; high resistance to downy mildew; very fine flavor (Shepherd's)

Hot-Weather Spinach Substitutes.

Basella Malabar Red Stem Summer Spinach Open-pollinated; a new vegetable introduced in 1987 from the Orient; harvest all summer; mild but not as flavorful as spinach; tolerates heat; vigorous; can grow up to 6'; easily trained on a trellis; ornamental red stems are also good in salads; not recommended in northern areas (Bountiful Gardens, Park, Seeds Blum)

New Zealand Everlasting Spinach *(Tetragonia expansa)* Open-pollinated; perennial; tastes like spinach; tolerates heat and drought; crisp green leaves; continuous harvest (widely available)

Red Orach Open-pollinated; also called "Mountain Spinach"; not really like any other listed above, but flavor is mild and sweet; use in salads and sandwiches like lettuce; can grow to 9' tall if allowed to go to seed; often grown as potherb in France and Asia; goes to seed quickly in warm weather but can be kept productive if you pinch out seed heads; pretty red seedheads are beautiful in arrangements; leaves are pretty red in salads (Seeds Blum)

Notes

GROWTH CONDITIONS

Germination Temperature: 70°–95°F
pH: 6.0–7.5
Planting Depth: in hills: ½"–1" vine: 72"–96"
Breadth: bush: up to 4 square feet vining: up to 12–16 square feet
Space Between Plants: in beds: 12"–18" in rows: 24"–28"
Space Between Rows: bush, 36"–60"
Water: Heavy.
Fertilizer: Heavy feeder; apply lots of compost; high N requirements.
Side-dressing: Apply compost midseason; in boron deficient soils, apply 1 teaspoon borax per plant.
Support Structures: Use an A-frame or trellis to grow vines upright.

Growth Temperature: 65°–75°F
Root Depth: 18"–6'
Height: winter: 12"–15" summer: 30"–40"

First Seed-Starting Date:

Days Germ	+	Days Transplant	-	Days After LFD	=	Days Count *Back* from LFD
7–10	+	28–42	-	21–28	=	14–24

Last Seed-Starting Date: (summer/winter varieties)

Days Germ	+	Days Transplant	+	Maturity	+	SDF	+	Frost Tender	=	Days *Back* from FFD
3	+	0 (direct)	+	40–50	+	14	+	14	=	71–81 (summer)
3	+	0 (direct)	+	80–110	+	14	+	14	=	111–141 (winter)

HARVEST

Cut all fruit except hubbard-types with a 1" stem. Don't ever lift squash by the stem. Treat even those with hard skins gently to avoid bruising. **Summer:** cut before 8" long, when skin is still soft, and before seeds ripen. **Patty Pans:** cut when 1"–4" in diameter and the skin is soft enough to break with a finger. **Winter:** cut when the skin is hard and not easily punctured, usually after the first frost has killed the leaves and the vine begins to die back but before the first hard frost.

STORAGE REQUIREMENTS

Cure winter squash after picking by placing in a well-ventilated, warm or sunny place for 2 weeks. If you cure fruit in the field, raise them off the ground and protect from rain. Or, dip fruit in a weak chlorine bleach solution (9 parts water:1 part chlorine), air dry, and store. Store only best fruit. Don't allow fruit to touch. Wipe moldy fruit with a vegetable-oiled cloth.

Fresh:

Temperature	Humidity	Storage Life
50°–60°F	60%–70%	4–6 months

Preserved:

Method	Taste	Shelflife (in months)
Canned	good	12+
Frozen	good	8
Dried	good	12+

GROWING TIPS

Squash is a warm-season crop, very tender to frost and light freezes. Plan an average of 2 winter plants per person, and 2 summer plants per 4–6 people. Winter squash doesn't transplant well, but can be sown inside in individual pots to minimize root disturbance. Squash is usually planted in small hills. To prepare, dig 18"-deep holes, fill partly with compost; complete filling with a mixture of soil and compost. Traditionally, 6–8 seeds are placed 1" deep in each hole (others recommended only 1 or 2 seeds due to high germination rate); when seedlings reach 3", thin to 2 seedlings. Raise fruits off the ground to prevent rot. Fabric row covers boost and prolong yields. In cooler climates, keep row covers on all season; when the female (fruit) blossoms open, lift the cover for 2 hours in early morning twice a week to ensure bee pollination, which is essential. To keep vines short for row covers, pinch back the end, choose the best blossoms, and permit only 4 fruits per vine.

Pests

Aphid, beet leafhopper, corn earworm, cucumber beetle, Mexican bean beetle, pickleworm, slug, snail, squash bug, squash vine borer, thrips, whitefly

Diseases

Alternaria leaf spot, anthracnose, bacterial wilt, belly rot, cottony leak, cucumber wilt, downy mildew, mosaic, powdery mildew, scab

Allies

Some evidence: corn
Uncertain: borage, catnip, goldenrod, marigold, mint, nasturtium, onion, oregano, radish, tansy

Companions

Celeriac, celery, corn, melon

Incompatibles

Potato, pumpkin (cross-pollinates with other *pepo* plants, which is only important if you are saving seeds; keep pumpkin distant or plant 3 weeks later)

SELECTED VARIETIES

Greenhouse

Aristocrat, Greyzini, Gld. Nugget, Grm. Globe, Ptty. Pan, Scallopini, Table King *(see* below).

Outdoor

Pepo. Almost all bush varieties are Pepo, including the most commonly grown such as summer squash, acorn, spaghetti, and pumpkin.

Summer

Aristocrat 53 days; hybrid zucchini; AAS winner; upright bush; early; high yields; excellent quality; dark green; smooth; long harvest (Jung, Nichols, Thompson & Morgan)

Cocozelle or Italian Vegetable Marrow 50 days; OP; slim zucchini; striped; very flavorful raw or cooked (Garden City, Johnny's, Nichols, Stokes)

Golden Bush Scallop OP; HL; long season; space-saving bush (Blum, Southern Exposure)

Gourmet Globe 50 days; hybrid zucchini or "apple squash"; compact bush; very early; small, round, flavorful fruits (Park, Shepherd's, Thompson & Morgan)

Greyzini OP; zucchini; high eating quality; long harvest (Stokes)

Patty Pan OP; flat with scalloped edges; excellent flavor; picky when very young, survives well even in English climate (Blum, Bountiful)

Scallopini Hybrid All American Bronze winner; best when 3" or less; good raw; boiled or fried (Jung, Stokes, Territorial)

Winter

Delicata or Peanut or Sweet Potato 100 days; OP; acorn type; oblong 8" fruits with dark green stripes; superb keeper; good taste; compact vines (widely available)

Gold Nugget 85 days; OP; runnerless bush plants; each plant bears about 4 slightly flattened orange fruits; 5" across; stores well (Blum, Johnny's)

Jersey Golden Acorn 80 days; OP; AAS winner; smaller; good for small gardens; when picked 1–3 days after flowering, the fruit tastes like corn with a sweet nutty flavor; also good when matured for winter storage (widely available)

Spaghetti Squash 100 days; OP; use pulp like spaghetti (widely available)

Table King OP; winter acorn; AAS winner; compact bush; dark green with small seed cavity; improves with storage (Garden City, Stokes, Territorial)

Winter Luxury Pumpkin OP; best for smooth, tasty pie fillings; ripens early; excellent keeper; high yields; about 10" fruit (Jung)

Maxima. These are excellent keepers, tolerant of borers, and include the largest fruit such as buttercup and banana.

Buttercup (Burgess strain) 105 days; OP; turban-shaped with light stripes; deep orange; rich, sweet, and very dry flesh; tastes like sweet potato; excellent keeper (widely available)

Blue Banana OP; best and sweetest banana; makes good pies; heirloom (Blum)

Mayo Blusher Large fruit turns pink when ripe; keeps well; good for low desert (Native Seed)

Red Kuri 92 days; beautiful red-orange; teardrop-shaped; good for pies and purees (Johnny's)

Moschata. The sweetest squashes, such as butternut, cushaws, and cheese, are all Moschata. They have high pest resistance and also have the highest vitamin content.

Early Butternut 92 days; hybrid; AAS winner; compact vines; high quality fruit; stores 2–3 months (widely available)

Magdalena Big Cheese Large; ribbed; flat pumpkin shape; good for low desert (Native Seeds)

Mixta. This is a Southern growing group like Moschata.

Cushaw 115 days; OP; green-striped; resists squash vine borer; light yellow flesh; good for pies; excellent canned (Blum, Gurney's, Field's, Southern Exposure)

Hopi "Vanta" Striped or solid green; thick hard shells (sometimes used for musical instruments); for high and low desert (Native Seeds)

KEY

OP = Open-pollinated
HL = Heirloom

Notes

GROWTH CONDITIONS

Germination Temperature: 60°–85°F
pH: 5.0–6.0
Planting Depth: 4"–6"
Breadth: 4–8 square feet

Growth Temperature: 70°–85°F
Root Depth: Length of the potato
Height: 12"–15"

Space Between Plants: in beds: 10"–12" in rows: 12"–16"
Space Between Rows: 36"–40"
Water: Dry to medium. Water well the first few days until anchored, then ease back on water.
Fertilizer: Light feeder. Low N. Before planting, place 1"–2" of compost in furrows.
Side-dressing: Once anchored apply high P fertilizer like bone meal, about 1 cup per 10 row-feet.

First Seed-Starting Date:

Days Germ	+	Days Transplant	-	Days After LFD	=	Days Count *Back* from LFD
8–12	+	42–56	-	7–21	=	43–57 (6 to 8 weeks)

Last Seed-Starting Date:

Days Germ	+	Days Transplant	+	Maturity	+	SDF	+	Frost Tender	=	Days *Back* from FFD
8–12	+	42–56	+	100–125	+	14	+	14	=	178–221

HARVEST

Some harvest after the vines are killed by frost, but most warn that frost damages the root. Always harvest on a dry day. Start digging a few feet from plant to avoid damage. Bruises or cuts as small as a broken hair root will shorten the shelf-life by serving as an entry point for fusarium surface rot. Dry for 1–3 hours on the ground. Do not wash unless absolutely necessary; never scrub.

STORAGE REQUIREMENTS

Cure sweet potatoes before dry storage to seal off wounds and minimize decay. Place in a warm, dark, well-ventilated area at 85°–90°F and high humidity for 4–10 days. Store in a cool place, making sure they don't touch. Temperatures below 55°F cause chill injury. Don't touch until ready to use.

Fresh:

Temperature	Humidity	Storage Life
55°–60°F	85%–90%	4–7 months

Preserved:

Method	Taste	Shelflife (in months)
Canned	good	12+
Frozen	excellent	6-8
Dried	good	12+

GROWING TIPS

The sweet potato is a warm-season crop, very tender to frost and light freezes. Plan an average of 5 plants per person. Other than extreme sensitivity to frost, sweet potatoes are easy to grow, mostly pest-free, and, once the transplants are anchored, drought hardy. Start slips with a sweet potato cut in half lengthwise. Lay the cut side down in a shallow pan of wetted peat moss or sand. Cover tightly with plastic wrap until sprouts appear, then unwrap. The slip is ready when it has 4–5 leaves, is 4"–8" tall, and has roots. A second method is to place a whole potato in a jar, cover the bottom inch with water, and keep warm. When leaves form above the roots, twist sprouts off and plant in a deep flat or, if warm enough, outdoors. A third method is to take 6" cuttings from vine tips in the fall just before frost. Place cuttings in water and, when rooted, plant in 6" pots set in a south window for the duration of winter. By late winter you can take more cuttings from these. To prepare the ground in April, fill furrows with 1"–2" of compost. Mound soil over compost to form at least 10" high ridges. This mini-raised bed optimizes both tuber size and quality, because tuber growth is easily hindered by obstructions in the soil. After all danger of frost is past, transplant slips into these ridges. Unlike potatoes, sweets are not true tubers and keep expanding as the vine grows.

Pests

Flea beetle, nematode, weevil, wireworm (Problems vary by region, so check with your extension agent.)

Diseases

Black rot (fungal), fusarium surface rot (storage), rhizoctonia, soil rot or scurf

Allies

Uncertain: radish, summer savory, tansy

Companions

None

Incompatibles

None

SWEET POTATO

SELECTED VARIETIES

Greenhouse

Bunch Port Rico, Vardaman *(see* below).

Outdoor

White. These white sweet potatoes, not very well known, have less beta-carotene but still more vitamin C than tomatoes. They are a good substitute for white potatoes.

Sumor Very white sweet potato; an excellent and more nutritious substitute for Irish white potato; some disease and insect resistance; stores well; must boil before removing skin (South Carolina Foundation Seeds)

White Delight Heavy yields; unusual white flesh; texture and sweetness resembles orange-flesh varieties (South Carolina Foundation)

Yellow-orange.

Allgold Moist flesh; resists viral disease; internal cork and stem rot; grows well in the Midwest; good keeper (Fred's)

Bunch Port Rico Compact vines to 18"; good for containers and greenhouses (Fred's)

Centennial 100 days; very popular; bright copper skins; high yields; keeps well; good for Northern climates; tolerates clay soils; resists wilt (Burpee, Jung, Park, South Carolina Foundation)

Excel Excellent flavor; earlier and higher yields; good shapes; good resistance to wilt; rootknot nematodes and soil insects (South Carolina Foundation)

Jewel 100 days; leading commercial variety; excellent keeper (up to 50 weeks); bright copper skin; highest yields of all; disease resistant; prefers sandy soil (Field's, Fred's, Jung, Park, South Carolina Foundation)

Southern Delight Dark orange flesh; high pest resistance, especially rootknot nematodes; resists diseases; excellent baking quality; introduced in 1988 (South Carolina Foundation)

Vardaman 110 days; a "bush" with short vines of only 4'–5'; resists fusarium wilt better than longer vined types; worth trying in the greenhouse (Field's, Jung, Park)

Notes

GROWTH CONDITIONS

Germination Temperature: 60°–85°F
pH: 5.8–7.0
Planting Depth: ½"
Breadth: 24"–36"

Growth Temperature: 70°–75°F
Root Depth: 8", some to 6'
Height: determinate: 3'–4' indeterminate: 7'–15'

Space Between Plants: in beds: 18" in rows: 24"–36"
Space Between Rows: 3'–6'
Water: Medium and deep watering until harvest. Even moisture helps prevent blossom end rot.
Fertilizer: Heavy feeder. Fertilize 1 week before and on the day of planting. Avoid high N and K at blossom time. Too much leaf growth may indicate too much N or too much water.
Side-dressing: Every 2–3 weeks apply light supplements of weak fish emulsion or manure tea. When blossoming, dress with a calcium source to prevent blossom-end rot.
Support Structures: Use a wire cage, stake, or trellis; most gardeners prefer cages.

First Seed-Starting Date:

Set out 2 to 4 weeks after the last frost. In Florida, Texas, and southern California, tomatoes can be transplanted in late winter and removed in summer when they stop bearing.

Days Germ	+	Days Transplant	-	Days After LFD	=	Days Count *Back* from LFD
7–14	+	42–70	-	14–28	=	28–56 (average 6 weeks/42 days)

Last Seed-Starting Date:

In Florida, Texas, and southern California, gardeners often plant fall crops.

Days Germ	+	Days Transplant	+	Maturity	+	SDF	+	Frost Tender	=	Days *Back* from FFD
7–14	+	42–70	+	55–90	+	14	+	14	=	132–202

HARVEST

Pick when fruit is evenly red but still firm. If warmer than 90°F, harvest fruit earlier.

STORAGE REQUIREMENTS

Wash and dry before storing. Pack no more than two deep.

Fresh:

Temperature	Humidity	Storage Life
ripe 45°–50°F	90%–95%	4–7 days
green 55°–70°F	90%–95%	1–3 weeks

Preserved:

Method	Taste	Shelflife (in months)
Canned	excellent	12+
Frozen	good	8
Dried	good	12+

GROWING TIPS

Tomatoes are a warm-season crop, very tender to frost and light freezes. Plan an average of 2–5 plants per person. All parts of the plant except the fruit are poisonous. Never plant near the walnut family trees (*see* Walnut on page 114). To start in flats, sow seeds at least ½" apart. Seedlings will be spindly with less than 12–14 hours of light per day. When seedlings have four leaves, transfer to a deeper pot and again when 8"–10" tall. Each time, place the uppermost leaves just above the soil line and remove all lower leaves. Transplant into the garden when the stem above the soil has again reached 8"–10" tall. Allow up to 10 days to harden off. Soil temperature should be at least 55°–60° to transplant, otherwise plants turn yellow, become stunted and are slow to bear. To transplant, pinch off the lower leaves again, and lay the plant on its side in a furrow about 2½" below the soil surface. This shallow planting speeds up growing since the plant is in warmer soil. Put in stakes on the downwind side of the plants. Some sources suggest that indeterminate and larger semi-determinate varieties be pruned of all suckers (tiny leaves and stems in the crotches of larger stems) because they may steal nourishment from the fruits. However, the Erie City Extension Service has shown that removing leaves decreases photosynthetic production. Hand pollinate in greenhouses.

Pests

Aphid, beet leafhopper, cabbage looper, Colorado potato beetle, corn borer, corn earworm, cucumber beetle, cutworm, flea beetle, fruit worm, garden centipede, gopher, Japanese beetle, lace bug, leaf-footed bug, mite, nematode, slug, snail, stinkbug, thrips, tomato hornworm, tobacco budworm, whitefly

Diseases

Alternaria, anthracnose, bacterial canker, bacterial spot, bacterial wilt, botrytis fruit rot, curly top, damping off, early blight, fusarium wilt, late blight, nematode, psyllid yellows, septoria leaf spot, soft rot, southern blight, spotted wilt, sunscald, tobacco mosaic, verticillium wilt.

Environmental disorders: blossom end rot, sunscald

Allies

Some evidence: cabbage

Uncertain: asparagus, basil, bee balm, borage, coriander, dill, goldenrod, mint, parsley, marigold, sage

Companions

Brassicas, carrot, celery, chive, cucumber, melon, marigold, nasturtium, onion, pea, pepper

Incompatibles

Corn, dill, fennel, kohlrabi, potato, walnut

SELECTED VARIETIES

Greenhouse

Coldset, Patio Prize, Small Fry, Sub-Arctic Plenty, Tiny Tim *(see* below).

Outdoor

Standard.

Ace 55 VF 70 days; H; DET; suited well for hot, dry areas in West (Burpee, Tomato)

Beefmaster VFN 80 days; H; IND; tomatoes up to 2 pounds; need staking (Park, Tomato)

Better Boy VFN 72 days; H; IND; midseason; popular; sturdy plant; large; meaty; resists sunscald; ranked well in 1987 by Auburn Agricultural station (Gurney's, Jung, Nichols, Tomato)

Bonny Best 76 days; OP; IND; early season; heirloom; meaty and good flavor; best grown in a wire cage (Nichols, Seeds Blum, Tomato Growers)

Brandywine 95 days; OP; IND; late; large, rich fruit; heirloom (Seeds Blum, Tomato)

Coldset OP; DET; medium fruit; withstands soil temperature of 50°F; can sow directly; doesn't tolerate wet; humid conditions well (Gurney's, Southern Exposure, Stokes)

Delicious VFN 77 days; OP; IND; midseason; very large fruit; good for slicing; little cracking (Burpee, Gurney's, Field's, Seeds Blum, Tomato Growers)

Early Girl VFF 54 days; H; IND; earliest slicing/canning; sweet-tart; improved variety has more disease resistance (Burpee, Gurney's, Jung, Nichols, Tomato Growers)

Floramerica VFFA 70 days; H; DET; AAS winner; developed in the South to resist 15 diseases; resists cold, heat, and humidity; good fresh or canned (Dam, Field's, Jung, Tomato)

Lemon Boy VFN 72 days; H; IND; lovely yellow; mild; adaptable (widely available)

Patio Prize VFNT 68 days; H; DET; bush; no staking; medium-sized fruit (4 ounces); excellent disease resistance (Park, Stokes, Tomato Growers)

Pink Ponderosa 80 days; OP; IND; late; very large; meaty and solid beefsteak fruit; low acid (Nichols, Seeds Blum, Stokes, Tomato Growers, William Dam)

Quick Pick VFFNT 68 days; H; IND; excellent flavor and texture; high yields (Tomato)

Rutgers VF 76 days; OP; DET; high disease resistance (widely available)

Sub-Arctic Maxi 62 days; OP; DET; early; sparse foliage for quick ripening; vigorous; no staking (Gurney's, Field's, Johnny's, Tomato Growers, Southern Exposure)

Yellow Oxheart F OP; stores 3–6 months; excellent flavor (Southern Exposure)

Cherry.
Most of these are determinate. Indeterminate are better flavored but need more space.

Chiapas Sprawling; survived curly top in low desert; prolific; for low desert (Native Seeds)

Pixie II VFT 52 days; H; DET; very early; compact; sturdy plant; meaty; 1¾" fruit; ideal for pots, small gardens, or greenhouse (Burpee, Tomato Growers, William Dam)

Small Fry VFN 65 days; H; DET; AAS winner; very early and prolonged yields; compact bush; excellent taste; good for salads and canning (Jung, Tomato Growers)

Sweet 100 65 days; H; IND; excellent sweet flavor; midseason; plants are tall and need staking; high yields over prolonged period; disease resistant; high vitamin C (widely available)

Tiny Tim 60 days; OP; DET; early; 15" plants; good for containers; fruit ¾"; not as sweet as large cherry types (Blum, Burpee, Southern Exposure, Stokes, William Dam)

Yellow Pear 75 days; OP; IND; pretty yellow; resists heat; meaty; great for soup; indeterminate; extremely prolific; requires significant staking and pruning; drought tolerant (Southern Exposure)

Sauce and Paste.
Most of these are determinate but can be staked.

Del Oro VFNA 72 days; H; DET; best disease resistance of paste types (Harris, Tomato)

Roma II VF 80 days; OP; DET; late season; compact plants; heavy bearer; very solid and meaty with few seeds; good canned whole and good for paste (readily available)

San Marzano 80 days; OP; IND; popular; rectangular pear-shaped fruit; meaty excellent paste tomato (widely available)

Super Italian OP; IND; midseason; meaty, excellent for paste; not good in droughts (Seeds Blum)

KEY

IND = Indeterminate
DET = Determinate
OP = Open-pollinated
H = Hybrid
V = Verticillium
F = Fusarium
N = Nematodes
T = Tobacco Mosaic
L = leafspot

Notes

Unlike most crops, you may solarize soil as you grow tomatoes because they're very heat tolerant. Solarizing helps control disease, particularly verticillium wilt. Wet the soil and cover with clear plastic (for the entire season for best results).

PART 2

Fruits and Nuts

Training an Espalier

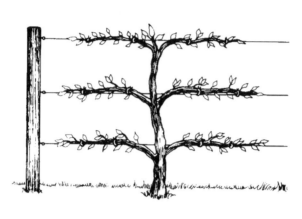

Six-arm Cordon

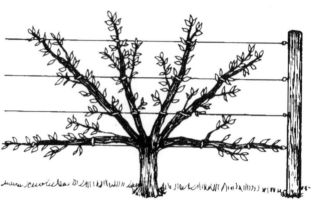

Fan

Training Grape Vines

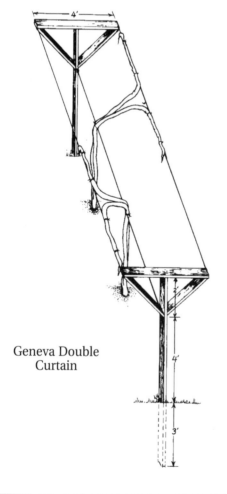

Geneva Double
Curtain

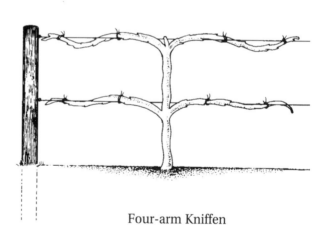

Four-arm Kniffen

Training Free-standing Fruit and Nut Trees

Central Leader

Dwarf Pyramid

Open Center

GROWTH CONDITIONS

Height: Dwarf: 8'–10' Semidwarf: 10'–20' Standard: 20'–30'
Spacing: Dwarf: 8' Semidwarf: 8'–20' Standard: 24'–30'
Root Depth: Very deep
pH: 6.0–6.5
Bearing Age: 3–4 years
Pollination: Most need cross-pollination; the pollinate cultivar can be grafted to main cultivar.
Chilling Requirement: 300–500 hours below 45°F.
Site: Full sun; south or south-east exposure; can withstand poor soil.
Water: Medium. Water deeply and let roots dry out between applications. Watering in fall and winter is very important. Mature trees are drought resistant and prefer dry summers.
Fertilizer: Heavy feeder. Low N for trees under 2 years. Appropriate new growth is 6"–10".
Side-dressing: Apply compost in late autumn.
Training: *Free-standing tree:* open center, vase *Espalier:* N/A
Pruning: Prune young trees minimally with little or no heading back, which delays bearing and stimulates extra leaf growth. When more mature, thin out crowded or competing branches, as well as the short, stubby spurs which bear nuts.

Pests

Boxelder bug, brown almond mite, codling moth, filbertworm, leaf-footed bug, mite, navel orangeworm, nematode, peach twig borer

Diseases

Bacterial canker, brown rot, crown gall, crown rot, leaf blight, leaf scab, peach leaf curl

Allies

Uncertain: caraway, coriander, dill, wildflowers

Incompatibles

None

HARVEST

Unlike walnuts, as almonds mature the outer hulls splits to expose the inner nuts; as the nuts dry, they fall to the ground. The nuts can also be knocked down onto canvas sheets. Don't harvest until the hulls of the nuts on the inner part of the tree have split open; they will be last. Spread nuts in a thin layer before hulling those that haven't fallen out of the hull. Unless wet, hull immediately.

STORAGE REQUIREMENTS

Place hulled nuts in water. Remove the rotten or diseased nuts that float. Dry immediately at 110°F. They're ready for storage when the kernels rattle in the shell, or, when unshelled, the nutmeat snaps when bent. Avoid big piles of nuts, which encourage rot.

Fresh or frozen (shelled or unshelled)

Temperature	Humidity	Storage Life
below 40°F	low	12+ months

GROWING TIPS

All almond trees, even the *dulcis*, which are grown for nuts, are pretty ornamentals. Their culture is very similar to the peach. Almonds bloom extremely early in the spring with white or pink blossoms, and are even more susceptible than peaches to bud damage from spring frosts. As a result, cold northern areas require hardy, late-blooming varieties. Before you plant, cultivate the soil as deeply as possible for the almond's deep roots. Rain and high humidity during the bloom season can interfere with pollination, reduce yields, and promote fungal and bacterial diseases. Also, in humid summers the hulls may not split. If your area is noted for this type of spring or summer, almonds may not be for you. Almonds thrive in long, dry summers supplemented by irrigation and can produce nuts for up to 50 years.

SELECTED VARIETIES

Nonpareil Good pollinator; the best almond; large thin shell; can be shelled by hand; regular bearer; one of the most widely grown in the U.S.; ripens early; hardiness similar to peach (Fowler, Van Well)

All-in-one Almond Semidwarf; self-pollinating; soft-shelled; very good to excellent quality; pollinates Nonpareil; zones 6–9 (Fowler, Stark)

Garden Prince Genetic dwarf; 10'–12'; self-fertile; low chill requirement; sweet and tasty kernels; bears young and heavily in climates without heavy February rains; zone 9 (Sonoma Apple, Stark)

Hall's Hardy Up to 20'; beautiful ornamental; good pollinator of others; late-blooming; good for the Northwest; most hardy almond. Bitter flavor can be leached out by boiling but the nuts are not recommended for eating since they were suspected of causing one case of cyanic poisoning (however, the amount eaten is unknown). This tree is self-pollinating, though it has better yields when planted near a peach or other almond. Hardy through zone 6 (Burpee, Gurney's, Henry Field's, Northwoods, Raintree)

ROOTSTOCKS

Almond seedlings grow slower than those grafted onto peach rootstock, but mature to a large height and produce well. They resist drought but are susceptible to crown rot, crown gall, and nematodes. Peach rootstocks produce rapidly growing trees that have a better survival rate than almond seedlings. Some are nematode resistant. All need irrigation. Marianna 2624 is a good semidwarfing rootstock (*see* Plum Rootstock Chart on page 108). The Almond X Peach Hybrid is a good rootstock for poor soils since it is vigorous with deep roots.

Notes

GROWTH CONDITIONS

Height: Dwarf: 6'–12' Semidwarf: 12'–18' Standard: 20'–40'
Spacing: Dwarf: 8'–20' Semidwarf: 15'–18' Standard: 30'–40'
Root Depth: 10' or more, with a spread 50 percent beyond drip line
pH: 6.5–7.0 (6.0–6.5 for bitter pit)
Bearing Age: dwarf and semidwarf: 2–3 years standard: 4–8
Pollination: Most require cross-pollination
Chilling Requirement: 900-1000 hours below 45°F, though some require less
Site: South-east exposure. Clay loam. To espalier, some experts suggest siting apples on an eastern wall or slope in very hot summer climates to avoid sunburn.
Water: Medium
Fertilizer: Low N for young trees. Appropriate new growth is 6"–14".
Side-dressing: Apply compost in late autumn and work into soil.
Support Structures: Branches may need support when fruiting; branch separators can increase yields.
Training: *Free-standing:* central leader *Wire-trained:* all cordons, espalier, fans, stepovers, palmettes
Pruning: Spur-types require little annual pruning since spurs bear for about 8 years, but each spring remove 1 out of 10 spurs and thin fruit by 10 percent. Tip-bearers fruit on 1-year old wood. For these, prune back some of the long shoots and some of the spurs. For bitter pit, a sign of unbalanced growth, remove the most vigorous shoots at the end of the summer.

HARVEST

For summer apples, pick fruit just before fully ripe, otherwise the apples become mealy. In the fall, pick fruit only when fully ripe. Make sure you pick with the stems, or a break in the skin will occur that will permit bacteria to enter and foster rot. Be aware that ripening apples give off small amounts of ethylene gas that may inhibit the growth of neighboring plants and cause early maturing of neighboring flowers and fruits.

STORAGE REQUIREMENTS

Wrapping in oiled paper or shredded paper helps prevent scald. Some apples stored over the winter develop a rich flavor that is excellent for pies. Israeli research shows that summer apples keep better if held at high temperatures several days before storage. Do not store apples with potatoes because apples will lose their flavor and potatoes will develop an off flavor.

Fresh:	Temperature	Humidity	Storage Life
	32°–40°F	80%–90%	4–8 months

Preserved:	Method	Taste	Shelflife (in months)
	Canned	good	12+
	Dried	good	12+

GROWING TIPS

Thousands of apple varieties have been grown since ancient times. Many are lost to posterity, but more varieties of apple still exist today than of any other fruit. Breeding for disease resistance has focused on the apple more than other fruits, so organic orchardists may have the greatest chance of success with this fruit. After the June drop and when the fruit is no more than 1" in diameter, thin to 8" apart, or remove about 10 percent of the total fruit. Also thin all clusters to just one fruit. The inclination of the apple branch is thought to determine its fruitfulness: the more horizontal, the more fruit. U.S. researchers have shown that shining red lights on apple trees for 15 minutes each night, beginning 2 weeks before harvest, delays fruit drop for 2 weeks. Other researchers are experimenting with inoculating bare roots with hairy root organism, previously thought to be a problem disease but now shown to promote early root growth and fruiting.

Pests

Aphid, apple maggot, cankerworm, codling moth, European apple sawfly, European red mite, flea beetle, fruit worm, gypsy moth, leafhopper, leafroller, mice, oriental fruit moth, pearslug, plum curculio, potato leafhopper, scale, tent caterpillar, weevil, whitefly, white grub, woolly apple aphid

Diseases

Apple scab, baldwin spot, canker dieback, cedar apple rust, crown gall, crown rot, cytospora canker, fire blight, powdery mildew, sunscald

Allies

Some evidence: buckwheat, *phacelia* genus of herbs (e.g., California bluebells), *eryngium* genus of herbs (e.g., button snakeroot and sea holly), weedy ground cover

Uncertain: dill, caraway, coriander, garlic, nasturtium, tansy, wildflowers, wormwood, vetch

Incompatibles

Mature walnut tree, potato

SELECTED VARIETIES

Early (Summer Apples)

Williams Pride (Co-op 23) Very early; large red fruit; 1988 Purdue release; best flavor of disease-resistant apples; immune to scab; resists mildew, cedar rust, and fire blight; stores 1 month refrigerated; naturally moderate-sized tree; tested in zones 5–6 (Raintree, Rocky Meadow, Stark)

Jerseymac Red fruit; one of the best early apples but bruises easily; susceptible to scab and blight; productive; naturally large tree (NYFT, Van Well, Windmill)

Redfree Large; bright red fruit; immune to scab and cedar rust; moderate resistance to mildew and blight; excellent flavor; naturally small tree (Adams, Raintree, Stark)

Midseason

Royal Gala, Imperial Gala, and Scarlet Gala Yellow background with red-orange blush; excellent quality; considered one of the best early apples; firm, sweet, and juicy; compact tree; prolific; heavy spur-bearing; hardy; excellent keeper; best on rootstocks and with cultural practices that maximize fruit size; susceptible to fire blight; zones 5–8 (Rocky Meadow, Stark, Van Well)

Gravenstein Yellow with red stripes; old favorite; great flavor; vigorous; bears biennially; ideal for sauce and cider; infertile pollen; requires pollinizer; loved on the West Coast (widely available)

Jonafree Red; good for fresh eating; immune to scab; resists fire blight and cedar apple rust; good keeper; high yields; vigorous and spreading tree; zones 5–8 (Adams, Stark)

Liberty Red with yellow; McIntosh-type; resists scab, mildew, rust, and fire blight; good dessert apple; naturally large tree; zones 4–8 (widely available)

Cox's Orange Pippin Historical apple; good fresh, baked, or as sauce; excellent for espalier; needs 600 hours or less chill; naturally medium-sized tree; hardy through zone 3 (Miller, NYFT, Northwoods, Raintree, Sonoma Apple, Windmill)

Freedom Red with yellow; very resistant to scab; resists mildew, rust, and fire blight; stores until January; one of the best for no-spray organic orchards; excellent pie apple; naturally large tree; zones 3–8 (Adams, Kelly, Miller, NYFT, Northwoods, Raintree, Windmill)

Late

"Braeburn" and later bearers need about 150 frost-free days for fruit to mature. Late ripeners tolerate temperatures as low as 29°F before internal freezing occurs, according to University of Minnesota Extension. If freezing does occur, let the apples thaw before harvesting, to prevent severe bruising.

Ashmead's Kernel Historical yellow apple with orange-brown blush; russet; natively large tree; excellent flavor fresh or juiced; excellent keeper; resists mildew; tart when tree ripe; mellows with storage; naturally moderate-sized tree; hardy through zone 3 (Northwoods, Raintree, Rocky Meadow, Sonoma Apple, Southmeadow, Windmill)

Jonagold Large yellow and red fruit; newer apple; cross between Jonathan and Golden Delicious; good taste fresh and in pies; stores until spring if kept at 31°F; heavy yields; naturally large tree; zones 4–8 (widely available)

Golden Delicious Universal pollinator; vigorous spreading tree; precocious; heavy crops; resists scab; crops well; susceptible to cedar apple rust; discovered in West Virginia (widely available)

Tydeman's Late Orange Excellent storage apple; reaches full flavor around Christmas; some say has better flavor than Ashmead's Kernel; naturally moderate-sized tree (Southmeadow)

Braeburn Yellowish with red blush; new from New Zealand; crisp; juicy; stores 6–12 months; bears young; manageable by homeowner because only moderately vigorous; susceptible to powdery mildew; doesn't appear susceptible to fire blight (Adams, Northwoods, Rocky Meadow, Stark)

Brown Russet Very late; russet with patches of green and red; good fresh, stored, or as sweet cider apple; resists scab and mildew; naturally moderate-sized tree (Raintree)

Crab (Crab apples are any apple smaller than 2" in diameter)

Dolgo Early; best all-purpose crab; excellent pollinator for all apples; excellent ornamental; excellent jelly; high disease resistance; needs chill 400 hours or less; naturally small to moderate-sized tree; hardy through zone 1 (Northwoods, NYFT, Raintree, Southmeadow, Windmill)

Notes

Rootstocks *See* pages 80–81.

Apple Rootstocks

Most growers now choose dwarf apples; standard trees grow very large, don't bear for years, and are difficult to harvest because of their height. To choose a rootstock you must know your soil type, drainage, and depth; then consider the specific variety's natural growing habit and size. These factors determine how much dwarfing you need in a rootstock. In rich, fertile soil all rootstocks grow more vigorously than predicted and need extra spacing. Buy smaller trees when possible because they suffer less transplanting shock, and are more productive and vigorous.

Most nurseries don't offer a choice of rootstocks for a particular variety, but choice can be found between nurseries. The purpose of these charts is not to help you make an independent decision; it is to help you conduct an informed discussion with the nursery. We urge you to seek and follow the nursery growers' advice.

Rootstock Name	Malling 27 EMLA 27/ M27	Poland 22 P22	Malling 9 EMLA 9/ M9	Malling 26 EMLA 26/ M26	MARK Mac-9
Size (percent of standard)	Minidwarf 15%–30%	Minidwarf 15%–30%	Dwarf 20%–40%	Dwarf 30%–50%	Dwarf 30%–45%
Height	4'–8'	5'–6'	8'–10'	8'–14'	8'–14'
Width	2'–8'	2'–8'	8'–10'	10'–14'	8'–12'
Best soil	Clay loam	—	Sandy and grainy loam	Sandy and grainy loams	Clay
Anchorage	Poor/stake	Poor/stake	Poor/stake	Fair/might stake	Good/no stake
Crown rot	VR	—	VR	S	R
Woolly aphid	LR	—	S	S	S to LR
Nematodes	—	—	S	—	—
Fire blight	R	—	VS	S	S
Powder mildew	MR	—	MR	MR	—
Hardiness	L	VH	—	VH	VH
Drought	—	—	—	—	—
Precocious	P	—	VP	VP	P
Other factors	Remove fruit first 2 years; stops growing when bears fruit; good for espalier when grafted to vigorous varieties	Roots are brittle; union with some types is brittle when young	Mice love this rootstock, so use tree guard; produces large fruit; defruit or thin fruit in first 2 years to prevent loss of leader	Can form root galls at graft union; defruit or thin first 2 years to prevent loss of leader; doesn't sucker much; produces large fruit	Open structure and roots well in stoolbeds; hardy to zone 4 but not as hardy as M26

We gratefully thank Robert Kourik for permission to reprint information on rootstocks from his book *Designing and Maintaining Your Edible Landscape Naturally* (*see* Bibliography).

KEY

R = Resistant   MR = Moderately Resistant   S = Susceptible

MS = Moderately Susceptible   L = Low Hardiness   H = Hardy

VH = Very Hardy   P = Precocious (early bearing)   VP = Very Precocious

M9/111	M7a Malling VII EMLA 7	MM106 Merton-Malling 106	MM111 Merton-Malling 111	Notes
Dwarf 25%–50%	Dwarf 40%–60%	Dwarf 55%–85%	Dwarf 65%–85%	
10'–15'	11'–20'	14'–21'	15'–24'	
10'–15'	12'–16'	14'–18'	15'–20'	
—	Most soils; avoid heavy clay	Sandy loam; avoid poor drainage	All soils; can also tolerate wet soils	
Good/no stake	Good/no stake	Fair to good	Very good/no stake	
R	L-MR	R	R	
R	LR	HR	—	
—	—	—	—	
S (in early years)	R	VR	—	
—	—	S	—	
—	VH	LH	VH	
Tolerant	Tolerant	Tolerant	Tolerant	
—	P	P	No	
Combines benefits of 111 and 9; bury rootstock so MM111 part is underground and M9 part is exposed	Susceptible to burr knot; better than M26 on wet soils; remove suckers each year	Susceptible to burr knot; good stock for spurs; fumigate site for nematodes, which spread union necrosis and ringspot. Stake in hardpan soil.	Smaller harvest than a stock like M106, but still productive; ideal for an interstem or under low vigor varieties	Stark Bro's Nurseries cautions that extremely dwarfing rootstocks (M27 and P22) won't do well for most gardeners. Miller Nurseries also notes that Malling 9 is very difficult for homeowners; its roots are shallow and brittle. It must be securely staked or the tree will blow over. The British Institute of Horticultural Research showed that wrapping M9 stems in July with black polyethylene film to 6" above ground increases root production.

GROWTH CONDITIONS

Height: Dwarf: 6'–7' Semidwarf: 12'–15' Standard: 20'–30'
Spacing: Dwarf: 8'–12' Semidwarf: 12'–18' Standard: 25'–30'
Root Depth: 50–100 percent farther than drip line
pH: 6.0–6.5
Bearing Age: 3–9 years
Pollination: Most are self-pollinating, but yields are higher with more than one variety.
Chilling Requirement: Very low, 350–900 hours, which results in early blooming.
Site: Not too rich or sandy. In the North, plant 12'–15' from the northern side of a building. This delays buds and minimizes late frost injury but ensures full summer sun. Avoid windy locations. *See* also Peach (page 100) about hydrogen cyanide.
Water: Medium.
Fertilizer: Appropriate new growth on a young tree is 13"–30"; on a bearing tree 10"–18". Since the tree is naturally vigorous, go easy on N.
Side-dressing: Apply compost or well-rotted manure mixed with wood ashes annually in the spring, before leaves appear.
Training: *Free-standing:* open center, dwarf pyramid. In colder areas use central leader.
    Wire-trained: fan
Pruning: If the tree bears fruit only in alternate years, prune heavily when over half of the flowers are blooming. Pruning encourages new spurs, each of which bears fruit for about 3 years. Prune yearly to encourage fruiting spurs. Remove wood that is 6 or more years old.

HARVEST

When all green color is gone and the fruit is slightly soft, twist and gently pull upward. If possible, harvest apricots when fully ripe. If plagued with animal problems, you may want to pick them slightly green and ripen them at 40°–50°F.

STORAGE REQUIREMENTS

For canning, use only unblemished fruits or all fruits in the container will turn to mush. For drying, split the apricot first and remove pit. If after drying the fruit is still softer than leather, store in the freezer.

Fresh:

Temperature	Humidity	Storage Life
60°–65°F		a few days
40°–50°F		3 weeks

Preserved:

Method	Taste	Shelflife (in months)
Canned	good	12+
Frozen (after partially drying)	excellent	12+
Dried	good	12
Jam	good	12+

GROWING TIPS

Apricots are good additions to the orchard. They're pretty (with glossy green leaves), easily managed, and one of the most drought-resistant fruit trees. They are, however, vulnerable to winter damage and their buds are very susceptible to late frost damage (*see* **Site**). Apricots grow vigorously and require annual pruning and thinning. After the natural fruit drop in late spring and when the fruit is about 1" in diameter, thin fruit to 3"–4" apart. Summer temperatures over 95°F cause pit burn, a browning around the pit. Apricots enjoy long lives of about 75 years.

Pests

Aphid, cankerworm, cherry fruit sawfly, codling moth, gopher, gypsy moth caterpillar, mite, peach tree borer, plum curculio, white fly

Diseases

Bacterial canker, bacterial spot, black knot, brown rot, crown gall, cytospora canker, scab, verticillium wilt

Allies

Some evidence: alder, brambles, buckwheat, rye mulch, sorghum mulch, wheat mulch

Uncertain: caraway, coriander, dill, garlic, nasturtium, tansy, wildflowers, wormwood, vetch

Incompatibles

Persian melon, plum. Also, don't plant where any of the following have grown in the previous 3 years: eggplant, oats (roots excrete a substance that inhibits the growth of young apricot trees), pepper, potato, raspberry, strawberry, tomato

SELECTED VARIETIES

Harcot Early ripening; freestone; firm and sweet; cold hardy; late blooming; vigorous; good resistance to perennial canker, bacterial spot, and brown rot; self-fertile; zones 5–8 (Kelly, NYFT, Northwoods, Windmill)

Sungold and Moongold Early midseason; very cold hardy for the North; developed by the University of Minnesota; recommended to pollinate each other; good fresh, canned, or as jam; zones 3–8 (Gurney's, Miller)

Lisa Sweet-Kernel or Sweet Pit Midseason; fruit and nut tree; edible kernel is sweet, easy to extract, stores well, and tastes similar to an almond; juicy; tree is compact; hardy; vigorous; self-pollinating; zones 5–8 (Gurney's, Miller, Raintree)

Precious Midseason; very hardy variety; original tree estimated over 100 years old; bears large crops even with cold winters, late frosts, and spring temperature fluctuations; sweet and juicy fruit; kernel usually has sweet almond flavor; disease resistant; self-fertile (Windmill)

Manchurian Bush Midseason; bush type; good for small areas; grows about 12'; juicy; sweet; a good choice if you don't know rootstocks; very hardy; tolerates both heat and cold; good fresh, dried, or as jam (Gurney's, St. Lawrence)

Aprium Late season; apricot-plum hybrid; self-fertile; medium-large, apricot-sized fruit; clear yellow skin; tree can be maintained at 10'; zones 6–9 (Northwoods, Raintree, Sonoma Apple, Stark)

Royal Blenheim Late season; grown in California; needs warm, dry weather during bloom; medium to large fruit; good fresh, canned, or dried; high yields; fruit is subject to pitburn in warmest springs; good pollinizer (Fowler, Sonoma Apple, Van Well)

Stark GoldenGlo Late season; genetic dwarf; 4–6'; productive; good dried or fresh (Stark)

ROOTSTOCKS

Generally, don't use peach rootstocks because they're susceptible to peach tree borer, root knot and lesion nematodes, root winter injury, and uneven growth, which weakens the graft. Try not to use plum rootstocks — those dwarfed on Nanking cherry *(P. Tomentosa)* or sand cherry *(P. Besseyi)*. Although more tolerant of wet soil, these sucker continuously and cause a different fruit flavor. Apricot rootstock offers the best chance for tree survival; it is resistant to nematodes, and has some resistance to peach tree borers.

Notes

GROWTH CONDITIONS

Height: 4'–10' when pruned

Spacing: Erect and Semierect Blackberry: 2'–3' in a row (suckers and new canes fill out row)
Trailing Blackberry: 6'–12' in a row (no suckers, but canes grow very long)

Root Depth: More than 12"

pH: 5.0–6.0

Bearing Age: 2 years

Pollination: Self-pollinating.

Chilling Requirement: Hours needed depend on the variety.

Site: Full sun; rich loam. Due to verticillium wilt, avoid planting where nightshade family plants were grown in the last 3 years. Plant at least 300 feet away from wild brambles (which harbor pests and diseases) and from raspberries (to prevent cross-pollination).

Water: Medium; drip irrigation is essential to avoid water on the berries, which is absorbed and dilutes flavor. Water regularly because of vulnerability to water stress.

Mulch: In summer, apply 4"–8" of organic mulch; in winter apply 4"–6" of compost.

Fertilizer: In spring, apply well-rotted manure or compost before canes break dormancy.

Training: A trellis is very important for disease and pest reduction, quality fruit, and easy harvest. For erect blackberries use a 4' top wire; for trailing blackberries use a 5' top wire. Fan out canes and tie with cloth strips.

Pruning: After harvest or in spring, cut out old canes done bearing.
Erect blackberries — thin to 5–6 canes per row-foot; to encourage branching, cut off the top 3"–4" when primocanes are 33"–40"; late the following winter, cut the lateral branches back to 8"–12" long.
Trailing blackberries — thin to 10–14 canes per hill; don't prune in the first year; in late winter cut canes back to 10'.

HARVEST

When berries slide off easily without pressure, harvest into very small containers so berries on the bottom won't be crushed. After harvest, cut back floricanes to the ground. For disease control, burn or dispose of all cut canes.

STORAGE REQUIREMENTS

Freeze within 2 days by spreading out berries on cookie sheets and freezing. When rock hard, store in heavy freezer bags. Refrigerated, they keep 4–7 days.

Preserved:

Method	Taste	Shelflife (in months)
Canned	excellent as jam	12+
Frozen	excellent	6

GROWING TIPS

Bramble fruits are very easy to grow. The keys to good yields are adequate spacing and light, and, because of shallow roots, good weed control and thick mulch. Rather than several short, close rows that limit berry development to only the upper cane parts, plant one long, narrow row that will produce berries to the bottom of the canes.

Blackberries are biennial. First-year green stems — primocanes — bear only leaves. Two-year-old brown stems — floricanes — produce fruit. Upright or erect canes are shorter, while trailing varieties (also known as dewberries in the South), grow flexible canes as long as 10'. Blackberries are usually hardy to zones 5–8; upright varieties are the hardiest.

Pests

Caneborer, mite, raspberry root borer, strawberry weevil, whitefly, white grub

Diseases

Anthracnose, botrytis fruit rot, cane blight, crown gall, powdery mildew, rust, septoria leaf spot, verticillium wilt

Allies

Some evidence: grape

Companions

If berries are planted down the center of a 3' bed, plant beans or peas in the first summer to keep the bed in production and to add organic matter and N to the soil.

Incompatibles

Black walnut, and all members of the nightshade family transmit verticillium wilt.

SELECTED VARIETIES

Trailing *(Rubus procerus)*

Dirksen Early; thornless; trailing; very sweet; hardy; vigorous; resists leaf spot, mildew, and anthracnose; zones 6–10 (Fowler, Henry Field's)

Hull Midseason; thornless; trailing; very sweet; good fresh or in pies; hardy; zones 5–8 (Burpee, Nourse, Rayner)

Chester Thornless Late season; trailing; large berry; productive; good fresh, frozen, canned, or as juice; firm; good keeping qualities; zones 5–8 (Burpee, Nourse, Raintree, Stark, Windmill)

Upright *(Rubus macropetalus)*

Darrow Early crop with smaller fall crop; upright; bred in the North; one of the top crops in the Northeast; large berries; low-acid fruit good for jelly; very cold hardy; zones 4–8 (Gurney's, Henry Field's, Kelly, Miller, Rayner, Stark)

Ebony King Early; upright; large purplish berry; sweet; withstands temperatures to -20°F; resists orange rust; zones 5–8 (Gurney's, Windmill)

Thornfree Midseason; semi-upright; from the USDA; hardy; plants don't sucker; tart flavor good for jam; some disease resistance; zones 6–8 (Kelly, Miller, Stark, Van Well)

PROPAGATION

Erect blackberry — by suckers. When dormant, dig up root suckers no closer than 6" to mother plant. *Thornless and trailing* — tip layering. Late in the season (August to September), bend and bury the primocane tips 4" deep in loose soil. In the spring, cut off the cane 8" from the ground and dig up the new plants.

Notes

GROWTH CONDITIONS

Height: Lowbush: 2'–4' Highbush: 5'–6'
Spacing: Lowbush: 3'–4' Highbush: 7'–8'
Rows: 10'
Root Depth: Very shallow, top 14" of soil
pH: 4.0–5.6
Bearing Age: 3–8 years
Pollination: All varieties require cross-pollination
Chilling Requirement: Low and Highbush: 650–800 hours below 45°F Rabbiteye: 200 hours
Site: Full sun; choose a site where plants won't be disturbed, away from paths, roads, and driveways
Water: Heavy and evenly moist
Mulch: 3"–6" acid mulches such as pine needles, peat moss, shredded oak leaves, or rotted sawdust
Fertilizer: Apply 1" of compost under mulch. Avoid high N, aluminum sulphate, or urea. If you must apply ammonium sulphate, use ½ ounce in year 1, and 1 ounce for every additional year thereafter.
Pruning: Don't prune until the third year after planting because blueberries fruit near the tips of 2-year and older branches. To prune, cut out diseased tips and, for larger fruit, cut branches back to where buds are widely spaced. Also cut out weak and diseased branches or canes, as they're called by commercial growers. Every 2 or 3 years you may need to cut the 5-year or older canes back to the main stem. Don't leave any stubs because suckers will be weaker than new canes growing from the roots. A good rule of thumb is to allow one branch per year of age plus one or two vigorous new branches. If new branch growth on an old bush (15 years) is thinner than ¼", cut out half of the new canes.

Pests

Apple maggot, birds, cherry fruitworm, fruit fly, mite, plum curculio, weevil

Diseases

Bacterial canker, cane gall, crown gall, mummy berry, *Phytophthera cinnomomi*, powdery mildew. Many problems are due to a lack of acidity.

Allies

None

Companions and Incompatibles

None

HARVEST

Leave berries on the bush 5–10 days after they turn blue. They're fully ripe when slightly soft, come off the bush easily, and are sweet. Pick directly into the storage bowl or container so that as little as possible of their protective wax is removed.

STORAGE REQUIREMENTS

Don't wash the fruit if you're going to freeze it.

Fresh:	Temperature	Humidity	Storage Life
	35°–40°F (refrigerated)	80%–90%	7 days

Preserved:	Method	Taste	Shelflife (in months)
	Canned	fair	
	Frozen	good	6
	As preserves	good	12+

GROWING TIPS

Blueberries lack abundant root hairs and have shallow, underdeveloped roots concentrated in the top 14" of soil. As a result, regular watering and thick mulch are critical to keep the weeds down. A very acid pH is necessary for the plant to extract iron and nitrogen from the soil. Most blueberry problems are caused by stress related to pH, either under- or overfertilization, or under- or overwatering. Plant 2-year-old bushes. When your plants arrive, do not put them in water. Follow directions and "heel in" until ready to plant. Try inoculating the roots with the beneficial *mycorrhizal* fungi, which increases yields significantly. Lowbush varieties are grown primarily in New England, highbush throughout the nation, and rabbiteye only in the South and West. Lowbush and rabbiteye require another variety for cross-pollination; highbush types don't, but yields increase with cross-pollination. To encourage root growth, remove all blossoms for a full 2–3 years. The delayed harvest will pay you back in higher yields and healthier plants. Blueberries mature about 50–60 days from pollination. For areas prone to late spring frosts, blueberries are a good choice, with strong frost resistance. Consider adding blueberries to your landscape as beautiful ornamentals.

SELECTED VARIETIES
Northern and Ornamentals
Highbush *(Vaccinium acorymbosum).*
Bluetta Very early; small-medium berry; 10–20 pounds/plant; compact; spreading; 3'–5'; good ornamental due to low stature; zones 5–7 (Hartmann's)

Blueray Early midseason; large berry; 10–20 pounds/plant; very sweet; leading U-pick; upright; 4'–6'; excellent ornamental; zones 4–7 (Fowler, Hartmann's, Miller, NYFT)

Bluecrop Midseason; large berry; 10–20 pounds/plant; upright, 4'–6', very hardy, drought resistant, leading highbush, excellent ornamental, zones 4–7 (widely available)

Elliot Late; small-medium berry; 10–20 pounds/plant; one of highest yielding blueberries; very tart until 60 percent of fruit are ripe; upright; 5'–7'; good ornamental; zones 4–7 (Hartmann's, Raintree)

Patriot Early; large berry; 10–20 pounds/plant; upright; 4'–6'; resists Phytophthera cinnomomi; good ornamental; very cold hardy; zones 3–7 (Fowler, Hartmann's, Henry Field's, Miller)

Northblue Midseason; large berry; 3–7 pounds/plant; 20"–30"; best with snow protection; good ornamental; very cold hardy; zones 3–7 (Hartmann's, Miller, Northwoods, NYFT, Raintree)

Lowbush *(Vaccinium angustifolium).*
Vaccinium Angustifolium Maine wild blueberry; ornamental and commercial uses; 6"–18"; spreads rapidly once established; excellent plant; zones 3–7 (Hartmann's)

Tophat Very beautiful and one of the best ornamentals; 20" high and 24" breadth; medium berry; profuse blooms; cold hardy; bonsai type; zones 4–7 (Hartmann's)

Wells Delight Late; creeping; 5"–8"; evergreen similar to holly; excellent low maintenance ground cover; zones 5–7 (Hartmann's, Raintree)

Southern and Ornamentals

Highbush.
All Southern highbush are self-pollinating and ripen 20–30 days earlier than Rabbiteye. Low chill varieties can be grown farthest South.

Sharpblue Early; large berry; 8–16 pounds/plant with irrigation; vigorous; 5'–6'; needs little chill; very good ornamental; zones 7–10 (Hartmann's)

Challenger Early midseason; medium berry; good quality and attractive fruit; slender and upright; 6'; needs little chill; good ornamental; zones 6–10 (Hartmann's)

Sunshine Late; medium berry; 5–10 pounds/plant; very hardy but needs little if any chill; excellent patio or pot culture; excellent southern ornamental; zones 6–10 (Hartmann's)

Rabbiteye *(Vaccinium ashei).*
Pollinate with another in same maturation group.

Climax Early midseason; large berry; 8–22 pounds/plant; very good quality; tall and spreading; 6'–10'; leading pollinator; good ornamental; zones 7–9 (Hartmann's)

Bonitablue Early midseason; large berry; 8–22 pounds/plant with irrigation; excellent quality; stores well; very sweet; upright; 6'–10'; very good ornamental; zones 8–9 (Hartmann's)

Woodard Midseason; very large berry; 8–16 pounds/plant; good in the northern South; good fresh or processed; not good commercial; good ornamental; zones 7–9 (Hartmann's, Stark)

Choice Late; small berry; 8–12 pounds/plant when irrigated; good quality; used in process market; upright; some spreading; 8'–12'; best Rabbiteye ornamental; zones 7–9 (Hartmann's)

Powderblue Late; large berries; 8–14 pounds/plant when irrigated; very good quality and flavor; upright; vigorous; 8'–12'; very good ornamental; zones 7–9 (Hartmann's)

Tifblue Late; large berry; 8–25 pounds/plant; vigorous; 8'–14'; excellent in Georgia and Texas; good ornamental; zones 7–9 (Hartmann's, Stark)

Notes

Propagation Layering — bend and bury the tip of a lower branch and cover with soil. Rooting hormone helps. The following spring, cut off the cane 8" from the ground and dig up the new plant.

GROWTH CONDITIONS

Height: Dwarf: 6'–10' Semidwarf: 12'–18' Standard: 15'–20'
Spacing: Dwarf: 8'–10' Semidwarf: 18'–20' Standard: 20'
Root Depth: 50 percent beyond dripline
pH: 6.0–6.5
Bearing Age: 2–7 years
Pollination: All sour types are self-pollinating.
Chilling Requirement: 800–1200 hours at below 45°F.
Site: Full sun to partial shade. A southern exposure or 12' from north-facing walls to delay blooming. Well-drained soil and good air circulation. Likes 4' of top soil. Don't plant on former apricot, cherry, or peach sites; when waterlogged, their roots release hydrogen cyanide, which may linger and hinder growth. Also don't plant between other fruit trees, because cherries bear at a time others may need to be sprayed.
Water: Heavy and even supply. Cherries are especially sensitive to water stress.
Fertilizer: Low N until 2 years old. Appropriate new growth is 12"–24" when young and 6"–12" bearing.
Training: *Free-standing:* central leader or open center *Wire-trained:* fan-trained against a south or north-facing wall, using the same method as for peaches. All sizes of sour cherries are suitable for training because they're not vigorous growers.
Pruning: The lowest branch should be about 2' off the ground and limbs about 8' apart. Both sour and sweet cherries bear on spurs as well as on 1-year-old wood. Sour cherries, however, produce several adjacent fruit blossoms on the 1-year-old wood, which cause future bare spaces that lack foliage. If there are too many of these lateral flower buds, trim 1"–2" off the branch ends in June to stimulate leaf buds. Sour cherry spurs bear 2–5 years.

HARVEST

Wait to pick until the fruit is fully ripe, which is when the flesh slides off the stem, leaving the pit behind.

STORAGE REQUIREMENTS

Use immediately, if possible; freeze sour cherries immediately.

Fresh:	Temperature	Humidity	Storage Life
	34°–40°F	high	soft flesh — 7 days
		firm flesh — 2–3 weeks	

Preserved:	Method	Taste
	Canned	good
	Frozen	good

GROWING TIPS

Sour cherries are the easiest cherries to grow because they're more tolerant than sweet cherries of cold winters and hot, humid summers. They also are less vigorous and therefore require less pruning. Cherries live about 30–35 years. For insect egg control, apply dormant oil spray every spring before the leaf buds open, covering all areas of the trunk and branches.

Pests

Apple maggot, blackberry fruit fly, birds, cherry fruit fly, cherry fruit sawfly, codling moth, peach leaf curl, peach tree borer, plum curculio

Diseases

Bacterial gummosis, black knot, black rot, brown rot, cherry leaf spot, crown rot, peach leaf curl, mildew, peach leaf curl, verticillium wilt

Allies

Some evidence: alder, brambles, buckwheat rye mulch, sorghum mulch, wheat mulch

Uncertain: caraway, coriander, dill, garlic, nasturtium, tansy, wildflowers, wormwood, vetch

Companions

Alfalfa, bromegrass, clover

Incompatibles

None

SELECTED VARIETIES

Montmorency Early; the standard of sour cherries; very large, bright red fruit; resists cracking; tart; semidwarfish tree; hardy to zones 2–3 depending on rootstock (widely available)

North Star Midseason; genetic dwarf only 6'-7'; small red fruit; more concentrated flavor than Montmorency; good for pies and jam; self-fertile; hardy; high yields; resistant to brown rot; great for the home garden due to size; zones 3–8 (widely available)

Meteor Late; natural semidwarf, 10'–14'; considered superior to Montmorency; very hardy; large fruit; good fresh, canned, frozen, baked, or juiced; hardy to zone 2 (Gurney's, Northwoods, NYFT, Rocky Meadow, Windmill)

ROOTSTOCKS

Mahaleb *(Prunus mahaleb)* rootstock is good for sour cherries. It produces trees 60–75 percent of standard size that are susceptible to root rot and gophers, less long-lived than Mazzard, but more resistant than Mazzard is to crown gall, drought, and cold injury. Colt rootstock produces semidwarfs, about 80 percent of full size, that may be more resistant to bacterial diseases and crown rot. North Star rootstock also produces semidwarfs that are hardy and resistant to wet soil. Elwood Fisher, master fruit gardener, uses North Star to dwarf other types of fruit trees as well. For other sour cherry rootstocks, especially GH 61-1, *see* **Sweet Cherry,** on page 90.

Notes

If possible, buy certified virus-free trees.

HOUGHALL COLLEGE LIBRARY

GROWTH CONDITIONS

Height: Dwarf: 6'–12' Semidwarf: 10'–15' Standard: 25'–40'

Spacing: Dwarf: 8'–10' Semidwarf: 15'–18' Standard: 25'–30'

Root Depth: 50 percent beyond dripline

pH: 6.0–6.5

Bearing Age: 2–7 years

Pollination: All sweet cherries, except Stella, must be cross-pollinated, although not all are compatible because of different bloom times. Further pollination difficulties arise because early spring flowers are receptive for only about 1 week. Also, a late frost or a wet spring can interfere with bee activity.

Chilling Requirement: 800–1200 hours below 45°F.

Site: Full sun; needs light and well-drained soil for successful survival. *See* **Growing Tips** below.

Water: Heavy and even supply. Cherries are particularly susceptible to water stress.

Fertilizer: Low N until 2 years old. Appropriate new growth is 22"–36" when young and 8"–12" bearing.

Training: *Free-standing:* central leader. *Wire-trained:* fan-trained against a south wall where the summer sun is not blistering hot, or 12'–15' away from a north wall.

Only dwarf sweet cherries are suitable for training.

Pruning: The lowest branch should be about 2' off the ground and limbs about 8' apart. Sweet cherries bear on spurs as well as on 1-year-old wood. Sweet cherry spurs produce for 10–12 years; exercise extreme caution when harvesting or pruning to avoid damaging them.

Pests
See **Sour Cherry,** (page 88)

Diseases
See **Sour Cherry,** (page 88)

Allies
See **Sour Cherry,** (page 88)

Companions
See **Sour Cherry,** (page 88)

Incompatibles
None

HARVEST

Wait until the fruit is fully ripe. Gently pull on the stem and twist upward. Be extremely careful not to damage or rip off spurs, as these bear for 10 or more years.

STORAGE REQUIREMENTS

Use immediately if possible. If not possible, place in an airtight container like a crisper and refrigerate. There is controversy over whether sweet cherries store best with or without their stems; experiment for yourself.

Fresh:

Temperature	Humidity	Storage Life
34°–40°F	high	soft flesh — 7 days firm flesh — 2–3 weeks

Preserved:

Method	Taste	Shelflife (in months)
Canned	good	
Frozen	poor	

GROWING TIPS

Standard sweet cherries grow very large and require consistent pruning in order to be managed properly. Cherries live about 30–35 years. For insect egg control, apply dormant oil spray every spring before the leaf buds open, ensuring that all areas of the trunk and branches are coated.

SELECTED VARIETIES

Red

Starkrimson Early; genetic dwarf, 12'–14'; self-pollinating; large fruit; very sweet; high yields; zones 5–8 (Stark)

Compact Van Early; fruit similar to the Bing; highly crack resistant; very hardy; large, excellent crops; zones 5–7 (Windmill)

Compact Stella Midseason; genetic dwarf, 8'–14'; self-pollinating; dark red fruit; zones 6–7 (Henry Field's, Miller, Stark, Windmill)

Lambert Midseason; flavor and looks of the Bing; later season, more resistant to cracking; excellent fresh or canned; hardy; high chill requirement; pollinated by Rainier (Northwoods, Sonoma Apple, Van Well)

Compact Lambert Midseason; same as Lambert, but only 7'–10'; suited for pot culture or in the ground; thrives in the Northwest (Northwoods, Raintree)

Parkhill Midseason; purplish soft flesh; excellent flavor; recommended by Southmeadow for the amateur home gardener; believed to be a seedling of Lambert (Southmeadow)

Lapins Sweet Cherry Late midseason; self-pollinating; Bing-type fruit; crack resistant; firm, meaty texture; from British Colombia; one of the best Bing-type for home orchards (Stark)

Spate Braun (Late Brown) Late; very large; very sweet; crack resistant; considered the best garden cherry for its size and texture; high yields (Southmeadow)

Yellow

Rainier Early; large fruit with red blush; like Royal Ann; firm, yellow-white flesh; resists splitting; productive; spreading tree (Northwoods, NYFT, Rocky Meadow, Sonoma)

Stark Gold Late; unusual yellow fruit with unique; tangy flavor; survived -30°F; attracts very few birds; crack resistant; pollinate with any other sweet cherry; zones 5–7 (Stark)

Compact Royal Ann Genetic dwarf; large, light yellow cherry with red blush; firm; good flavor; can maintain under 10' (Raintree)

Duke Cherries

The Duke cherry, not widely grown since the beginning of the 20th century, is still available. Duke cherries are hardier than sweet cherries and excellent substitutes. Their fruit is yellow-red, soft, and juicy. Pollination is less difficult than with sweet cherries. If you can't grow sweet cherries because the climate is too cold, you might try these. (Windmill)

ROOTSTOCKS

Mazzard *(Prunus avium)* rootstock is good for sweet cherries. It is a vigorous grower, produces large trees, is slow to bear, and is tolerant of wet soil. Mazzard is particularly good in the West, Northwest, and areas of the East where moisture is sufficient and winter hardiness is not a problem. GM61, a new rootstock from Belgium, is considered by some to be the best overall dwarfing stock for cherry. Its trees are 50–60 percent of standard size; they can be maintained below 15', are hardy to at least -20°F, are spreading and precocious, do well in heavier soils, and are good for both sweet and sour. Trees propagated on GM61 are available from Northwoods, Raintree, Rocky Meadow, and Stark Nurseries. For information on other rootstocks, *see* **Sour Cherry**, (page 88).

Notes

Select certified virus-free trees, if possible.

GROWTH CONDITIONS

Height: 30'–40'

Breadth: 20'

Spacing: 8' if thinned out in 5 years; 20' if thinned out to 40' in 20 years; 40' if not thinned

Root Depth: Deep

pH: 5.0–6.0

Bearing Age: 3–4 years

Pollination: All require cross-pollination; plant two of the same or different varieties.

Chilling Requirement: Low number of hours are required for nut blossoms development.

Site: Full sun. Preferred soil is light and sandy, but it can be rocky or silty as long as it isn't alkaline or very dry. Soil must be very well-drained. Avoid frost pockets, areas that are subject to soil compaction, and sites with potential disruption of the root system.

Water: Medium; however, established trees are fairly drought resistant.

Fertilizer: Medium feeder. Use low N for trees under 2 years; you don't want rapid growth when the tree is young. Unlike some nuts, the chestnut likes to be fed throughout its life and produces better quality nuts with regular feeding. If you want to use lime to add calcium, make sure the pH is 5.0–5.5 initially, as the chestnut thrives in acid soil.

Side-dressing: Apply compost in late autumn, or rotted manure and leaf mold in the early spring.

Training: *Free-standing:* central leader *Wire-trained:* N/A.

Pruning: Prune young trees minimally, just enough to train the tree to a single trunk and basic scaffold; too much pruning stimulates extra vegetative growth and delays bearing.

Pests

Chestnut weevil, gall wasp (in Georgia), mite, nut curculio, squirrel

Diseases

Chestnut blight, blossom end rot, oak wilt

Allies, Companions, and Incompatibles

None

HARVEST

Use thick gloves to protect your hands from the spines of the outer chestnut hull. To minimize daily gathering, when the burs begin to crack open in late summer, pick or knock down small bunches of them onto a harvest sheet. For final ripening, store the burs at 55°–65°F for about 1 week or until they split open. If unable to pick them in bulk, you must gather fallen nuts each day, for chestnuts are particularly susceptible to rapid degradation by fungi and bacteria on the ground.

STORAGE REQUIREMENTS

The chestnut can be eaten raw if cured first to maximize the nut's free sugar. To cure, dry de-burred nuts in a shady, warm, dry place for 1 to 3 days until the nut texture is spongy. To roast, cut an X in the shell and cook at 400°F for 15 minutes. If not eaten immediately, store uncured nuts in a cold place that is either dry or has high humidity but no free moisture. A good method is to mix freshly harvested and dehulled nuts with dry peat moss, pack in plastic bags, seal, and refrigerate. You can also dry and grind nuts into a baking flour.

Fresh : (uncured)	Temperature	Humidity	Storage Life
	32°F	high, but no free moisture	6–12 months

GROWING TIPS

The Chinese chestnut is an attractive, globe-shaped landscape shade tree. It also offers rot-resistant timber and regular annual crops of one of the sweetest nuts. In early summer, the tree is decked with pretty (but odiferous) yellow catkins, and its glossy, dark green serrated leaves cling late into the fall. Chestnut fungal blight swept through North America in the early 1900s, destroying nearly all American *(C. dentata)* and European *(C. sativa)* chestnuts, both of which are now planted on the West coast where blight is less a problem. The Chinese chestnut, introduced in 1853, resists blight and grows well in zones 5–8 in a wide variety of soil and climatic conditions, although it's grown primarily in the East and Northwest. Like the peach, it is hardy to about -20°/20°F, but, unlike the peach, late blooming permits it to escape spring frosts. For rot-resistant poles, chestnuts can be coppiced: cut down the tree to stimulate sucker growth, let suckers grow to desired pole thickness, and cut again. Chestnuts can live 50 or more years.

SELECTED VARIETIES

Chinese and Chinese Hybrids

Suited for east of the Rocky Mountains, where blight is widespread.

Au-leader Grafted Chinese variety; large nut; good flavor; hardy; disease-resistant; grows only 25'–35'; zones 4–9 (Stark)

Crane 32 nuts/pound; flavor and storage quality is excellent when cured; good annual bearer; good anywhere from north Florida to the Great Lakes region; hardy to -20°F (Nolin River)

Douglass Chinese-American hybrid; well-filled nuts; good flavor; available as graft or seedling from different nurseries; zones 5–7 (Grimo, Windmill)

Eaton Ornamental and high quality nut tree; 30–40 nuts/pound; good texture, flavor, and sweetness; need 2–3 trees for a good crop; originally from Connecticut; good from northern Florida to Michigan and Wisconsin; zones 5–6 (Nolin River)

Layeroka Chinese-European hybrid; combines blight resistance of Chinese with timber and nut quality of European; very hardy; good for commercial orchards; early ripening; available as graft or seedling from different nurseries; not a very big nut; zones 6–7 (Grimo, Northwoods, Raintree, Saginaw, Windmill)

Manchurian Chinese-American hybrid; flavor and nut size of American; vigorous grower; hardy to -28°F (Miller)

Sleeping Giant Good quality nut; also good for timber; spreading crown; originally from Connecticut; not prone to frost problems (Nolin River)

American (C. dentata)

Suited only for the Northwest where blight is not a problem.

American seedlings Excellent; huge timber tree (Grimo, Northwoods, Raintree, St. Lawrence)

European (C. sativa)

Suited only for areas west of the Rocky Mountains.

European seedlings Planted widely on West Coast (Northwoods)

Notes

Most seedlings do better than grafted trees in the northern zones (5–6).

GROWTH CONDITIONS

Height: 20'

Breadth: 15'

Spacing: 15'–20' for trees 3'–5' for hedges

Root Depth: Unlike other nut trees, this has no taproot.

pH: 6.5

Bearing Age: 2–4 years

Pollination: All need cross-pollination.

Chilling Requirement: Medium-high hours.

Site: Full sun in maritime climates; partial shade in very sunny, hot climates. In the East, choose a northern, cold exposure to delay premature bloom. Can adapt to clay and sand, but prefers deep, fertile, well-drained soil. Must avoid low frost pockets or poorly drained areas.

Water: Medium; water well in times of bad drought. In maritime climates like the Northwest, mature trees rarely need watering. Sawdust mulch helps keep moisture in the soil.

Fertilizer: Heavy feeder, but do not fertilize unless foliage is pale and growth is slow. Appropriate new growth is 6"–9".

Side-dressing: Apply compost in late autumn and organic mulch in early spring.

Training: *Free-standing:* open center *Wire-trained:* N/A

Pruning: To grow a shrub, cut excessive sucker growth yearly. For a tree, prune to establish a central leader and basic scaffold, and remove all suckers. Nuts develop on 1-year-old wood, so prune lightly every year to stimulate new growth. Make thinning-out cuts only where branches are cut back to their base, not in half or stubbed off.

Pests

Blue jay, filbert bud mite, filbertworm, filbert weevil, squirrel

Diseases

Crown gall, Eastern filbert blight, filbert bacterial blight, powdery mildew *(Note:* Eastern filbert blight should not be excluded as a possible problem in West Coast growing regions. It was first found on the West Coast in the Williamette Valley of Oregon in 1986.)

Allies

None

Companions

None

Incompatibles

None

HARVEST

Nuts usually turn brown and ripen by late summer, but an immature husk, shaped like a barely opened daffodil blossom, prevents them from dropping for almost another month. The nut is ripe when it readily turns in the husk if pressed. When ripe, you can either hand harvest the husks, or wait until nuts drop to the ground (and risk competing with the squirrels and birds).

STORAGE REQUIREMENTS

Place hulled nuts in water; remove the rotten and diseased nuts that float to the top. Dry and cure by spreading nuts in one layer and leaving them in a cool, dry, well-ventilated place for several weeks. They're ready for storage when the kernels rattle in the shell, or, when unshelled, the nutmeat snaps when bent. Avoid big piles of nuts, which encourage rot.

Fresh:	Temperature	Humidity	Shelf Life
	shelled: 65°–70°F	low	several weeks
	unshelled: 34°–40°F	low	several months

Preserved:	Method	Taste	Shelflife (in months)
	Frozen (shelled)		12+

GROWING TIPS

Filberts, also known as hazelnuts, are unusual because they can be grown as shrubs, hedgerows, or trees. An ideal size for home growers, they are generally hardy. However, very early blooming renders them very susceptible to late frosts. In the Northwest, they never go fully dormant. Filberts tend to bear in alternate years, depending on how much new wood was produced and how much was pruned out the prior year. In areas that are subject to temperatures of 5°F or lower, they do not produce nuts consistently. In the first 2 years, protect young tree trunks from sunscald. Filberts produce numerous suckers that are easily used for propagation and good for coppice management (*see* **Chestnut,** page 92). Delicious in baked goods, filberts are also high vitamin and protein snacks.

SELECTED VARIETIES

European species (C. avellana). Commonly known as filberts, these are a major commercial crop in the Northwest, grow best in maritime climates, and are the kind of nut usually found in supermarkets. They have been occasionally grown in the East, but generally do poorly there due to Eastern filbert blight.

Butler Good pollinizer for **Ennis;** medium-large nut; good flavor; smooth kernel; moderate bud mite resistance; very hardy (Northwoods)

Ennis European; replaces the prime commercial **Barcelona** cultivar; more productive; very few blanks; larger nut; smooth kernel; moderate hardiness and moderate bud mite resistance (Northwoods, Raintree)

Royal Filbert European; large nuts; thin shells; pollinate with Barcelona; zones 5–8; best for the East (Miller, Stark)

American species (C. americana). Most often known as hazelnuts, these species grow in native, wild hedgerows throughout the northern U.S. and southern Canada. American hazelnuts are usually smaller than the European nut. The American species serves as a host for Eastern filbert blight fungus but is very tolerant of its attack.

American Bear early; less than 15' tall; pretty ornamental; good nuts; yields better with 2 (Kelly)

Hazelberts. These nuts are a cross between the European filbert and American hazelnut, combining the large European nut size with American hardiness and early ripening.

Fingerlakes Super Hardy Large nut; productive; early bearing; hardy; resists aphids and bud mites (Miller)

Gellatly Early bearing; hardy (Grimo)

Grimo Productive tree; available grafted, layered, or seedling (Grimo, Windmill)

Hambleton Well-filled nut; available grafted or layered (Windmill)

Turkish Trazel (cross of *C. colurna* **and** *C. avellana)* Excellent small shade tree and nut producer; shapely; good flavor; only 20'–30' tall; hardy to -25°F (Gurney's, Raintree)

Notes

When buying a filbert or hazelnut, make sure it is intended to be a nut-bearing tree. Many are grown only as ornamentals and may be poor nut bearers. Nuts from grafted or layered trees are generally higher quality than those from seedling trees.

GROWTH CONDITIONS

Height: Pruned: 12'–20' Unpruned: 50'–100'
Spacing: 8' is best; 7' in shallow soil and 10' in deep soil
Root Depth: In deep soil they can easily extend 12'–40'.
pH: 6.5–7.0
Bearing Age: 3–4 years
Pollination: All are self-fertile with the exception of a few muscadine vines.
Chilling Requirement: None
Site: Best on a 15° south-facing (SE or SW) slope.
Water: Low to dry. To harden the vines for winter, don't water much after August.
Fertilizer: Apply compost only at the beginning of the growing season or during blooming. When applied late in the season, nitrogen delays ripening, inhibits coloring, and subjects vines to winter injury if they keep growing too long into the fall. American grapes and hybrids are especially sensitive to N-deficiency in the early spring and during blooming.
Training: Refer to diagrams on page 74. For vigorous vines, the less common Geneva double curtain method provides the best aeration, most sun, and highest yields. Plant vines down the center, prune each to 2 trunks, and grow trunks to long, 6'–8' cordons on upper wire. Train the first vine to the front wire, the second to the back wire, and so on. The more common 4-arm Kniffen method provides an attractive privacy screen but shades the lower vine parts. For both methods, bury 9' end-posts 3' in the ground. Use heavy galvanized #11 wire.
Pruning: To spur prune European vines, consult other sources. Cane prune all others as follows. (1) Cut out water spouts which are shoots on more than 2-year-old wood. (2) Remove winter-damaged wood. (3) Cut out last year's fruiting cane. (4) Identify canes receiving the most sun by their darker wood and closely spaced nodes; select the thickest to bear this season's fruit, and cut back to only 8–15 nodes. (5) For each selected fruiting cane, choose a cane nearby as a renewal spur for next year's fruit; cut back to 2 buds. Each year replace the fruiting arm with a cane from a renewal spur, and select new renewal spur for the following year.

Pests

Leafhopper, grape berry moth, Japanese beetle, phylloxera root aphid, plum curculio, mealybug, mite, rose chafer

Diseases

Anthracnose, black rot, botrytis fruit rot, crown gall, downy mildew, leaf spot, powdery mildew, Pierce's disease (spread by leafhoppers)

Allies

Some evidence: blackberries *(Rubus sp.)*, Johnson and Sudan grass *(see* caution on Johnson Grass in chart on page 235).

Uncertain: chives, hyssop

HARVEST

Cut bunches when fruits are fully colored, sweet, and slide off easily, and the stems and seeds are brown. Grapes don't ripen further once picked. For raisins, use a hydrometer and harvest when the grapes reach 20 percent soluble solids. A lower percentage significantly decreases raisin weight and quality.

STORAGE REQUIREMENTS

Cool to 50°F as soon as possible after picking and spread out fruit bunches in single layers. Dry in the sun under clear polyethylene; this shortens drying time and yields better raisins with higher levels of sugar and vitamin C than raisins dried in an oven. Dry until stems shrivel slightly, then store in trays no more than 4" deep.

Fresh:	Temperature	Humidity	Storage Life
	40°F	slightly humid	2–3 months

Preserved:	Method	Taste	Shelflife (in months)
	Jelly	good	
	Frozen	poor	
	Dried	excellent	
	Juice	good	12+

GROWING TIPS

Grape vines need well-drained soil and should have at least 20" of topsoil. They don't need very fertile soil because of vigorous, extensive roots; vines that grow more slowly also develop more "character." Plant vines at the same depth as grown in the nursery. Mound soil over the crown to prevent wind damage, except in the West because of possible crown rot. Cut out all but 1 or 2 stems (with 2–3 buds each) for the central trunk. Grape roots prefer warm soil, so mulch with stones or black plastic to raise soil temperature. If vines overbear, thin flowers before berries form.

SELECTED VARIETIES

American

Pure strains are rich in pectin, best for jelly, and renowned for a "foxy" flavor (cloyingly sweet, like the Concord) that, if possible, wine-makers avoid. Newer hybrids are good fresh and for wine.

Red.

Swensen Very early; good for Northern states; hardy to -40°F with occasional winter injury; for table and wine; good for cold storage; zones 3–7 (NYFT, St. Lawrence, Raintree, Windmill)

Reliance Early; seedless; fruity; high yields; stores to 3 months; hardy to -10°F without protection; resists anthracnose; black rot; powdery and downy mildew; good fresh; zones 4–8 (Burpee, Gurney's, Kelly, Miller, NYFT, Raintree, Stark)

Canadice Early; seedless; very good flavor; high yields; keeps on vine a long time; very disease resistant; hardy to -15°F without protection; for table, jelly, or wine (widely available)

Vanessa Early; seedless; high quality; vinifera character; hangs in compact clusters; from Vineland Ontario Station; has survived -25°F (NYFT, Raintree, Southmeadow, Windmill)

Einset Midseason; high yields; stores well; resists botrytis; flavor has a hint of strawberry; good fresh or dried as raisins; hardy to -5°F; zones 5–8 (NYFT, Raintree)

Saturn Midseason; excellent flavor; high yields; good fresh or as dessert wine; hardy; disease resistant; hardy to -5°F without protection; zones 5–8 (Miller, NYFT, Raintree, Stark)

Catawba Very late; high vigor; susceptible to mildew; keeps for up to 2 months; for wine, juice, jelly, and also table; hardy to -10°F; zones 5–8 (Burpee, Miller, Southmeadow, Windmill)

White.

Himrod Early, low yields; very vigorous; great for home garden; stores well; excellent fresh flavor; good for raisins; hardy to 0°F without protection; zones 5–8 (widely available)

Interlaken Early, small berries; high yields; excellent flavor fresh; excellent raisins; hardy to +5°F without protection; zones 5–8 (Kelly, Miller, NYFT, Raintree, Southmeadow)

Kay Gray Extremely hardy; medium berry; mild fruity flavor; disease resistant; good fresh or as juice or wine; vigorous; hardy to -15°F without protection (NYFT, St. Lawrence)

Cayuga Late; high vigor; moderately susceptible to mildew; for juice and jelly; very high quality wine; hardy to -5°F without protection; zones 4–7 (Miller, NYFT)

Muscadine (var. *rotundifolia*)

Indigenous to the American Southeast, these require a warm, moist climate and are good for jelly, juice, and wine. They require cross-pollination, so plant two varieties.

Fry Gold-yellow; large berry; very sweet; vigorous; high yields; good fresh; zones 7–9 (Burpee)

Carlos Bronze; large berry; self-pollinating; disease resistant; very vigorous; makes sparkling wines; zones 7–9 (Burpee)

Hybrids (French Hybrids, American-European Hybrids)

These represent an attempt to obtain the best of both worlds: European taste and American hardiness and disease resistance.

Aurore (Seibel 5279) Gold-pink berry; early; moderate vigor; high yields; for wine, juice, jelly, and table; hardy to -10°F without protection; zones 6–7 (widely available)

Seibel 9110 Gray-yellow berry; crisp; meaty; delicious table grapes; adherent skins; needs protection from severe winters (Southmeadow)

European and California (var. *vinifera*). Low in pectin, these require a frost-free season of 170–180 days and are not hardy below 10°F without protection. Most wines are made from Vinifera or the American-European hybrids. Among the many varieties, these are hardiest.

White Riesling One of hardiest wine grapes; for cool climates; zones 5–9 (NYFT, Van Well)

Cabernet Sauvignon Black; very seedy; for a cool climate and long growing season; red wine; cane prune; zones 5–9 (Fowler, Henry Field's, NYFT)

Notes

Grape seeds secrete growth hormones within the berry, so commercial growers spray seedless grapes with growth hormones. Homegrown, unsprayed, seedless grapes will be smaller.

GROWTH CONDITIONS

Height: Up to 30' long vines

Spacing: Between plants: 10'–20' Between rows: 15'–20' Male and female: within at least 100'

Root Depth: Shallow (which means they're susceptible to crown and root rot in wet areas)

pH: 6.0–6.5

Bearing Age: 3–5 years, except for self-pollinating types, which can bear 1 year after planting

Pollination: Cross-pollination between male and female vines required; 1 male can pollinate 8 female vines.

Chilling Requirement: Vines benefit from 400–600 hours below 45°F.

Site: Full sun (minimum 6 hours), except for the *A. kolomikta* which likes partial shade in hot climates. Wind protection is important. Prefers rich, fertile soil, but will tolerate heavy soil. In any soil, good drainage is imperative. Avoid soggy, low areas. Best spot is to the north of a building or tree to delay bud break. Cover vines if frost threatens in spring or fall.

Water: Heavy. Drip irrigation is best. Overhead sprinkling can protect fruit and foliage from frosts.

Fertilizer: Heavy feeder. Apply slow acting organic fertilizers, very thick compost, or well-rotted manure in late winter and spring, several inches away from the crown. Don't fertilize past mid-June. Kiwi needs high K, and also Mg to prevent K-induced deficiency. Never apply Boron, as above-optimum levels can be severely toxic.

Side-dressing: Apply twice during the growing season; use only mildly nitrogenous substances.

Training: Requires trellis, arbor, T-bar fence, pergola, wall, or chain-link fence to support fruiting vines. Supports for females should be 6' tall, and for males 7' tall. Stake when planting.

Pruning: Similar to grapes. Kiwis fruit on the base 6 buds of this season's fruiting shoot, off of 1-year-old wood. On planting, prune the main stem back to 4–5 buds. The first summer allow the vine to grow freely. Cut back females to 6' and males to 7', and remove all but 2 or 4 of the strongest cordons for each. The second winter, head back female cordons to 8–10 buds, and males to ½ that length (4–5).

Pests

No significant pests reported in North America

Diseases

No significant diseases reported in North America

Allies

None

Companions

None

Incompatibles

None

HARVEST

Allow fruit to ripen on the vine until the first signs of softening; it should give with a little finger pressure. Clip hardy kiwi with some stem. Snap off fuzzy kiwi, leaving the stem on the vine. Even minor damage causes ethylene production, which prematurely softens other fruit. In dry climates, you can let the kiwi dry on the vine; they will become intensely sweet and keep about 6 weeks.

STORAGE REQUIREMENTS

Remove soft, rotten, or shriveled fruit on a regular basis from fresh storage. Freeze whole kiwis in plastic bags; or freeze ¼" unpeeled slices and then pack in plastic bags. To dry, peel the fruit, cut drying process in half, dry at 120°F for 2 hours; repeat it the next day.

Fresh:	Temperature	Humidity	Storage Life
(whole)	32°F	85%–95%	2 months (hardy)/4 months (fuzzy)

GROWING TIPS

Kiwi is a productive and tasty candidate for the home grower — but only if proper attention is paid to site, water, support, and pruning. The buds, young shoots, and fruit of all species — regardless of hardiness — are very frost tender and need to be protected when temperatures fall below 30°F for any length of time, in spring or fall. Cover at night to protect from frost damage, or use overhead sprinkling until temperatures surmount 32°F. Frost-damaged fruit emit ethylene gas in storage, thereby hastening the softening of other fruit. Kiwi vines can bear for 40–50 years. Yield and fruit size are optimized by light pruning and fruit thinning, rather than heavy pruning and no thinning. Thin before flowers open to about 60 fruit/square meter.

SELECTED VARIETIES

Very Hardy (A. kolomikta)

Hardy to zone 3 (-40°F), these are beautiful plants. The male has variegated leaves, and females display some variegation too. Northwoods Nursery brought 7 "Arctic Beauty" varieties back from the Soviet Union in 1987, only one of which is listed below. Fruits are smaller than fuzzy kiwi and are smooth-skinned.

"Arctic Beauty" Ornamental male with no fruit; good for zones 3–7 (Gurney's)

Krupnopladnaya Very large fruit; productive; good flavor; 14 percent sugar; high vitamin C (Northwoods)

Hardy (A. arguta)

Hardy to zone 4 (-25°F), native to northern China. The fruit is smaller than fuzzy kiwi and its smooth skin can be eaten like a grape's.

Issai Self-fertile Japanese variety; ideal for limited spaces; fruit will be larger with pollination although it will then have seeds; zones 5–9 (Burpee, Field's, Hartmann's, Northwoods, Stark)

74–49 Proven vigorous and reliable in Virginia; large fruit; aromatic; sweet (Northwoods)

Ananasnaja Means pineapple-like in Russian; very sweet fruit with a hint of mint flavor; brought from Belgium to the Northwest; actually a hybrid of Arguta and Kolomikta (Hartmann's, Northwoods, Raintree)

Miller's Kiwi Sweet; vigorous; hardy; fully rooted plants (Miller)

Tender or Fuzzy Kiwi (A. deliciosa)

Native to China and first commercially grown in New Zealand. This fuzzy fruit is hardy to zones 8–10 (5°–10°F), and can be grown as far north as the Pacific Northwest and British Columbia, Canada, or cultivated in greenhouses.

Blake Self-fertile; early ripening; medium fruit; productive (Northwoods, Raintree)

Hayward The variety usually found in supermarkets; good for warm areas of the maritime Northwest (Northwoods)

Saanichton 12 Large fruit; the hardiest fuzzy variety; same flavor and size of store kiwi; grown on Vancouver Island, British Columbia, Canada for 30+ years (Northwoods, Raintree)

PRUNING

General Female Winter Pruning Guidelines. Cut out damaged wood, curled or twining growth, and all wood that has fruited two seasons. Select fruiting arms that have short internodes (less than 2" apart), are 10"–14" apart, and are well-exposed to sunlight; cut these back to 8 buds.

General Female Summer Pruning Guidelines. Select next season's fruiting arms, remove other shoots, cut out erect water shoots, and shorten curled or tangled growth. Make sure enough light passes through to cast patterns on the ground below.

General Male Pruning Guidelines. Cut back flowering arms after blooming in July to 20"–24"; if necessary, trim again in August-September to 29"–31". Trim vines in winter.

Notes

One male can fertilize up to eight female vines; tag them to be sure you always know which is which. Try to buy larger plants since they have a higher survival rate. Otherwise, you may want to start small, rooted cuttings in 5-gallon containers.

GROWTH CONDITIONS

Height: Dwarf: 4'–10' Standard: 15'–20'
Spacing: Dwarf: 12'–15' Standard: 15'–25'
Root Depth: Shallow, over 90 percent in top 18". Roots won't branch out if planted too deeply.
pH: 6.0–6.5
Bearing Age: 2–3 years
Pollination: Most self-pollinate, but yields will be higher with cross-pollination.
Chilling Requirement: Most need 600–900 hours below 45°F.
Site: Full south or southeast exposure, whether or not espaliered. Will not survive on heavy clay soils. Do not plant on former apricot, cherry, or peach tree sites; when waterlogged, their roots release hydrogen cyanide that may linger in the soil and hinder growth.
Fertilizer: Low N when under 3 years. Appropriate new growth is 12"–15" when young, and 8"–18" when bearing.
Training: *Free-standing:* open center *Wire-trained:* fan, against a south-facing wall
Pruning: Unlike apple, peach bears fruit on 1-year-old wood only and should be pruned to encourage new growth. Cut out branches that shade or cross each other, intrude on the center, or are winter-damaged. Remove at least one-third of the previous year's growth, or too much fruit will be set. Every few years, cut out some older wood. Cut upright-growing shoots back to the outward-pointing buds.

HARVEST

Pick when the fruit is firm, almost ready to eat, and easily slides off the stem by tipping or twisting. Never pull it directly off or you'll bruise the peach and hasten spoilage. If fruit has a mild case of brown rot, harvest only those peaches that are infected and dip them in hot water for 7 minutes at 120°F (alternatives: 3 minutes at 130°F; 2 minutes at 140°F). This kills the fungi without harming the fruit, and prepares it to be stored for further ripening.

STORAGE REQUIREMENTS

To freeze the fruit: peel, pit, and cut it in halves or slices. Pack it with some honey mixed with lemon or a pectin pack. Peaches don't store well in a root cellar.

Fresh:	Temperature	Humidity	Storage Life
	50°–70°F	low	3–14 days

Preserved:	Method	Taste	Shelflife (in months)
	Canned	fair	
	Frozen	good	6+
	Dried	fair	12+

GROWING TIPS

Peaches are considered one of the hardest fruits to grow — particularly for growers who don't use chemical sprays — because of multiple pests and an early bloom period that makes it extremely susceptible to frost damage. Spraying white paint on the trees, buds and all, in mid-January can help delay blooming by up to 5 days; this is often enough to make a big difference in flower survival and fruit set, according to Rutgers University. Use flat-white, interior latex paint to avoid damaging the trees. Plant at about the same depth that it was grown in the nursery; its upper roots should be only a few inches below the soil surface. Thinning is crucial to a good harvest. After the June drop, but before the fruit is 1¼" in diameter, thin to: (a) 1 fruit per 30–40 leaves, (b) 1 fruit per 10" on early-ripening varieties, or (c) 6"–8" on late-ripening varieties. "Cling" varieties are firm, best for canning, but rarely available to homegrowers. "Freestone" varieties don't can well; the flesh separates from the pit when ripe and is soft. Peach trees live a mere 8 years in the South and 18 years in the North; poor drainage renders even shorter life cycles.

Pests

Aphid, birds, cherry fruit sawfly, codling moth, gopher, gypsy moth caterpillar, Japanese beetle, mite, oriental fruit moth, peach tree borers, peach twig borer, plum curculio, root lesion nematodes, tarnished plant bug, tent caterpillar, weevil, whitefly

Diseases

Bacterial canker, bacterial spot, brown rot, crown gall, cytospora canker, peach leaf curl, scab, verticillium wilt

Allies

Some evidence: alder, brambles, buckwheat, goldenrod, lamb's-quarters, ragweed, rye mulch, smartweed, sorghum mulch, strawberry, wheat mulch

Uncertain: caraway, coriander, dill, garlic, nasturtium, tansy, wildflowers, wormwood, vetch

Bird control: A border of dogwood, mulberry, or other aromatic fruit, all of which birds prefer

Incompatibles

None

SELECTED VARIETIES

Yellow Flesh

Redhaven Early; good fresh, frozen, and canned; almost fuzzless; requires thinning early; hardy wood and buds; disease resistant; not good for warm winters; 950 hours chill; zones 5–8 (Adams, Fowler, Kelly, NYFT, Sonoma, Southmeadow, Stark)

Compact Redhaven Same as Redhaven, but semidwarfed to 10'; tolerates bacterial spot and leaf curl; 850 hours chill (Stark, Van Well)

Frost Midseason; medium fruit; semi-freestone; good flavor; highly resistant to leaf curl; good in Pacific Northwest (Northwoods, Raintree)

Harrow Beauty Midseason; a beautiful tree and fruit; good fresh; excellent flavor; hardy; medium vigor; very open; spreading; productive; tolerates bacterial spot and brown rot; 850 hours chill (NYFT, Windmill)

Sunhigh Midseason; large oblong fruit; very good flavor; sweet and melting flesh; susceptible to bacterial spot; 750 hours chill; best in East (Adams, Cumberland, Southmeadow)

Canadian Harmony Midseason; large fruit; good flavor; some resistance to bacterial spot; good for California and Northwest; 850 hours chill (Adams, Cumberland, Kelly)

Madison Late midseason; good fresh and canned; sweet; juicy; thin skins; very hardy; vigorous; hardier than Redhaven; tolerates frost during blooming; good bud hardiness; 850 hours chill (Adams, Cumberland, Kelly, NYFT, Stark)

Biscoe Late; medium fruit; good flavor; well-formed tree; vigorous; productive; highly resistant to bacterial spot; 850 hours chill (Cumberland)

Rio Oso Gem Late; large fruit; good fresh, frozen, and in pies; reported non-browning; large showy flowers; naturally smaller tree; vigorous, 850 hours chill (Adams, Fowler, Sonoma)

Jerseyglo Late; large fruit; hardy and easy to manage; very resistant to bacterial spot

Stark Encore Very late; medium-large fruit; excellent flavor; very resistant to bacterial leaf spot; buds are cold hardy (Stark)

White Flesh

Babcock Early; small-medium fruit; very sweet; low acid fruit; requires heavy thinning; good in California (Fowler)

Raritan Rose Early; large fruit; excellent fresh; firm flesh; tender; juicy; honeysweet; hardy buds; very vigorous; susceptible to brown rot; 950 hours chill; best in East (Adams)

Champion Midseason; old variety; medium fruit; excellent fresh; extremely tender and juicy flesh; very hardy; vigorous (Miller, Southmeadow)

Genetic Dwarf Peaches and Nectarines

Stark Sensation Early; 4'–6'; good fresh, canned, or frozen; good for Midwest; zones 5–8, also zone 4 if potted (Stark)

Nectar Babe Early; nectarine will grow less than 6'; easily grown in pot; keep rain off to avoid peach leaf curl; Honey Babe is best pollinator (Fowler, Raintree)

Honey Babe Early midseason; 3'–5'; flesh is yellow; firm; sweet; delicious; for container growing; keep rain off to avoid leaf curl; good in Northwest (Northwoods, Raintree)

Garden Beauty Midseason; clingstone nectarine; for tub planting (Windmill)

ROOTSTOCKS

See Plum Rootstock Chart on page 108, since most are the same for peaches. Peaches do best on a peach seedling rootstock, which produces standard trees. Standard trees can be kept small by pruning. Elberta rootstocks are not hardy for the North.

Notes

GROWTH CONDITIONS

Height: Dwarf: 8'–15' Semidwarf: 15'–20' Standard: 30'–40'
Spacing: Dwarf: cordon — 3' pyramid — 5' fan — 15' espalier — 15' Semidwarf: 20' Standard: 30'
Root Depth: Deep
pH: 6.0–6.5
Bearing Age: 2–4 years
Pollination: All require cross-pollination.
Chilling Requirement: Most need 600-900 hours below 45°F.
Site: Full south or south-east exposure.
Water: Heavy and constant supply; ground irrigation especially important to minimize fire blight.
Fertilizer: Avoid high N; pears need a lot of boron, so periodically check soil for deficiency.
Support Structures: Limb spreaders strengthen joints, and encourage earlier blossoming and higher yields. More than other fruits, pear branches sag with fruit and may need to be tied up.
Training: *Free standing:* central leader for Comice and Anjou. Open center for Bartlett, Bosc, those with flexible limbs, and those susceptible to fire blight. *Wire-trained:* all cordons, espalier, stepover, palmettes.
Pruning: Cut as little as possible because every cut exposes tissue to fire blight.

HARVEST

Pick when pears are at least 2" in diameter. Don't allow European varieties to ripen on the tree as they'll become mealy and coarse. Handle very carefully; although they appear hard, they'll bruise easily. Asian pears should ripen on the tree.

STORAGE REQUIREMENTS

Some pears require lengthy storage before they begin to ripen, and some will never ripen if left in cold storage too long. After cold storage, ideal ripening temperature is 60°–70°F; some pears won't ripen after cold storage if the home temperature is too high. If you wish to avoid the need for cold storage, place pears in a paper bag with ripe apples or pears; they emit ethylene gas, which stimulates the final stages of fruit ripening.

	Minimum Storage Life at 30°–32°F	Maximum Storage Life at 30°–32°F	Maximum Storage Life at 40°–42°F
Anjou:	2 months	4–6 months	2–3 months
Bartlett:	none	1½ months	2–3 weeks
Bosc:	none	3–3½ months	2–2½ months
Comice:	1 month	2½–3 months	1½–2 months
Seckel:	none	3–3½ months	none

GROWING TIPS

Pears can tolerate heavy clay soils better than most other fruits. Their blossoms are fairly frost resistant and won't be injured by temperatures as low as 28°F. European pears don't usually need thinning because of a low "set" ratio, the number of blooms producing fruit. Asian pears should be thinned to 1 fruit per cluster to avoid overbearing. The higher the temperature right after blooming, the sooner the fruit will mature, generally in 106–124 days after blooming. Pear trees are among the longest-lived fruit trees, sometimes achieving as many as 200–300 years.

Pests

Aphid, apple maggot, cherry fruit fly, codling moth, European apple sawfly, flea beetle, gypsy moth, mite, oriental fruit moth, pear psylla, pearslug, plum curculio, tarnished plant bug, tent caterpillar, thrips, weevil, whitefly

Diseases

Bitter pit, blossom blast (Boron deficiency), cedar apple rust, crown gall, crown rot, cytospora canker, fire blight, pear decline, pear curl, scab

Allies

Some evidence: alder, brambles, buckwheat, rye or sorghum or wheat mulch

Uncertain: caraway, coriander, dill, garlic, nasturtium, tansy, wildflowers, wormwood, vetch

Incompatibles

None

SELECTED VARIETIES

European *(Pyrus communis)*

Harrow Delight Very early; medium-large fruit; juicy; melting; hardy; productive; good fire blight resistance; zones 5–7 (NYFT, Raintree, Rocky Meadow, Stark, Windmill)

Moonglow Early; Comice seedling; Bartlett type; good fresh, in pies, or canned; upright; heavy spurs; hardy; strong pollinator of other pears; vigorous; wide climate tolerance; good fire blight resistant; zones 5–8 (Jung, Miller, Southmeadow, Stark)

Harvest Queen Early; new Bartlett type (slightly smaller fruit); identical flavor and appearance to Bartlett; very fire blight resistant (NYFT, Windmill)

Collette Early midseason; very high-quality fruit; long bearing for several months; good fresh and canned; hardy to -10 to -15°F (Miller, Windmill)

Seckel Midseason; self-fertile; very small fruit; yellow-green with russet cover; "sugar pear"; fresh or canning; keeps well; productive; very hardy; some fire blight resistance; zones 5–8 (widely available)

Orcas Midseason; large fruit; yellow with red blush; great fresh, canned, or dried; extremely productive; scab resistant; good for the Northwest (Raintree)

Comice Late; Oregon-grown winter pear; large fruit; top flavor; vigorous; some fire blight resistant (or moderate susceptibility); erratic crops; requires storage before ripening; good storage pear; a low chill requirement makes it suitable also for Southern California — it prefers milder climates with less summer heat but is grown commercially in Southern California; zones 5–9. (widely available)

Beurre Bosc Late; large pear; brown russet over green or yellow; long-necked; perfumed and melting flesh; excellent keeper; large and vigorous tree can grow up to 25'; does well in heavy clay soils; can withstand hot summer temperatures and resists cold winters (Adams, Kelly, Miller, Raintree, Sonoma, Southmeadow)

Magness Late; needs pollinator; Comice-Seckel seedling; medium-large fruit; delicious flavor and melting; juicy flesh; slightly russeted; more spreading than most pears; cross-pollinates with Asian varieties; resists fire blight; zones 5–8 (Burpee, Rocky Meadow, Sonoma, Southmeadow, Windmill)

Asian *(Pyrus serotina)*

All are attractive ornamentals

Hosui Early; medium fruit; golden, juicy, and crunchy; excellent flavor like butterscotch; becoming a leading commercial variety in California; resists fire blight; zones 6–9 (Adams, Miller, Raintree, Sonoma, Stark)

Chojuro Late midseason; medium oblong fruit; brown and russeted; rich aromatic flavor; crisp like apples; can keep until March; medium-sized tree; spreading and vigorous; will pollinate with Seckel and Bartlett (Miller, Raintree, Sonoma, Van Well)

ROOTSTOCKS

Quince is the most dwarfing rootstock, but isn't as hardy as the pear, increases the tree's susceptibility to fire blight, needs staking, and doesn't do well in poorly drained soils. It has some resistance to pear decline and pear root aphids. If fire blight is a problem for you, but you must use quince for achieving the most dwarfed tree, choose varieties that have the highest natural fire blight resistance. One superior root stock, a cross of Old Home and Farmingdale (OHxF), offers resistance to fire blight, pear decline, and better tolerance of heavy, wet soils. For standard trees, the most common rootstock is the Bartlett seedling, which is hardy to winter cold but very susceptible to fire blight, nematodes, pear root aphids, and pear decline.

Notes

GROWTH CONDITIONS

Height: 75'–100'

Spacing: 25'x25' to 70'x70' (depending on the variety)

Root Depth: Very deep

pH: 5.8–7.5

Bearing Age: 3–4 years in the South, 8–10 years in the North

Pollination: Self-fertile, but nuts will be higher quality with cross-pollination.

Chilling Requirement: Most require some chilling but the hours depend on the variety.

Site: Full sun and rich, well-drained soil.

Water: Medium, but during drought periods water up to 3"–4" per week.

Mulch: Avoid sawdust.

Fertilizer: Low N when young.

Side-dressing: Apply compost in late winter-early spring.

Training: *Free-standing:* central leader *Wire-trained:* N/A

Pruning: At planting, cut back ⅓ to ½ of the top, about 2"–3" above a bud facing the prevailing wind. Cut out crowded or crossed branches.

Pests

Aphid, birds, fall webworm, hickory shuckworm, pecan casebearer, pecan weevil, scale, squirrel, walnut caterpillar

Diseases

Canker dieback, crown gall, liver spot, pecan bunch, root rot, scab, sunscald

Allies

None

Incompatibles

None

HARVEST

Gather nuts from October to January. As the pecan matures, the outer hull splits to expose the inner nut; as the hull dries, the nut tends to fall out to the ground. For most varieties, however, the limbs must be shaken to encourage nut drop. Spread a canvas sheet on the ground to collect the nuts. Don't start harvesting until the hulls of the nuts on the inner part of the tree have split open; they will be last.

STORAGE REQUIREMENTS

Place hulled nuts in water, and remove the rotten and diseased nuts that float to the top. Dry and cure by spreading nuts in one layer in a cool, dry, well-ventilated area. They're ready for storage when the kernels rattle in the shell, or when unshelled nutmeats snap when bent. Store unshelled nuts in attics or cool underground cellars, where they'll keep for a year. Store shelled nuts in plastic bags with holes, or in tightly sealed tin cans that are lined with paper and have a hole punctured in the side beneath the lid. Shelled nuts can also be stored in the refrigerator or freezer for up to a year.

Fresh:	Temperature	Humidity	Storage Life
	34°–40°F	dry	12+ months

GROWING TIPS

The pecan is a member of the walnut family and is usually cultivated in mild, warm regions. In order to produce filled nuts, the tree requires a long, hot growing season averaging 75°–85°F, with a minimum average of 1000 Cooling Degree Days and 140–250 frost-free days. Midwest states are more suited for nut production than Northeastern states like Connecticut because, despite being at the same latitude, they usually experience higher summer temperatures. The four major groups of pecan cultivars are adapted to the Southwest, Southeast, and "North" (*see* definition under *Varieties.*) Pecans tend to bear in alternate years. They bloom in late spring and summer. High humidity at bloom time can hinder pollination, increase disease and, at harvest time, cause nuts to sprout while still in the husks. In choosing cultivars, note that vigorous growers usually bear heavily, and trees that break dormancy in late spring will suffer the least frost damage. Also, the smaller the transplant, the less injury to the tap root.

SELECTED VARIETIES

South-West Region (arid climates)

Pawnee Early nut maturity; large nuts; well-filled nut; vigorous with long unbranched limbs that later branch with strong angles; good producer; bears throughout tree; more scab resistant for growing in more northern areas; plant with Posey (Fowler, Nolin River)

Posey Early nut maturity; good for more northern areas; plant with Pawnee (Nolin River)

Mohawk Early; large nuts; good flavor; vigorous; upright and spreading; partially self-fertile; replaces Mahan; very good producer; may be good for northern California but may not fill well there; best in Southwest, zones 7–9, and southern edge of 6 (Fowler, Nolin River, Stark)

Cheyenne Matures to only 35'–45'; thin shells; heavy crops at an early age; best pollinated with Stuart; best suited for Southwest but has been grown in the East; zones 7–9 (Stark)

South-East (humid climates)

Candy Vigorous; prolific; scab resistant (locally available)

Stuart High yields; thin-shelled nuts; spreading branches; vigorous; prone to disease; also grows in the West; zones 7–10 (Gurney's, Henry Field's, Stark)

North (short season)

The "North" refers to the northern part of the pecan growing region such as Indiana, Illinois, Iowa, Missouri, Kentucky, Tennessee, and Kansas. Pecans can be grown further north — through southern New England and the Northwest — but they will never produce filled nuts there.

Fisher Good producer as far north as Scranton, Pennsylvania area; good flavor; medium nut; good cracker; zones 5–7; grow with Lucas (Grimo, Nolin River)

Lucas Good medium nut; cracks and fills well; high yields; good as far north as Scranton, Pennsylvania; grow with Fisher (Nolin River)

Greenriver Late; very good producer; medium nut; good south of Ohio River as far north as southern Indiana, Illinois, and Missouri; scab resistant; pollinates with Major (Nolin River)

Major Medium-large nut; large yields; thin shell; easy cracker; scab resistant; pollinates with Greenriver; good in Tennessee, Kentucky, Virginia, and as far north as southern Indiana, Illinois, and Missouri; zones 6–9 (Henry Field's, Nolin River, Stark)

Starking Hardy Giant Self-pollinating; yields even after winters of -20°F; very large nuts; thin shells; good nut but not heavy bearer; larger yields when cross-pollinated (Stark)

Hican

This is a cross between shellbark hickory and pecan, is reputedly easier to grow in Northern areas than pecan is, and is a good ornamental. Its nuts generally favor the hickory flavor. Plant several varieties for full crops. Nolin River carries a bunch of varieties. You may not want to grow Hicans if you have a lot of hickory trees nearby, as hickory weevils are reputed to like Hicans. Also, a Hican's productivity may depend on your climate and what you use as a pollinator.

James Hican Matures to 60'; zones 6–8 (Stark)

Burton Self-pollinating; medium nut; good producer and bears young; thin shell; good for South and Midwest as far north as northern Indiana, Illinois, and Ohio (Grimo, Nolin River)

Notes

Look for grafted trees, which produce sooner than seedling stock.

GROWTH CONDITIONS

Height: Dwarf: 3'–5' Semidwarf: 14' Standard: 16'–30'
Spacing: 8'–12' Semidwarf: 12'–20' Standard: 20'–25'
Root Depth: Depends on rootstock, generally shallow
pH: 6.0–8.0
Bearing Age: European: 4–5 years Japanese: 2–3 years
Pollination: European are usually self-pollinating; Japanese need cross-pollination.
Chilling Requirement: European need 700–1000 hours below 45°F, while Asian need 500–900 hours.
Site: *See* Incompatibles. Plums need at least 8 hours of sun and well-drained soil. *European and Damson:* heavy loam and south or southeast exposure. *Japanese and Beach:* sandy loam, and northern slope, or 12'–15' north of a building to minimize premature bloom and frost loss.
Water: Medium. Consistent watering is critical. Avoid watering in autumn, except in droughts.
Fertilizer: Low N in first 3 years. They may need K and Zinc supplements. Appropriate new growth for European plums is 16"–18" when young, and 10"–14" when bearing fruit. Appropriate growth for Asian plums is 18"–20" when young, and 15"–18" when bearing.
Side-dressing: In the spring, apply a layer of compost or mixture of well-rotted manure and wood ashes.
Support Structures: Forked prop to hold up heavy fruiting branches.
Training: *Free-standing:* open center for Japanese; central leader or dwarf pyramid for European. *Wire-trained:* fan.
Pruning: Never prune in the winter. Trees are best pruned only after the tree starts to bear fruit. Europeans require little pruning while Japanese require harder pruning. Fruit is on spurs 2"–6" long that live 5–8 years, so don't prune these.

HARVEST

Plums turn color 20–30 days before harvest. Pick when the fruit starts to soften and comes off with a slight twist. Be careful not to injure the spurs. *European plums:* for fresh eating, pick when ripe; for cooking, pick underripe. *Japanese plums:* always pick underripe; if allowed to fully ripen on the tree, they will be mushy and overripe.

STORAGE REQUIREMENTS

Ripen Japanese plums at 60°–65°F; if not too soft, they can be stacked.

Fresh:	Temperature	Humidity	Storage Life
	37°–40°F	90%	2 weeks

Preserved:	Method	Taste	Shelflife (in months)
	Canned	good	12+
	Frozen	good	12+
	Dried	good	12+

GROWING TIPS

Plums are naturally smaller than apple, pear, or peach trees and, as a rule, grow well wherever pears do. For a stone fruit, plums have an unusual range of flavors, sizes, and shapes. Japanese plums, now common in the stores, are very juicy and soft, and make excellent dessert fruits. European plums are much sweeter, though, and dry well as prunes. Plum curculio greatly damages plums. Thin fruit no later than two months after full bloom. For both European and Japanese, allow only one fruit per spur or cluster. While usually self-thinning, European plums may need to be thinned to 2"–3" apart. Thin Japanese plums, a more vigorous tree, to 4"–5" apart. When thinning, destroy all fruit with the curculio's crescent-shaped, egg-laying scar.

Pests

Aphid, apple maggot, birds, cankerworm, cherry fruit fly, cherry fruit sawfly, European apple sawfly, fall webworm, flathead borer, mite, oriental fruit moth, peach tree borers, peach twig borer, pearslug, plum curculio, weevil, whitefly

Diseases

Bacterial spot, black knot, brown rot, cherry leaf spot, crown gall, cytospora canker, peach leaf curl, powdery mildew, verticillium wilt

Allies

Some evidence: alder, brambles, buckwheat; rye, sorghum or wheat mulch

Uncertain: caraway, coriander, dill, garlic, nasturtium, tansy, wildflowers, wormwood, vetch

Incompatibles

Don't plant where the following have grown in previous 3 years: cocklebur, eggplant, ground cherry, horse nettle, lambs quarters, pepper, pigweed, potato, raspberry, strawberry, tomato, weeds in nightshade family

SELECTED VARIETIES

European

These are the sweetest plums; pollinate them with other Europeans, Damsons or Americans.

Stanley Late midseason; self-fertile; freestone; vigorous; productive; resists bacterial spot; very susceptible to black knot; good fresh, canned, cooked, or dried; zones 5–7 (widely available)

Green Gage (Reine Claude) Late; self-fertile; yellow-green fruit; juicy; very sweet; compact tree; not for warm winters; susceptible to brown rot; good fresh, frozen, or canned (widely available)

Count Althann's Gage Late; cling; leading European dessert plum; sweet; juicy; golden flesh resists bacterial spot; moderate resistance to black knot; zones 5–7 (Southmeadow)

Pearl Late; red-speckled yellow fruit; yellow flesh; extremely sweet; tender and melting flesh; tree is moderately upright; thought to be unsurpassed by Southmeadow (Rocky Meadow, Southmeadow)

Damson *(P. institia)*

Very small and tart, these are best suited for preserves and cooking.

Shropshire Damson (French Damson) Late; cling; genetic semidwarf; good for jelly; very resistant to bacterial spot; very susceptible to black knot; productive; vigorous; zones 5–7 (NYFT)

Japanese *(P. salicina)*

Very juicy and soft, these make excellent fresh eating; some can also be canned and cooked. Generally they like warmer climates. Cross with other Japanese or Americans.

Shiro Early; yellow fruit; hardy; prolific; low tree; moderately resistant to bacterial spot and black knot; susceptible to bacterial canker; leaf scald and brown rot; extremely juicy; excellent sweet flavor; clingstone; good fresh, canned, or cooked; zones 5–9 (widely available)

Weeping Santa Rosa Early; very ornamental; self-fertile; easy to keep at 8' or espaliered; large fruits; rich sweet-tart flavor; good pollinator; low chill (Northwoods, Raintree, Sonoma)

Ozark Premier Early midseason; red skin; yellow flesh; very tasty; sweet; large fruit; resists bacterial spot, canker, and black knot; susceptible to leaf scald and brown rot; zones 5–9 (Adams, Stark)

Redheart Early midseason; red; juicy; firm flesh; excellent flavor; holds quality canned or frozen; good pollinator; cross with Elephant Heart; zones 5–9 (Stark, Windmill)

Burbank Midseason; red-purple firm fruit; dwarf; somewhat drooping; needs thinning; hardy; prolific; resists bacterial spot and black knot; susceptible to bacterial canker, brown rot, and especially to leaf scald; pollinate with Shiro; zones 6–9 (Burpee, Miller, Stark, Windmill)

Elephant Heart Late; self-fruitful; red; very juicy; good flavor and quality; vigorous; hardy; prolific; cross with Redheart (Fowler, Rocky Meadow, Southmeadow, Windmill)

American Hybrid

Bred especially for Northern areas, these pollinate Americans or Japanese.

Toka Midseason; very hardy; medium fruit; firm flesh; good fresh (Jung, Windmill)

Beach *(P. maritima)*

These plums are good in very poor soil and extremely hardy. Pollinate with other Beach.

Miller's Beach Small shrub or tree; once established can withstand long droughts, extreme cold, and most diseases; great for jam and jelly; good windbreak (Miller)

Other Varieties

Pluot Early; a cross of plum and apricot; reputed best tasting new fruit; ripens midsummer, cross with Japanese, Plumcot, or Aprium (*see* **Apricot**); zones 6–9 (Stark, Raintree)

Notes

Rootstocks *See* chart on pages 108–109.

Plum Rootstocks

Unlike apple trees, standard size plum trees are naturally smaller and can be kept small through pruning. Because of this, a very dwarfing rootstock is not essential for espalier work. Pay attention to variety characteristics, too, as each has a different growing habit. For example, a Japanese plum — which is naturally more vigorous — might be better on a more dwarfing stock than, say, would a European plum. Buy smaller trees when possible because they suffer less transplanting shock; in several years they're more productive and vigorous than a larger transplant.

Most nurseries don't offer an in-house choice of rootstocks; your choices of rootstocks usually depends on the variety of nurseries in your area. The purpose of these charts is not to enable you to make an independent decision, but to help you conduct an informed discussion with the nursery grower. We urge you to seek and follow the nursery grower's advice on what will be good for your soil, climate, space, and desired variety.

Rootstock Name	P. besseyi (Western Sand Cherry)	P. tomentosa (Nanking Cherry)	Pixie (P. domestica)	St. Julien (P. americana)	Citation	Marianna 2624
Size (percent of standard)	Dwarf 20%–35%	Minidwarf 15%–25%	Dwarf 30%–40%	Dwarf 70%–80%	Dwarf 70%–75%	Semidwarf 90%
Height	3'–5'	2'–4'	6'	10'–15'	14'	16'
Width	3'–5'	2'–3'	5'	13'	13'	14'
Best soil	Loam	Loam	Loam	Sandy loam	Sandy loam	Clay loam
Anchorage	Poor	Poor	Good	Good	Good	Good
Crown rot	HR	HR	LR	LR	LR	MR
Oak root fungus	—	—	—	S	—	MR
Nematodes	—	—	MR	—	MR	R
Crown gall	—	—	—	—	S	MR
Bacterial canker	S	S	MR	R	—	HS
Hardiness	H	H	—	H	—	—
Mice	—	—	—	S	—	MR
Borer	—	—	—	—	—	—
Precocious	—	VP	P	—	—	—
Other factors	Lives less than 8 years	Lives less than 10 years	Rootstock promotes small fruit	Good disease resistance; citation can replace this	Good disease and pest resistance	

We gratefully thank Robert Kourik for permission to reprint information on rootstocks from his book *Designing and Maintaining Your Edible Landscape Naturally* (*see* Bibliography).

KEY

R = Resistant   MR = Moderately Resistant   S = Susceptible

MS = Moderately Susceptible   L = Low Hardiness   H = Hardy

VH = Very Hardy   P = Precocious (early bearing)   VP = Very Precocious

Myrobolan	Myrobolan 29c	Nemagaard (P. persica)	Bailey (P. americana)	Notes
Standard 100%	Standard 100%	Augmented 110%	Standard 100%	
18'	18'	20'	18'	
16'	16'	18'	16'	
Clay loam	Clay loam	Clay loam	Sandy loam	
Excellent	Fair	Very good	—	
MR	MR	LR	—	
MS	MS	S	—	
R	S	R	—	
MR	HS	S	—	
S	S	S	R	
—	—	—	H	
S	S	MR	—	
S	S	HS	—	
—	—	—	—	

GROWTH CONDITIONS

Height: 5'–10'

Spacing: Red and Yellow: 2'–4' in a row (suckers and new canes will fill out row)
   Black and Purple: 3'–4' in hills (no suckers, but need room for branching canes)

Root Depth: 12"

pH: 5.5–7.0

Bearing Age: 2 years

Pollination: Self-pollinating

Chilling Requirement: Most require some chilling, but the amount depends on variety.

Site: Full sun; rich loam; good drainage; east-facing spot sheltered from late afternoon sun. Plant at least 300 feet away from any wild brambles, which harbor insect and disease pests. Also keep at a distance from different types of berries to minimize cross-pollination.

Water: *see* **Blackberry**, page 84.

Mulch: *see* **Blackberry**, page 84. One gardener with a 60-year-old patch layers 8"–10" of leaf mulch in autumn, and some wood ashes in winter to counter leaf acidity. He rarely needs to water.

Fertilizer: *see* **Blackberry**, page 84.

Training: A trellis is important for disease and pest reduction, quality fruit, and easy harvest. Place bottom wire at 2', middle wire at 3', and top wire at 4' for black and purple, or 5' for red and yellow. Fan out canes and tie with cloth strips.

Pruning: After harvest or in the spring, cut out thin, weak, spindly, or sick canes, and ones finished bearing. *Red and yellow:* thin to 8 canes per 3 row-foot, or 4"–6" soil per cane. "Topping off" canes lowers yields, so don't do it unless the cane is taller than 6'. Cut out most sucker growth. *Everbearers:* cut to 5–7 canes per hill. To encourage branching, when primocanes are 18"–24" cut off the top 3"–4" of the cane ("topping off"). In late winter, cut lateral branches back to 8"–12" long.

HARVEST

When berries slide off easily without pressure, harvest into very small containers so berries on the bottom won't be crushed. After harvesting, cut floricanes to the ground; on everbearers cut the tips of primocanes. Burn or destroy all canes for disease control.

STORAGE REQUIREMENTS

To freeze, spread berries out on cookie sheets and freeze within 2 days of harvest. When rock hard store in heavy freezer bags. Refrigerated, berries keep 4–7 days.

Preserved:

Method	Taste	Shelflife (in months)
Canned (as jam)	excellent	12+
Frozen	excellent	6
Dried	good	

GROWING TIPS

Red raspberries are the hardiest bramble fruit. *See* notes under **Blackberry** (page 84) about yields, rows, floricanes, and primocanes. The everbearing raspberry cane bears annually; its floricanes bear a summer crop, and primocanes bear in the fall on their tips. The bottom of the primocane matures to bear the following summer as the floricane. For continuous harvest, try growing biennials for a spring crop and everbearers for a bumper fall crop (*see* **Pruning**).

Pests

Aphid, birds, caneborer, flea beetle, fungus beetle (in ripe fruits), Japanese beetle, mite, raspberry root borer, sap beetle, strawberry weevil, tarnished plant bug, weevil, whitefly

Diseases

Anthracnose, botrytis fruit rot, cane blight, cane gall, crown gall, leaf curl, leaf spot, mosaic, rust, powdery mildew, verticillium wilt

Allies

Uncertain: garlic, rue, tansy

Companions

See **Blackberry**, page 84

Other Benefits

Raspberries, unlike most other plants, do tolerate the juglone in black walnut roots.

Incompatibles

Don't plant where nightshade family was grown in last 3 years because of verticillium wilt.

SELECTED VARIETIES

Red *(R. idaeus)*

Heritage Everbearing; tall canes but usually sturdy enough to grow without stakes; medium berry; excellent quality; very hardy; zones (4)5–8 (widely available)

Titan Early; thornless; firm; sweet and juicy; mild flavor; trellis recommended; high yields; resists diseases and pests; zones 5–7 (Henry Field's, Kelly, Miller, NYFT, Nourse, Stark)

Killearney Early; large and firm; disease resistant; one of hardiest raspberries; zones 3–8 (Burpee)

Latham Midseason; large firm berry; excellent flavor; good fresh, frozen, or canned; prone to virus, so buy virus-free; zones (3)4–8 (Gurney's, Henry Field's, Kelly, Miller, Nourse, Rayner, Stark)

Taylor Midseason; conical large berry; very firm; excellent flavor; good quality; vigorous; hardy (NYFT, Miller, Windmill)

Chilliwack Midseason; new from British Columbia; excellent for wet sites; resists root rot; large firm berry; very sweet; productive; suited to Northwest (Northwoods, Raintree)

Yellow *(R. idaeus)*

Golden West Midseason; large berry; upright canes; vigorous; disease resistant; good fresh, frozen, and as jam; also pretty ornamental (Raintree)

Fallgold Everbearing; sweet and juicy berry; vigorous; hardy; zones 4–8 (Burpee, Gurney's, Henry Field's, Jung, Miller, Northwoods, Raintree)

Purple (cross of red and black raspberry)

Royalty Late midseason; juicier than black raspberry; sweeter than Brandywine purple raspberry; high yields; very hardy; resists insects and immune to raspberry aphid that carries mosaic; can be tip-layered but this one is best propagated by suckers; gourmet; good fresh and for jam; zones 4–8 (Jung, Kelly, Miller, Northwoods, NYFT, Nourse, Rayner, Stark, Windmill)

Black *(R. occidentalis)*

Bristol Very early; large firm berry; vigorous upright canes; no staking needed; leading variety in Finger Lakes area; zones 5–8 (Miller, NYFT, Nourse, Rayner, Stark)

Jewel Very early; large glossy berry; high quality; high yields; not susceptible to any serious disease; only mildly susceptible to mildew; hardy (Kelly, NYFT, Nourse, Rayner)

Cumberland Midseason; large glossy fruit; excellent flavor; long picking season into fall; very hardy; zones 5–8 (Burpee, Gurney's, Henry Field's, Van Well)

Notes

Always select certified disease-free stock. Black and purple types are better for preserves. **Propagation** Red and yellow by suckers; black and purple by layering. *See* **Blackberry,** page 84.

GROWTH CONDITIONS

Space Between Plants: 8"–15"
Height: 8"–12"
Root Depth: Shallow, up to 8"

Space Between Rows: 2'–5½'
Breadth: 6"–12"
pH: 5.5–6.8

Bearing Age: *Everbearing* (including newer "day neutrals"): at end of first summer planted.
  Junebearing: 1 year after planting; in the deep South, fall-plantings may bear in early spring.
Pollination: Self-fertile
Chilling Requirement: Most require chilling hours, but the amount depends on variety.
Site: Good drainage. North-facing, sunny slope to delay blossoms in areas susceptible to late frost. The previous fall, prepare beds with 5 pounds manure per 10 square feet; repeat whenever renewing.
Water: Medium.
Mulch: Apply 3"–4" after ground is frozen hard, remove in spring, and replace in hot weather. Do not cover crowns. University studies in New Hampshire show that row covers through the winter, rather than mulch, produce higher yields. Pull off covers during April bloom (replace if frost is expected).
Fertilizer: Low N; apply very lightly and often rather than in two heavy feedings.
Thinning: When runners get too prolific for a solid 7"–8" spacing, cut off excess runners.

HARVEST

A few days before harvest you may want to apply foliar calcium chloride. Canadian research shows this can lengthen storage life by slowing ripening and delaying development of gray mold. Pick all berries as soon as ripe — whether damaged or not — to prevent disease. Handle very gently to avoid bruising. Berries picked with green caps last longer in storage.

STORAGE REQUIREMENTS

Do not wash or remove green caps.

Method	Taste	Shelflife (in months)
Canned	not good	
Frozen	excellent	12+
Dried (as fruit leather)		
As jam	excellent	12+

GROWING TIPS

Plan about 24 plants to feed a family of four strawberry lovers. Junebearer strawberries yield a single crop in June or July and make lots of runners. Everbearing strawberries yield a first crop in June or July and a second in late summer/early fall; they require summer daylight of 15 or more hours (unless it is a newer "day neutral" type). If you suffer late spring frosts, choose varieties that flower late and tolerate high humidity. When planting, cover all roots but keep the upper ⅔ of the crown above the soil line. To promote a healthier, more productive plant, deflower all Junebearers the first year and everbearers only in their first late-spring flowering time. For a bumper fall crop, however, you may deflower everbearers in June every year. Most strawberry plants reproduce by runners. These can be pinched off to produce larger berries but lower yields, or trained to 7"–10" for smaller berries but higher yields.

Strawberries tend to become less productive each year, so beds are often renewed by various methods. For a perennial bed, try the "spaced runner system." Space plants in rows 2'–4' apart; train runners to 7"–8" apart by pinning them down with clothespins or hairpins. Cut off excess runners to maintain spacing. In year 2, train runners into the central paths. Immediately after harvest in year 2 or 3, mow down the original 2- or 3-year-old plants, till in several times, spread lots of compost, till a final time, and mulch with chopped leaves or compost every 2 weeks until fall. Every 2–3 years the pathways and growing beds trade places. University of Wisconsin studies show enhanced yields when "Regal" perennial rye grass is grown as a living mulch and mowed to 2"–3" two or three times per year.

Pests

Aphid, birds, earwig, flea beetle, garden webworm, Japanese and June beetles, mice, mite, nematode, pill bug, slug, snail, sap beetle, strawberry beetle, strawberry crownborer, strawberry leafroller, strawberry weevil, strawberry root weevil, tarnished plant bug, white grub, wireworm

Diseases

Anthracnose, botrytis fruit rot, leaf blight, leaf spot, leaf scorch, powdery mildew, red stele, root rot, septoria leaf spot, verticillium wilt, walnut bunch, yellows (virus)

Allies

Uncertain: borage, thyme

Companions

Bush beans, lettuce, onion family, sage, spinach

Incompatibles

All *Brassicas*

SELECTED VARIETIES

Junebearers

These are usually the highest quality berries yielding 1 crop per year in late spring or early summer.

Earliglow Early; this sets the standard for all others; medium-large berry; best flavor of all; good fresh, canned, and frozen; resistant to red stele, verticillium, leaf spot, and leaf scorch; best from North Carolina to New England to Missouri (Burpee, Jung, Miller, Nourse, Rayner)

Surecrop Early midseason; good choice for beginners; large and firm; good fresh, canned, and frozen; very verticillium resistant; resists leaf spot, scorch, red stele, and drought; vigorous even in poor soil; good coast to coast; zones 4–8 (Burpee, Henry Field's, Kelly, Miller, Nourse, Rayner, Stark)

Allstar Midseason; easy to grow; good fresh, frozen, and U-pick; high quality; very hardy; consistent high yields; resists red stele, leaf scorch, powdery mildew, and verticillium wilt (somewhat); good in Northeast, mid-Atlantic, and west to Missouri (Burpee, Kelly, Miller, Nourse, Rayner)

Catskill Midseason; very large berry; soft; sweet; good dessert and freezing quality; very resistant to verticillium wilt; good in colder areas of New England, south to central Pennsylvania, and west to Minnesota (Miller, Nourse, Rayner)

Jewel Late; introduced in 1985; very high-quality, large fruit; good fresh and frozen; hardy; not resistant to red stele or verticillium wilt, but has low incidence of fruit rots and foliar diseases; good from Nebraska to Maine, and south to Maryland and Ohio (Kelly, NYFT, Nourse)

Sparkle Late; medium berry; good frozen or for preserves; resists red stele and harsh winters; good in Northeast, west to Wisconsin, and in the Rocky Mountain region (Burpee, Gurney's, Henry Field's, Kelly, Miller, Nourse, Rayner)

Lateglow Late; medium berry; firm; sweet and aromatic; high yields; strong resistance to red stele and verticillium wilt; tolerates leaf spot, leaf scorch, gray mold, and powdery mildew (Burpee, Jung, Nourse, Rayner)

Everbearers

These plants produce 2 main crops per year; for 1 large and late crop, just pick off all early summer blossoms. The standard everbearer needs 15 or more hours of daylight, but a newer breed — "day-neutral" everbearers — are not supposed to be affected by day length.

Fort Laramie Large berry; good flavor; tolerates -30°F without mulch; pretty in hanging baskets; hardy in mountain states and high plains, and also good in Southern states (Field's, Gurney's, Jung, May)

Ozark Beauty Standard everbearer; large berry; need to keep runners to 2 or 3 to ensure large fruit; good fresh or frozen; extremely productive; good Maine to Missouri and on the West Coast; wide climate adaptability; zones 4–8 (Field's, Fowler, Gurney's, Jung, Kelly, May, Miller, Stark)

Sequoia Very large berry; excellent flavor; vigorous; resists many diseases; tolerates some soil alkalinity; good for the West Coast; can be grown in desert climates as winter annual (Fowler)

Tristar "Day Neutral"; early and continuous crop through fall at about 6-week intervals; heaviest crop in the fall; medium and firm; good fresh and frozen; very sweet; resists red stele and verticillium; tolerates leaf spot and scorch; can be grown in towers or hanging baskets because runners bloom and bear before rooting; good in Northeast, Midwest, and throughout West; zones 5–8 (Field's, Gurney's, Jung, Northwoods, Nourse, Rayner, Raintree, Stark)

Notes

Try to buy certified virus-free plants.

_____

_____

_____

_____

_____

_____

_____

_____

_____

_____

_____

GROWTH CONDITIONS

Height: 20'–80'
Breadth: 20'–40'
Space Between Plants: 10'. When 10" in diameter (about 25 years), thin to 22'–50'.
Root Depth: Very deep.
pH: 5.5–7.0; for Persian: 6.0–7.0
Bearing Age: 3–5 years for nuts; 10–20 years to produce veneer for market.
Pollination: All walnuts require cross-pollination.
Chilling Requirement: All require some chilling hours.
Site: Full sun; deep, well-drained loam. Don't plant anywhere near vegetable garden or orchard.
Water: Medium.
Fertilizer: Don't fertilize the first year. In following years, apply compost or well-rotted manure. When 10 years old, apply ½ pound boron (borax) in deep bar holes for steady nut production.
Training: *Free-standing:* central leader   *Wire-trained:* N/A
Pruning: Unlike most fruit and nut trees, prune in the fall. Don't start until 4–5 years old. Cut out dead or diseased wood, and crossed or competing branches.

HARVEST

Due to the indelible stains imparted by the husks, always wear gloves. Remove the outer husks within 1 week of harvest; let dry for several days, after which the husks will be easy to remove. There are three methods to de-husk the nut. (1) Use a corn sheller equipped with a flywheel and pulley, driven by ¼ hp motor. (2) Spread a single layer in a wooden trough on a driveway and run a car or tractor over them, which splits the husk easily. (3) Take them to a professional huller.

STORAGE REQUIREMENTS

Rinse off hulled nutshells and place in water. Remove the rotten and diseased nuts that float to the top. Dry and cure by spreading in one layer in a cool, dry, well-ventilated area. They're ready for storage when the kernels rattle in the shell — 1–3 weeks — or when unshelled kernels snap when bent. Store shelled nuts in plastic bags with holes, or in tightly sealed tin cans lined with paper (with a hole punctured in the side of the can beneath the lid), or freeze. Store unshelled nuts in an unheated shed over the winter; in spring move them to a cool place.

Fresh:	Temperature	Humidity	Storage Life
	32°–36°F	60%–70%	1 year

Preserved:	Method	Taste	Shelflife (in months)
	Frozen (shelled)	excellent	24

GROWING TIPS

Black walnut and butternut roots excrete an acid (juglone) that inhibits the growth of many plants, so plant far away from vegetables and flowers. Weed control is vital to the initial years of walnut tree growth. All walnuts benefit from mulching. Walnut trees grown for nut crops require large crowns; those grown for veneers need a straight trunk. To grow for both, veneer requirements prevail, so prune for straight growth.

Carpathian walnuts grow rapidly, about 4'–5' per year. Black walnuts, the largest *Juglans*, bear nuts that are high in protein and polyunsaturated oils and should be used sparingly in cooking. Grafted trees usually yield 3–4 times higher kernel filling than seedlings. Butternuts, or white walnuts, are the hardiest *Juglans*, don't require as much water, and also have a rich buttery taste. Buy as small a tree as possible to minimize injury to the taproot which, in *Juglans*, is very straight and long. True nut flavor and quality may not emerge for 2–3 years after bearing, so don't judge trees prematurely.

Pests

Aphid, bluejay, codling moth, fall webworm, mouse, navel orangeworm, squirrel, walnut caterpillar, walnut husk fly, walnut maggot

Diseases

Crown gall, walnut anthracnose, walnut blight, walnut bunch

Allies

Some evidence: weedy ground cover

Companions

Autumn olive, black locust, European alder, soybean, popcorn (for the first few years), raspberry

Other Tip

Walnuts do better in mixed plantings than in a monoculture walnut grove.

Incompatibles

Apple, azalea, potato, tomato (which is particularly sensitive to walnut root acid)

SELECTED VARIETIES

Black *(J. nigra)*

Purdue No.1 Superior tree; the only known patented hardwood; from Purdue University; very thin shell; extra-large meat size; also excellent for timber; Indiana Walnut Products has a program to buy the nuts back from you (Indiana Walnut Products)

Emma Kay An excellent variety; high kernel filling; thin shell; excellent cracking; good flavor; heavy yields; good in the Midwest (Grimo, Nolin River, Saginaw)

Thomas Oldest grafted black walnut; one of largest nuts; well filled; high quality; very hard, thin shells; good cracking; early and heavy yields; good in Northern and Western regions where anthracnose is not a problem; zones 5–9 (Fowler, Gurney's, Grimo, Miller, Saginaw, Stark)

Thomas Myers Good straight tree for timber and good nuts; heavy bearer; large nuts crack well; good through zone 8 and as far north as Massachusetts, Southern Wisconsin, and Michigan (Nolin River)

Weschcke Good flavor; high yields; one of hardiest black walnuts; pollinates Bicentennial; good for the far North (Grimo, St. Lawrence, Windmill)

Bicentennial Excellent timber type; nuts as hard as Thomas; large nut; precocious; vigorous; one of hardiest black walnuts; good for the far North (Grimo, St. Lawrence, Saginaw)

Persian (also called English or Carpathian) *(J. regia)*

Because they leaf early, Persian walnuts grow best where peach trees don't suffer frost-kill. Carpathian refers to its namesake mountain range in Poland from where many Persian walnuts were imported; now it usually just refers to "hardy" cultivars.

Hansen Bears young; self-fruitful; thin shell; good flavor; small-to-medium nut; resists anthracnose and husk maggot; naturally small; hardy; widely planted in the East; considered one of the best; especially good for Great Lakes area (Grimo, Nolin River, Saginaw, Windmill)

Colby Early maturing; medium nut; thin shell; good flavor; hardy; especially good for Great Lakes area (Grimo, Nolin River)

Champion Natural dwarf, growing to only 35'; thin shell; tasty nut; hardy; zones 5–9 (Stark)

Himalaya Very hardy; a good-quality nut; good for the far North (Grimo, Windmill)

Franquette Common cultivar in Northwest; tight nut resists worms; medium-large elongated nuts; high quality; thin smooth shells; tree leafs out and blooms late; slow maturing; not hardy in colder parts of the Northwest; good for the West and Northwest (Fowler, Northwoods, Raintree)

Spurgeon Large, flavorful nuts; reliable producer; productive; leafs out late; best cultivar for pockets where late spring frosts are a problem; benefits from pollination by Franquette; good for Northwest (Northwoods, Raintree)

Butternut *(J. cinerea)*

For location in the Ohio valley and southward, choose varieties with "clean foliage" for anthracnose resistance. Increasingly scarce, these offer high-quality lumber. Hardy in zones 3–7.

Creighton Good cracking qualities; medium nut; late vegetating; clean foliage; vigorous; rated number one in Indiana in 1988 (Nolin River, Saginaw)

Kenworthy Large nut; good flavor; good cracking; vigorous; hardy (Grimo, Windmill)

Loumis "Bountiful" Self-pollinating; 40'–50'; mild; thin shell; high yields; zones 4–7 (Stark)

Heartnut *(J. sieboldiana)*

A Japanese ornamental walnut, these grow fast and bear nuts that hang in strings or clumps of 10–15. The heart-shaped nutmeat is the sweetest of all walnuts, with no bitterness; it is high in protein, and easy to extract. The tree bears even in poor soils.

Heartnut Grows 40'–60'; cross-pollinate with Butternut and Buarnut; zones 5–9 (Northwoods, Miller, Stark; Nolin River, Saginaw & Windmill carries specific cultivars)

Other Varieties

Buarnut or Butterheart (butternut X heartnut) Disease resistant; nuts are similar to butternut; zones 4–7 (Grimo, Miller, Northwoods, St. Lawrence, Saginaw, Windmill)

Notes

PART 3

Herbs

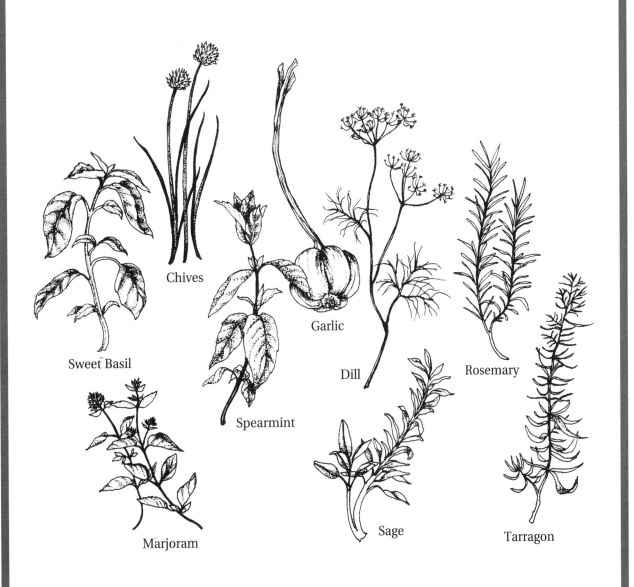

Sweet Basil

Chives

Spearmint

Garlic

Dill

Rosemary

Marjoram

Sage

Tarragon

GROWTH CONDITIONS

Germination Temperature: 75°–86°F
pH: 5.5–7.0
Planting Depth: ¼"
Breadth: 20"–30"

Growth Temperature: Hot
Root Depth: 8"–12"
Height: 18"–24"

Space Between Plants: in beds: 10"–12" in rows: 12"–18"
Space Between Rows: 15"–25"
Site: Full sun; protected site
Water: Low, but evenly moist
Fertilizer: Light feeder
Side-dressing: Not necessary
Propagation: By seed

First Seed-Starting Date:

Days Germ	+	Days Transplant	-	Days After LFD	=	Days Count *Back* from LFD
3–9	+	7–14	-	14	=	9 days before LFD to 4 days after LFD

Last Seed-Starting Date:

Days Germ	+	Days Transplant	+	Maturity	+	SDF	+	Frost Tender	=	Days *Back* from FFD
3–9	+	7–14		+	30–50	+	14	+	14		=	68–101

HARVEST

Pick continuously before the flower buds open. Keep blossoms clipped and pruned in order to encourage continuous bushy growth. Cut in the morning after the dew has dried. Cut the top growth up to 6" below the flower buds or ends. Don't wash the leaves unless necessary, or you'll wash away aromatic oils.

STORAGE REQUIREMENTS

Leaves can be used fresh, dried, or preserved in oil (must be refrigerated) or vinegar. To dry, find a warm, dry, dark place and hang bunches of snipped stems with leaves or spread leaves on a wire mesh. When thoroughly dry, strip leaves off stems. Do not crush or grind leaves until you're ready to use. Store in the dark in airtight containers or freezer bags. Some people feel basil stored in oil or vinegar is much better than dried. If storing frozen pesto, don't add garlic until ready to serve since garlic can get bitter in the freezer.

Method	Taste	Storage Life
Fresh	excellent	3–5 days (*see* **Growing Tips**)
Frozen	excellent (particularly for pesto)	
Dried	fair — good (relative to fresh basil)	

GROWING TIPS

Basil is an annual warm-season herb, very tender to frost and light freezes. It transplants easily and can also be grown easily in a greenhouse. Continuous harvest benefits this herb because pruning fosters a bushier plant. Rosalind Creasy reports that a study by the University of California at Davis recommends never putting basil in the refrigerator; they found that basil lives better in a glass of water and kept at room temperature. Basil is one of the more popular herbs for seasoning a wide range of dishes, fresh or dried. In the experience of some culinary experts, dried basil has very little flavor compared with fresh basil. It is, perhaps, hard to compare the flavors of fresh and dried as they are so different and can also give different effects in a dish. No basil lover, however, will ever pass up fresh for dried. There are quite a wide range of basil varieties, from purple to lime green, curly to ruffled-edged leaves, and smooth to hairy leaves. An ingredient in the liqueur Chartreuse, basil varies widely in flavor from the minty to hints of clove and cinnamon.

Pests

Japanese beetle, slug, snail

Diseases

Botrytis rot, damping off

Companions

Pepper, tomato

Other Benefits

Basil is said to repel flies, mosquitoes, and to improve growth and flavor of vegetables.

Incompatibles

Cucumber, rue, snap beans. Basil is also alleged to lower cabbage yields and cause a higher incidence of white flies in snap beans.

SELECTED VARIETIES

Greenhouse

All varieties work well.

Outdoor

Cinnamon *(O. var.)* Similar to sweet basil; cinnamon flavor; from Mexico (widely available)

Dark Opal Basil 18"; purple-bronze foliage; dark purple flowers; very ornamental; good for seasoning; colors vinegars purple (Fox Hill, Nichols, Richters, Sandy Mush)

Green Ruffles *(O. basilicum* "**green ruffles**") 24"; pretty curly and serrated large leaves (Burpee, Dabney, Richters)

Holy *(O. sanctum,* **purple Tulsi form)** Whole plant has reddish-purple tint; deep, spicy clove scent (Companion Plants, Fox Hill, Sandy Mush)

Lemon *(O. citriodorum)* 12"; intense lemon flavor; ideal for tea; compact bush-type (widely available)

Lettuce Leaf *(O. basilicum crispum)* 18"; large broad crinkled leaves to 4" long; rich flavor, not as strong as sweet basil (Companion Plants, Nichols, Richters, Sandy Mush, Seeds Blum)

Mammoth Basil *(O. basilicum)* Extremely large leaves; sweet fragrance and tasty (Richters)

Mayo/Yaqui Basil *(O. basilicum)* Do not grow with other basils if saving seed; good for low desert (Native Seeds)

Mrs. Burns famous Lemon Basil *(O. basilicum)* Pure strain; readily self-seeds; plant spring and fall; for low and high desert; some consider superior to other sweet basils (Native Seeds)

Piccolo Verde Fino Small leaves; intense true basil flavor; slightly minty; favored for pesto because it maintains flavor better after flowering than others (Casa Yerba, Companion Plants, Fox Hill, Richters, Nichols)

Purple Ruffles AAS winner; large, very ruffled and fringed leaves; dark purple leaves and pink flowers; beautiful ornamental; also good culinary (Burpee, Fox Hill, Nichols, Richters, Seeds Blum)

Spicy Globe Great fragrant edging plant and for pots; maintains small mound shape all season; white flowers; good culinary uses (Dabney, Fox Hill, Richters, Seeds Blum)

Sweet Basil *(O. basilicum)* 16"; a fast grower; tasty and one of best basil flavors; classic pesto basil (widely available)

Thai Green leaves with purple flowers and stems; good for Southeast Asian cuisine (Nichols)

Notes

GROWTH CONDITIONS

Germination Temperature: 70°F
pH: 5.5–7.0
Planting Depth: ¼"–½"
Breadth: 12"–18"

Growth Temperature: Warm
Root Depth: Long taproot
Height: 2'

Space Between Plants: in beds: 6" in rows: 12"–18"
Space Between Rows: 18"–24"
Site: Full sun to light shade
Water: Low, but evenly moist
Fertilizer: Light feeder
Side-dressing: Not necessary
Propagation: By seed and cuttings

First Seed-Starting Date:

Days Germ	+	Days Transplant	+	Days Before LFD	=	Days Count *Back* from LFD
17	+	0 (direct)	+	0–7	=	17–24

Last Seed-Starting Date:

Days Germ	+	Days Transplant	+	Maturity	+	SDF	+	Frost Tender	=	Days *Back* from FFD
17	+	0 (direct)	+	55	+	14	+	N/A	=	86

HARVEST

When the seeds are brown and before they begin to fall, snip the stalks. Tie in bundles and hang upside down in a warm, dry, airy place. Place paper-lined trays under the stalks to collect falling seeds, or cover them with a paper bag and let the seeds drop into the bag. Shaking the stalks may also be necessary to dislodge the seeds. After a few weeks, when the fallen seeds are thoroughly dry, store them in an airtight jar.

STORAGE REQUIREMENTS

Store in airtight jars in a cool, dark place.

Method	Taste
Frozen	Caraway leaf doesn't freeze well
Dried	Seed is excellent dried

GROWING TIPS

Caraway is a biennial warm-season herb, tender to frost and light freezes. It is commonly grown as an annual in most areas of the country, except for northern California where it apparently doesn't grow well. Sow it directly, as it doesn't transplant well, or transplant while still small. It flowers in the spring and produces seed in its second summer — or in its first summer if sown in the fall. Caraway roots, which are long taproots, can be eaten like carrots. The leaves can be used in salads, soups, or stews. The oil is used to flavor Kümmel, a German and Russian liqueur, as well as Aquavit.

Pests

Carrot rust fly

Diseases

None

Companions

Coriander, fruit trees, peas

Other Benefits

Caraway is supposed to be good for loosening the soil, and is reputed to attract beneficial insects to fruit trees.

Incompatibles

Fennel

SELECTED VARIETIES

Greenhouse

Caraway should grow well in the greenhouse if grown in a pot deep enough to accommodate its taproot.

Outdoor

The single cultivar of caraway is widely available.

Notes

GROWTH CONDITIONS

Germination Temperature: 60°–70°F
pH: 5.5–7.0
Planting Depth: ¼"–½"
Breadth: 6"–8"

Growth Temperature: Hot
Root Depth: Bulb clumps
Height: 6"–18"

Space Between Plants: in beds: 6" in rows: 5"–8"
Space Between Rows: 12"
Site: Full sun to a little light shade
Water: Average
Fertilizer: Light feeder
Side-dressing: Not necessary
Propagation: Division or seed; divide plant in mid-May every 3 years into clumps of 6 bulbs

First Seed-Starting Date: Chives mature in 50 days, whether or not transplanted.

Days Germ	+	Days Transplant	+	Days Before LFD	=	Days Count *Back* from LFD
10–14	+	21–42	+	0	=	31–56

HARVEST

After the plant is 6" tall, cut some of the blades down to 2" above the ground to encourage plant production. Herbs should be cut in the morning after the dew has dried. Rather than cutting chive tips, cut near the base of the greenery so new, tender shoots will emerge. Do not wash the cuttings or aromatic oils will be lost.

STORAGE REQUIREMENTS

Chives are best fresh or frozen, but can also be dried. To dry, tie them in small bunches and hang upside down in a warm, dry, dark place. Do not crush or cut up until ready to use. Store the stem whole, if possible. If harvested with the flower, chives can be stored whole in white vinegar to make a pretty light lavender, mildly flavored vinegar for gifts. Another storage method — recommended by Alan Gouin as an excellent way of preserving chive flavor — is to layer 1" of kosher salt alternately with 1" of chives in a glass jar. Pack down each layer with a spoon. Use these chives in any dish, just as you would fresh chives; they're reportedly especially good in soups. The brine can also be used to flavor soups and other dishes.

Method	Taste
Frozen	excellent
Dried	fair-good

GROWING TIPS

Chives are a perennial warm-season herb, hardy to frost and light freezes. This herb likes rich and well-drained soil. Chives are virtually foolproof since they suffer no diseases or pests. After several years you can divide them for expansion, and in the autumn you can dig up a clump to pot indoors for continuous winter cutting. Chives blossom midsummer and are an attractive addition to the garden. If allowed to bloom, cut them back after flowering so new shoots will come up in spring. Chives also thrive in a cool greenhouse or on a kitchen windowsill.

Pests
None

Diseases
None

Companions
Carrot, celery, grape, peas, rose, and tomato

Other Benefits
Chives are a putative deterrent to Japanese beetles, black spot on roses, scab on apples, mildew on cucurbits, and aphids on celery, lettuce and peas.

Incompatibles
Beans, peas

SELECTED VARIETIES

Greenhouse

All chives grow well in a cool greenhouse or on a windowsill.

Outdoor

Chive Common strain; mild onion flavor; great in salads, soups, potatoes, eggs, cheese, and fish dishes (widely available)

Curly Chive *(Allium senescens var. "glaucum")* Ornamental; not edible; deep pink flowers (Companion Plants)

Garlic Chive *(Allium tuberosum)* Mild onion-garlic flavor; broader leaves than common strain; from Japan; pretty white flowers (widely available)

Grolau Chive Similar to the common strain but developed for indoor growing; excellent in greenhouses; productive when cut continuously; good strong flavor (Nichols)

Mauve Garlic Chive Same as the garlic chive but with pretty mauve flowers (Richters)

Yellow Garlic Chive Same as the garlic chive but with light yellow flowers (Richters)

Notes

GROWTH CONDITIONS

Germination Temperature: 50°–70°F
pH: 6.0–7.0
Planting Depth: ¼"–½"
Breadth: 6"–12"

Growth Temperature: Cool
Root Depth: 8"–18"
Height: 12"–21"

Space Between Plants: in beds: 6"–8" in rows: 8"–12"
Space Between Rows: 12"–15"
Site: Full sun to partial shade
Water: Average
Fertilizer: Light feeder; N reduces flavor.
Side-dressing: Not necessary
Propagation: By seed

First Seed-Starting Date:

Days Germ	+	Days Transplant	+	Days Before LFD	=	Days Count *Back* from LFD
12	+	30	+	7–21	=	49–63

Last Seed-Starting Date:

Days Germ	+	Days Transplant	+	Maturity	+	SDF	+	Frost Tender	=	Days *Back* from FFD
6	+	21	+	55	+	14	+	0	=	96

Pests
Carrot rust fly

Diseases
None

Companions
Caraway, eggplant, fruit trees, potato, tomato

Other Benefits
Coriander is supposed to enhance anise growth. It is also a putative companion to fruit trees because it is supposed to attract beneficial insects.

Incompatibles
None

HARVEST

For fresh leaves, snip the stalks with smaller immature leaves for best flavor. Herbs should be cut in the morning after the dew has dried. Cut the top growth up to 6" below the flower buds or ends. Do not wash or aromatic oils will be lost. For seeds, harvest when the seeds and leaves turn brown but before seeds drop. Cut the whole plant.

STORAGE REQUIREMENTS

The leaves store poorly unless preserved in something like salsa, where its flavor can still fade in a day. But coriander seeds keep well in airtight jars. To dry seeds, tie the plant upside down in a warm, dry, dark place for several weeks until the seeds turn brown. Place stalks in a paper bag and thresh until all seeds are removed from stems. Sift out seeds from chaff. Another method to finish the drying process is to remove the seeds from stems and dry them in a slow oven (100°F) until they turn a light brown. You can smell the difference between properly air-dried or roasted coriander seed and seed that is still green. For best flavor, don't grind the seeds until ready to use. Store seeds in a cool, dark place in an airtight jar.

Method	Taste
Fresh	Cuttings last well 3–7 days refrigerated in water that is refreshed daily
Frozen	Some report excellent for leaf, some report poor
Dried	Excellent for seed, poor for leaf

GROWING TIPS

Coriander is an annual cool-season herb, tender to frost and light freezes. In some warmer climates, coriander is self-seeding. It grows easily, although it does go to seed quickly when the weather turns hot. For a steady supply of the leaf try sowing in succession every 1–2 weeks. If you're growing it for seed, you'll need to stake the plant. Put in stakes at the time of sowing or transplanting. Mulch coriander early and heavily to keep weeds down. All parts of the coriander are edible, including the root which tastes like the leaves but has an added nutty flavor. Unlike most herbs, fresh coriander leaf is usually either loved or hated. Make sure your guests can tolerate fresh coriander before including it in a dish. Coriander is supposed to attract useful insects, and coriander honey is apparently famous for its flavor. You can make imitation coriander honey by adding a small amount of coriander oil to clover honey.

SELECTED VARIETIES

Greenhouse

Coriander grows well in the greenhouse.

Outdoor

Chinese Coriander Especially good for fresh leaf production because it doesn't bolt as quickly (Richters)

Coriander (standard) Fresh leaves are delicious in salsa and Latin, Indian, Chinese, and many other cuisines; the seeds are traditional in curry, chili, and some baked goods, and are a great addition to soups, stews, and Indian dishes; good in all areas, including high and low desert; self-seeding in warmer climates (widely available)

Slow-bolt Coriander Especially good for fresh leaf production because it doesn't go to seed as quickly (Seeds Blum, Shepherd's)

Vietnamese Coriander *(Polygonium odoratum)* Not a true coriander; almost identical to native smartweed or knotweed; a perennial in some climates; tastes remarkably similar to true coriander; can be grown indoors with sufficient light (Companion Plants, Richters)

Notes

GROWTH CONDITIONS

Germination Temperature: 50°–70°F
pH: 5.5–6.5
Planting Depth: ¼"–½"
Breadth: 24"

Growth Temperature: Hot
Root Depth: Very long taproot
Height: 3'–4'

Space Between Plants: for leaf: 8"–10" for seed: 10"–12"
Space Between Rows: 18"–24"
Site: Full sun, sheltered from wind
Water: Average
Fertilizer: Light feeder; might need one application of compost or slow release fertilizer.
Side-dressing: Not necessary
Propagation: Seed

First Seed-Starting Date: Sow every 3 weeks for a continuous supply of leaves.

Days Germ	+	Days Transplant	-	Days After LFD	=	Days Count *Back* from LFD
14	+	21–30	-	14	=	21–30

HARVEST

Cut the tender feathery leaves close to the stem. Herbs should be cut in the morning after the dew has dried. Do not wash or aromatic oils will be lost. Dill foliage has the best flavor before the flower head develops and when used the same day it's cut. If you want to harvest dill seed, let the plant flower and go to seed. Harvest when the lower seeds turn brown and before they scatter. The lower seeds on a head will brown first: the upper ones can dry inside. Finish drying by tying stems and hanging upside down in a cool, dark, dry place, or place in a paper bag with holes cut in the sides. Sift to remove the seed from chaff.

STORAGE REQUIREMENTS

Fresh dill keeps for up to 3 days in a jar, stems down in water, covered with plastic. It will store for up to 3 months layered with pickling salt in a covered jar in the refrigerator. To use, just brush off salt. To freeze, store on the stem in plastic bags. Cut off what you need and return the rest to the freezer. To dry the leaves, spread them over a nonmetallic screen in a dark, warm, dry place for several days. Then store in an airtight container. Don't crush or grind until ready to use.

Method	Taste
Frozen	Good for foliage
Dried	Good for foliage, excellent for seeds

GROWING TIPS

Dill is an annual or perennial warm-season herb, very sensitive to light freezes and frost. If it's not grown in a protected spot, make sure you stake it to prevent the wind from knocking over the tall stalks. Dill doesn't transplant easily because of its long taproot, so don't transplant once it grows beyond seedling stage. If it's not planted early enough, seed may not develop until the beginning of the second year. It can be grown in the greenhouse if you provide a container large enough for its roots — at least 6"–8" in diameter — and pot it in rich soil. In the garden, if allowed to go to seed without complete harvest, it will reseed itself and grow as a perennial. As a seed it's used primarily for pickling. As dill weed, it's used to flavor sauces, fish, meats, soups, breads, and salads. To keep the best flavor, try snipping the weed with scissors instead of mincing with a knife.

Pests

Carrot rust fly, green fly, parsleyworm, tomato hornworm

Diseases

None

Companions

All *Brassicas,* fruit trees

Other Benefits

Some gardeners report that, in orchards, dill helps attract beneficial wasps, bees, and flies that pollinate blossoms and attack codling moths and tent caterpillars. Others report it may help cabbage by repelling aphids, spider mites, caterpillars. There is, however, no scientific study or proof.

Incompatibles

Carrot, fennel (cross-pollinates with dill), tomato

SELECTED VARIETIES

Greenhouse

Dill grows well in the greenhouse. *(See* **Growing Tips***)*

Outdoor

Aroma Dill This offers larger yields and a better aroma (Sandy Mush)

Bouquet Dill Best grown for dill seeds for pickles and potato salads; a more compact and attractive plant than the common strain (Nichols, Shepherd's)

Dill Old-fashioned dill; used for dill pickles and sauerkraut (widely available)

Dukat Dill Best for its fresh leaves; originally from Finland; slow-bolting; flavor is mellow and aromatic; never bitter; excellent with shrimp, fish, and cucumbers (Dabney, Shepherd's)

Indian Dill *(Anethum sowa)* Seeds used in Indian curries; leaves used in rice and soups; little more bitter than the common strain, smaller plant (Companion Plants, Sandy Mush)

Notes

GROWTH CONDITIONS

Germination Temperature: 60°–80°F
pH: 5.5–7.0
Planting Depth: ¼" (just barely covered with soil)
Breadth: 12"–18"

Growth Temperature: Cool
Root Depth: Taproot
Height: up to 4'–5' (may need staking)

Space Between Plants: slim fennel: 6" Florence fennel: 10"–12"
Site: Full sun and rich, well-drained soil
Water: Low, but evenly moist. Water in times of drought.
Fertilizer: Light feeder
Side-dressing: Not necessary
Propagation: By seed; divide and replant established plants every 3 years.

First Seed-Starting Date:

Days Germ	+	Days Transplant	+	Days Before LFD	=	Days Count *Back* from LFD
6–17	+	10–28	+	26	=	42–71

Last Seed-Starting Date:

Days Germ	+	Days Transplant	+	Maturity	+	SDF	+	Frost Tender	=	Days *Back* from FFD
6–17	+	0 (direct)	+	60–70	+	14	+	14	=	94–115

Pests
Carrot rust fly

Diseases
None

Companions
Most vegetables

Incompatibles
All beans, caraway, coriander (prevents seeds from forming), dill (cross-pollinates with fennel), pepper, tomato

HARVEST

For leaf clippings, you can start to cut the leaves once the plant is established. For fennel stems and bulbs, wait until the plant begins to bloom, pinch off the blooms, and allow the stems and bulb to fatten several more days. Cut them off at the base and use while fresh. For seeds, allow plant to bloom. When the seeds turn brown, cut off the entire seed head and place in a paper bag. Fennel seeds are very delicate and fall easily from the plant, so be sure to cut seedheads before seeds are blown away. Dry in a warm, dark place for several weeks.

STORAGE REQUIREMENTS

Store seeds and dried leaf clippings in airtight jars in a cool, dark place. Dried leaf clippings lose their flavor over time. Stems and bulbs can be stored for 1–2 weeks in the refrigerator. You might also peel and store the stems in white vinegar with black pepper corns for use in salads.

Method	Taste
Frozen	Good for leaf clippings
Dried	Excellent for seed

GROWING TIPS

Fennel is a perennial warm-season herb, half-hardy to frost and light freezes. This herb is best sown in succession plantings in the spring, as it tends to bolt in hot summers. For a fall crop, sow in July. If you're growing Florence fennel — renowned for its swollen and tender anise-flavored stalks — mound the soil a little bit around the base to promote more tender, blanched stalks. Fennel stems are a more common culinary item in Europe than in the United States. They're delicious raw in salads, steamed, sauteed with a little butter and wine, or added to soups, stews, and fish dishes. Fennel leaves are thought by some to improve digestion, and fennel tea is believed to have antiflatulent and calming effects. Fennel seeds are delicious in breads, sausages, pizza and tomato sauce, stews, and fish and chicken dishes.

SELECTED VARIETIES

Greenhouse

All varieties of fennel should grow well in the greenhouse.

Outdoor

Sweet Fennel *(F. vulgare).* Grown primarily for leaves and seeds.

Bronze *(F. vulgare dulce* var. *rubrum)* Pretty coppery leaves; ornamental and flavorful seeds; may tend to be biennial (Burpee, Companion Plants, Nichols, Richters, Seeds Blum, Shepherd's)

Green Leaf Can be grown for leaves, seeds, and stalks (Cook's)

Red Leaf Bronze leaves; known for ornamental and culinary uses (Cook's)

Sweet *(F. vulgare dulce)* Grown primarily for seeds and leaves, but stalks can be eaten as a vegetable; popular in Italy (Companion Plants, Dabney, Fox Hill, Nichols, Richters)

Finnochio or Florence Fennel. Best for swollen roots and stalks.

Florence *(F. vulgare* var. *azoricum)* Develops nice crisp, anise-flavored stalks; fall-maturing; usually grown as an annual (Burpee, Dabney, Fox Hill, Richters)

Herald High bolt resistance; grow for plump, sweet bulbs (Thompson & Morgan)

Zefa Fino Good bulbing variety; from Switzerland (Cook's)

Notes

GROWTH CONDITIONS

Germination Temperature: 60°–80°F
pH: 4.5–8.3
Planting Depth: 1"–2" (pointed end up)
Breadth: 6"–10"

Growth Temperature: Cool
Root Depth: Bulbs: 2"–2'
Height: 1'–3'

Space Between Plants: in beds: 3" in rows: 4"–6"
Space Between Rows: 12"–15"
Site: Full sun
Water: Low. For perennial bulbs withhold all water during summer, except in arid, dry areas (*see* **Growing Tips**).
Fertilizer: Light feeder; use compost and liquid seaweed extract.
Side-dressing: Not necessary
Propagation: Usually propagated by cloves (easiest method), though garlic can be started by seeds.

First Clove-Starting Date: Cloves can be planted about 6 weeks before the last frost.

Days Germ	+	Days Transplant	+	Days Before LFD	=	Days Count *Back* from LFD
7–14	+	0 (direct)	+	14–21	=	21–35

Last Clove-Starting Date: Cloves can be planted in autumn for harvest in spring.

Days Germ	+	Days Transplant	+	Maturity	+	SDF	+	Frost Tender	=	Days *Back* from FFD
7	+	0 (direct)	+	90	+	14	+	0	=	111

HARVEST

Green garlic shoots, a gourmet treat in many places, can be cut from the bulbs going to flower and used like scallions. Garlic bulbs are ready to harvest when the tops turn brown and die back. Do not knock the tops down to hasten harvest: some research indicates this practice shortens storage life. Withhold water and, in a few days, dig carefully to lift the plants. The tops usually are not strong enough to pull, with the exception of the perennial garlic (*see* **Perennial Method**). Do not bruise bulbs or they'll get moldy and attract insects when stored.

STORAGE REQUIREMENTS

Cure bulbs in the sun for several days to 2 weeks to harden the skins and dry. To braid, keep the tops on. Otherwise, clip off dried leaves and the root bunches. Store in paper bags, net bags, or nylon stockings, tying a knot between each bulb in the stocking.

Method	Temperature	Humidity	Storage Life
Fresh	32°F	65%–70%	6–7 months

GROWING TIPS

Garlic is an annual or perennial cool-season crop, hardy to frost and light freezes. Plant cloves in rich, deep, moist well-drained soil in a sunny location. Although it can be started from seed, it's easiest to grow from individual cloves. Garlic bulbs mature in an average of 6–10 months. Cloves may be planted in either fall or spring, but fall plantings yield larger bulbs the next summer than spring plantings harvested in the fall. You may have to add compost to the soil before planting. Remove flower buds if they develop. Early cultivars store poorly and have inferior quality.

Perennial Method: One Washington State gardener has a garlic patch that hasn't been planted or plowed for 20 years. His method: when the garlic is about 2' tall, pinch off the seed buds that develop or garlic won't form. Do not water at all during the summer (except in arid, dry climates, where you should water regularly). Harvest only the large plants by simply pulling them (no digging necessary). The smaller plants die back and emerge again the following year. After harvest, lightly till the surface with a hand cultivator and uproot weeds. Water well to germinate weed seeds, then cultivate again to get rid of young weeds. In October spread a 3"–4" leaf mulch. In spring garlic will grow through the mulch again.

Pests

Nematode

Diseases

Botrytis rot, white rot

Companions

Beet, *Brassicas*, celery, chamomile, fruit trees, lettuce, raspberry, rose, savory, tomato

Other Benefits

Garlic spray has been found to have some antifungal powers in controlling downy mildew, cucumber and bean rust, bean anthracnose, early tomato blight, brown rot of stone fruit, leaf spot of cucumber, bacterial blight of beans, and soft-bodied insects such as aphids and leafroller larvae.

Incompatibles

All beans, peas

SELECTED VARIETIES

Greenhouse

None; garlic doesn't do well in the greenhouse.

Outdoor

Artichoke Garlic Very early; cloves are layered like artichoke leaves; purple skin; fairly large (Seeds Blum)

California White Easy to grow; stores like onions; very mild flavor (Henry Field's, Jung)

Elephant Garlic *(Allium ampeloprasum)* Milder than regular garlic and about 6 times larger; hardy for fall planting; developed and named by Nichols; bake whole, roast, or use fresh in salads and other dishes where a mild garlic is desired (widely available)

Italian Garlic or **Rocambole** or **Serpent Garlic** *(A. sativum ophioscordon)* Mild garlic flavor; easy to peel; above ground bulblets and below ground bulbs are prized in Europe; the stems bearing the small bulblets are looped (Richters, Sandy Mush, Seeds Blum)

Nichols Silverskin Noted for its strong flavor; size and easy peeling (Fox Hill, Nichols)

Nichols Top Set Pungent flavor; harvest medium bulbs at end of season; small bulblets at the top of each plant can be kept for early spring or fall planting (Nichols)

Notes

Culinary Proverb: "Anything not benefiting from the addition of chocolate will probably benefit from the addition of garlic."

GROWTH CONDITIONS

Germination Temperature: N/A
pH: 6.5–7.0
Planting Depth: Cover roots properly
Breadth: up to 5'

Growth Temperature: Hot
Root Depth: Deep
Height: 14"–3'

Space Between Plants: in beds: 2' in rows: 4'–6'
Space Between Rows: 6'
Site: Full sun, can be stony, protected from wind.
Water: Low.
Fertilizer: Light feeder. Lime may be needed to make sure soil is basic enough.
Side-dressing: Not necessary.
Propagation: Cuttings or seed. Lavender is seldom started from seed because of its long germination time. In summer use cuttings 2"–3" long from the side shoots. Make sure there is some older wood on cutting. Place cuttings in moist, sandy soil in a shaded cold frame 3"–4" apart. When they're 1 year old plant in well-drained, dry soil that is protected from severe frost. The first year plants should be pruned to keep from flowering and encourage branching.

Pests
Caterpillars

Diseases
Fungal diseases

Companions
None

Other Benefits
Lavender leaves are reputed to repel insects.

Incompatibles
None

HARVEST

Don't cut until the second year planted outside. Pick the flowers when in blossom but just before full bloom, usually in August. On a dry and still day, cut early in the day after the dew has dried. Cut the top growth up to 6" below the flower spikes. Do not wash them or aromatic oils will be lost.

STORAGE REQUIREMENTS

To dry, tie branches in small bunches and hang upside down in a warm, dry, dark place. Then remove the flowers from the stems and keep whole in storage.

Method	Results
Dried	Excellent; remains aromatic for a long time

GROWING TIPS

Lavender is a perennial warm-season herb, hardy to frost and light freezes in zones 5–8. It likes full sun and light, well-drained soil. Lavender can be grown easily in containers in the greenhouse or on windowsills, and trained to different forms. Besides serving as a pretty border plant, dried lavender flowers are touted as a good moth repellant, and lavender oil is used as an additive to soaps and sachets. For the best oil production lavender needs hot, dry weather from May through August. Oils have been used for centuries for a wide variety of things from curing lice, repelling mosquitoes, and embalming, to use in porcelain lacquers, varnishes, and paints. Lavender is also used to make a light perfume: Add rose petals, lavender flowers, and jasmine flowers to distilled vinegar and store in airtight bottles. In the kitchen, lavender flowers and leaves can be used to flavor jellies and vinegars. Author Rosalind Creasy tells us that in southern France (Provence), lavender is added to herb mixes for salads. She also raves about lavender ice cream which, in her book *Cooking From The Garden*, she describes as having a "unique lemony-perfume taste."

SELECTED VARIETIES

Greenhouse

Tender varieties can be grown inside.

Outdoor

Hardy English-types.

English Lavender *(L.a.* or *L. vera)* 3'; the hardiest lavender; considered the best for culinary uses, perfumes, soaps, and oils; spreading; bushy growth; silvery grey and narrow leaves; light purple flowers; good for northern climates (Companion Plants, Dabney, Nichol, Richters, Sandy Mush)

Grey Lady *(L.a.*"Grey Lady") 18"; fast, compact growth; grey foliage; lavender-blue flowers; hardy (Companion Plants, Sandy Mush)

Jean Davis *(L.a.*"Jean Davis") 18"; dainty compact mounds; low growth; bluish foliage; pink flowers; very hardy; excellent for borders and formal gardens (Dabney, Sandy Mush)

Rosy *(L.a.* "Rosea") 18"; attractive; compact plant; pink flowers; good for borders and formal gardens (Companion Plants, Richters)

True Lavender 3'; very hardy; good for clipped borders (Sandy Mush)

Tender types. Good for frost-free areas; may also be dug up and potted as a winter house plant.

French or **Fringed Lavender** *(L. dentata)* 3'; very green toothed leaves; very fragrant foliage; provides more but lower quality oil with camphor-rosemary scent (Companion Plants, Dabney, Richters, Sandy Mush)

Spanish Lavender *(L. stoechas)* 30"; beautiful grey foliage with green overtone; toothed and narrow leaves; aroma is strong and resinous — reminds some of turpentine; flowers bloom nearly all year; light purple flowers; excellent year-round pot plant (Companion Plants, Sandy Mush)

Spike *(L. latifolia)* Coarse, broad leaves; oil is used in soaps; high oil yields (Richters)

Notes

GROWTH CONDITIONS

Germination Temperature: 65°–75°F
pH: 6.5–7.0
Planting Depth: 0"; tiny seeds need light and should not be covered
Breadth: 10"–12"
Space Between Plants: in beds: 6"–8" in rows: 8"–10"
Space Between Rows: 15"
Site: Full sun
Water: Low
Fertilizer: Light feeder
Side-dressing: Not necessary

Growth Temperature: Hot
Root Depth: 6"–12"
Height: 1'–2'

Propagation: Seeds, cuttings, root division. If you propagate by seed, either sow seeds directly outside after all danger of frost has passed, or start seeds indoors and then transplant in clumps of three, spaced 6"–8". Germination takes 8–14 days. Pinch back plants before they bloom. After the first year, you can divide the plant roots, and pot them for your winter windowsill or greenhouse.

Pests
Aphid, spider mite

Diseases
Botrytis rot, damping off, rhizoctonia

Companions
Sage. Marjoram is also alleged to generally improve the flavor of all vegetables.

Incompatibles
Cucumber

HARVEST

Pick marjoram all summer and, if you want, cut it down to 1" above the ground. In the North don't cut it back severely in the fall as it will weaken the plants. Herbs should be cut in the morning after the dew has dried. Cut the top growth up to 6" below the flower buds or ends. Do not wash or aromatic oils will be lost.

STORAGE REQUIREMENTS

To dry, tie the cuttings in small bunches and hang upside down in a warm, dry, dark place. When dried, remove the leaves from the stems, and store whole. Do not crush or grind until ready to use. Store in air-tight jars in a dark place.

Method	Taste
Frozen	Good
Dried	Excellent; retains much of its flavor

GROWING TIPS

Marjoram is a perennial or annual warm-season herb, very tender to frost and light freezes. It is winter hardy only in the South, zones 9–10, so most gardeners will want to grow it outdoors as an annual, or in pots to bring them indoors through the winter. Marjoram likes full sun and soil that is light, dry, and well-drained. Also, note marjoram's requirement for very low-acid soil. This herb has played many roles over the centuries, from medicinal and culinary purposes, to aromatic uses in closets and sachets, to serving as a green wool dye. Don't confuse sweet marjoram with "wild marjoram" or the perennial oregano *(O. vulgare)*. Sweet marjoram is used for cooking while the "wild marjoram" is used for medicinal purposes.

SELECTED VARIETIES

Greenhouse

Any variety can be grown in a cool greenhouse in the winter, but its flavor will be milder.

Outdoor

Golden Marjoram *(O. marjorana "Aurea")* Crinkled; yellow-white leaves; attractive border plant; not strongly scented; not good for culinary uses (Companion Plants)

Pot Marjoram *(O. onites)* 12"–15"; pretty plant; spreads slowly in all directions; attracts bees; profuse blooms in late summer; stronger flavor than true marjoram; hardier than marjoram; larger flowers (Companion Plants, Fox Hill, Nichols)

Sweet or **Knot Marjoram** 12"–24"; best culinary variety, good in soups, salads, vinegars, and Italian, French, and Portuguese cuisines; an infusion is said to be good for coughs and sore throats; keeps well on a sunny windowsill through winter; small, oval, grey-green leaves (widely available)

Notes

GROWTH CONDITIONS

Germination Temperature: 65°–75°F
pH: 6.5–7.5
Planting Depth: 0"; tiny seeds should not be covered
Breadth: 12"

Growth Temperature: Hot
Root Depth: Shallow
Height: 12"–24"

Space Between Plants: in beds: 18"
Space Between Rows: 18"–20"
Site: Full sun
Water: Low
Fertilizer: Light feeder
Side-dressing: Not necessary
Propagation: Root division in spring, or cuttings and seeds. The easiest method is to take cuttings in summer and root them in sandy compost. Seeds germinate in about 4 days.

Pests
Aphid, leafminer, spider mite

Diseases
Botrytis rot, fungal disease, rhizoctonia

Companions
All beans, cucumber, squash

Incompatibles
None

HARVEST

One gardener claims that a first harvest when the plant is a mere 6" tall fosters bushy growth. When the plant is budding proliferously in June, she cuts the plant severely so that only the lower set of leaves remains. The plant reportedly leafs out again in a couple weeks. Then she cuts it back severely again in August. For times of highest oil content (for best flavor), *see* **Growing Tips.** Generally, herbs should be cut in the morning after the dew has dried. Cut the top growth up to 6" below the flower buds or ends. Do not wash the leaves or aromatic oils will be lost.

STORAGE REQUIREMENTS

To dry, tie the cuttings in small bunches and hang upside down in a warm, dry, dark place. When dried, remove the leaves from the stems, and keep leaves whole for storage. Store in airtight jars in a dark place. Don't crush or grind until ready to use.

Method	Taste
Frozen	Good
Dried	Good

GROWING TIPS

Oregano is a perennial warm-season herb, hardy to frost and light freezes through zone 5. It likes full sun and well-drained, average soil. Flowering doubles the concentration of oil in oregano leaves, so for the strongest flavor don't harvest until the plants start flowering. For non-flowering varieties, harvest in the late spring as the oil concentrations rise steadily in the spring and then decline. Even the late spring peak flavor of these varieties, however, doesn't compare with the oil levels in autumn flowering varieties. So, for the strongest-flavored oregano, choose a variety that is autumn flowering. It's difficult to get a good-flavored oregano; it's best to start from a cutting or plant that you have tasted or one that has an established track record. The best is *O. heracleoticum*.

SELECTED VARIETIES

Greenhouse

Any variety will do well in the greenhouse.

Outdoor

Compact Oregano *(O. compacta Nana)* 2"–3"; excellent ground cover in sunny areas; strong flavor; does well in a cool window in winter (Sandy Mush)

Dark Oregano 2'; excellent seasoning; larger and darker leaves; more upright than standard (Fox Hill, Sandy Mush)

Golden Creeping Oregano *(O.* var. *Aureum)* 6"; decorative golden ground cover; needs winter mulch; very mild oregano flavor (Companion Plants, Dabney, Fox Hill, Richters, Sandy Mush)

Greek Oregano *(O. var. hirtum/O. hirtum/O. heracleoticum)* 18"; excellent flavor; white flowers; bright green leaves; good for drying (widely available)

Italian Oregano *See* **Thyme;** this has a strong oregano flavor but is actually a thyme.

Mexican Oregano *(Lippia graveolens)* Not a true oregano but listed here for its oregano flavor; often sold in Mexico and the Southwest as true oregano; used in Southwest chili and Mexican dishes; very strong flavor resembling oregano; can be grown into a miniature tree in a greenhouse or bright window (Companion Plants, Dabney, Fox Hill, Richters, Seeds Blum)

Mt. Pima Oregano *(Monarda austromontana)* Used as commercial oregano in Mexico; wild plant with an unusual flavor; for low and high desert (Native Seeds)

Oregano Tytthantum (Khirgizstan Oregano) 18"; excellent flavor; bushy growth; glossy green leaves; pink flowers (Sandy Mush)

Seedless Oregano *(O. Viride)* 18"; excellent seasoning; as strong as Greek oregano but sweeter and less biting; leaves resemble sweet marjoram (Companion Plants)

Notes

GROWTH CONDITIONS

Germination Temperature: 50°–85°F
pH: 6.0–7.0
Planting Depth: ¼"
Breadth: 6"–9"

Growth Temperature: 60°–65°F
Root Depth: Shallow–4'
Height: 12"–18"

Space Between Plants: in beds: 4" in rows: 6"–12"
Space Between Rows: 12"–36"
Site: Full sun to partial shade
Water: Low
Fertilizer: Heavy feeder
Side-dressing: 2–3 times during the season, apply compost or spray with liquid seaweed.
Propagation: Seed

First Seed-Starting Date:

Days Germ	+	Days Transplant	+	Days Before LFD	=	Days Count *Back* from LFD
11–42	+	7–14	+	10	=	28–66

Last Seed-Starting Date:

Days Germ	+	Days Transplant	+	Maturity	+	SDF	+	Frost Tender	=	Days *Back* from FFD
11–42	+	7–14	+	63–76	+	14	+	14	=	109–160

Pests

Cabbage looper, carrot rust fly, carrot weevil, nematode, parsleyworm, spider mite

Diseases

Crown rot, septoria leaf spot

Allies

Uncertain: black salsify, coriander, pennyroyal

Companions

Asparagus, corn, pepper, tomato

Incompatibles

None

HARVEST

Cut as needed. To keep it productive, frequently cut back the full length of the outside stems and remove all flower stalks. Herbs should be cut in the morning after the dew has dried. Cut the top growth up to 6" below the flower buds or ends. Do not wash the leaves or aromatic oils will be lost.

STORAGE REQUIREMENTS

To dry, tie the cuttings in small bunches and hang upside down in a warm, dry, dark place. When dried, remove the leaves from the stems and keep whole for storage. The drying job can be finished, if you prefer, in the oven or microwave. Store in airtight jars in a dark place. Don't crush or grind until ready to use.

Method	Taste
Frozen	Good for curly parsley
Dried	Good for broad leaf Italian

GROWING TIPS

Parsley is a cool-season biennial herb, hardy to frost and light freezes. It is notorious for taking a long time to germinate. There are several methods to speed things along: soak the seeds overnight or for 48 hours; refrigerate the seeds; freeze the seeds; or pour boiling water over the soil plug before covering it. If you soak the seeds for longer than overnight, change the water twice. Make sure you discard the water, since it will contain some of the germination inhibitor, furanocoumarin. If you let some of the plants go to seed late in the season, they may produce seedlings that can be lifted and grown on the windowsill for next year's crop. Parsley is hardy but will usually go to seed in its second year, so it's most often grown as an annual. While some say it's hard to transplant, you can direct sow or transplant it from pots. An excellent source of vitamin C, iron, and minerals, parsley is more than a pretty garnish. Its refreshing flavor is a great addition to soups, salads, sauces, and many dishes.

SELECTED VARIETIES

Greenhouse

Any variety thrives in a cool greenhouse.

Outdoor

Plainleaf Group *(P. crispum neapolitanum).* Best for drying, or to use in soups and stews.
Giant Italian 2'–3'; thick stalks, great in soups, stews, and salad (Nichols)
Italian Broad Leaf or **Single Italian** Stronger flavor than the curled; best for drying; flat dark green leaves (Companion Plants, Dabney, Richters)
Plain or **Single-leaf Parsley** Earlier maturing than others; deeply cut, bright green leaves; excellent flavor (Nichols, Richters, Shepherd's)

Curled Group *(P. crispum).* Best for garnishing.
Decora Best for warm climates; hot weather doesn't slow growth; deep-green curled leaves; thick leaves; good aroma and flavor (Richters)
Exotica or **Forest Green** Grows vigorously even in cool weather; deep-green curled leaves; good aroma and flavor (Nichols, Richters)
Mosscurled Standard curly variety; bright green; good aroma and flavor; best for freezing (Companion Plants, Dabney, Nichols, Richters)

Hamburg Group *(P. crispum tuberosum).*
Parsnip Rooted or **Hamburg** The parsnip-like root of this variety can been added to soups and stews; leaf can be used but its flavor isn't rich (Burpee, Nichols)

Notes

GROWTH CONDITIONS

Germination Temperature: 65°–75°F
pH: 6.0–7.0
Planting Depth: ¼"
Breadth: 12"–24"

Growth Temperature: Hot
Root Depth: 12"–24"
Height: 2'–6'

Space Between Plants: 12"–24"
Site: Full sun; good drainage essential
Water: Low
Fertilizer: Light feeder
Side-dressing: 2–3 applications per season of liquid seaweed.
Propagation: Stem-tip cuttings taken in the spring or fall root easily in sandy compost. It's not recommended to propagate from seed because the seeds are unreliable and lose viability rapidly. If you do start from seeds, however, use seeds that are less than 2 weeks old. Rosemary seeds take a long time to germinate — up to 3 weeks — so be patient. Make sure the seed pots have excellent drainage, but don't let the soil dry out.

Pests

In the greenhouse: spider mite and whitefly

Outdoors: mealybugs and scale

Diseases

In humid climates fungal botrytis rot, rhizoctonia

Companions

All *Brassicas*, beans, carrot, sage

Other Benefits

Rosemary is alleged to deter bean beetles, cabbage moth, and carrot rust fly.

Incompatibles

Cucumber

HARVEST

When the plant matures you can harvest it all year. Cut 4" branch tips, but do not remove more than 20 percent of the plant's growth. Herbs should be cut in the morning after the dew has dried. Do not wash them or aromatic oils will be lost.

STORAGE REQUIREMENTS

To dry, tie cuttings in small bunches and hang upside down in a warm, dry, dark place. When dried, remove the leaves from the stems, and keep whole for storage. Store in airtight jars in a dark place. Do not crush or grind until ready to use.

GROWING TIPS

Rosemary is a perennial warm-season herb, very tender to light frost and freezes. It is very tolerant of a wide variety of soil conditions ranging from 4.5 to 8.7 pH, and anywhere from 12–107 inches of water per year. Rosemary likes a sunny location and does not transplant well. If grown from seed, do not harvest for 3 years. It benefits from frequent pruning at any time of year, and can be trained into interesting shapes. Don't hesitate to cut it back severely. "Dr. Rosemary," nurseryman Thomas De Baggio in northern Virginia, recommends that above zone 8 rosemary be grown in pots year round and brought indoors for the winter, as most varieties are hardy to only 15°–20°F. There is only one variety, "Arp," that is hardy to -10°F and can be grown outdoors above zone 8. If you grow "Arp" outside, support its limbs and shield it with burlap in the winter (polyethylene can build up heat underneath), leaving the top open to minimize fungal disease. Overwatering causes tips to turn brown, followed by all leaves browning and dropping off. For pest problems try a soap-based insecticide or a homemade solution of 5 tablespoons liquid soap per 1 gallon of water. Spray both tops and bottoms of leaves.

SELECTED VARIETIES

Greenhouse

Any variety; rosemary grows beautifully in the greenhouse.

Outdoor

Culinary.

Common or **Upright Rosemary** *(R. officinalis)* Over 6'; hardy to 15°F; the only rosemary good for cooking (Dabney, Nichols, Richters)

Ornamental. Most of these can be used for culinary purposes but are better ornamentals.

Arp *(R.o. "Arp")* 5'; hardiest cultivar to -10°F; grey-green leaves; shrubby; very fragrant, light blue flowers; ornamental (Dabney, Fox Hill)

Benendon Blue or **Pine-Scented** or **Augustissimus** 2'–5'; hardy to 20°F; very strong pine-like aroma; dark blue sparse flowers; tall; narrow growth habit; used in potpourri; the only non-culinary variety (Companion Plants, Fox Hill, Richters, Sandy Mush)

Blue Boy 2'; hardy to 20°F; smallest habit and leaves of any rosemary; especially suited for indoor growing; good on windowsills and for bonsai; prostrate type; mild fresh fragrance; light blue flowers abundant in summer (Companion Plants, Dabney, Fox Hill)

Creeping or **Prostrate Rosemary** *(R.o. prostratus)* 6"–12"; hardy to 20°F; excellent for bonsai; espalier; hanging baskets and living wreaths; its long branches twist and curl; short and narrow leaves; mild fragrance; pale blue flowers; blooms almost year round (Companion Plants, Dabney, Sandy Mush)

Joyce deBaggio or **Golden Rain** 5'; hardy to 20°F; gold-edged leaves; strong fragrance like common rosemary; dark blue sparse flowers; compact; bush; self-branching; very pretty landscape specimen; looks gold from a distance (Companion Plants, Dabney)

Notes

GROWTH CONDITIONS

Germination Temperature: 60°–70°F
pH: 6.0–7.0
Planting Depth: ¼"
Breadth: 15"–24"

Growth Temperature: Warm
Root Depth: Shallow
Height: 12"–40"

Space Between Plants: in beds: 18"–20"
Space Between Rows: 3'
Site: Full sun; good drainage essential
Water: Average
Fertilizer: Light feeder
Side-dressing: An occasional spray of liquid seaweed will benefit the plant.
Propagation: Layering, stem cuttings, seed. Crowns of old sage plants can rarely be divided successfully, but dividing may work on younger plants. For seeds, start indoors 1–2 months before the last frost or sow directly outdoors 1–2 weeks before the last frost. They germinate in about 21 days. Transplant outdoors about 1 week before the last frost. In the fall, take a 4" cutting and root it for planting the following spring.

Pests

Slug, spider mite, spittlebug

Diseases

Powdery mildew, rhizoctonia, verticillium wilt

Companions

All *Brassicas*, carrot, marjoram, rosemary, strawberry, tomato

Other Benefits

Sage can be used to deter cabbage moths and carrot flies.

Incompatibles

Cucumber, onion family

HARVEST

If you want to keep these plants through winter, harvest lightly in the first year, no later than September. Herbs should be cut in the morning after the dew has dried. Cut the top growth up to 6" below the flower buds or ends. Don't wash the leaves unless necessary; you'll wash away aromatic oils.

STORAGE REQUIREMENTS

To dry, tie cuttings in small bunches and hang upside down in a warm, dry, dark place. When dried, remove the leaves from the stems, and keep whole for storage. Store in airtight jars in a cool, dry, dark place. This herb can also be frozen in airtight containers.

GROWING TIPS

Sage is a perennial shrub, hardy to -30°F, if covered. In the North, cover with a loose mulch of hay or evergreen boughs. A June-bloomer, sage likes well-drained and moderately rich soil, though it will tolerate poor soil and drought. Sage seeds store and germinate poorly. When started from seed, it takes about 2 years to grow to a mature size. Most gardeners start sage from cuttings or division, using the outer, newer growth. Some gardeners advise that you replace your sage plants every several years when they become woody and less productive. Sage has putative antibacterial activity and has been used as a natural preservative for meats, poultry, and fish. It also supposedly works better as a preservative with rosemary, rather than alone. Distilled sage extracts have been made into antioxidants that are used to increase the shelflife of foods. Some research also indicates that sage lowers blood sugar in diabetics, and may have estrogenic properties, which could explain the popular folklore that sage dries up milk. Fresh sage has a lemony and slightly bitter flavor, while dried sage has a more musty flavor.

SELECTED VARIETIES

Greenhouse

Any variety; sage grows well in the greenhouse.

Outdoor

Blue or **Cleveland Sage** *(S. clevelandii)* 3'; royal blue flowers; pleasant aroma; good for culinary and potpourris; from Southern California (Companion Plants, Dabney, Fox Hill, Richters)

Clary or **Muscatel Sage** *(S. scleria)* 2'–4'; fragrant; very ornamental; masses of white or pink flowers; large, hairy, toothed leaves, used to make Muscatel wine; this variety is said to have medicinal value — some say an infusion of its seeds make a good eyewash; grows well in heavy soils (Companion Plants, Dabney, Fox Hill, Nichols, Sandy Mush, Seeds Blum)

Common or **Garden Sage** 2'–3'; grey-green pebbly leaves; pale blue flowers; good culinary herb for meat, stuffings, sausage, omelettes, cheese, and bean dishes; said to have medicinal values (Companion Plants, Dabney, Richters, Sandy Mush)

Golden Sage *(S. off. "Aurea")* 18"; hardy to 20°F; chartreuse-yellow on edges of dark green leaves; good culinary and border plant; compact growth (Companion Plants, Richters, Sandy Mush)

Pineapple Sage *(Salvia elegans)* 2'–4'; brilliant red flowers with pineapple scent; attracts hummingbirds; good culinary sage for drinks, chicken, jams, and jellies; good indoor plant; needs good light indoors (Companion Plants, Dabney, Richters, Sandy Mush)

Purple Sage *(S. off. "purpurea")* 18"; compact; aromatic red-purple foliage; good culinary sage for stuffings, sausage, eggs, soups, and stews; needs winter mulch; good in or outdoors in full sun (Companion Plants, Fox Hill, Richters, Sandy Mush)

Tri-color Sage *(S. off. "tricolor")* 2'–3'; hardy to 20°F; variegated white, purple, and green leaves; true sage flavor; very showy; excellent border plant where hardy; needs winter mulch (Companion Plants, Fox Hill, Richters, Sandy Mush)

Notes

"Why should a man die if he has sage in his garden." (This tribute to sage's reputed ancient medicinal uses appears in the catalogue of Dabney Herbs.)

GROWTH CONDITIONS

Germination Temperature: 75°F
pH: 6.0–7.0
Height: 12"–36"

Growth Temperature: Warm
Planting Depth: Cover roots
Breadth: 24"

Space Between Plants: in beds: 18" in rows: 2'
Site: Full sun to partial shade
Water: Average
Fertilizer: Light feeder
Side-dressing: Not necessary
Propagation: Cuttings, divisions, seed. French tarragon cannot be grown from seed, so if you grow tarragon seeds it is the less aromatic, more common Russian tarragon. To propagate French tarragon, take cuttings or divisions in the early spring and transplant 2' apart.

Pests

None

Diseases

Downy mildew, powdery mildew, rhizoctonia (root rot)

Companions

Tarragon is alleged to enhance the growth of most vegetables.

Incompatibles

None

HARVEST

Begin harvest 6–8 weeks after transplanting outside. The leaves bruise easily, so handle gently. Herbs should be cut in the morning after the dew has dried. Cut the top growth up to 6" below the flower buds or ends. Don't wash, for the aromatic oils will be lost.

STORAGE REQUIREMENTS

To dry, tie cuttings in small bunches and hang upside down in a warm, dry, dark place. When dried, remove the leaves from the stems, and keep whole for storage. The leaves will brown slightly during the drying process. Do not crush or grind until ready to use. Store in airtight jars in a dark place. Other ways to store fresh tarragon are to preserve it in white vinegar (which preserves flavor better than drying), or to freeze the leaves in airtight plastic bags.

Method	Taste
Frozen	Good (better than dried)
Dried	Fair

GROWING TIPS

Tarragon is an aromatic, perennial herb, hardy to frost and light freezes through zone 4. It likes full to partial shade in rich, sandy, well-drained loam. The plants should be divided every 2 or 3 years for flavor and vigor. All flower stems should be removed to keep the plant productive. Tarragon most often fails due to soil that is too wet or too acidic. It can be grown in containers in the greenhouse or on a windowsill as long as you ensure good drainage. The only tarragon worth growing is French tarragon, but it is somewhat harder to find than Russian tarragon. Tarragon is an excellent flavor enhancer in vinegars, salad dressings, and chicken, cheese, and egg dishes.

SELECTED VARIETIES

Greenhouse

Tarragon does well with 16 hours of light over a 6-week period at 40°F.

Outdoor

French Tarragon *(A. dracunculus* **var.** *sativa)* Classical French Tarragon; cannot be grown from seed; best if shaded during hottest part of the day; divide every 4–5 years to maintain flavor; narrow pointed leaves (Burpee, Companion Plants, Fox Hill, Richters, Sandy Mush)

Russian Tarragon *(A. dracunculus)* Not recommended; almost flavorless; tarragon seeds are always this variety (widely available)

Tarahumara (Mt. Pima Avis, aka: Mexican Mint Marigold) *(Tagetes lucida)* A substitute for tarragon; perennial native to Mexico; used as a tea; wonderful aroma; for low and high desert (Native Seeds)

Notes

_____

_____

_____

_____

_____

_____

_____

_____

_____

_____

_____

_____

_____

_____

_____

_____

GROWTH CONDITIONS

Germination Temperature: 60°–70°F
pH: 5.5–7.0
Planting Depth: 0"–¼"
Breadth: 18"–3'

Growth Temperature: Warm
Root Depth: 6"–10"
Height: 3"–12"

Space Between Plants: 8"–12"
Site: Full sun to partial shade
Water: Average
Fertilizer: Light feeder
Side-dressing: Not necessary
Propagation: Cuttings, divisions, layering, seed. *Seeds:* start indoors 2–3 weeks before the last frost, keeping seeds dry and uncovered. *Layering, divisions, and cuttings:* snip 3" from fresh new green growth, place in wet sand, keep moist for 2 weeks, and transplant when rooted. The best time for divisions or cuttings is spring, although they also can be taken through early summer.

Pests

Aphid, spider mite

Diseases

Botrytis rot, fungal diseases, rhizoctonia (root rot)

Companions

All *Brassicas,* eggplant, potato, strawberry, tomato

Other

May repel cabbageworm and whitefly

Incompatibles

Cucumber

HARVEST

Cut as needed before the plant blossoms in midsummer. Or harvest the entire plant by cutting it down to 2" above the ground; the plant will grow back before the season ends. The second harvesting method, however, renders the plant less hardy for the winter. Herbs should be cut in the morning after the dew has dried. Cut the top growth up to 6" below the flower buds or ends. Do not wash the leaves or aromatic oils will be lost.

STORAGE REQUIREMENTS

To dry, tie cuttings in small bunches and hang upside down in a warm, dry, dark place. When dried, remove the leaves from the stems, and keep whole for storage. Do not crush or grind leaves until ready to use. Store in airtight jars in a dark place or freeze in airtight containers.

Method	Taste
Frozen	Fair
Dried	Excellent

GROWING TIPS

Thyme is a perennial herb, hardy to frost and light freezes through zones 5–9. It likes full sun, and does well in light and dry to stony, poor soils. Good drainage is always essential or the plant will be susceptible to fungal diseases. Keep it sheltered from cold winds. It may not survive severe winters unless covered or heavily mulched. The plant may become woody and straggly in 2 to 3 years. Either replace it or try cutting back three-fourths of the new growth during the growing season to rejuvenate it and keep it bushy. French thyme is difficult to propagate by cuttings, but, can be accomplished by the following method: Prune the plant severely in mid-June, and take small ½" to 1" softwood cuttings in mid-July; root the cuttings in a sand bed, and cover the bed with a milky white plastic "tent" 6"–8" above the top of the cuttings; mist the cuttings once a day at midday.

SELECTED VARIETIES

Greenhouse

Any variety does well, but keep foliage dry to prevent rot.

Outdoor

Caraway *(T. herba-barona)* 4"; rapid spreader, good ground cover and in rock gardens; rose flowers; used for meats, soups, and vegetables (Companion Plants, Dabney, Nichols, Richters)

Common, Garden or **English** *(T. vulgaris)* 14"; small upright shrub; source of antiseptic oil, Thymol; common, English, and French variations are most often used in cooking and also are excellent bee plants (Companion Plants, Dabney, Fox Hill, Nichols, Sandy Mush)

Creeping *(T. glabrescens)* 6"; main use as a good ground cover; a dense mat with purple flowers; fast spreader; early bloomer (Companion Plants)

English, German or **Winter** *(T. vulgaris* var.) 8"; broad dark green leaves; robust growth habit (Companion Plants, Fox Hill, Richters, Sandy Mush)

French or **Summer** *(T. vulgaris* var.) 12"; greyer and sweeter than the English; needs some winter protection; pink flowers; trim upright plants (Companion Plants, Dabney, Fox Hill, Nichols, Richters, Sandy Mush)

Italian Oregano Thyme 10"; strong oregano taste and aroma; tender perennial (Companion Plants, Nichols, Sandy Mush)

Lemon and Golden Lemon *(T. citriodoratus)* 12"; low-growing with strong lemon scent delicious in teas, or fish and chicken dishes; not as hardy as other thymes; may need winter protection; the Golden Lemon variation has sharply defined yellow edges on leaves and is a beautiful plant (Companion Plants, Dabney, Fox Hill, Nichols, Richters, Sandy Mush)

Mother-of-Thyme or **Creeping** *(T. praecox* subsp. *articus)* 2"; beautiful ground cover; good bee plant; rose-purple flowers; dark green leathery leaves; used in formal herb gardens, between stepping stones, and on earth benches; releases fragrance when stepped or sat on; comes in red-flowered and lemon variations (Dabney, Richters, Sandy Mush)

Silver *(T. vulgaris "Argenteus")* 10"; somewhat sprawling, striking plant; pretty white margins on green leaves; pale blue flowers; flavor like common or garden thyme; good for edging and hanging baskets (Companion Plants, Dabney, Fox Hill, Richters, Sandy Mush)

Notes

PART 4

Macro- and Microdestructive Agents

Organic Remedies

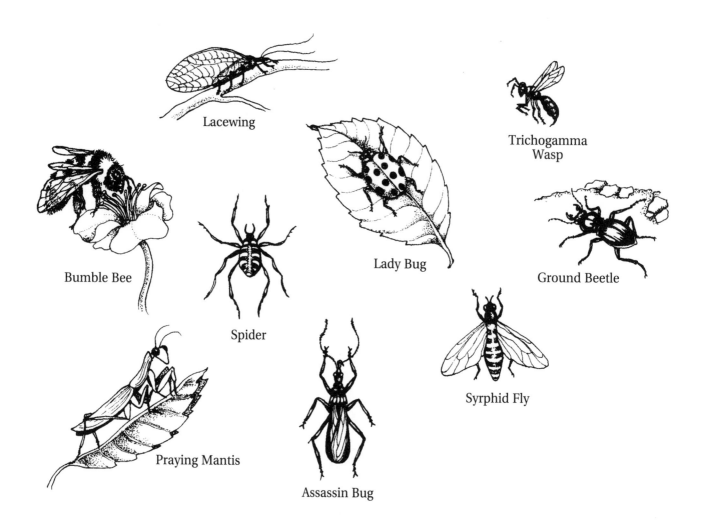

Lacewing

Trichogamma
Wasp

Bumble Bee

Spider

Lady Bug

Ground Beetle

Praying Mantis

Assassin Bug

Syrphid Fly

Selected Beneficial Insects

Insect	Benefits
Assassin bugs	Eat immature insects.
Bumble bees	Pollinate blossoms, from which fruits and vegetables develop. One of nature's best helpers for our food supply.
Ground beetles	Eat caterpillars, cutworms, some species of slugs and snails, and soft-bodied larvae.
Lacewing wasps	Eat aphids, corn earworms, mealybugs, mites, leafhopper nymphs, thrips, caterpillar eggs, scales, and whiteflies.
Ladybugs	Eat aphids, mealybugs and small insects. Different species of ladybugs prefer different insects.
Praying mantis	Eat aphids and small insects.
Syrphid flies (Hover flies and Flower flies)	Eat aphids, leafhoppers, mealybugs, and mites, scales, and small insects.
Spiders	Eat insects and other pests.

Wasps — parasitoid (nonstinging)

Braconids	Parasitize aphids, larvae of moths, butterflies, and many beetles.
Chalcid	Parasitize aphids, mealybugs, scales, and larvae of beetles, moths, butterflies.
Ichneumonid	Parasitize moth and butterfly larvae.
Pediobius foveolatus	Parasitize Mexican bean beetle larvae.
Trichogramma	Parasitize and eat eggs of the corn borer, cabbage looper, codling moth, and many caterpillars.

(Additional beneficial insects are mentioned in the following charts.)

An Ounce Of Prevention...

Prevention and a self-sustaining, balanced ecosystem are the organic gardener's most important tools for minimizing diseases. Without preventive measures, the advantages of organic gardening quickly diminish. As with people, preventive medicine in plants means adopting a holistic approach *from the beginning.* Some diseases and insects can be minimized by breaking the pest cycle through proper garden siting, crop rotation, intercropping, and soil maintenance. Other pests can be minimized by ensuring good plant nutrition, because healthy plants are less susceptible to attack.

Realistic expectations are intrinsic to this holistic approach. False expectations can lead to ghost gardens gone to seed or to habitual quick chemical fixes. Abandon at the outset the idea of picture-perfect produce. Even a healthy garden with an advantageous balance between predators and prey suffers some damage through the growing season.

As garden steward, your role is to determine the severity of the damage, the factors promoting the damage, and to decide what action — if any — is worth taking. Damage does not necessarily mean lower yields.

Most plants can lose up to twenty percent of their foliage and still match yields of those with no foliage loss.

If you can identify an imbalance, you might be able to take long-term remedies. Events seemingly out of your control, such as unusually prolonged wet periods that promote fungus, might be addressed over the long term by improving soil drainage and ventilation. In the short term, however, often the best single remedy is to prevent further garden contamination: Remove and destroy the infected plants.

An organic garden is an object of sentiment, not sentimentality. It may be hard to trash a plant you lovingly nurtured and nourished, but the needs of the whole garden can outweigh those of one plant. The remedy necessary to make a plant that is weak, diseased, or unsuitable for your micro-environment grow may be more deleterious to you and your garden than the benefits warrant. Outdoors, where nature's balancing act prevails, a philosophical embrace of imperfection and a "tough love" policy toward diseased plants are both critical.

A garden in its totality, from microorganisms in the soil to birds, resembles more the acquisition of a pet than of a sofa. A garden is like a complex living organism that takes time to understand. Several years may be needed to build a productive soil and resident population of beneficial organisms. It also takes time to learn which varieties are suited to your micro-environment. A neighbor one mile up the road may have perfect conditions for your favorite tomato, but you may not be able to grow it well because of microenvironmental variations.

If you can learn to accept some imperfections, some diseases, some insects, and some failures, your garden can be a continual source of nutritive food, relaxation, and pleasure.

Planning Ahead

Don't be an attractive target.

A healthy body, by definition, is less susceptible to disease.

*Don't let the nose of the camel in the tent because
the rest of the body may soon follow.*

Garden Location

For any garden selecting the right location may be the key step toward preventing plant disease.

Direct sun. Choose a location that receives bright sunlight most of the day — **especially morning sun** in humid areas, so that dew dries as rapidly as possible. This will help minimize the growth and spread of fungal and bacterial pathogens.

Good drainage. Choose a garden site that drains well. If it doesn't already drain well, mix materials into your soil that will improve the drainage, such as humus. This is important so that the plant roots don't become water-logged and, therefore, oxygen-starved and severely stressed. Poor drainage also increases your chances of root rots and various soil-borne diseases.

Soil Condition

Soil is "alive" — full of organisms, large and small. Your role as caretaker is to encourage a healthy diversity of organisms and nutrients. One of the best guidelines in organic gardening is, "feed the soil, not the plants."

Healthy soil helps you grow healthy plants. Avoid dumping large quantities of chemical fertilizers on your soil. Although they may help plant growth temporarily, they can kill beneficial soil organisms, such as earthworms, and, in the long run, can deplete the soil. Earthworms are a major way to feed the soil and thereby promote healthy plant growth. (*See* pages 3-4 for more information on earthworms.) As steward, you can enrich your garden soil by taking the following steps.

- **Import earthworms,** if your soil doesn't already have them.

- **Enrich your soil** with peat humus, compost, and composted manure. These ingredients are available from many of the suppliers listed in Appendices B and C.

- **Minimize tilling depth.** After the initial tilling, double-digging, or other preparation of your garden bed, don't till more than a few inches deep (unless absolutely necessary); going deeper may kill or disturb earthworms and other soil organisms. There are a few exceptions to this rule, as noted in the animal pest charts on pages 183–228.

- **Avoid soil compaction.** Don't walk on your garden soil, if possible. Some gardeners lay 6 to 12 inches of straw to avoid compaction where heavy machinery is used.

- **Sow cover crops** after a harvest to replenish the soil; use a legume or grass, such as cowpeas or winter rye. Cover crops help retain soil moisture, improve soil texture, and increase organic matter; legumes will also return nitrogen to the soil.

- **Use raised beds** where possible: they automatically help you achieve multiple goals, such as good drainage, minimal soil compaction, and aeration. Contained raised beds also help minimize the spread of disease organisms by localizing them to the infected bed. (*See* page 7 for more information on raised beds.)

- **Solarize garden soil** if your garden develops a soil-borne disease problem. Solarization is accomplished by creating a kind of mini-hothouse that raises soil temperature to 130°–140°F for several days. Temperatures higher than this kill beneficial organisms. There are different methods, depending on how large and deep an area you wish to solarize. An easy way to solarize your soil is to loosen the soil in midsummer, thoroughly drench it with water and let it sit overnight. The next day, cover the soil with 4-mm–thick clear plastic, stretch the plastic tight, and seal the edges with rocks or soil. Allow the soil to heat up for 4–6 weeks; then remove the plastic and plant as usual. For other methods consult sources in the Bibliography.

- **Pasteurize potting soil** used in extensive greenhouse operations and to start seeds in flats, pots, or other containers. Otherwise, use unpasteurized soil mix. Also, pasteurization may not be necessary if you use potting soil taken from uncultivated areas or fields growing grains or forage. An easy way to pasteurize is to place a 1 to 1½ inch layer of soil in shallow pans, and bake for one hour at 220°F. Or, cover the soil with foil, stick in a meat thermometer so it doesn't touch the pan's bottom or sides, and bake at 350°F until soil temperature reaches 180°F. Turn off the heat and let the soil remain in the oven another 30 minutes. When cool, store soil in tightly sealed plastic bags.

Plant Location and Selection

Consider your garden plot a place to encourage *diversity* of life, large and small. The soil is alive with microbial organisms, many of them disease pathogens. One of the best ways to minimize these pathogens is to interrupt or discourage their life cycle. The following practices will help you achieve this goal.

- **Rotate your crops.** At a minimum, plant the same vegetable in the same soil site only once every other year (a 2-year rotation). If possible, routinely rotate on a 3–8 year basis. "Same soil site" is defined as a radius of 10 feet from where the vegetable has been planted. So, rotation can occur within the same growing bed as long as it is at least 10 feet away from where it was the previous year.

- **Intercrop.** Try to avoid "monocrops" — crops of, say, just corn or beans. Space and time permitting, if you want to grow a large amount of one vegetable, try planting it in several different places, or breaking up a large patch with plantings of another vegetable. Intercropping discourages some pests from having an easy feast on their favorite food. In fact, studies have shown that random mixing of plant cultivars in a stand greatly reduces disease severity. Also, certain vegetables may grow better in one spot than another, so experimentation with placement may be helpful.

- **Test different varieties** of the same crop. Each variety of a particular vegetable has slightly different growing habits and different disease and insect resistance. One variety may thrive where another dies. The more varieties you try, the higher intrinsic resistance your garden has to widespread disease and insect damage. Over time, you will identify the varieties that fare best in your particular microclimate.

- **Encourage good air circulation** by giving each plant adequate space to grow to maturity. Prune trees and canes annually to prevent overcrowding limbs and branches. In some cases, you may need to remove entire trees if the area becomes too crowded.

- **Select varieties that are resistant or tolerant** to the problems specific to your climate — fungal, bacterial, viral, or insect. Your extension agent or local organic association should be able to tell you what the predominant pest problems are in your area. For some diseases, selecting resistant varieties is the only prevention and remedy.

- **Buy certified disease-free seed or plants** whenever possible. For certain eastern U.S.-predominant diseases, buying seed grown west of the Rockies is an important preventive measure.

Prevention Strategies

A stitch in time saves nine.

If it ain't broke, don't fix it.

Most of the following defensive actions are *also organic remedies* for a host of different disease or animal pests. If you adopt these practices *at the outset,* your need for the rest of the information in this section will be minimal. Some steps may be free, some inexpensive, some more expensive. Do what you can, when you can, choosing options that are congruent with your goals. A purple martin house, for example, may be expensive because its construction is complex. But, it will last twenty years and greatly reduce your need for any insecticidal spray — chemical or organic. Bluebird or bat houses, by contrast, can be easily built of scrap lumber or bought for a small price and, in sufficient numbers, may accomplish the same goal.

Plant Maintenance

These steps are critical for prevention. They also, as a group, are the most common and important *remedies* for disease or insect damage. If you do experience disease or insect problems, go over this list; if there is a step you haven't already taken, implement it as a remedy.

- **Avoid deep planting** where fungal root rot (rhizoctonia) is a problem. Shallow planting encourages early emergence of seedlings and gives them a better chance of survival.

- **Water from below** by some form of irrigation. A cheap method is to use gallon-sized plastic jugs with the bottoms cut out. Lodge the necks upside down in the soil at intervals appropriate to the plants' needs, and fill with water. More expensive methods include soaker and emitter tubes. Watering from below helps prevent and remedy fungal disease by discouraging its growth and minimizing its spread through water droplets. It is also more efficient than regular watering and reduces evaporative loss.

- **Water before noon** to let the plants dry off in the middle of the day, before nightfall. This, too, discourages fungal growth.

- **Don't work around or touch wet plants.** Diseases are frequently transmitted by human hands and tools, so this preventive measure is standard cultivation practice.

- **Don't touch healthy plants after working with diseased plants**, for the same reasons as above.

- **Avoid high nitrogen fertilizers,** which not only can harm soil organisms, but can push the plant to put its energy into leafy growth, not fruits.

- **Feed the soil with compost**. For some diseases, a major remedy is to spread 1 inch or more of compost through the garden. See page 4 for more information.

- **Mulch** is another occasional remedy for fungal, bacterial, and certain insect pest problems. Apply several inches of mulch in the spring and 4 to 6 inches in autumn, after harvest (*see* following note on **Fall Cultivation**). For more information on mulch, *see* page 10.

- **Control weeds** in and around the garden that can harbor insect and disease pests. If you weed regularly in the early summer months, you should not experience a severe weed problem during the rest of the season. Removing perennial weeds and thistles within 100 yards of the garden is considered a remedy for several diseases.

- **Remove rotting or dead leaves, stalks, weeds, and plants**, which can be a breeding ground for pests. Clean the garden of fall leaves, too, even though you may not be growing any fall crops.

- **Remove piles of wood, garden debris,** or other potential breeding grounds for pests to a spot away from the garden.

- **Don't allow large, stagnant pools of water.** Small birdbaths and running water are not a problem.

- **Mow grass in orchards,** where the grass is a potential breeding ground. One "natural" orchard plan involves planting companion grasses, or plants that attract beneficial insects, and allowing them to naturalize. Most orchards, however, are surrounded by orchard grass, which should be kept mowed to discourage pests.

- **Disinfect tools** periodically, even if there's no sign of disease. When working with diseased plants, always disinfect tools between pruning cuts.

- **Shade plants in extremely hot weather** if they wilt continuously; use a shading material such as cheesecloth. If they wilt one day, that doesn't mean they will die the next. But, don't be afraid to shade your plants. Recent NASA studies indicate that plants integrate light over time, and that long, sunny summer days provide more light than they require. If plants are wilting from heat stress, also make sure they receive adequate water.

- **Protect plants from freezes** with any light material whenever a freeze is anticipated. Even newspaper works.

- **Harvest fruits and vegetables promptly when ripe.** Allowing fruits and vegetables to stay on the stem too long promotes certain diseases.

- **Remove plants immediately after harvest.** Don't allow harvested plants to just sit in the garden. Remove them (if they're not diseased) and add them to the compost pile, or, where appropriate, work them back into the soil.

- **Fall cultivation.** After plants have been harvested and the garden cleaned of plant debris, leave the soil completely bare for a few days. For normal purposes, cultivate the soil no more than 3 inches. For certain insect pest problems, cultivate the soil to a depth of 6 to 8 inches to expose eggs and larvae for birds and other predators. Two weeks later, lightly cultivate the soil a second time with a rake, this time only 2 inches deep. Leave bare for a few more days, then plant a cover crop, or apply a layer of winter mulch 4 to 6 inches deep.

- **At all times, remove and destroy infected or diseased leaves, canes, or the entire plant when necessary.** For some disease and insect pests, removing the infected leaves may be sufficient. For other pests, which may be systemic, removing the affected leaves may not be sufficient. If all other measures discussed in this section fail to control the problem, you may need to resort to various sprays — whether simple home remedies, insecticidal soaps, or more harsh remedies such as the copper-based fungicides and botanical sprays.

Helpful Supports and Devices

These devices may seem unnecessary, but they can make the difference between the presence or absence of a problem. In some cases, they are recommended as remedies to specific disease or animal pests.

- **Borders** of certain plants around vegetable beds have been found by some research to be helpful in maintaining garden health. Planted in small ratios relative to the garden bed size, try planting borders of dead nettle, valerian, hyssop, lemon balm, and yarrow.

- **Trellises, stakes, A-frames, teepees,** and other forms of plant support accomplish multiple goals. Not only do they make the most efficient use of growing space, but they promote better light penetration and air circulation; both of these factors help minimize disease. Supports also make it much easier to prune and harvest. Use these supports for vegetables like tomatoes, pole beans, peas, cucumbers, melons, and squash. Melons and large squash can be supported on trellises with something like panty hose. If grown on the ground, melons should be raised off the soil with steel cans or plastic containers to minimize rot. Cane fruit — such as blackberries, raspberries, and grapes — also grow effectively when trellised.

- **Row covers** are helpful throughout the growing season. In spring and fall, they keep your crops warm and protected from frost, prolonging your season. In spring and summer, they are an easy and effective protection against insect attack. Before applying row covers, however, make sure that harmful insects are not trapped underneath. Row covers are usually a light-weight woven material, such as polyester or polyvinyl alcohol, that allows in air, light, and water, and requires no supports. An additional way to keep the beds warm under row covers is to fill simple plastic jugs with water and place them every few feet along the rows. The jugs absorb heat during the day and radiate the stored heat through the night.

- **Wire cages, stakes, and water-based white paint** are critical aids to saplings. Wire cages provide an effective barrier against animals. When planting the sapling, install a ½- to ¼-inch hardware cloth around the trunk, extending 4" below ground to prevent rodents from burrowing under, and rising 18 to 24 inches above ground to prevent rabbit damage (especially in winter months). Make sure the wire is spaced a couple of inches away from the trunk to allow for growth. For trees on dwarf rootstock characterized by poor anchorage, place a 4- to 6-foot stake close to the trunk before filling the planting hole with soil, and attach with special ties that permit growth and flexing. Tree trunks can be painted anytime, but if done while young, it will help prevent sunscald or winter injury — a condition promoted by sunny winter days and resulting in cracks or cankers.

- **Electrical fences or other barriers** against large animals, such as deer, are almost essential in rural areas. Many a gardener has gone to bed with a prospering garden and awakened to find devastation. Some gardeners initially feel the problem doesn't warrant the expense, only to change their minds once their entire garden — flowers and vegetables alike — are wiped out in short order. For suggestions on different types of barriers, see the remedies for deer in the animal pest chart on page 195.

Attract Beneficial Animals

Birds, bats, bees, predatory and parasitic wasps, ladybugs —these are just a few of the beneficial animals that are critical to a self-sustaining garden. Beneficial animals are one of the easiest ways to prevent disease and to deter animal pests that spread disease. Beneficial animals save you both money and time (and time *is* money). To attract beneficial insects, plant herbs, flowers, and clovers around the borders of your garden. (For more information on beneficials, *see* pages 5–6 and also page 151.)

In the beginning, your ecosystem may not contain all of the beneficial animals that you want or need. You may want to import beneficial insects to fight a specific problem. Such a practice is part of *Integrated Pest Management* (IPM), a relatively new concept in crop management. IPM relies extensively, but not exclusively, on precisely timed releases of beneficial insects to fight pest problems. Backyard gardeners who don't have the opportunity or inclination to investigate the proper timing or method of releasing purchased beneficial insects shouldn't bother with this remedy, because their money will most likely be wasted. However, if you wish to experiment and can follow through on the timed releases, importation of beneficials can be an effective remedy. Beneficial insects are listed, where applicable, in the animal pest chart on page 183; suppliers can be found in Appendix C. We urge you to consult the supplier and follow their instructions on both quantity and timing to ensure success.

Some purists feel that the importation of beneficial insects disrupts the development of a balanced local ecosystem. This argument has some merit. However, some beneficials can be self-limiting: when their food source dies, they die. Ideally, a self-sustaining garden should not need imported help, but you may decide to resort to imported beneficials for acute infestations. The decision depends on your individual goals and, as discussed previously, the amount of damage you're willing to tolerate. Most important, if the first and second lines of defense have been implemented, the probability of extensive damage to any single crop or crop variety is low.

Identifying the Problem

*If you hear hoofbeats,
look for horses not zebras.*

Identification may seem an improbable defensive action, yet it is absolutely vital. If you see water spots on your ceiling, you don't immediately replace the roof; it may be a simple problem of condensation due to inadequate ventilation of the roof rafters. When you develop a fever, you don't instantly resort to penicillin. Similarly, when plants get sick, it is essential to diagnose the problem accurately before taking action. What you may think is a fungus may simply be a lack of phosphorus.

The most common garden problems are frequently the simplest ones to fix: over- or underwatering, inadequate nutrients, poor drainage, or lack of ventilation. Take the time to examine the problem carefully.

The remainder of this part on disease and animals pests is intended primarily to help you narrow down the possible causes of your plant problem and to help you conduct informed discussions with professionals. And, if you wish to experiment with your garden — and you do not have an investment in saving every plant, maximizing yields, or obtaining picture-perfect produce — the following guidelines and remedies can be a source of fun, discovery, and learning. If you are a market gardener with an investment in yields — quality and quantity — it is vital to obtain an accurate diagnosis from a professional before implementing a remedy. Remember, advice and soil tests from extension agents are free.

Regular Monitoring

The most important guideline is to monitor your garden daily, if you have time, or at least weekly. Act quickly to prevent a pest or disease from becoming a problem, starting with the most benign methods of control, which are also usually the easiest and least expensive. The simplest methods include handpicking and trapping, or spraying plants with strong jets of water to clear off bugs. Work your way up from these to stronger methods, such as biological predators. If the problem becomes very serious, you might try stronger controls like botanical insecticides — but use them sparingly and only as a last resort. (*See* the warning under **Botanical Controls** on page 166.) The key is to find the control for your garden that is both the most effective and the most benign.

Systematic Examination Of The Environment

Before attempting diagnosis, you must first learn how to observe. Begin by taking a general accounting of the plant and determining the parts that are affected. The following are just a few examples of what you might look for.

- **Leaves:** Inspect edges (margins), veins, top side, and bottom side. Notice wilting, general coloration and distortion (curling, crinkling), holes, spots, eggs, and insects.

- **Blossoms and fruits:** Check petals, blossom end of the fruit, and skin. Look for spots, discolorations, decay, cuts, holes, premature drop, lack of fruit setting, eggs, and insects.

- **Stems or bark:** Examine from the soil level to the top, even slightly below soil level. Notice cuts, cracks or splits in the tissue, blisters, growths (cankers or galls), discoloration, wilting, stunting, twisting, spindly growth, sticky coating, gummy exudate, spots, eggs, and insects.

- **Roots and surrounding soil** (if the plant is sufficiently diseased, you may wish to dig it up): Check the length and breadth of main roots and root hairs. Notice nodules, knots, decay, underdevelopment, twisting or distortions, eggs, cocoons, and insects.

Start With Basics, Not Zebras

After examining the plant and its environment, consider the basics, not the unusual. Start with the most common garden problems — water, nutrients, drainage, air circulation — even if insects or disease are clearly present. Many pests don't attack a plant unless it is already weakened and stressed. Before reaching for the fungicide, check to see if the roots are too wet and compacted to get oxygen. Global garden destruction can be due to animals, such as deer and rodents. And global garden sickness can be caused by acid rain, pollution, or smog — modern afflictions we often forget in diagnosis.

CHART

Identifying and Treating Common Problems

Problem	Symptoms/Where it Occurs	Diagnostic Tools/Remedies
Water *Too much*	The soil around the stem is soaked. Mold, moss, or fungus may be growing on top of the soil. Other symptoms include wilting, yellowing, and dead leaf margins.	**Diagnostic Tools:** Why guess? Buy a simple moisture meter to find out whether the root medium is too wet or dry. Buy a rain gauge and mount it where it can be easily checked.
Too little	Plants wilt due to loss of tissue turgor, which is maintained by water pressure. Leaves may eventually brown and die. With prolonged water shortage, growth is stunted.	**Remedies:** ▪ Earthworms ▪ Compost *Do the obvious:* If it's too wet, let the root medium dry out; too dry, provide more water.
Walnut Wilt	Roots of black walnut and butternut trees secrete an acid (juglone) that is toxic to tomato, potato, pea, cabbage, pear, apple, sour cherry, and others. Plants can suddenly wilt and die. Their vascular systems brown, which may cause a false diagnosis of fusarium or verticillium wilts.	**Diagnostic Tools:** If affected plants are growing near a black walnut or butternut tree, the acid from the tree roots is most likely the problem. **Remedies:** ▪ Remove the tree, or plant the garden a distance from the tree that exceeds the height of the tree.
Nitrogen (N) *Too little*	Nitrogen is essential for all phases of growth. Because it can be rapidly depleted, garden soil needs a slow constant supply such as compost provides. Slow growth. Lighter green leaf color is followed by yellowing tips, usually starting at the bottom of the plant. Leaf undersides may become blue-purple. Plant eventually becomes spindly, and older leaves drop. Fruits are small and pale before ripening, and overly colored when ripe. **Where:** Widespread.	**Diagnostic tools:** Soil test kit **Remedies:** ▪ Earthworms ▪ Compost (slow release) ▪ Foliar spray of diluted fish emulsion or other liquid fertilizer ▪ Fish meal (slow release) ▪ Composted manure (slow release) ▪ Hoof and horn meal (slow release) ▪ Cottonseed meal (medium release) ▪ Blood meal (fast release) *Avoid:* Urea, the various nitrates, ammonium phosphate
Too much	Lush, green foliage. Little or no fruit, because the plant is putting all of its energy into growth. **Where:** Usually occurs when there is an excess of fast-acting fertilizer.	

Problem	Symptoms/Where it Occurs	Diagnostic Tools/Remedies
Phosphorus (P) *Too little*	Phosphorus is essential for proper fruiting, flowering, seed formation, and root branching. It also increases the rate of crop maturation, builds plant resistance to disease, and strengthens stems. Leaf undersides have blue-red spots that expand to entire leaf. Darkened leaves develop a blue-green tinge. Green crops have reddish purple color in stems and leaf veins. Fruiting crops are leafy, with fruits setting and maturing late, if at all. **Where:** Widespread, except in the Northwest. Most severe in the Southeast from the Gulf of Mexico to North Carolina.	**Diagnostic Tools:** Soil test kit **Remedies:** ■ Earthworms ■ Compost ■ Bone meal (slow release) ■ Soft phosphate (even slower release) ■ Phosphate rock (very slow release) *Avoid:* Phosphoric acid, superphosphates, highly soluble compounds
Potassium (K) *Too little*	Potassium is essential for regulating water movement in plants and helps with production of sugars, starches, proteins, and certain enzyme reactions. It also increases cold-hardiness, especially in root crops. Leaves at the plant base turn grayish green. Leaf edges yellow, brown, or blacken, and curl downward. Black spots appear along leaf veins. New leaves curl and crinkle. Flowers and fruit are small and inferior. Stems are hard and woody. Plant and roots are stunted. Leaves may turn bronze, yellow-brown, or mildly bluish. **Where:** Most common east of the Mississippi and in coastal fog areas; most severe in parts of Texas through Florida, and north to Virginia.	**Diagnostic Tools:** Soil test kit **Remedies:** ■ Earthworms ■ Compost ■ Greensand (very slow release) ■ Crushed granite (very slow release) ■ Rock potash (slow release) ■ Kelp meal (medium release) ■ Wood ash (fast release, caustic) ■ Feldspar dust *Avoid:* Potassium chloride
Magnesium (Mg) *Too little*	Magnesium is important for chlorophyll production and respiration. Lower, older leaves yellow between the leaf veins and eventually turn dark brown. Leaves get brittle and curl upward. Fruit matures late. Symptoms usually appear in late season. **Where:** Occurs in acidic soils, leached, sandy soils, or soils high in potassium and calcium.	**Diagnostic Tools:** Soil and pH tests **Remedies:** ■ Earthworms ■ Compost ■ Seaweed meal ■ Liquid seaweed (foliar spray)
Calcium (Ca) *Too little*	Calcium is necessary for water uptake and proper cell development and division. Newer, upper leaves turn dark green, sometimes curl upward, and leaf edges yellow. Weak stems, poor growth, early fruit drop, fruit cracking. Fruits develop water-soaked decaying spots at the blossom end. Examples are Blossom End Rot in tomato, Tip Burn in lettuce, Black Heart in celery, and Baldwin Spot in apple and pear flesh (brown spots under the skin and bitter flesh).	**Diagnostic Tools:** Soil and pH tests **Remedies:** ■ Earthworms ■ Compost ■ Ground limestone (slow release), applied once in the fall ■ Ground oyster shells (slow release) ■ Crumbled egg shells (slow release) ■ Avoid fertilizers high in nitrogen and potassium ■ Wood ashes, applied once in spring *Avoid:* Quick lime, slake lime, hydrated lime

Problem	Symptoms/Where it Occurs	Diagnostic Tools/Remedies
Boron (B) *Too little*	**Where:** Present in acidic, leached, very dry soils, or soils high in potassium. Boron is important for cell wall formation and carbohydrate transport. Bushy growth from lower stems. Newer shoots curl inward, turn dark, and die. Young leaves turn purple-black. Leaf ribs get brittle. Fruit develops cracks or dry spots. **Where:** Occurs in eastern U.S., especially in alkaline soils.	**Diagnostic Tools:** Soil and pH tests **Remedies:** ■ Granite dust (slow release) ■ Rock phosphate (slow release) ■ Liquid kelp foliar spray (fast acting) ■ Boric acid spray on newly opened fruit blossoms (.02 pound to 1 gallon water)
Iron (Fe) *Too little*	Iron is important for chlorophyll formation. Similar to nitrogen deficiency, but leaf yellowing is between the veins and starts first on upper, not lower, leaves. **Where:** Occurs often in soils with pH above 6.8.	**Diagnostic Tools:** Soil and pH tests **Remedies:** ■ Compost ■ Lower soil pH to 6.8 or less ■ Add peat moss manure (lowers pH) ■ Glauconite (source of iron) ■ Greensand (source of iron)
Acid Soil *pH below 6.0*	Nitrogen, phosphorous, and other nutrient deficiencies appear because an acid medium makes them less biologically available. The plant performs poorly and exhibits multiple symptoms. Excess aluminum and manganese, because an acid medium makes these more biologically available. **Where:** Common in areas with acid rain, especially in the Northeast.	**Diagnostic Tools:** Soil and pH tests **Remedies:** ■ Earthworms ■ Compost ■ Ground dolomitic limestone (slow release, contains magnesium and calcium) ■ Ground calcitic limestone (slow release, no magnesium and calcium) ■ Wood ashes (fast release, caustic) ■ Organic material, because lime speeds decomposition of organic matter
Alkaline Soil *pH above 7.0*	Micronutrient deficiencies. Poor plant performance.	**Diagnostic Tools:** Soil and pH tests **Remedies:** ■ Earthworms ■ Compost and other organic materials ■ Gypsum (calcium sulphate) ■ Aluminium sulphate ■ Powdered sulphur
Drainage *Too much* *Too little*	Sandy soils do not sufficiently retain water. Long-standing puddles. Slowly melting snow.	**Diagnostic Tools:** Dig a gallon-sized hole and fill with water. Let it drain, fill a second time with water, and time how long it takes the hole to drain. More than 8 hours indicates poor drainage. **Remedies (for both conditions):** ■ Earthworms ■ Compost or other organic matter (helps soil retain and drain water)

Problem	Symptoms/Where it Occurs	Diagnostic Tools/Remedies
Poor Ventilation	Plants wilt due to heat stress. Dew dries very slowly. Mold, moss, mildew, and other symptoms of too much moisture.	**Remedies:** ■ Stake plants, or use some support structure to keep plant erect ■ Prune trees and plants; remove suckers between stem crotches ■ If the garden is too crowded, remove weakest, smallest, or least-desired plants
Ozone (O₃) (a major photochemical irritant in smog)	Plants become more brittle and generally attract more insects. One theory suggests ozone alters amino acid and sugar levels, making the plant more attractive to pests.	**Remedies:** ■ No known remedy for smog pollution. If gardening in a smog-polluted area, do everything possible to maintain soil and plant health, and don't assume that the plant is diseased.

*For more detailed information on remedies, see the *Glossary of Organic Remedies* on pages 165–172.

Micro- and Macropests

Microdestructive agents are called micro because they cannot be seen by the naked human eye. They include fungi, bacteria, and viruses. By contrast, macrodestructive agents are those you can visibly see and identify, from whiteflies to deer.

Identification of macropests is much easier and normally possible without the aid of a professional. Micropests are another matter. A definitive diagnosis of most microscopic organisms cannot be made without specialized training, and sometimes, without laboratory tests. The difficulty is compounded by the fact that microscopic organisms share numerous symptoms. Several broad differences do exist. A fungus infection frequently results in mold growth, whereas bacteria may cause bad-smelling plant parts. Mottled coloring in the leaves is often a symptom of a virus. These differences are not reliable for diagnosis, however, because they don't always accompany the disease. When a definitive diagnosis is necessary, consult a trained professional.

The Blue-Cheese Syndrome. A garden is much like blue cheese, that contains about thirteen critical microorganisms which produce its distinctive taste and texture. In blue cheese, about half of these are fungal, half bacterial. Similarly, every garden contains a wide variety of micro- and macroorganisms, all acting and interacting to produce healthiness or disease. In the advanced stages of disease, therefore, there is probably no such thing as a "pure" infection by a single organism or even a single family of organisms. Disease is usually promoted by a host of factors, from nutrients to microbial activity. Once a plant is weakened, it can be attacked by several different organisms simultaneously.

The good news is that some organic remedies are broad-spectrum; they help attenuate different types of diseases. Many of these remedies are also the same good preventive practices mentioned previously — such as ensuring good soil drainage, or watering from below to prevent further contamination through water droplets. One of the most basic broad-spectrum remedies is to remove and destroy diseased leaves, fruit, branches, or plants. The lesson here is that once the basics have been ruled out — and disease has been ruled in — a thorough and accurate diagnosis of the major pathogens responsible for the disease may not be necessary if the broad-spectrum remedies work.

Differential diagnosis is important, however, when insect vectors play a role, for the insects then can be controlled. A differential diagnosis is also especially critical any time the gardener wants to use remedies specific to a particular disease, such as a botanical, mineral, or other chemical spray. Finally, a large-scale or commercial gardener who has constraints far beyond that of the backyard gardener usually must seek professional help with diagnosis before implementing remedies.

The following is only a broad outline of micro- and macroagents, symptoms, and promoting factors and remedies. It is neither a definitive list nor a substitute for professional advice or textbooks. A single plant may exhibit only one or multiple symptoms. And, there are occasional exceptions to the promoting factors and remedies. Remember, most of the remedies listed are also the same good *preventive* garden practices discussed in the preceding sections on the First and the Second Lines of Defense.

Overview of Symptoms and Remedies

	Symptoms	Promoting Factors/Remedies

Fungal Diseases	*Fungal-specific symptoms:* Mold on any plant part; may be fuzzy, flat, or colored. This group of diseases also includes the Blights, which are characterized by rapid withering or tissue decay with no apparent rotting. The Blights are perhaps the most difficult to identify because they can mimic each other and often deviate from specific symptoms.
	
	Spots (on leaves, stems or bark, or fruit and flowers): watery, soft, sunken, dry, shriveled, colored.
	
	Leaves: Yellowed, wilted, fallen, defoliation, curled, wrinkled.
	
	Fruit: Shriveled, misshapen.
	
	Flowers: Spots, discolored petals.
	
	Stems: Rot (decay), sunken areas, girdling, watery blisters, and other types of cankers, cracks, and dark swellings.
	
	Roots: Rot (decay), discoloration, knots, cankers.
		Promoting Factors Usually fostered and spread by prolonged periods of rain, moisture, dew, humidity. Spread by tools, gardeners, wind, seeds (sometimes), and insects. Can be soil-borne, and harbored in plant debris. Some fungal pathogens can live up to 15 years in the soil.
		
		Immediate Remedies
		■ Remove and destroy diseased plants, or parts of plants.
		■ Water from below.
		■ Don't touch plants when wet, to avoid spreading disease.
		■ Disinfect hands after working with diseased plants.
		■ Disinfect tools between cuts.
		■ Improve ventilation.
		■ Keep orchard grass mowed.
		■ Spray fruit trees with liquid seaweed every 2 to 3 weeks, to prevent spread of fungus; this coats fruits with a protective filament.
		■ For some fungal problems, you can spray with copper-based fungicides, Bordeaux mixture, sulfur, or lime-sulfur. Never use sulfur on apricots or high doses on *cucurbits,* which are sensitive to sulfur and will be injured. Copper can kill earthworms.
		■ For certain fruit tree fungi, follow a spray program starting in spring when the tree is dormant, such as that recommended by Necessary Trading Company (*see* Appendix C).
		■ Find out which spray is appropriate for the disease.
		
		Long-Range Remedies
		■ Import earthworms.
		■ Compost.
		■ Use long crop rotations of 3 to 5 years for all the fungal wilts.
		■ Plant in a well-drained area.
		■ Solarize garden soil (especially effective for controlling verticillium wilt).
		■ Select resistant varieties.
		■ Where recommended, use hot water seed treatment as follows:
		    Brassicas — place seeds in water at 122°F for 25 minutes.
		    Solanaceae — 122°F for 30 minutes.
		    Celery — 118°F for 30 minutes.
		■ For fruit trees, paint trunk and lower limbs to reduce cold injury, because disease spreads through injury.
		■ Don't prune trees until buds swell, because disease may spread through dead buds and bark cuts.
		■ Prune limbs or canes 4" below the infection (cankers, galls), and disinfect tools between cuts.
		■ Increase organic matter in soil to discourage wilts.
		■ Store harvested produce in well-ventilated, cool, dry areas.
		■ To heal the soil where diseased plants have been removed, the application of soil taken from underneath birch trees or surrounding birch roots is thought to have beneficial effects.

	Symptoms	**Promoting Factors/Remedies**
Bacterial Diseases	*Bacteria-specific symptoms:* Bad smells associated with fruit, roots, stems, or leaves.	**Promoting Factors** Usually spread by rain and some beetles (e.g., cucumber beetles, flea beetles).

Bacterial Diseases

Bacteria-specific symptoms: Bad smells associated with fruit, roots, stems, or leaves.

Circular and angular spots (on leaves, stems and bark): Sunken, raised, and water-soaked tissue may drop out of spots, leaving holes.

Leaves: Yellowed, curled, wilted, stunted.

Fruit: Slimy, spots.

Blossoms: Withered, dead.

Stems: Lesions, wilted, blackened, dead, wartlike growth, oozing.

Roots: Soft, slimy.

Promoting Factors Usually spread by rain and some beetles (e.g., cucumber beetles, flea beetles).

Immediate Remedies
- Apply insecticidal soap spray at specific site of infection.
- Remove and destroy infected plants.
- Disinfect tools.
- Don't touch plants when wet.
- Clean cultivation.
- For trees, prune out infected parts, disinfect tools between cuts, and destroy removed parts.
- Where severe, remove and destroy tree. If feasible, solarize soil.
- Where recommended (usually for fruit trees), spray with a copper-sulfur blend. (This can kill earthworms.)
- Where recommended (usually for vegetables), apply micronized sulfur.

Long-Range Remedies
- Import earthworms.
- Compost.
- Plant resistant varieties.
- Crop rotation.
- Hot water seed treatment:
  Carrots — 122°F for 10 minutes
  Solanaceae — 122°F for 25 minutes
- In the East, use seed grown west of the Rockies (free of bacterial blight).
- Improve soil drainage.

Viral Diseases

Virus-specific symptoms: Mottled coloring in leaves.

Leaves: Mottled coloring; misshapen growth; yellowing; curling downwards; crinkling; unusual narrow, pointed, or fernlike leaves; veins may disappear.

Fruits: Misshapen, premature ripening.

Blossoms or flowers: Misshapen, underdeveloped, few.

Stems: Stunted, twisted, misshapen.

Promoting Factors Usually spread by insect or human vectors (e.g., aphids, cucumber beetles, grasshoppers, leafhoppers, thrips, smokers for tobacco mosaic, human hands, and tools).

Immediate Remedies
- Control insect vector.
- Disinfect tools and hands before working with plants.
- Remove and destroy infected plants, or parts of plants.
- Clean cultivation.

Long-Range Remedies
- Import earthworms.
- Compost.
- Plant resistant varieties.
- Remove weeds that harbor insect vectors.
- Plant in areas protected from wind to minimize aphid contamination.
- Use closer spacing where leafhoppers are a problem.

Insect Pests

Visible presence of insect (but those that suck plant juices are harder to spot).

Immediate Remedies
- Handpick bugs off plants.
- Remove and destroy eggs.
- Use traps, most are insect-specific.
- Mulch, where appropriate.
- Remove and destroy heavily infested plants.

Symptoms	Promoting Factors/Remedies
Insect Pests *(continued)*	

Insect Pests *(continued)*

Leaves: Chewed or ragged holes, defoliation, tunnels, blotches, skeletonization, wilting, webbing, leaf drop, eggs on upper or lower leaf sides.

Fruit: Small, round- or other-shaped holes, premature drop.

Flowers: Malformed.

Stems and bark: Holes or sunken area, severed, weak, stunted or distorted, wilted.

Roots: Malformed, poorly developed, eaten, decay in storage.

■ Clean cultivation.
■ Where appropriate, apply sprays of insecticidal soaps, oils, etc.
■ Spray fruit trees with liquid seaweed every 2 to 3 weeks, which masks fruit scent and protects the trees against insect damage.

Long-Range Remedies
■ Import earthworms.
■ Compost.
■ Plant resistant varieties.
■ Use row covers before pest emerges.
■ Use fall cultivation.
■ Encourage insect-eating birds and other beneficial animals.
■ Solarize soil, if feasible.

(Note: For more detailed information on remedies, see the following *Glossary.)*

A Glossary of Organic Remedies

The following is a detailed description of the common remedies for micro- and macropests that are referred to in the charts in abreviated form. Suppliers of these remedies are listed in Appendix C.

Bacillus thuringiensis (Bt). Something akin to the wonder drug of organic growing, Bt is a bacterium that was discovered in 1901. It comes in a powder form that is biodegradable and alleged to be so safe that it can be sprayed or dusted right up to the day of harvest. It works by paralyzing the insect's gut. Bt specifically kills leaf-eating caterpillars and leaves unharmed other insects, animals, and birds. Now, new strains of Bt are being isolated which target specific larvae, such as the new M-One that attacks Colorado potato beetle larvae.

☛ ***Warning:*** As with any "antibiotic," legitimate concern exists that exclusive or immoderate use of Bt will foster Bt-resistant pests in future generations. In fact, such resistance has already been confirmed in at least one moth pest. Many specialists, however, believe that if such problems develop, new strains of Bt can be developed to conquer the newly resistant pests. This argument, of course, was the very same as that used by pharmaceutical companies about new forms of penicillin to combat penicillin-resistant bacteria. What is generally not realized is that, although new forms of penicillin were successfully developed, the toxicity to humans of the newer penicillins exceeded the original by ten to twelve times. The allergic response to the original penicillin was less than 1 percent and "improved penicillins" run up to 10 to 20 percent *severe* allergic responses. As a consequence, noncommercial growers may decide, like we did, not to use Bt, or if necessary to use it only as a last resort.

Beneficial nematodes. Unlike the various nematodes that cause damage, beneficial nematodes such as *Neoplectana carpocapsae* are a fast and totally safe control for various pests. A number of species and varieties of beneficial nematodes exist. As juvenile-stage microscopic organisms, these parasites inject the insect with bacteria that kill the host within 24 hours. They don't harm humans, plants, pets, birds, earthworms, honeybees, or beneficial insects. A self-limiting control, they seek out soil grubs (young phase of certain insects), feed, reproduce and, when their food supply is exhausted, die. Only effective in the juvenile stage, these nematodes can be stored in the refrigerator for up to 2 months.

Beneficial nematodes must be applied at sufficient rates to be effective, about 50,000 per foot of standard row, or per square foot in raised beds. Numerous destructive pests are susceptible to these nematodes, including borers, weevils, cutworms, cucumber beetles, and even gypsy moths. One quart is sufficient for about 50 square feet and sells for about five dollars —just sprinkle the mixture where the pests are a problem. Also, one source suggests using nemotodes in compost heaps to eradicate harmful larvae.

Beneficial insects and plants. Beneficial insects are attracted to flowering *Umbelliferae*, such as dill and carrots in their second year, yarrow, sweet cicely, and fennel. For more information on beneficials, please see pages 151 and 5 to 6. The Henry Doubleday Research Association in Coventry, England, has shown that the following beneficial insects are attracted to the noted plants:

- Hover fly — pot marigolds, *Nemophilia*, bush morning glory, poached-egg plant *(Limnanthes douglasii)*

- Parasitic wasps and flies — yarrow *(Achillea)*, flowering fennel and carrots, angelica

- Lacewings and parasitic wasps — mustard

Botanical controls. These are insecticides that are derived from naturally occurring sources, and are considered "organic" by many people because of their alleged lack of persistence in the environment. Botanicals are also generally thought to be relatively safe for birds, pets, humans and other wildlife. Some of the new synthesized chemicals, however — which are not considered organic — seem to be gentler on beneficial insects in and above the soil than some of the older "organic" sprays. Minerals, such as copper, are not strictly speaking botanicals, but they are included under this rubric for easy reference.

WARNING: WHAT GOES UP MUST COME DOWN

Remember that substances that may damage insects above the soil may also damage beneficial organisms in the soil. Such remedies may treat the plant at the expense of the ecosystem. Wherever possible, we have noted the possible effects remedies may have on beneficial organisms above and in the soil.

Some perspective may be important. Most garden vegetable plants last for a year, whereas the soil takes years to build into a healthy medium. If you drive out beneficial organisms in order to get rid of a pest problem one year and harm the soil in the process, there is a distinct possibility that your garden will have even more problems the following year — and require even more remedial measures. This is the kind of vicious cycle that leads to open-field hydroponics, discussed on pages 1 to 2.

Although there may be times you wish to use these remedies to save some plants, we urge you to do so with consideration for the soil. This means applying the remedy in the smallest effective quantities, and in the smallest area necessary for control. Massive preventive spraying is usually neither necessary nor recommended for the backyard gardener. Commercial growers and orchardists may have no choice at the moment, but the backyard gardener does.

☞ **Warning:** No insecticide — botanicals included — should be used unless your crops have suffered significant damage. Regardless of how safe the insecticide is reputed to be, the introduction of botanical poisons, minerals, or other substances alters your garden's natural system of checks and balances. Rotenone and pyrethrins can kill beneficial organisms in and above the soil just as easily as the pests you're trying to eradicate. Ryania and sabadilla are somewhat less treacherous to beneficial insects. "Significant damage" is a matter of personal interpretation. But, bear in mind that most plants can lose up to 20 percent of their foliage and still produce yields equal to those of plants with no foliage loss.

Even when significant damage occurs, you might consider the size of the area you will need to spray and the value of your crop, compared to the potential damage to the ecology of the rest of your garden.

At all times insecticides and fungicides should be used as an absolute last resort, after all other methods have failed. When used, apply the botanical control just to the leaves, plants, or areas that are affected, and at the minimal concentrations necessary to do the job.

For more information, see the information that follows about copper, neem, pyrethrum, rotenone, ryania, and sabadilla.

Bug Juice. Considered an old home remedy, this may or may not be effective. It is thought that some insects release a pheromone upon death to warn their kind away. But, this practice might also help spread disease to other plants. If you wish to try it experimentally, capture ½ cup of the pest, crush it, and liquefy it with 2 cups of water. Strain to remove particles for spraying. Do not use a household blender — use an old blender jar, or mortar and pestle specifically for garden use. Spray both sides of leaves and stems.

Clean Cultivation. *See* **Plant Maintenance** on page 155. Generally, clean cultivation means you should remove and destroy all infected plants or parts of plants, and clean out weeds, dead and rotting vegetation, piles of junk, and plants that are finished bearing. Destroy diseased plants by burning (where permitted), burial, or some other appropriate means. Remove stagnant pools of water or piles of brush, lumber, or stones near the garden. Don't work around or touch wet plants, particularly when they're diseased. Don't add diseased plant material to compost piles.

> ## BAD TIMES FOR APPLYING PESTICIDES
>
> Pesticides such as botanicals and homemade sprays, soaps, and oils should not be applied under *any* of the following conditions.
>
> - In the rain
> - In windy conditions
> - In intense sunlight
> - In the middle of hot, dry days (pesticide may volatilize before reaching insect or leaf)
> - When mixed with non-compatible materials
> - On open blossoms, when bees are present
> - When plant is moisture-stressed (too much or too little)
> - When leaf is wet with dew (unless such moisture is specifically recommended to assist adherence)

Cooking Oil Spray Mix. The USDA recommends the following home oil spray for controlling aphids, white flies, and spider mites: 1) Mix 1 tablespoon of plain dishwashing liquid detergent with 1 cup of cooking oil; 2) Add 1 to 2½ teaspoons of this oil/detergent solution to 1 cup of water; 3) Spray directly onto plants every 10 days.

The USDA finds this spray works well on carrots, celery, cucumber, eggplant, lettuce, pepper, and watermelon, but may burn squash, cauliflower, and red cabbage.

Copper. (*See* the warning included under **Botanical Controls.**) Copper is usually considered a fungicide, and can be dusted, sprayed, or combined with other substances, such as rotenone. It is an effective control of fungal and bacterial diseases such as anthracnose, all blights, brown rot, downy and powdery mildews, leaf spot, rust, and scab. The main problem with using copper in a self-sustaining garden is that it has been shown to kill earthworms through drips and fallen leaves. For a more detailed discussion of the effects of copper and other substances on earthworms, *see The Earthworm Book* by Jerry Minnich (listed in Bibliography).

Crop Rotation. At a minimum, plant the same vegetable in the same soil site only once every other year — rotating on a 2-year basis. Some diseases require a longer minimum rotation. "Same soil site" is defined as within a radius of 10 feet from where the vegetable was previously planted. So rotation could occur within the same growing bed as long as the new site is at least 10 feet away from where the same crop was the previous year, or from where there is refuse from the planting. If possible, routinely rotate on a 3- to 5-year basis.

Diatomaceous Earth (DE). This is an insect remedy with very low toxicity. Diatomaceous earth is a hydrophilic (water-loving) form of silicon dioxide (sand) that rapidly takes up water. Harvested from riverbeds, it is made of petrified skeletons of water-dwelling microorganisms known as diatoms. It works by desiccating insects.

Apply a dusting of diatomaceous earth after a light rain, dew, or after lightly spraying plants with water. Dust all plant surfaces, starting from the base and moving upward. You can also spray diatomaceous earth in a weak insecticidal soap solution (¼ pound DE to 5 gallons water to 1 teaspoon insecticidal soap), which helps the spray adhere to plant surfaces. Fruit trees can be painted with the the same solution. Whether dusted or sprayed, reapply after rainfall. DE is effective against most soft-bodied insects (aphids, mites, slugs, etc.), but also may work with some beetles and weevils.

Fall Cultivation. Leave the soil completely bare for a few days. Cultivate soil to a depth of 6 to 8 inches to expose eggs and larvae for birds and other predators. Two weeks later, lightly cultivate the soil a second time with a rake, this time only 2 inches deep. Leave bare for a few more days, then plant a cover crop, or apply a layer of winter mulch 4 to 6 inches deep.

Garlic Spray. This falls into the category of old-home remedies, which means it may or may not work for you. Garlic has been found to have some antifungal properties (*see* the **Other Benefits** listed for garlic on page 130), but the methods of extraction and quantities necessary haven't been widely tested. This spray should be treated as experimental. *See* **Hot Pepper Spray,** for ideas on how to prepare garlic spray.

☞ *Warning:* Earthworms will not eat onion family plants, so this spray could drive them away from the area sprayed.

Greenhouse Grower Warning. Studies have shown that the residues of some pesticides may linger longer than specified when used in greenhouses. Therefore, safe reentry time may be longer than expected. Greenhouse growers should contact the manufacturer to see if the pesticide has been tested under conditions similar to those in your greenhouse.

Handpick. This is often the most effective control. Use gloves at all times to prevent allergic reactions. To kill bugs, drop them into soapy water, boiling water, or water that has some insecticidal soap in it. Small amounts of kerosene or oil work, but are harder to dispose of in an ecologically safe way.

Horticultural Oil. The two horticultural grades of oil work by suffocating mature insects, larvae, and eggs. The older and heavier grade of horticultural oil, sometimes called dormant oil, is applied to fruit trees in early spring or fall while the trees are still dormant. If applied to large areas of a plant, foliage oil can severely injure or kill the plant by clogging leaf pores, thereby preventing respiration. The newer and lighter grades of horticultural oil, sometimes called superior horticultural oil, are less injurious to some plants because they evaporate more quickly. They can be used up to one month before harvest, as long as soil moisture is adequate, relative humidity favors evaporation, and the plant is relatively healthy. Woody ornamentals are most likely to tolerate this oil in their foliage state. To test whether a plant will tolerate the superior oil, spray it on a few leaves. After several days, leaf tips and margins will yellow if the plant is damaged by the oil. Horticultural oils are considered relatively safe to humans and other warm-blooded animals and to beneficial insects.

Hot Pepper Spray. Red peppers have been shown to contain an active ingredient called capsaicin that repels onion fly maggots when as little as one milligram was sprinkled around the plant base. It is also thought to be effective against other insects as well. It apparently does not work well in monocultures, but works well in gardens with a variety of plants where insects have a choice of feeding sites. Capsaicin kills nerve fibers in mammals, so it may be effective against insect pests by affecting their nervous system. Capsaicin is available commercially, or you can make your own.

Following are two recipes.

(1) Chop, grind, or blend hot peppers. Mix ½ cup of ground hot peppers with 2 cups of water. Strain to remove particles.

(2) Mix together 2 tablespoons garlic powder; 1 to 2 tablespoons tabasco sauce or Louisiana hot sauce; dash of liquid dishwashing detergent; and 2 cups of water. Because of the soap, the spray sticks better to leaves and bugs and works well against many soft-bodied insects such as aphids, white flies, mealy bugs, and most larvae (except that of gypsy moth). This effective recipe is from horticulturist Carl Totemeier, Ph.D.

Application: spray the plant twice, with an interval of two to three days in between. The spray must make physical contact with the pest to be effective. Pepper spray usually repels — not kills — the bugs.

☞ *Warning:* The effects of capsaicin on beneficial insects and earthworms are not well-known.

Hot Water Seed Treatment. Place seeds in a cheesecloth bag; place bag in water at the designated temperature. Stir continuously, adding hot water periodically to keep water temperature even. Don't pour hot water directly on the seeds. When finished, remove the seeds and immerse them in cold water. Drain and dry.

Insecticidal Soap Spray. This is not the same thing as homemade soap; it is not effective for household cleaning. Insecticidal soap is based on fatty acid salts that penetrate insect cell membranes. They work best on soft-bodied insects such as aphids, mealybugs, mites, and whiteflies. It biodegrades in two to fourteen days, and the residue on the plant is considered ineffective once dry.

Insecticidal soaps are specifically formulated to attack only harmful pests and, unless specified, are not harmful to pets, humans, or most beneficial insects. In fact, they have been used in conjunction with beneficials such as *Encarsia formosa* and ladybug larvae. Insecticidal soaps are better for plants than household soap sprays are because they usually won't burn plant leaves, lack the added ingredients of household soaps, and have active ingredients (fatty acid salts) present in known quantities. Any phytotoxic symptoms appear within the first 48 hours of spraying, so if you're unsure whether the soap will burn or injure a plant, test it on just a few leaves and wait for two days to see if wilting, yellowing, or other symptoms of burn appear.

Insecticidal soap only works on contact, so it must be sprayed directly on the pest. Spray only those areas affected by the pest, not the entire patch of plants — not necessarily even the entire plant. Coat all sides of the infested plant surfaces. This is called spot spraying.

Insecticidal soap is generally not very effective against hard-bodied insects, but the addition of isopropyl alcohol increases its effectiveness because the alcohol carries the soap through the pest's protective coating to its body. Add ½ cup isopropyl alcohol to every 4 cups of insecticidal soap. Some commercial insecticidal soaps come premixed with some alcohol, even though they may not advertise this fact.

Don't spray insecticidal soap at temperatures over 90°F or in the full sun. Don't spray newly rooted cuttings, new transplants, or blooming fruit and nut trees. It's best to spray in the early morning. Rinse all soap residues off any plant that begins to wilt in the first few hours after spraying.

Neem. Available under various labels such as Margosan-O, Bioneem, Neemisis, neem is a relatively new botanical insecticide derived from the neem tree of arid, tropical zones in Asia and Africa. The active ingredient — azadirachtin — is unlike most other botanical poisons which act on the stomach or nerves. Neem acts as a feeding deterrent and interrupts normal hormonal activity so that insects cannot molt properly; they die in their own skin. Neem does not persist in the soil and is not known to be toxic to mammals, birds, or beneficial insects, including honeybees. It has been found to be effective against the Colorado potato beetle, gypsy moth, grasshopper, Japanese beetle, and Mexican bean beetle.

Pyrethrum. (*See* the warning included under **Botanical Controls.**) This botanical poison is derived from the pyrethrum flower, a member of the chrysanthemum family. This is considered a "knockout" contact insecticide and stomach poison which works by paralyzing the insect. If the insect receives less than a lethal dose, however, it may revive. Pyrethrum is considered safe for warm-blooded animals and relatively safe for honeybees and ladybug larvae, but only because it degrades within six hours in temperatures over 55°F. It is often used in combination with Rotenone, and is effective against most greenhouse pests, especially flying insects such as whitefly. Use this one with extra special caution; if possible, use ryania or sabadilla before using pyrethrum. Spray at dusk when honeybees are less active, and don't spray at all if a heavy dew is expected. The foliar spray is considered less harmful to bees than the dust application.

Rotenone. (*See* the warning included under **Botanical Controls.**) A botanical poison refined from the root of a tropical plant. It can also be found in the roots (5 percent concentration) of a native weed, Devil's shoestring (*Tephrasis virginiana*), which Native Americans have used as a fish poison. It is used at two concentrations, one percent for the more easily killed insects, and five percent for the more difficult bugs. It kills beneficial insects just as easily as harmful insects and is extremely toxic to fish. If possible, use ryania or sabadilla before using rotenone. It degrades within three to seven days in the presence of light and oxygen.

Row Covers. Row covers are an extremely effective prevention against egg-laying insects. They are made of light-weight material that lets in air, light, and water. Cover your transplants immediately or when specified for pest emergence times. Seal edges to the ground and leave on all season, unless otherwise noted. Allow extra material to accommodate the growth of the tallest plant covered. For plants that need pollination, such as most cucumbers, you can lift the edges of the row covers during bloom time for two hours in the early morning, twice a week. This is all the time bees and other pollinators need to do their good work. When the blooming time is past, secure the row cover edges again until harvest time.

Note: Do not use row covers if the pest was seen in that spot the previous season and it overwinters or lays eggs in the soil. Also, row covers usually raise the temperature underneath, which is helpful for extending your growing season in spring and fall. However, if you plan to keep the covers on through the warm season — especially if you live in one of the southern growing zones — the temperature rise may not be beneficial to plants that don't tolerate heat well. Tufbel is reputed to be one of the best row covers. The suppliers listed in Appendix C offer a variety of row covers.

Ryania. (*See* the warning included under **Botanical Controls.**) This is a botanical poison refined from the South American ryania shrub. As a contact and stomach poison, it controls pests by making them extremely sick. It is considered safe to humans and other warm-blooded animals and plants. It is also considered less toxic to beneficial insects — including honeybees — than other botanical controls. The foliar spray is less harmful to bees than the dust application. Ryania degrades quickly, so it can be used close to harvest.

Sabadilla. (*See* the warning included under **Botanical Controls.**) This botanical poison is derived from the seeds of a South American lily. A very old insecticide dating back to the 16th century, Sabadilla is a powerful contact and stomach poison. It is considered somewhat less harmful than other botanicals are to beneficial insects, although honeybees are vulnerable. Applied as a dust, humans and pets may experience irritated mucous membranes and sneezing fits.

Soap Spray (homemade). This is not the same thing as insecticidal soap sprays (*see* listing). Tests of various types of household soap sprays show that they differ considerably in their effectiveness against bugs, and in the degree to which they burn plant leaves. Start off with 2 to 3 tablespoons of soap per gallon of water; never use more than 4 tablespoons, which will burn the plant leaves. Test different soaps to determine the brand and concentration needed to avoid burning the leaves. Another option is to rinse the plant one to two hours after you have sprayed; this should prevent harm to the plant but still affect the insects. Avoid soaps that are dyed or perfumed. Soap flakes, although harder to prepare, seem to be the least damaging to plants. Some liquid dishwashing soaps are mild enough to be left on the plant without rinsing. Soap spray is a contact insecticide (*see* **Insecticidal Soap Spray**).

☛ *Warning:* Unless you are absolutely sure that the home soap you use is biodegradable, you may do more harm than good if you spray it widely. Spot spraying, however, should not be a problem. Commercial manufacturers may label a kitchen soap "biodegradable," but the question is: Under what conditions and in how many years? The label may be appropriate for a septic tank, but whether the soap will biodegrade rapidly in the soil should be checked with the manufacturer. When in doubt, use an insecticidal soap that is designed to biodegrade rapidly and to target specific pests.

Soap and Lime Spray. Mix agricultural lime at the rate of ¼ to ½ cup per gallon of water. Add 2 to 3 tablespoons of insecticidal soap per gallon. The soap helps the lime adhere to insect bodies. The lime can dry out very small insects, kill some small insects and mites, and irritate adults. Test the spray first on a small area of the plant, since some plants may react adversely to these materials.

Wait several days before judging the results and deciding to spray the remainder of the plant. As with other soap sprays, you should spot spray to avoid harming beneficial insects.

Stem Collar. These are used to create a physical barrier to crawling pests. To make them, use wax paper cups, which don't fall apart easily in the rain, or some other weather-resistant material, such as cardboard or tar paper. To prepare the cups, cut a hole in the bottom of each one for the stem; cut slits radiating out from the hole to permit stem growth. Place inverted around the base of the stem. Sink the cup's edges at least 1 inch into the soil. For other materials, simply cut a 3 to 4 inch collar, push it 1 inch into the soil, and fasten the sides together securely. Toilet paper tubes work fine and eventually disintegrate.

Sticky Bands. Sticky bands are wrapped around tree trunks to trap larvae, egg-laying females, or other pests. Use wide cotton batting, burlap, or heavy paper — at least 6 inches wide. Place around the tree trunk at about chest height. Cover the batting with a 6 to 12 inch piece of tar paper coated with Tanglefoot, or with a mixture of either pine tar and molasses, or resin and oil. Wrap tightly and secure with wire or a tie. Renew the sticky substance periodically. If you're trapping larvae, remove the bands and destroy the larvae once a week in warm weather, or every 2 weeks in cool weather. If you're trapping a crawling insect that is not bearing or laying eggs (e.g., aphids), clean as necessary and renew the sticky substance.

Sticky Balls. These traps may be best as an early-warning device to detect the presence of pests in sufficient numbers to require other action. Usually red, these balls are hung in trees as both early warning and control devices. As a monitoring device, count the pests trapped every two to three days and recoat the ball every two weeks. As a pest control, use one to four balls per tree, depending on the tree size; clean and recoat as needed; and remove all balls after four weeks to avoid catching too many beneficial insects.

Sticky Traps. These traps may work best as an early warning device to detect the presence of pests in sufficient numbers to require other action. For monitoring, count the pests trapped every two to three days; recoat the traps every two weeks. These traps are usually yellow or white boards, about 8x10 inches, coated with a sticky substance such as Tangle Trap or petroleum jelly. Do not use motor oil (recommended by some), because it will change the board's color. Place the traps adjacent to susceptible plants; do not place them above the plants. Clean and recoat as needed. Try not to use these more than three to four weeks at a time to avoid capturing more beneficial insects than are necessary. In a greenhouse, place the traps at the canopy height of the plants.

Synthetic Pesticides. Designed for quick results and long-lasting activity, synthetics are totally man-made poisons often acting on the nervous systems and digestive tracts of insects. Some synthetics are considered milder and less toxic than the more "natural" botanical poisons. They are considered less safe for organic growing, however, because their breakdown products often persist in the soil longer and are more toxic than their original formulation. Some synthetic pesticides persist so long that they can be found in soils more than 20 years after their application. Botanicals are favored in organic growing because they don't persist in the environment and their breakdown products are safer.

Traps. Traps are an easy, nontoxic way to monitor and control many different insects. They usually use pheromones and visual colors that attract the targeted bug. Monitoring is useful to determine when the insect emerges, where it comes from, and how many are present — before resorting to chemical remedies. Generally, traps are a safe and cost-effective tool for a self-sustaining garden. Traps are available for such insects as the slug, Japanese beetle, codling moth, gypsy moth, oriental fruit moth, corn earworm, cherry fruit fly and husk fly, apple maggot (*see* **Sticky Balls**), some scales, and more.

Some Caveats on Traps: Some traps that are not pheromone-specific may capture some beneficial insects along with the harmful ones; consequently, they shouldn't be left out longer than recommended. Some pheromone traps that work over long distances may actually attract more of the targeted insect to your garden than you already had. Some pheromone traps are best suited to large commercial operations. Before investing in traps, consult your supplier on your particular situation and whether traps are best placed in the garden or away from it.

Identifying and Remedying Specific Micro- and Macropests

The following two charts outline in detail how to identify and remedy a range of diseases, and the insect and animal pests that may affect your plants. However, these charts are not meant to discourage you; most diseases should not be a problem if you rotate crops, destroy diseased material from garden areas, use resistant varieties, and start with pathogen-free transplants. As for insects, most gardens experience very few — usually no more than three to five major pests. Proper controls adopted in a timely fashion should minimize major threats to your crops. Also, remember that plants can lose up to twenty percent of their foliage and still produce yields equal to those of plants with no foliage loss.

Only when you have made a positive identification of the microscopic destructive agent should you use remedies specific to that disease. Specific disease remedies, such as botanical sprays, are generally more injurious to the ecosystem than the broad-spectrum, preventive remedies discussed on pages 155–157. An application of a special remedy that doesn't target the appropriate disease is not only a waste of money and time, but potentially harmful to the plant and ecosystem. An antibacterial spray, for example, when used inappropriately could wipe out the beneficial bacteria above and in the soil. These balances in and above the soil take time to build, and should not be sacrificed lightly. If you are ready to spray or use some other pest-specific remedy, it's worth the time to first consult a textbook, extension agent, or other professional to ensure that you have correctly identified the pest.

Prevention is by far the best approach for both disease and insect control; it is most critical with diseases. Postinfection remedies for specific macropests are often more varied and usually include some easy, nontoxic methods that don't harm beneficials above or in the soil.

In these charts we have tried to avoid — or at least minimize — controls that might be difficult to administer, could potentially harm the earthworms and soil microorganisms, or could cause ecological imbalances in future years. Not everyone, however, agrees on the use of certain substances. Whenever in doubt, we have tried to err on the side of safety.

A WORD ABOUT WEEDS

It is often said a weed is any plant that grows where it is not desired. Some people keep meticulous gardens, weeding every last whisper of grass or dandelion green from the garden throughout the season. Research in north central California has shown that such meticulous care may not be necessary, and may even be harmful. Hoeing and other forms of weeding were shown — in some cases — to reduce yields. The research concluded that cucumbers, lettuce, and cauliflower need only two weeks of weeding in order to be well-established. A balanced approach to weeds, then, might be to weed meticulously during the first few weeks of plant establishment. Then follow your own aesthetic.

Another way to deal with weeds is to solarize your soil, which kills some weed seeds. Research studies have also found radish juice to be an effective herbicide; if you can find a source, radish juice added to the growing medium will completely inhibit germination of some important weed species.

Controlling Diseases

Notes On Using this Chart

Selection Criteria: The diseases in this chart were included only if they met the following criteria: (1) The remedies for the disease goes beyond the remedies mentioned in the earlier parts of this chapter (to avoid unnecessary repetition); (2) Insects are known to spread the disease organism (the disease may be attenuated by insect control); and (3) The disease organism is especially virulent and the affected plants need to be removed immediately.

Pathogens: Diseases in different plants may share a common name (e.g., bacterial wilt) but they are often caused by different pathogens. Consequently the "same" disease may have distinct symptoms in different plants. To make matters more difficult, sometimes even the same pathogen causes different symptoms in different species. To simplify matters for the backyard gardener, we group diseases by their common names and describe the different symptoms, where possible.

Remedies: In addition to the specific remedies listed in this chart, remember not to work with plants when wet, and to practice clean cultivation as described on page 167 — helpful remedies for many diseases.

☛ **Warning:** Diseases are much more difficult to diagnose accurately than insect pests. This chart is included primarily to indicate how serious a problem disease identification may be, given the similar symptoms shared by a wide variety of diseases, and to help you conduct a more informed discussion with professionals. It is not intended to be a final diagnostic tool. Before you use botanical or other sprays, or institute large-scale or costly remedies, it is vital that you make an accurate diagnosis. The following precautions are strongly urged: (1) If attempting a diagnosis on your own, read the descriptions for all possible diseases listed in the plant entry; don't stop at the first one that seems to match the symptoms of your plant; (2) Because this chart presents a *selection* of diseases, consult other texts as well, listed in the **Bibliography**; (3) When in doubt, take a plant sample to a local professional to obtain a diagnosis.

Disease Plants Affected	Description of Symptoms How It is Spread/Where It Occurs	Organic Remedies
Armillaria Root Rot (also known as: Honey Mushroom, Mushroom Root Rot, Oak Root Fungus, Shoestring Fungus) *Fruit trees* *Nut trees* *Ornamentals*	**Fungus:** White, fan-shaped fungus appears between the bark and wood. Lower trunk decays. Crown is girdled by fungus. Mushrooms appear in autumn around the plant base. Roots rot and die slowly. If stressed by other factors, the tree will die suddenly. Fungus spreads underground 1 foot at a time. **Where:** Occurs in western states, Atlantic coast, Florida, and Gulf Coast. Worst in heavy, poorly drained soils.	■ In mild cases: remove the soil around rotted trunk areas; cut out dead tissue; let trunk dry out through the summer and replace soil when a freeze approaches. ■ In severe cases: remove the plant, stump, and, if possible, the roots.
Asparagus Rust *Asparagus*	**Fungus:** Leaves and stems develop orange-red spots or blisters which, in time, burst open with orange-red spores. Tops yellow and die prematurely. Spread by wind and spores. **Where:** Widespread. Worst in moist seasons.	■ Cut, remove and destroy affected tops. ■ Do not start new plantings next to old plantings. ■ Destroy wild asparagus. ■ *See* last three remedies listed under **Bean Rust.**
Aster Yellows	*See* **Yellows**	*See* **Yellows**

Disease Plants Affected	**Description of Symptoms** How It is Spread/Where It Occurs	**Organic Remedies**
Bacterial Canker (also known as: Bacterial Blast, Bacterial Gummosis) *Almond* *Apricot* *Blueberry* *Cherry* *Peach* *Tomato*	**Bacteria:** *Almond, apricot, peach* — Small purple spots develop on leaves, black spots on fruits, and cankers on twigs. *Cherry* — Leaves wilt and die. Cracks and stems may ooze in spring and fall. Limbs may die. *Blueberry* — Stems develop reddish-brown to black cankers, and nearby buds die. Plants eventually die. *Tomato* — Oldest leaves turn downward first, leaflets curl and shrivel. Only one side may be affected. A stem cut lengthwise may reveal discoloration of creamy white to reddish-brown. Young infected fruits are stunted and distorted. Fruits may develop small, white round spots. Transmitted by wind, rain, infected seeds, and debris. It enters through skin wounds. **Where:** Widespread, especially in cool, windy, moist weather.	*Tomato* ▪ Hot water seed treatment at 122°F for 25 minutes. ▪ Plant resistant varieties or certified seed. ▪ Rotate crops. *Trees* ▪ Prune immediately. Between cuts disinfect tools and hands. If uncontrollable by pruning, destroy tree.
Bacterial Wilt (also known as in corn: Stewart's Disease) *Beans* *Corn* *Cucurbits* *Eggplant* *Tomato*	**Bacteria:** *Beans* — Seedlings usually die before 3 inches tall. Mature vines wilt, especially midday, and die. *Cucurbits* — Plants wilt rapidly and, even while green, can die. Cut stems produce oozy strings. This bacteria blocks the plant's vascular system. *Corn* — Plants may wilt, and leaves can develop long water-soaked or pale yellow streaks. A cut in the lower stem oozes yellowish droplets that can be drawn out into fine, small threads. *Tomato* — Plants wilt and die rapidly, starting with young leaves first. Lower foliage may yellow slightly. A lengthwise stem cut reveals an oozy gray-brown core. Transmitted in beans by seeds; in *cucurbits* by both cucumber beetles; in corn by the corn flea beetle. The pathogen affecting beans and tomatoes overwinters in debris. **Where:** *Corn* — Central, South, and East. *Solanaceae* — South. *Cucurbits* — Northeast and North Central states. Some wilts are fostered by moist soil and soil temperatures above 75°F.	▪ *Corn and cucurbits* — control the insect vector (*see* Description of Symptoms). ▪ Immediately remove and destroy infected plants. ▪ *Beans and tomato* — plant only certified wilt-free seeds. Rotate crops on a 4–5 year basis. Fumigate soil. ▪ Plant resistant varieties.
Bean Rust *Bean*	**Fungus:** Leaf undersides develop small, red-orange to brown blisters full of spores. Leaves yellow, dry, and drop prematurely. Spores are spread by wind and water. **Where:** Occurs along the Eastern seaboard and in irrigated areas in the West. Fostered by relative high humidity for 8–10 days.	▪ Don't reuse vine stakes. ▪ Use long crop rotations. ▪ If necessary, apply a sulfur spray every 7–10 days until 1 month before harvest. ▪ Use heavy mulch and drip (not overhead) irrigation to minimize spreading disease through splashing. ▪ Select resistant varieties.

Disease Plants Affected	Description of Symptoms How It is Spread/Where It Occurs	Organic Remedies
Black Heart *Celery* *Potato*	**Environmental:** *Celery* — A low calcium-potassium ratio causes spreading brown, water-soaked areas on leaves. *Potato* — Low oxygen levels at the tuber center cause purple, black or gray areas. **Where:** Widespread, but rare in the Northwest and north central states.	■ *Celery* — Make sure the soil contains adequate calcium. ■ *Potato* — Improve soil drainage to reduce chances of it recurring. Don't leave potatoes in or on very hot soil (over 90°F).
Black Knot *Apricot* *Cherry* *Plum*	**Fungus:** Coal black, hard swellings appear on twigs and limbs. Growths develop in late summer as olive green, then blacken. They can be 2–4 times the thickness of the branch. Limbs weaken. Trees die slowly. The disease is detected the year after infection. Spread by wind and rain. Harbored in the tree knots. **Where:** Occurs east of the Mississippi.	■ Cut off all twigs and branches at least 4 inches below swellings. Destroy cuttings. Cover wounds with paint or wax. ■ Remove all infected wild cherry and plum. ■ Where significant damage is expected, spray with a lime-sulfur or Bordeaux mix at the first bud stage. ■ Plant resistant varieties.
Blotch Disease (also known as: Sooty Blotch) *Apple* *Citrus* *Pear*	**Fungus:** Only skins are affected. Fruits are still edible. Mottled, irregular shaped spots (up to ¼") appear. "Cloudy fruit" has spots that run together. **Where:** Occurs in the eastern, central, and southern states to the Gulf of Mexico.	■ Scrub citrus fruit skins. ■ Peel skins off fruits other than citrus before eating. ■ Prune and space trees for better air circulation. ■ Prune and destroy infected twigs.
Canker Dieback *Apple* *Pecan*	**Fungus:** *Apple* — Watery blisters on bark. Oval dead patches (1"–1') may become sunken. Eventually leaves yellow. *Apple and pecan* — Branches wilt and die from the tip down. **Where:** Widespread. For apples, especially a problem in moist springs and early falls. For pecans, may be caused by inadequate water in winters or heavy soils with poor drainage.	■ Avoid wounding tree trunks and stems. ■ Cut off infected branches well below infection. ■ For small cankers, gouge out with sharp knife and treat with tree paint or Bordeaux paste. Disinfect tools between cuts. ■ Destroy all pruned matter. ■ *Pecan* — Ensure adequate drainage in hardpan soils, and deep watering in sandy soils.
Cedar Apple Rust *Apple* *Pear*	**Fungus:** Light yellow spots on leaves become bright orange spots. Fruits may also develop spots. Cedar Apple Rust has a 2-year life cycle. Transmitted in wind and rain by spores from red cedars and junipers. **Where:** Occurs in the eastern and central states, and Arkansas.	■ Remove all red cedars, junipers, wild apple, and ornamental apples within 300 yards of infected trees. **Or** plant a windbreak between the disease hosts and apple trees. ■ *See* the last three remedies listed under **Bean Rust.** (Copper may be used, but can harm earthworms.)
Celery Mosaic *Celery*	**Virus:** Leaves turn yellow and mottled green. Stalks are stunted, twisted and narrow.	■ Control aphids. ■ Destroy infected plants.

Disease Plants Affected	Description of Symptoms How It is Spread/Where It Occurs	Organic Remedies
Cherry Leaf Spot **and** **Plum Leaf Spot** (also known as: Yellow Leaf in cherry) *Cherry* *Plum*	**Fungus:** Purple spots on leaves, followed by bright yellow foliage. Spots often drop out of leaves, followed by defoliation. Heavy fruit drop in plums. Very damaging. Harbored in debris and spread by wind. **Where:** Occurs east of Rockies; particularly bad in warm, wet conditions.	▪ Destroy fallen leaves and fruit; pinch off infected leaves. ▪ A spray of wettable sulfur from petal fall to harvest is virtually the only control. ▪ Fall cultivation of soil — no more than 2 inches — reduces spore spread.
Common Mosaic *Beans*	**Virus:** Severely stunted plants with few pods. Mottled green, elongated leaves crinkle and curl downwards at the edges. Infection occurs usually near bloom time. Plants eventually die. Spread by aphids and gardeners. Overwinters in perennial weeds like Canadian thistle. **Where:** Widespread.	▪ Control aphids. ▪ Destroy infected plants, no matter how mildly affected. ▪ Remove all perennial weeds within 150 feet of the garden. ▪ Plant resistant varieties.
Cottony Rot (also known as: Pink Rot and Watery Soft Rot in cabbage, White Mold in beans) *Beans* *Cabbage* *Celery* *Lettuce*	**Fungus:** *General* — White mold develops, and small, hard black bodies form on or within the mold. *Beans* — Stems develop water-soaked spots, branches and leaves follow. White mold develops in these spots. *Cabbage and Lettuce* — Stem and leaves near ground become water-soaked, leaves wilt, and plant collapses. White mold grows on the head. *Celery* — White, cottony growth appears at stalk base. Stalks rot and taste bitter. Spread by small black bodies, which can survive in soil for up to 10 years. **Where:** Widespread. Most common in cool, moist conditions.	▪ Remove and destroy infected plants, if possible before black bodies form. ▪ Plant in well-drained soil; raised beds help greatly. ▪ *Beans and celery* — Where flood irrigation is feasible — usually in muck or sandy soil — flood the growing area for 4–8 weeks, or alternate flooding and drying, which kills the black bodies. ▪ Rotate with immune or resistant crops such as beets, onion, spinach, peanuts, corn, cereals, and grasses. Avoid successive plantings of beans, celery, lettuce, or cabbage.
Crown Gall *Almond* *Apple* *Apricot* *Blackberry* *Blueberry* *Cherry* *Filbert* *Grape* *Peach* *Pear* *Pecan* *Plum* *Raspberry* *Walnut*	**Bacteria:** Fruit trees and brambles weaken and produce small, poor fruit. Galls are swellings that circle roots and crowns, and sometimes are several inches in diameter. Galls can be spongy or hard. Plants can survive for many years but are very susceptible to other stresses. Transmitted through wounds in the roots, crowns, and stems by tools and soil water. **Where:** Widespread.	▪ *Brambles* — Destroy canes and plants with symptoms. ▪ *Trees* — Prune galls and treat with tree surgeon's paint or a bactericidal paint. Cover with soil after painting. Destroy infected portions. Disinfect hands and tools between cuts. ▪ Remove badly infected trees, trunks, and roots and destroy. Don't plant another susceptible tree in infected location for 3–5 years. ▪ Propagate fruit trees only by budding. ▪ Select resistant rootstocks. ▪ Use Gall-trol or Norbac 84-C at planting (competitive bacteria). ▪ Ensure good soil drainage.
Crown Rot	*See* **Southern Blight**	*See* **Southern Blight**

Disease Plants Affected	Description of Symptoms How It is Spread/Where It Occurs	Organic Remedies
Crown Rot *Almond* *Apple* *Cherry* *Pear*	**Fungus:** Late in the season one or more branches turn reddish. Leaves turn yellow or brown, and wilt. Dead bark tissue appears at the soil line, with sunken and sometimes girdling cankers. Like collar rots and damping off, this fungus attacks at or below the soil surface. **Where:** Widespread where trunks are wet at the soil line.	■ Rake soil away from tree crown and, if necessary, expose upper roots. This improves air circulation and may correct the problem. ■ Avoid standing water or continuously wet conditions around the trunk. ■ Allow soil to dry out thoroughly between watering. ■ Avoid deep planting of new young trees.
Cucumber Mosaic (also known as: CMV, Mosaic) (in spinach: Yellows) *Cucurbits* *Lettuce* *Pepper* *Potato* *Raspberry* *Spinach* *Tomato*	**Virus:** *General* — Yellow-green mottling and curled foliage. Plants are weak, stunted, may have few blossoms, poor fruit, and may die. Fruits are misshapen and mottled. Distorted leaves are common. *Pepper and Tomato* — Older leaves look like oak leaves and develop large yellowish ringspots. Affected leaves can drop prematurely. Fruits develop concentric rings and solid circular spots, first yellow then brown. Fruits flatten and roots are stunted. *Potato* — Tubers may develop brown spots, and the plant yellows and dies. *Raspberry* — Dry, seedless, crumbly fruit. Canes may droop, blacken, and die. *Cucurbits* — Leaf margins can curl downward, and cucumbers and summer squash fruits become mottled yellow-green. Spread by aphids (in *cucurbits,* lettuce, pepper, tomato) striped or spotted cucumber beetles (in *cucurbits),* and gardeners. It overwinters in many perennial weeds. **Where:** Widespread.	■ Control appropriate insect vector — aphids or cucumber beetles *(See Description of Symptoms.)* Apply row covers until blossom time to prevent aphids and cucumber beetles. ■ Remove and destroy infected plants and, if severe, surrounding plants. ■ Remove all perennial weeds within 150 feet of the garden. ■ Plant resistant varieties.
Curly Dwarf *Artichoke*	**Virus:** Stunted plants. Spread by aphids and leafhoppers. **Where:** Pacific coast and southern coast of Texas.	■ Control aphids and leafhoppers. ■ Remove and destroy all infected plants. ■ Remove all milk thistle and other nearby weeds.
Curly Top (CTV) (also known as: Western Yellow Blight in tomato) *Beans* *Beet* *Cucurbits* *Pepper* *Spinach* *Tomato*	**Virus:** *General* — Stunted plants have numerous small leaves that pucker, crinkle, curl, and yellow. Fruits are few, dwarfed, or may ripen prematurely. *Beans* — Leaves are also darker green. Young plants may die, but older plants usually survive. Plant produces few or dwarfed pods, and looks bushy. *Cucurbits* — Leaves may also be mottled. *Tomato* — Branches are also very erect; leaflet veins turn purple; plant turns a dull yellow. Spread by beet leafhoppers. **Where:** Widespread.	■ Control beet leafhoppers. ■ Apply row covers until blossom time to reduce leafhoppers. ■ Prune and destroy infected parts of plants immediately. If serious, remove and destroy all infected plants and all nearby plants. ■ Grow tomatoes away from beets, spinach, melons or other leafhopper hosts. Also, space them closely to discourage leafhoppers. ■ Select resistant varieties.

Disease Plants Affected	Description of Symptoms How It is Spread/Where It Occurs	Organic Remedies
Enation Mosaic (also known as: Pea Virus I, Leaf Enation) *Pea*	**Virus:** Young leaves become mottled. Leaf undersides develop small outgrowths known as enations. Vine tips become misshapen and internodal distance shortens. Stunted plants have few, if any, pods. Pods may have yellow seeds. Extremely damaging. Spread primarily by aphids; overwinters in various clovers, vetch, and alfalfa. **Where:** Widespread, but particularly a problem in the Northwest.	■ Control aphids. ■ Plant early to avoid high aphid populations. ■ Select resistant varieties.
Fire Blight *Apple* *Pear*	**Bacteria:** Infected shoots turn brown and black, as though scorched by fire. Lesions may ooze orange-brown liquid. Blossoms wither and die. Reddish, water-soaked lesions develop on bark. Spread by aphids, psylla, bees, and rain. Enters through blossoms or new growth. **Where:** Widespread, particularly in areas of high humidity, dew, and rain. Bacteria remain dormant through the winter inside cankers.	■ Control aphids and psylla. ■ Remove and destroy all suckers and infected branches. Research shows control is most effective when infected areas are removed as soon as seen, no matter what the season. Cut at least 12 inches below point of visible wilt. After each cut, disinfect tool in bleach solution (1:4 dilution). In winter, repeat and treat cuts with asphalt-based dressing. ■ Spray the tree regularly while in bloom with a solution of four percent Clorox (4 ounces Clorox in 3 gallons water). This sterilizes the blossoms so that the bees do not spread the blight. ■ Avoid heavy pruning or high nitrogen fertilizer. Both stimulate rapid twig growth. ■ Check soil acidity. The more acid the soil, the more prone to fire blight. ■ If significant damage occurs, spray with a copper-sulfur blend labeled for fire blight. ■ Plant resistant varieties.
Fusarium Wilt (also known as: Fusarium Yellows or Yellows) *Asparagus* *Brassicas* *Celery* *Lettuce* *Melon* *Pea* *Potato* *Spinach* *Sweet Potato* *Tomato* *Turnip* *Watermelon*	**Fungus:** *General* — Yellowing, stunting, and wilting (often rapid). Lower leaves may wilt first. Plants usually die, but seedlings can die quickly. In some plants, a sliced lower stem may reveal discoloration originating from the roots. *Celery* — Ribs also redden. *Muskmelon* — One side of the vine develops a water-soaked yellow streak near the soil line, which darkens to brown. *Potato* — In storage, blue or white swellings may develop on brown decayed areas. Spread by water, tools, and seeds. The disease can live in soil for 20 years. Thrives in warm, dry weather. **Where:** Widespread, but occurs mainly east of the Rockies. Worst in the South; in light, sandy soil; and in dry weather with temperatures of 60°–90°F. Temperatures above 90°F retard the disease.	■ Remove and destroy infected plants. ■ Ensure good soil drainage. ■ Don't plant susceptible crops for 8 years in places where fusarium was last seen; rotate crops on a regular basis as a preventive measure. ■ Solarize garden soil, where possible; sterilize potting soil. ■ Select resistant varieties — one of the best controls. ■ *Asparagus* — Use seed labeled "treated with a Clorox solution" (available in New Jersey).

Disease Plants Affected	Description of Symptoms How It is Spread/Where It Occurs	Organic Remedies
Leaf Blight (also known as: Bacterial Blight) *Carrot*	**Bacteria:** *Carrot* — Spots on seedling leaves start out yellow-white. In time they turn brown and look water-soaked. **Where:** Occurs in Arizona, Iowa, Indiana, Michigan, New York, Oregon, and Wisconsin.	▮ Hot water seed treatment: 126°F for 25 minutes. ▮ Plant disease-free seed. ▮ At harvest, remove and destroy carrot tops. ▮ Rotate on a 2–3 year basis.
Oak Wilt *Chestnut* *Oak*	**Fungus:** Water-soaked spots form on leaves — usually along the tip and margin. Leaves turn brown and fall off. Symptoms start in the top of the tree then move to the trunk, which develops short, bulging, vertical splits in the bark. A very serious disease in Chinese chestnut. White oak is a major reservoir for the fungus but tolerates the disease better. **Where:** Occurs in states bordering the Mississippi; west to Oklahoma, Kansas, Nebraska; east to Pennsylvania; and south to all states in the Appalachian Mountains.	▮ Once this disease is identified, immediately cut and destroy tree. Remove the stump and major roots. ▮ The fungus is thought to enter through wounds that penetrate the tree bark — so you might try dressing wounds with a fungicide or tree paint as soon as they are spotted.
Orange Rust *Blackberry* *Raspberry*	**Fungus:** Yellow spots appear on both sides of leaves in early spring. Several weeks later, the leaf underside ruptures with masses of orange-red powdery spores. Spread by wind. Overwinters in plant stems and roots. **Where:** Widespread	▮ Remove and destroy all infected canes, roots, suckers, and wild berries within 500 yards. ▮ Mulch heavily with straw and leaf mold. ▮ Apply lots of compost in autumn with extra P and K. (Low P and K encourages rust.) ▮ Select resistant varieties.
Pear Decline *Pear*	**Mycoplasma:** Transmitted by the pear psylla. Especially affects those on oriental rootstocks. Tree weakens and slowly dies.	▮ Control pear psylla. ▮ Use only *P. communis* rootstock.
Pecan Bunch *Pecan*	**Mycoplasma:** Symptoms are similar to Walnut Bunch. **Where:** Occurs in Arkansas, Kansas, Louisiana, Georgia, Mississippi, Missouri, New Mexico, Oklahoma, and Texas.	*See* **Walnut Bunch.**
Phytophthera cinnamomi *Blueberry (Highbush)*	**Fungus:** Leaves yellow; leaf margins turn brown, wilt, and fall off. Stunted growth. You may also see a "flag" branch on an otherwise healthy-looking bush (dead branch with dried leaves still attached). Lives indefinitely in all soil types, except perhaps sand. Most prevalent in wet soils with poor drainage. **Where:** Emerges in hot, moist conditions, especially in Florida, Georgia, Arkansas.	▮ Best prevention is to grow plants in raised beds to ensure good drainage. ▮ Avoid stressing the plant with under- or overfertilization or over-watering. ▮ Cut down the infected part of the bush all the way to the ground; remove and destroy.

Disease Plants Affected	Description of Symptoms How It is Spread/Where It Occurs	Organic Remedies
Psyllid Yellows *Potato* *Tomato*	**Toxic Substance Released by Tomato Psyllid:** *Potato* — Young leaves yellow or redden, brown, and die. Sprouts emerge on young tubers and form new tubers, creating eventually a chain of deformed tubers. *Tomato* — Older leaves get thick and curl upward. Young leaves turn yellow with purple veins. Plant is dwarfed and spindly. Developed fruit is soft. If the plant is attacked while young no fruit will appear.	■ Clear away Chinese lantern and ground cherries, both of which are hosts. ■ Control the tomato psyllid — garlic spray may work.
Scab (many different strains) *Almond* *Apple* *Apricot* *Beet* *Cucumber* *Melon* *Peach* *Pecan* *Potato* *Pumpkin* *Squash* *Watermelon*	**Fungus:** Symptoms vary in different plants. The disease develops rapidly at 70°F. *Beet and Potato* — Ugly corky, wartlike lesions on the outside of roots. Tubers are still edible if damaged areas are removed. *Cucurbits* — Leaves develop water-soaked spots and can wilt. Stems can develop small cankers. Immature fruit develop gray concave spots which darken, become deeper, and develop a velvety green mold. *Fruit trees* — When fruit is half-grown, small, greenish, dark spots eventually turn brown. Branches and twigs may develop yellow-brown spots. Fruit can crack. *Pecan* — In spring when leaves unfold, irregular, olive-brown to black spots appear, usually on leaf undersides. Concave spots appear on nuts. Nuts and leaves drop prematurely. Spread among fruit and nut trees primarily by wind. Overwinters in fallen leaves and dead twigs. Dry soil favors this fungus, so keep soil moist but not soggy. **Where:** Widespread, particularly in the humid Southeast. Fostered by humidity.	■ Remove and destroy all diseased leaves, plants, and fruit. Mow under trees. Research shows chopping or burning apple leaves soon after they have dropped in the fall can significantly lower scab spore survival. ■ *Beets and potatoes* — Lower soil pH to below 5.5. ■ *Fruit trees* — Spray or dust with sulfur 3 weeks after petal drop, and repeat 2 weeks later. ■ *Pecans* — Remove all leaves, shucks, and dead leaves. Burn, if legal. Hot composting methods will destroy the organism. ■ Ensure good drainage. ■ *All vegetable crops* — Rotate on a 3-year basis at minimum. ■ *Melons* — Ensure full sun by planting in a sunny location. ■ Plant soybeans in infested soil and turn under. ■ Select resistant varieties. ■ Grow chives near the affected plant roots. ■ Apply composted pigeon droppings to plant soil. ■ Spray trees in spring and early summer with Equisetum (horsetail) tea.
Smut (different strains) *Corn* *Onion*	**Fungus:** *Corn* — Stunted or misshapen stalks. Smut develops anywhere on the leaves, stalks, ears, or tassels. Ugly white or gray galls are covered with a shiny milky membrane that ruptures and releases more black spores. *Onions* — Black spots on leaves or bulbs. Cracks containing black powder appear on the sides of spots. Onion seedlings may die in a month. If not infected by the time its first true leaves appear, the seedling will usually escape this disease. **Where:** Most likely to occur in climates with hot dry season and dry spring followed by a wet spell. Spores survive for years. *Onion* — Prevalent in northern states.	■ *Corn* — Remove and destroy smut balls before they break. If severe, remove and destroy infected plants. Remove all stalks in fall. Control corn borers when tassels first appear to reduce injury. ■ Avoid manure fertilizer, which may contain spores. ■ Rotate crops on a 3+ year basis. ■ Select disease-resistant corn and disease-free onion sets. ■ If you can produce it reliably, you might sell young corn smut to specialty restaurants, a new gourmet item.

Disease Plants Affected	Description of Symptoms How It is Spread/Where It Occurs	Organic Remedies

Southern Blight
(Sclerotium rolfsii)
(also known as:
Crown Rot, *Sclerotium*
Root Rot, Southern Wilt)
   Artichoke
   Bean
   Okra
   Peanut
   Pepper
   Soybean
   Tomato
   Watermelon
 	
*Known to infect 200
plant species.*
	Fungus: Leaves yellow, wilt, and drop, starting at the bottom, followed by vine wilt and death. White mold grows on the stem at or near the soil line. The white mold may harden and crust over.
	Round, yellow, tan, or dark brown bodies the size of mustard seeds appear on lower stems and on soil, and may develop white mold growth. Some fruits and roots develop round lesions. Storage rot may occur in cabbage, squash, potato, and sweet potato.
	
	This fungus can spread over the soil to other plants. It overwinters 2 to 3 inches below the soil line in the mustard seedlike bodies.
	
	Where: Prevalent in southern states below 38° latitude, coast to coast. This fungus prefers warm soil (80°F or higher), moisture, and sandy soils low in nitrogen.
		■ In warm climates, immediately dig up infected plants and destroy. In cool climates — above 38° latitude — some suggest this disease may not need controls.
		■ Black plastic mulch is reported by Auburn University in Alabama to help control this disease, and is an easier control than soil solarization.
		■ After harvest, plow in the plant stubbles deeply.
		■ Rotate crops, and don't plant susceptible vegetables near each other.
		■ Solarize soil.
		■ Use wide spacing.
		■ Plant early where there is a history of southern blight.

Southern Wilt	*See* **Southern Blight**	*See* **Southern Blight**
Spotted Wilt *Tomato*	**Virus:** Leaves develop small orange spots. Older leaves brown and die. Plant is stunted. Green fruits can develop yellow spots that develop concentric zones of brown, green, pink, or red shading. Transmitted almost entirely by thrips. **Where:** Widespread.	■ Control thrips. Use a reflective mulch such as aluminum foil or black plastic sprayed with aluminum. ■ Grow two plants per pot and set out together. Only a maximum number of plants per given area get infected, so yields can be kept high.
Stewart's Disease	*See* **Bacterial Wilt**	*See* **Bacterial Wilt**

Sunscald
(also known as:
Winter Injury)
   Apple
   Cherry
   Onion
   Pecan
   Pepper
   Tomato
	Environmental: The southwestern side of the plant warms during the day, then cells rupture during cold nights. Vegetables develop white or yellow wrinkled areas. Onions get bleached and slippery tissue during curing. Fruit tree bark darkens and splits open in long cracks or cankers.
	
	Where: Widespread. Dark tree bark is the most susceptible. Worst in drought years with cold, sunny, winter days.
		■ *Fruit trees* — Shade bark by covering with burlap, or apply a white interior latex paint.
		■ *Vegetables* — Keep as much foliage as possible to shade fruit, so don't prune suckers at the plant base. If necessary, prune above the first group of leaves above fruit.
		■ *Onions* — Don't cure in the direct sun.

Tobacco Mosaic (TMV)
   Eggplant
   Pepper
   Tomato
	Virus: Misshapen leaves in young plants. Dark green mottled leaves tend to be pointed or fernlike; leaves may curl and wrinkle, and have a grayish coloring. In the final disease stage, leaves drop, branches die, and fruits yellow and wrinkle. Very difficult to control.
	
	Spread by tools and hands (especially smokers'). Virus is known to live in cured tobacco for up to 25 years.
	
	Where: Widespread.
		■ Never smoke near plants; have smokers scrub hands before touching plants.
		■ Destroy infected and nearby plants. Clear nearby perennial weeds.
		■ Disinfect all tools.
		■ Spray infected seedlings with skim milk or reconstituted powdered-milk solution. Spray until seedlings are dripping.
		■ Select resistant varieties.

Disease Plants Affected	Description of Symptoms How It is Spread/Where It Occurs	Organic Remedies
Walnut Bunch (also known as: Witches Broom, Brooming Disease) *Strawberry* *Walnut*	**Mycoplasma:** *Walnut* — Lateral buds don't remain dormant, but produce bushy, densely packed shoots and undersized leaves, often two weeks earlier than healthy branches. Few nuts are produced. Nuts are shriveled, soft-shelled, poorly developed and have dark kernels. Diseased shoots enter dormancy in fall, very late. *Strawberry* — Symptoms are on shoots only. On swollen stems deformed shoots are bush- and broomlike. Occurs on woodland borders and where balsam fir is present. **Where:** Prevalent in the Northeast and Midwest.	■ *Walnut* — Removing all diseased branches can be an effective control. Make cuts well back from the infected area. Disinfect tools. ■ *Walnut* — Propagate only from disease-free trees. ■ *Strawberry* — Remove all infected berries and plants. ■ *Strawberry* — Eliminate nearby balsam firs.
Western Yellow Blight	*See* **Curly Top**	*See* **Curly Top**
Winter Injury	*See* **Sunscald**	*See* **Sunscald**
Yellows	**Fungus:** *See* **Fusarium Wilt**	*See* **Fusarium Wilt**
Yellows *Beet* *Celery* *(similar virus)* *Spinach*	**Virus:** Leaves yellow, starting at tips and margins. Outer and middle leaves can get thick and brittle. Stunted plants and roots. Spread by aphids. **Where:** Occurs in California, Oregon, Washington, Utah, Colorado, Michigan, Nebraska, Ohio, Maryland, and Virginia.	■ Control aphids, using a reflective mulch such as black plastic sprayed with aluminum. ■ Don't plant winter spinach near beets. ■ Plant vegetables in protected areas to minimize aphids spreading by wind.
Yellows (also known as: Aster Yellows) *Broccoli* *Carrot* *Celery* *Lettuce* *Onion* *Tomato* *Strawberry*	**Mycoplasma:** Young leaves yellow. Top growth is yellow and bushy like witches' broom. Older leaves may become distorted. Carrot tops turn reddish-brown in mid- to late season. Flowers may be absent, green, underdeveloped, misshapen, or fail to produce seed or fruit. Immature leaves are narrow and dwarfed. Stunted plants. Sterile seeds. Vegetables ripen prematurely. Yields and quality are severely affected. Spread by leafhoppers, particularly the six-spotted leafhopper. **Where:** Widespread, but particularly destructive in the West, where it affects over 200 plant species.	■ Control leafhoppers; eradicate weeds to destroy leafhopper eggs, especially early in the season. ■ Immediately remove and destroy infected plants and plant residues. ■ Plant tolerant varieties.

Controlling Insects and Animals

Notes on Using this Chart

Clean cultivation. Clean cultivation and sanitation practices are assumed (*see* pages 155 and 167). Both are important to the prevention and control of many diseases and insects.

Damage not requiring control. When assaulted by chewing pests, plants can tolerate up to 20 percent defoliation without significant loss in yield or quality. The exception is plants whose leaves are the product — such as spinach or cabbage.

Remedies. The use of aluminum foil mulch for prolonged periods may result in aluminum leaching into the soil. If you're planning on leaving the mulch on for long periods, consider a substitute, such as black plastic sprayed with reflective aluminum paint.

Allies. Ally listings in this chart should be checked against the chart on **Allies and Companions** on pages 231–238, because an alleged ally may help only one of the crops listed. Also, remember that while an ally may effectively deter one insect pest it may, at the same time, attract others.

KEY

* Plants most frequently attacked by the insect.

** Remedies that should be used experimentally, as their effectiveness may depend on the severity of the problem and on your method of application. (Most of these haven't been formally tested.)

Macropest Plants Affected	Description of Symptoms and Pest Monitoring Its Presence/Where It Occurs	Organic Remedies
Aphid (many species) *Many herbs* *Most fruits* *Most vegetables*	Foliage curls, puckers, or yellows. Plants can be stunted or distorted. Cottony masses may appear on twigs of trees and shrubs. Presence of sticky "honeydew," which attracts ants and supports black, sooty mold. Aphids of different species suck leaves, fruit, stems, bark, and roots. Tiny (¹⁄₁₆"–¹⁄₈") soft-bodied insects are pear-shaped, and can be brown, black, pink, white, or green. They have long antennae and two tube-like projections from the rear, and may have wings. Aphids transmit many viral diseases. The phylloxera aphid attacks grapes and nearly wiped out the French wine industry in the 1800s.	▪ Symptoms may result from too much nitrogen or pruning. Check for the presence of aphids. ▪ Use row covers. ▪ Control aphids and ants — which carry aphid eggs — with sticky bands, sticky yellow traps, or yellow pans filled with soapy water. ▪ Keep grass mowed around garden. ▪ A reflective mulch like aluminum foil repels them. Application of fermented extract of stinging nettle is thought to repel black aphids.** ▪ *Homemade Sprays:*** **A.** Forceful water jets 2–3 times per day. **B.** Bug juice. **C.** Garlic, onion or pepper. **D.** Oxalic acid from leaves of rhubarb or spinach (boil 1 pound of leaves for 30 minutes in 1 quart of water; strain; cool; and add a touch of soap (not detergent). **E.** Tomato or potato leaf juice. ▪ *Other Sprays:* **A.** Light or superior horticultural oil (3 percent solution), applied in the plant's dormant or active phase. **B.** Insecticidal soap. **C.** Strong lime solution spray. **D.** Cooking oil spray mix, as recommended by USDA. Make sure all sprays contact the aphids. ▪ Dust with diatomaceous earth to dry up aphids — or with calcium to control ants.

continued

Macropest / Plants Affected	Description of Symptoms and Pest Monitoring Its Presence/Where It Occurs	Organic Remedies
Aphid, *continued*	**Where:** Widespread; produces 20 or more generations per year. The phylloxera aphid is primarily a problem in the West (e.g., California and Arizona) where European vines are grown.	■ Fall cultivation. ■ Rotate crops (more effective with root-feeding species). ■ *Biological Controls:* Larvae and adults of the green lacewing and ladybug. Syrphid fly larvae, minute pirate bug, damsel bugs, big-eyed bugs. ■ *Botanical Controls:* Sabadilla dust, rotenone (1 percent solution), pyrethrin. ■ *Allies (see chart on pages 231–238):* Anise, broccoli, chives, clover, coriander, cover crops of rye and vetch, fennel, French beans, garlic, lamb's quarters, nasturtium, onion family, tansy.
Apple Maggot *Apple* * *Blueberry* *Cherry* *Pear* *Plum*	Slight cavities and holes indicate eggs are present. Brown streaks on fruit skins. Premature fruit drop. After fruit falls or is picked, flesh becomes brown pulpy mess. Very damaging. Small (¼") white-yellowish worms hatch in mid- to late summer. They create winding brown tunnels as they feed inside fruit. Once the fruit falls, larvae emerge to pupate in the soil. The adult is a small black fly with yellow legs, a striped abdomen, and zigzag black markings on its wings. Females lay eggs in puncture wounds in fruit. **To Monitor:** Prepare traps by mixing 2 teaspoons ammonia, ¼ teaspoon soap flakes, and 1 quart water. Hang in jars on the sunny side of trees, shoulder high. Ten jars per orchard should give a good picture of the maggots' presence. Count the flies every 2–3 days. **Where:** Northeast, west to the Dakotas, and south to Arkansas and Georgia. Produces 1 to 2 generations per year.	■ Red sticky balls. Hang these on perimeter trees at shoulder height, with about 4 balls per tree. ■ Make a control trap of 1 part molasses/9 parts water; add yeast; and pour into wide-mouthed jars. When fermentation bubbling subsides, hang the jars in trees.** ■ Remove and destroy badly infested fruit or feed it to animals. Drop mildly damaged fruit into water to kill maggots; these are okay for cider. ■ Fall cultivation. ■ *Biological Controls:* Beneficial nematodes, applied in late summer to early fall. ■ *Botanical Controls:* Rotenone (5 percent solution).
Asparagus Beetle *Asparagus*	Defoliation. Misshapen spears. Adult beetles eat leaves, fruit, and spears. The small (¼") metallic blue-black beetle, with three yellow-orange squares on each side of back, lays dark shiny eggs the size of specks on leaves and spears. Eggs develop into orange larvae with black heads and legs, then green-gray grubs with dark heads. Beetles overwinter in garden trash. **Where:** Widespread, but rare in the Pacific coastal areas, the Southwest, Florida, and Texas. Produces 2 generations per year in cold areas, 3–5 in warm areas.	■ Use row covers. ■ Harvest regularly in the spring. ■ Vacuum adults off ferns. Immediately empty the bag and destroy the bugs, or they can crawl back out. ■ Fall cultivation to destroy over-wintering pests. ■ In autumn, let chickens in the garden to eat beetles. ■ *Biological Controls:* Encourage birds, and import ladybugs, chalcid and trichogramma wasps, and *Encarsia formosa.* ■ *Botanical Controls:* Ryania, rotenone (1 percent solution). ■ *Allies (see chart on pages 231–238):* Basil, parsley, marigold, nasturtium, tomato. Also, beetle allegedly dislikes bone meal.

Macropest Plants Affected	Description of Symptoms and Pest Monitoring Its Presence/Where It Occurs	Organic Remedies
Bean Jassid	*See* **Potato Leafhopper**	*See* **Potato Leafhopper**
Bean Leaf Bettle *Bean** *Pea*	Holes in leaves, particularly young seedlings. Adult beetles feed on leaf undersides and on seedling stems. Larvae attack roots, but usually don't affect the plant. Not a frequent pest. The adult is a small (¼") reddish-tan beetle with 3–4 black spots on each side of its back. It lays eggs in the soil at the base of seedlings. Larvae, slender and white, feed on roots. **Where:** Present primarily in the Southeast. Produces 1–2 generations per year.	■ Use same controls as for **Mexican Bean Beetle.** ■ *Biological Controls:* Ladybugs and lacewings eat the eggs. Beneficial nematodes, mixed into seed furrow and in mulch, may kill larvae and emerging adults. ■ *Botanical Controls:* Rotenone (1 percent solution).
Beet Leafhopper (also known as: Whitefly, in the West) *Beet** *Bean** *Cucumber* *Flowers* *Spinach* *Squash* *Tomato*	This leafhopper spreads curly top virus. Symptoms of curly top are raised leaf veins, stunted plants, small, wartlike bumps on the leaf undersides, and curled, brittle leaves. For a description of this and other leafhoppers, *see* **Leafhopper.** **Where:** West of Missouri and Illinois, except not in coastal fog areas. Produces up to 3 generations per year.	*See* **Leafhopper controls.**
Birds *Fruits* *Nuts* *Many vegetables*	Can be major pests of all fruits and berries, and corn and peas. **Where:** Occurs everywhere.	■ *Trees* — Netting must be held out away from the tree by supports. Otherwise they peck through the netting. Secure the netting tightly around the bottom. For more complete protection you can use cheesecloth, which is harder to peck through. ■ *Growing beds* — Use row covers over corn and peas. ■ *Corn seed* — Spread lime down seed rows.** Plant corn seeds deeper than usual, or mulch heavily. Erect several taut strands of black thread or fishing line over each seed row. Or, start seeds inside and transplant once established. ■ *Mature corn* — When silks brown, tie small rubber bands over each ear. ■ Construct growing boxes that are screened on all sides. ■ For berries and other large plants, erect around the plant a Teepee structure out of lumber or poles, and drape netting over it. ■ *Strawberries* — Paint large nuts red and place in the strawberry patch before fruit has ripened. Some gardeners report birds tire of pecking at these fake berries before the real thing ripens.** ■ Scare-eye balloons have been reported to be effective.**

Continued

Macropest Plants Affected	Description of Symptoms and Pest Monitoring Its Presence/Where It Occurs	Organic Remedies
Birds, *continued*		■ Mulberry and elderberry trees offer berries in the fall that birds eat before anything else.** Mulberry grows rapidly to a breadth of 50'–60'. ■ Use noise-making devices to scare birds away. One gardener reported that talk shows with human voices worked best.**
Blackberry Sawfly *Blackberry*	Rolled and webbed leaves. Adults are small wasp-like flies with two pairs of transparent wings hooked to each other. They lay white eggs on leaf undersides in May. Blue-green larvae (¾") roll leaves closed with webs and feed inside the webs through July. They then drop to the ground to pupate in the soil.	■ Use sticky traps to catch adults. ■ Handpick eggs and larvae in spring. ■ *Botanical Controls:* Rotenone (1 percent solution); pyrethrin.
Blister Beetle	*See* **Striped Blister Beetle**	*See* **Striped Blister Beetle**
Boxelder Bug *Almond* *Ash* *Boxelder* * *Maple* *	Damaged foliage and twigs. Medium-sized (½") bugs suck plant juices. They look like squash bugs, but are brown with red markings. Nymphs are bright red. **Where:** Present wherever boxelders grow.	■ Remove any nearby female boxelder trees. ■ Insecticidal soap spray, though this isn't a very effective control of hard-bodied insects.
Brown Almond Mite	*See* **Mite**	*See* **Mite**
Cabbage Butterfly	*See* **Imported Cabbage Worm**	*See* **Imported Cabbage Worm**
Cabbage Looper *Bean* *Brassicas* *Celery* *Lettuce* *Parsley* *Pea* *Potato* *Radish* *Spinach* *Tomato*	Ragged holes in leaves. Seedlings can be destroyed. Worms bore into the heads of all cabbage family plants. This large (1½") pale green worm with light stripes down its back doubles up or "loops" as it crawls. It hides under leaves in hot, dry weather. The worm overwinters as a green or brown pupa in a thin cocoon attached to a plant leaf. The adult moth (1½") is night-flying, brownish, and has a silver spot in middle of each forewing. It lays greenish-white round eggs, singly, on leaves. Eggs hatch in 2 weeks and the looper feeds for 3–4 weeks. **To Monitor:** Use pheromone traps to monitor population levels of adult moths, starting soon after planting. **Where:** Widespread. Produces 4 or more generations per year.	■ Use row covers all season. ■ Handpick loopers. ■ Plant spring crops to avoid the cabbage looper peak. ■ Stagger planting dates to avoid entire crop susceptibility. ■ Hot pepper spray.** ■ Spray with soap and lime, or dust wet plant with lime. ■ In the deep South, practice a thorough fall cultivation and also rotate crops on a 3 to 5 year basis. This insect doesn't overwinter in the North, so these steps aren't necessary. ■ Make viral insecticide from loopers infected with nuclear polyhedrosis virus (NPV). Loopers are chalky white, sluggish or half-dead, may be on top of leaves or hanging from undersides. They turn black and liquefy within days. Capture three and make bug juice. Spray from three bugs covers ¾ acre. Loopers take 3–6 days to die, but one spraying can last entire season. *Note:* Spray only when it is cool and damp, and when you see that loopers are not hiding under leaves.

continued

Macropest / Plants Affected	Description of Symptoms and Pest / Monitoring Its Presence/Where It Occurs	Organic Remedies
Cabbage Looper, *continued*		■ Encourage predators such as toads, bluebirds, chickadees, robins, and sparrows. ■ *Biological Controls:* Bt, applied every 2 weeks until heads form (for broccoli and cabbage). Lacewings and trichogramma wasp. ■ *Botanical Controls:* Sabadilla; rotenone (1 percent solution); pyrethrin. ■ *Allies (see chart on pages 231–238):* Dill, garlic, hyssop, mint, nasturtium, onion family, sage, and thyme.
Cabbage Maggot *Brassicas* *Pea* *Radish* *(Late spring)* *Turnip*	Seedlings wilt and die. Stems are riddled with brown, slimy tunnels. Stunted, off-color plants. The maggot transmits both bacterial soft spot and black leg. The adult resembles a housefly, but is half the size and has bristly hairs. It emerges from an underground cocoon in spring at cherry blossom time, in early summer, or in autumn. It lays eggs on plant stems near the soil line or in cracks in the soil. The small (⅓"), white, legless worm with a blunt end attacks stems below the soil line. To overwinter, maggots pupate 1"–5" deep in the soil and emerge on the first warm spring day. In season, each life cycle takes about 6–7 weeks. **To Monitor:** Yellow sticky traps are a good early warning device for adults. Another method is to take a scoop of soil from the plant base; place it in water; and count the eggs that float to the top to determine the extent of the problem. **Where:** Widespread, particularly in western and northern United States. It thrives in cool, moist weather. Produces numerous generations per year.	■ Use row covers in early season. ■ Maggots don't like alkaline environment. Circle plants with a mixture of lime and wood ashes (moistened to prevent blowing) or diatomaceous earth.** Replenish after rain. Mix wood ashes into the surrounding soil. Do not replenish more than one or two times; continued use of wood ashes raises the pH excessively by its addition of potassium. ■ Use a 12" square of tar or black paper to prevent larvae from entering the soil. ■ Plant very early spring or in fall to avoid maggot peak in May and early June. ■ *Biological Controls:* Beneficial nematodes are effective when applied before planting. ■ *Allies (see chart on pages 231–238):* Clover, garlic, onion family, radish, sage, and wormwood.
Cabbage Moth	*See* **Imported Cabbage Worm**	*See* **Imported Cabbage Worm**
Cabbageworm (also known as: Cross-striped Cabbageworm) *Cabbage*	*See* **Imported Cabbage Worm** New worms are gray with large round heads. Mature worms (⅔") are green to blue-gray with long dark hairs and at least three distinct black bands across each segment. The adult moth is small, pale yellow with mottled brown on its forewings. **Where:** Widespread.	*See* **Imported Cabbage Worm**

Macropest Plants Affected	Description of Symptoms and Pest Monitoring Its Presence/Where It Occurs	Organic Remedies
Caneborer (also known as: Rednecked Cane Borer) *Blackberry* *Raspberry*	**Caneborer** Large cigar-shaped swellings on canes. Where cane joints swell, the cane may break off and die. Blue-black beetles (⅓") with coppery red thorax appear in May, and lay eggs in June in cane bark near a ragged or eaten leaf. Flat-headed larvae bore into canes and cause swellings or galls in late July and August. Cut open galls to find creamy white grubs. **Where:** Present in the Northeast; other types are prevalent in other parts of the United States.	▪ Cut out all canes with swellings and burn or destroy.
Cankerworm, Fall and Spring (also known as: Inchworm, Measuring Worm) *Apricot* *Apple* * *Cherry* *Elm* *Maple* Oak Plum	Skeletonized leaves. Few mature fruit. Trees may look scorched when damaged by the spring variety. Defoliation may occur 2–3 years in a row. Small worms (1") are green, brown or black, have a yellow-brown stripe down their back, and drop from trees on silky threads when ready to pupate. They pupate 1"–4" deep in the ground in cocoons near the trees. Male adults are grayish moths. Females are wingless. In the spring they lay brownish-gray eggs in masses on tree trunks or branches, or in the fall brown-purple egg masses beneath the bark. Eggs hatch in 4–6 months. **Where:** Widespread. The fall variety is worst in early spring in California, Colorado, Utah, and northern United States. The spring variety is worst in the East, Colorado, and California.	▪ Use sticky bands from October to December — and again in February — to catch wingless females crawling up trees to lay eggs. Renew sticky substance periodically. ▪ Encourage predators such as bluebirds, chickadees, and nuthatches. ▪ Spray horticultural oil before leaves bud in spring. ▪ *Biological Controls:* Trichogramma wasps work on spring species. Chalcid wasps. Bt, applied every 2 weeks from the end of blossom time to 1 month later. ▪ *Botanical Controls:* Sabadilla.
Carrot Rust Fly *Caraway* *Carrot* *Celery* *Coriander* *Dill* *Fennel* *Parsley* *Parsnip*	Stunted plants. Leaves wilt and turn yellow. Soft rot bacteria in the carrot. Small (⅓"), yellow-white larvae burrow into roots and make rusty-colored tunnels. The adult fly is slender, shiny green, and lays eggs at the plant crown in late spring. **Where:** Widespread, but mostly a problem in northern and Pacific Northwest states. Produces several generations per year.	▪ Use row covers all season. ▪ Fall cultivation and early spring cultivation disrupt overwintering maggots. ▪ Rotate crops. ▪ Avoid early planting. Plant all target crops after maggot peak. ▪ Yellow sticky traps. British horticulturists have shown these traps are most effective for this pest when placed at a 45° angle. ▪ Sow seeds with used tea leaves.** ▪ Spread wood ashes (moistened to prevent blowing), pulverized wormwood, or rock phosphate around the plant crown to repel egg-laying.** ▪ *Allies (see chart on pages 231–238):* Black salsify (oyster plant), coriander, lettuce, onion family, pennyroyal, rosemary, and sage.

Macropest Plants Affected	Description of Symptoms and Pest Monitoring Its Presence/Where It Occurs	Organic Remedies
Carrot Weevil Beet Carrot* Celery Parsley Parsnip	Zigzag tunnels in the tops and roots of plants. Defoliation. Small (⅓"), pale, legless, brown-headed worms tunnel into roots and celery hearts. The tiny (⅕") dark brown, hardshelled adult is snout-nosed, and overwinters in garden litter and hedgerows. **Where:** Present east of the Rockies. Produces 2–3 generations per year.	■ Use row covers all season. ■ Fall cultivation. ■ Rotate crops. ■ Encourage chickadees, bluebirds, juncos, and warblers. ■ *Biological Controls:* Beneficial nematodes when plants are very small. ■ *Botanical Controls:* Sabadilla, rotenone (5 percent solution).
Carrotworm	*See* **Parsleyworm**	*See* **Parsleyworm**
Celery Leaftier (also known as: Greenhouse Leaftier) Celery* Kale Many Other Plants	Holes in leaves and stalks. Leaves folded and tied together with webs. Medium (¾"), pale green-yellow worms, with white stripe down the length of their backs, eat a host of vegetables. They web foliage together as they feed, and eventually pupate in silky cocoons inside webs. The adult is a small (¾"), brown nocturnal moth. It lays eggs that look like fish scales on leaf undersides. They can do great damage, but don't usually appear in large numbers. **Where:** Widespread, but worst in the Northeast and southern California. Most destructive in greenhouses. Produces 5–6 generations per year in warm areas, 7–8 in greenhouses.	■ Handpick and destroy pests. Also pick damaged or rolled leaves where leaftier may be hiding inside.
Celeryworm	*See* **Parsleyworm**	*See* **Parsleyworm**
Cherry Fruit Fly Cherry Pear Plum	Small, disfigured fruit. Premature fruit drop. Rotten flesh with maggots feeding inside. These black fruit flies resemble small houseflies, with yellow margins on the thorax and 2 white crossbands on the abdomen. They emerge in early June and feed for 7–10 days by sucking sap. They then lay eggs in developing fruit through small slits. The maggots are yellow or white small worms with two dark hooks on their mouths. They feed inside fruit, then drop to the ground and pupate for 6 months 2"–3" deep in the soil. Pupae overwinter in the soil. **To Monitor:** Use sticky red balls or pheromone traps to monitor population levels. **Where:** Widespread, except in the Southwest and Florida.	■ Fall cultivation after the first several frosts will expose pupae to predators. ■ *See* first three remedies listed for **Apple Maggot.** ■ **Biological Controls:** Braconid wasps.

Macropest Plants Affected	Description of Symptoms and Pest Monitoring Its Presence/Where It Occurs	Organic Remedies
Cherry Fruit Sawfly *Apricot* *Cherry* *Peach* *Plum*	Fruits shrivel and drop. Small (⅛") adult wasp-like flies have two pairs of transparent wings hooked together and yellow appendages. Small (¼") larvae are white with brown heads. They bore into young fruit and feed on seeds. They exit fallen fruit to pupate and overwinter in silken cocoons in the ground. **Where:** Present on the Pacific coast.	■ Shallow 2" cultivation around trees to expose pupae. ■ *See* controls for **Blackberry Sawfly.**
Cherry Fruitworm *Cherry*	Rotten flesh with larvae feeding inside. Can be very damaging. The small, gray adult moth lays single eggs on cherries in May and June. Small (⅜") pinkish larvae hatch in 10 days and bore into fruit where they feed. They overwinter in the stubs of pruned branches or in bark crevices. They are distinguished from the cherry fruit fly maggot by their black head and caterpillar-like body. **Where:** Prevalent in Colorado, and north and west of Colorado. Produces 1 generation per year.	■ *Biological Controls:* Bt, sprayed in the first week of June.
Cherry Slug	*See* **Pearslug**	*See* **Pearslug**
Chestnut Weevil (also known as: Snout Weevil) *Chestnut*	The adult (5⁄16"–½") has a very long snout (proboscis), as long or longer than its body. It emerges from April to August, and in August deposits eggs into the bur through a tiny hole. Larvae feed on kernel tissue for 3–5 weeks, sometimes hollowing out the interior, then leave the nut. Larvae are legless, white, plump, and curved like a crescent moon. Mature larvae overwinter 3"–6" below ground. **Where:** Wherever Asian Chestnuts are grown. This pest completes a life-cycle in 1–2 years.	■ Collect all fallen nuts every day and immerse in hot water (122°F) for 45 minutes to kill all larvae. This prevents larvae from entering the soil and continuing the cycle. ■ Plant away from woods or forest from which squirrels and other rodents can bring in infested nuts. ■ Fall cultivation. Also, chickens can help clean up larvae.
Click Beetle	*See* **Wireworm**	*See* **Wireworm**
Codling Moth *Almond* *Apple** *Apricot* *Cherry* *Peach* *Pear* *Walnut (English)* *continued*	Holes and tunnels in fruit, with brown fecal material at the core and a brown mound at the hole opening. Sometimes forms cocoons in bark crevices. Large (1") larvae is white tinged with pink, has a brown head, and a voracious appetite. Adult moths (¾") are gray-brown with dark brown markings on lacy forewings, fringed back wings, and dark brown edging on all wings. They lay flat white eggs, singly, on twigs on upper leaf surfaces.	■ In spring, band tree trunks with several thicknesses of 6"-wide corrugated cardboard. Exposed ridges must be at least 3⁄16"-wide and must face tree. This gives larvae a place to spin cocoons when they leave fruit. Remove and kill larvae once a week in warm weather, once every 2 weeks in cool weather. Continue through harvest. Burn cardboard. ■ Use sticky bands to catch larvae. ■ Make a trap for larvae of 2 parts vinegar/1 part molasses in wide-mouth jar.** Hang three to four traps per tree, 8" below the limb. Clean and replenish daily.

Macropest Plants Affected	**Description of Symptoms and Pest** Monitoring Its Presence/Where It Occurs	**Organic Remedies**
Codling Moth, *continued*	Eggs hatch in 6–20 days, and larvae tunnel into and out of fruit. Pupae overwinter in tough cocoons built in cracks of loose bark, fences, buildings, or garden debris. **To Monitor:** Use pheromone traps to determine population levels. More than five moths per trap per week indicates that controls may be needed. **Where:** Widespread. Produces 2 generations per year; the first generation attacks immature fruit, the second attacks mature fruit.	■ In spring, scrape off all loose rough bark from trunk and limbs. Catch scrapings and destroy. Seal pruning wounds. ■ Apply soap and lime spray, or fish oil spray, to entire tree before leaves appear in late winter, and, later, to tree trunk and base weekly. ■ Apply horticultural oil spray before buds open. Be sure to cover all surfaces of the tree. ■ Encourage woodpeckers in the winter with one suet ball per tree. ■ *Biological Controls:* Two or three sprays of Bt, applied 3 to 4 days apart at peak egg-laying time, is very effective. Three timed releases of trichogramma wasps — the first at petal fall, the second 3–8 weeks later, and a final release 5–8 weeks later in early fall — is also helpful. Beneficial nematodes help most when sprayed on wet tree trunks and nearby soil in late winter. ■ Pheromone-based mating disruption devices should be commercially available soon, but may not be effective in small orchards. ■ *Botanical Controls:* Ryania, sabadilla, pyrethrin. ■ *Allies (see chart on pages 231–238):* Cover crops of the buckwheat, clover, and daisy families; dill; garlic; wormwood.
Colorado Potato Beetle *Eggplant* * *Pepper* *Potato* * *Tomato* *	Skeletonized leaves and complete defoliation. Adults and larvae chew foliage. Small (⅓"), yellow, hardshelled beetles have orange heads with black dots and black stripes down their backs. They lay bright yellow eggs on leaf undersides. Eggs hatch in 4–9 days and become plump red larvae with black spots and black heads. **Where:** Widespread, but mostly a problem in the eastern United States. Rarely a problem in southern California through Texas, Louisiana, and Georgia. Produces 1–3 generations per year.	■ Use row covers in early season. ■ Handpick immediately, when sighted, and crush adults and egg masses — a very effective control. ■ Apply thick organic mulch to impede the movement of overwintered adults to plants. Beetles walk more than fly during early season. Potatoes can be started in thick mulch above ground. ■ Fall cultivation. ■ Where different potato and tomato varieties are grown, resistant varieties will be less susceptible. If only one resistant variety is grown, however, even this will be consumed. All eggplants are susceptible. ■ Timed plantings to avoid beetles. Plant potatoes as early as possible to allow sufficient plant growth to withstand attack of overwintered adults. ■ Foliar spray of fish wastes was shown by University of Maine studies to repel these bugs. They used Biostar. ■ A University of Delaware study showed that ground tansy — diluted 1:100 (leaf to water weight ratio) and used as a foliar spray — dramatically reduced bug feeding.

continued

Macropest Plants Affected	Description of Symptoms and Pest Monitoring Its Presence/Where It Occurs	Organic Remedies
Colorado Potato Beetle, *continued*		■ Garlic, onion, and pepper sprays, applied directly on beetles, are irritants.** ■ Foliar sprays of hydrogen peroxide (1 tablespoon/1 gallon water) applied directly on active adults provide fair control. Do not apply in direct sunlight in the heat of the day. ■ A dusting of diatomaceous earth dries out beetles. Soap and lime spray is also thought to dry out beetles, but generally soap is not effective against hard-bodied insects. ■ Sprinkle fine-milled bran on leaves at the first sign of beetles.** (Found effective by an Ohio gardener.) ■ In the fall, let chickens into the garden to eat beetles and larvae. ■ Encourage predators like songbirds, toads, and ground beetles. ■ *Biological Controls:* Ladybugs, lacewings, and *Edovum puttleri* eat the eggs. Beneficial nematodes. Two-spotted stink bug *(Perillus bioculatus)*. New Bt strains (M-One, Trident, Foil) are very effective if applied in the larval stage. Once the larvae are too big, it doesn't help much. ■ *Botanical Controls:* Sabadilla, rotenone (5 percent solution). ■ *Allies (see chart on pages 231–238):* Bean, catnip, coriander, dead nettle, eggplant, flax, horseradish, nasturtium, onion family, and tansy. Since beans are allegedly noxious to this bug, and potatoes repel the Mexican Bean Beetle, they might be companions.
Corn Borer	*See* **European Corn Borer**	*See* **European Corn Borer**

Corn Earworm (also known as: Vetchworm, Cotton Bollworm, Tomato Fruitworm, Tobacco Budworm)
    Bean
    Corn (sweet) *
    Pea
    Peanut
    Pepper
    Potato
    Squash
    Tomato
 	
 continued
	Ragged holes in tender leaves. Eaten tassels and damaged pods on developing fruits. Chewed silk and damp castings near the silk. Damaged kernels, often at the ear tip. Extremely destructive.
	
	 Large (1½" to 2"), light yellow, green, red, or brown caterpillars; striped, with "spines" at bands; feed first on leaves and corn silk. They feed on kernels and exit through the husk to pupate. Feeding lasts about 1 month, when they drop to the ground and pupate 3"–5" deep in the soil.
	
	 The adult (1½") grayish-brown moth feeds on flower nectar. It lays 500–3,000 tiny, single, ribbed, dirty white eggs on host plants.
	
	 This pest is most numerous 2–3 weeks after a full moon. Some say corn should ideally silk during the full moon. Its numbers are reduced by cold winters and wet summers.
		■ Mineral oil, applied just inside the tip of each ear, suffocates the worms. Apply only after silk has wilted and started to brown at the tip, or pollination will be incomplete. Use ½ of a medicine dropper per small ear, ¾ of a dropper per large ear. You might add red pepper to the oil to see if it increases the effectiveness. Apply two or more applications of oil, spaced at 2 week intervals.
		
		 ■ Fall cultivation. In the spring, cultivate the top 2 inches of soil.
		
		 ■ Handpick worms after silks brown.
		
		 ■ Time plantings to avoid worms. In northern states, early plantings that silk before mid-July often avoid attack.
		
		 ■ Plant resistant varieties with tight husks. Or clip husks tightly with clothespins. You can also try covering ears with pantyhose.

Macropest Plants Affected	Description of Symptoms and Pest Monitoring Its Presence/Where It Occurs	Organic Remedies
Corn Earworm, *continued*	**Where:** Widespread, but primarily a problem in southern and central states. Produces 2–3 generations per year.	■ The USDA recently showed petunia leaves contain a natural repellant. ■ Spray light or superior horticultural oil (2–3 percent solution). Bt added to the oil spray will increase its effectiveness. ■ *Biological Controls:* Minute pirate bugs. Lacewings. Trichogramma wasps and Tachinid flies lay eggs in the moth eggs and prevent hatching. Inject beneficial nematodes into infested ears; they seek out and kill worms in 24 hours. Bt can be applied to borers before they move into the stalks. Then wettable Bt, applied every 10–14 days, is effective. ■ *Botanical Controls:* Ryania, rotenone (1 percent solution), pyrethrin. Use pheromone traps to identify moth flight paths before spraying. Spray moths before they lay eggs. ■ *Allies (see chart on pages 231–238):* Corn, marigold, and soybean.
Corn Maggot (also known as: Seedcorn Maggot) *Bean* *Corn (sweet)* * *Pea*	Damaged seeds that fail to sprout. Poor, stunted plants. Small (¼"), yellow-white larvae, with long heads tapering to point, tunnel into larger vegetable seeds. The adult is a small gray-brown fly that lays eggs in April through May in the soil and on seeds and seedlings. **Where:** Widespread. Produces 3–5 generations per year. Worst injury occurs early in cold, wet soil that is high in organic matter.	■ Delay planting until soil is warm; avoid planting early in soils high in organic matter and manure. ■ Plant seeds in shallow furrows to speed emergence. ■ If damage is heavy, replant immediately. Seeds will germinate before the next generation of adults emerge. ■ *Allies (see chart on pages 231–238):* Rye.
Corn Rootworm (Northern and Western) *Corn (sweet)*	Weak plants with damaged silks and brown tunnels in the roots. Adult yellow-green beetles are small (¼") and emerge in late July and August. They feed on corn silks and other plants. They lay eggs in the ground in late summer near corn roots. Eggs hatch in late spring. Small (½") narrow, wrinkled white worms with brown heads feed only on corn and burrow through corn roots. **Where:** The western variety is active in the upper Midwest, and East to Pennsylvania and Maryland. The northern variety is active in New York to Kansas and South Dakota. Produces 1 generation per year.	■ Crop rotation. If beetles are found feeding on silks then plant sweet corn in a different location next year.
Corn Rootworm (Southern)	*See* **Cucumber Beetle** (Spotted)	*See* **Cucumber Beetle**

Macropest Plants Affected	Description of Symptoms and Pest Monitoring Its Presence/Where It Occurs	Organic Remedies
Cucumber Beetles — **Striped and Spotted** (Spotted also known as: Southern Corn Rootworm) *Asparagus* *Beans (early) ** *Corn (sweet) ** *Cucumber ** *Eggplant* *Muskmelon ** *Pea* *Potato* *Pumpkin ** *Squash ** *Tomato* *Watermelon ** *Some fruit trees*	Both types eat stems and leaves of *cucurbits* before the first true leaves emerge. Spotted beetles also eat flowers and fruit. Adults transmit bacterial wilt of *cucurbits,* brown rot in stone fruit, cucumber mosaic, and wilt. Larvae feed on the root system. Small (⅓"), thin white larvae with brown heads and brown ends feed for 2–6 weeks on roots and underground stems. Heavy larvae populations can reduce plant vigor and damage melon rind surfaces next to the ground. Adults of both types are small (¼") with black heads and yellow or yellow-green backs. Striped beetles have three black stripes down the back. Spotted beetles have eleven to twelve black spots scattered across the back. Both lay yellow-orange eggs in the soil near host plants. Beetles tend to congregate on one leaf or plant, so it may be possible to remove a selected plant and destroy large quantities. Midsummer adults feed on upper plant parts, while autumn adults feed on fruits, then weeds and trees. Striped adults are the most destructive and eat mostly *cucurbits.* Break a cucumber plant stem, put it back together, pull it back apart and see if strings (looking like pizza cheese) form. If so, it has bacterial wilt. This test is not so easy with other *cucurbits.* **Where:** Widespread east of the Rockies, but most serious in the South and where soils are heavy. Produces 1 generation per year in cold areas; 2 in warm climates.	■ Use row covers from the time of sowing or transplanting to bloom time. Lift edges during bloom time for 2 hours in early morning — just twice per week — to allow pollination; secure edges again until harvest. ■ Vacuum adults with a hand-held vacuum at dusk. Empty into a plastic bag immediately, or they'll crawl out. ■ Select resistant varieties. ■ Transplant strong seedlings. ■ Fall cultivation. ■ Circle plants with a 3"–4"-wide trench, 3" deep. Fill with wood ashes, moistened to prevent blowing.** Don't get on plants. ■ Handpick beetles. ■ Apply thick mulch. ■ Lime is thought to dry out these beetles. Apply one of the following directly on beetles: soap and lime spray, lime dust (hydrated or plasterer's lime), or a spray containing equal amounts of wood ashes and hydrated lime mixed in water. Soap alone isn't very effective against hard-bodied insects. ■ Spray of hot pepper and garlic.** ■ Sprinkle onion skins over plants.** ■ Time plantings to avoid bugs. ■ Plant zucchini or yellow squash to trap early infestations.** ■ Encourage song birds. ■ *Biological Controls:* Lacewings and ladybugs eat eggs. To kill adults, apply beneficial nematodes in the seed furrows, around roots, and in mulch. ■ *Botanical Controls:* Sabadilla, rotenone (1 percent solution), pyrethrin. ■ *Allies (see chart on pages 231–238):* Broccoli, catnip, corn, goldenrod, marigold, nasturtium, onion skins, radish, rue, tansy.
Cutworm *Bean* *Brassicas* *Corn (sweet)* *Cucumber* *Eggplant* *Lettuce* *Melon (seedlings)* *Peanut* *Pea* *Pepper*	Severed stems, straight across, at or below soil surface. Plants wilt and collapse. Buds, leaves, and fruit may also be eaten by the variegated cutworm. Large (½") soft-bodied larvae are gray or brownish larvae with bristles. They curl into a circle when disturbed. They feed at night for several weeks and burrow into the soil during the day. The last generation overwinters as naked brown pupae in the soil.	■ Stem collars. ■ Plant transplants inside ½-gallon milk cartons, with bottoms cut out and rim about 1" out of the soil. ■ Diatomaceous earth sprinkled around the base of each plant, and worked slightly into the soil, is very effective. ■ Sprinkle cornmeal or bran — ½ teaspoon per plant — around stem in a circle leading away from the stem.** Worms eat this and die.

continued

Cutworm, *continued* *Potato* *Radish* *Tomato* *All seedlings*	Adults are night-flying moths with ragged blotches like paint drips on their wings. They lay egg masses on leaves, tree trunks, fences, and buildings. Eggs hatch in 2–10 days. **Where:** Widespread. Produces up to 5 generations per year.	■ Make a trap of equal parts of sawdust (pine is best) and bran, add molasses and a little water. At dusk, sprinkle several spoonfuls near plants. The sticky goo clings to their bodies and dries, making them food for prey.** ■ Create barriers by making a 3"–4" wide trench, 2"–3" deep; fill with wood ashes — moistened to prevent blowing — crushed egg shells, oak leaves, or cornmeal or bran (½ teaspoon per plant). ■ Fall cultivation. Following fall cultivation, allow chickens into the garden to clean out exposed pests. ■ Handpick at night with light. ■ Encourage birds and toads. ■ University of British Columbia student Greg Salloum claims cutworms will starve before eating plants treated with extracts of pineapple weed or sage brush. ■ *Biological Controls:* Apply beneficial nematodes at a rate of 50,000 per plant. Apply Bt. Lacewing, braconid, and trichogramma wasps. Tachinid flies. ■ *Allies (see chart on pages 231–238):* Shepherd's purse and tansy.
Deer *Azalea* *Fruit trees* *Holly* *Juniper* *Rose* *Saplings* *Vegetables*	Large quadruped mammal. They have two large and two small toes on each foot — a distinct print. **Where:** Widespread.	■ *Fences:* Serious deer fences need to be electrified with seven strands, at 8", 16", 24", 40", 50" and 60". An alternative is to use a one-wire electric fence, but only if you bait the fence. All electrified fences work best if baited. Bait with attached pieces of aluminum foil smeared with peanut butter; this attracts deer, shocks them, and trains them to stay away. An effective nonelectric fence is two 4' high fences spaced 5' apart, with bare ground between. Deer aren't broad jumpers and realize that, once they get into the middle section, there isn't enough room to clear the second fence. An alternate nonelectric is a fence inclined horizontally. Research at the Institute of Ecosystem Studies, New York Botanical Garden, in Millbrook, New York, shows that deer won't jump a horizontal fence. ■ Tie bags with 1 ounce of human or dog hair, dried blood meal, or fish heads, to orchard trees and along perimeters of melon and sweet potato patches.** This allegedly provides protection for 10 months. ■ Make a spray of 2 egg yolks in 1 quart of water; spray fruit tree foliage.** One farmer claims trees weren't bothered the entire season.

continued

Macropest / Plants Affected	Description of Symptoms and Pest / Monitoring Its Presence/Where It Occurs	Organic Remedies
Deer, *continued*		■ Lay chicken wire squares wherever you find deer droppings; deer will avoid the area.**
		■ Hanging soap in outer tree limbs is reported by some to work.** Some suggest Camay, some Safeguard, some say any brand will work. Be warned, however, that groundhogs love soap.
		■ The product named Hinder reputedly works when sprayed on leaves and branches. Commercial deer repellant was found unreliable in intense browsing areas in a Virginia study.
		■ Maintain dogs to keep deer away.
		■ Use automated blinking lights at night to keep them away.**
		■ Old, smelly shoes are reputed to be effective deterrents when placed around the garden perimeter.**
		■ Plant a border of plants that deer won't eat, such as Fritillaria.
Diamondback Moth *Brassicas*	Small holes in outer leaves. Usually a minor pest. Small (⅓"), green-yellow larvae with black hairs chews leaves. When disturbed it wriggles and drops to ground. Gray-brown adult moth (¾") has fringed back wings, with a diamond that shows when the wings are at rest. **Where:** Widespread.	■ Apply soap and lime spray directly on worms; before harvest, spray 3 days in a row to kill new worms. ■ Southernwood is an herbal repellant.** ■ *Biological Controls:* Lacewings and Trichogramma wasps. ■ *Botanical Controls:* Sabadilla; Rotenone and pyrethrum work against larvae. ■ *Allies (see chart on pages 231–238):* Cabbage, tomato.
Earwig *Bean (seedling)* *Beet (seedling)* *Cabbage (Chinese)* *Celery* * *Corn (sweet)* * *Flowers* *Lettuce* *Potato* * *Strawberry* *	As a beneficial, it can scavenge larvae, slow-moving bugs, and aphids. As a pest, it feeds on soft plant tissue such as foliage, flowers, and corn silks. It can be particularly damaging to seedlings. Symptoms are round holes in the middle of leaves. Nocturnal, slender, brown, beetle-like insect (¾") with sharp pincers at its tail. It usually crawls, but can fly if it takes off from a high place. Hides under and in things during the day. **Where:** Widespread, but primarily a pest in the West, particularly the San Francisco Bay area and northern California areas.	■ Probably best left alone in areas where they're not a serious problem. ■ In areas where they're a serious problem, trap and kill. Good trap locations are moist, tight areas where they spend the day. Try rolled-up moistened newspapers, rolls of moistened corrugated cardboard, or bamboo. Collect and dispose of pests in the morning. ■ If very bad, use commercial earwig bait.
Eelworm	*See* **Nematode**	*See* **Nematode**

Macropest Plants Affected	Description of Symptoms and Pest Monitoring Its Presence/Where It Occurs	Organic Remedies
European Apple Sawfly *Apple* *Pear* *Plum*	Premature fruit drop. Brown scars on fruit skin. Small wasplike adult flies are brown and yellow with two pairs of transparent wings hooked together. They emerge at blossom time. Larvae are white worms with seven forelegs that bore into fruit and leave chocolate-colored sawdust on the fruit surface. Worms then drop to the ground where they pupate through the winter in the ground. **Where:** Present in Connecticut, Massachusetts, New Jersey, New York, Rhode Island. Produces 1 generation per year.	▌Clean up fallen fruit and destroy larvae by placing them in a sealed black bag in a sunny location. ▌*Botanical Controls:* Ryania. Rotenone (1 percent solution), applied at petal fall and again 1 week later.
European Corn Borer (also known as: Corn Borer) *Bean (green)* *Chard* *Corn (sweet)* * *Pepper* *Potato* *Tomato*	Broken tassels and bent stalks. Sawdust castings outside small holes. This pest bores into ears and feeds on kernels at both tips and butt ends. It bores into the stem and fruit parts of pepper, potato, and green beans. It can attack the stems, foliage, and fruits of over 260 different plants. Extremely destructive. The gray-pink or flesh-colored caterpillar (1") has brown spots on each segment and a dark brown head. The adult, night-flying, yellowish moth (½") has dark wavy bands across its wings, and lays clumps of white eggs on leaf undersides. Eggs hatch in up to 1 week. Larvae overwinter in corn stubble. Pupae are reddish brown grubs. **To Monitor:** Use blacklight traps to monitor populations before spraying moths. Catches of more than 5 moths per night warrant sprays applied every 4–5 days, starting at full tassel. **Where:** Widespread, except in the Southwest and far West. Produces 1–3 generations per year, depending on the climate.	▌Remove and destroy all plant debris. ▌Fall cultivation destroys larvae. Plants must be destroyed and turned under at least 1" beneath the soil line. ▌Avoid early plantings which are more susceptible to larvae attack. ▌Handpick by slitting damaged tassels and removing borer. ▌Plant resistant varieties. Small-stemmed, early season types are less tolerant of borer injury. ▌Cover ears with pantyhose. ▌Encourage predators such as toads, downy woodpeckers, phoebes, swallows. ▌*Biological Controls:* Trichogramma wasps parasitize eggs. Braconid wasps. Tachinid flies. Ladybugs and lacewings eat the eggs. Release Trichogramma when adults are first caught in a monitoring trap. Bt is also effective. ▌*Botanical Controls:* Ryania, sabadilla, rotenone (1 percent solution), pyrethrin. ▌Apply Bt and botanical controls at tassel emergence if moth activity is high. Repeat sprays every 4–5 days until silks turn brown. ▌*Allies (see chart on pages 231–238):* Clover, peanuts.
European Red Mite	*See* **Mite**	*See* **Mite**

Macropest Plants Affected	Description of Symptoms and Pest Monitoring Its Presence/Where It Occurs	Organic Remedies
Fall Armyworm and Spring Armyworm *Bean* *Corn (sweet) *** *Cabbage*	Chewed leaves, stems, and buds. The fall species also bores into ears and feeds on kernels; it can be very destructive to late plantings. The spring species is a large (1½") tan, brown, or green caterpillar found early in the season in the whorl leaves of corn. The fall armyworms have three light yellow hairline stripes from head to tail, and on each side a dark stripe below which is a wavy yellow stripe marked with red. Heads have a prominent V or Y. Both species usually feed on cloudy days and at night, but the fall species also feeds during the day. The adult gray moth of the spring species has one yellow or white spot on each forewing. Each lays up to 2,000 eggs on corn and grasses. Eggs hatch in 7 days, and the cycle continues. Further generations feed through late summer. **Where:** The spring species is widespread, but most serious in warm climates where there is more generation turnover. The fall species overwinters in the South and migrates to Northern states every year in June and July. Produces 3–6 generations per year.	■ Encourage natural predators such as birds, toads, and ground beetles. Skunks also prey on these, but you may not want to attract them. ■ In case of a serious problem, dig a steep trench around the garden.** Armyworms will be trapped inside and can be destroyed by putting them in boiling water or in water laced with insecticidal soap (don't use kerosene — it is toxic to the soil and difficult to dispose of safely). ■ Alternate rows of corn with sunflowers to discourage population movement.** ■ *Biological Controls:* Lacewings, ladybugs, and other insect predators eat eggs and young larvae. The new Hh strain of beneficial nematodes *(Neoplectana carpocapsae)* is effective against the larval stage. Ichneumon and braconid wasps. Tachinid flies. Bt is effective against the larvae.
Fall Webworm *Fruit trees* *Pecan*	Large silken tents or nests on ends of branches. Tents include foliage, unlike tentworms. Very damaging. Trees can be stripped and die. This yellowish caterpillar (1¼"), has long, light brown or whitish hairs, a dark stripe down its back, and is dotted with small black spots. It builds gray cocoons in secluded sites, fences, bark, or garden debris. White or green eggs are layered in clusters of 200–500 on leaf undersides. Adult white moths, with black or brown spotted wings, emerge in spring and late summer. **Where:** Widespread. Produces 2 generations per year.	■ Cut off and destroy nests. Burn where permitted. Otherwise destroy nests by putting them in boiling water or water laced with insecticidal soap (don't use kerosene — it is toxic to the soil and difficult to dispose of safely). Pick off leaves with eggs and destroy. ■ *Biological Controls:* Trichogramma wasps eat eggs. Bt is also effective.
Filbert Bud Mite *Filbert*	Buds swell through the summer and fall to 2–3 times their normal size. They will be easily recognized by December, with thousands of mites feeding per bud. Swollen buds open, dry, and drop prematurely in the spring. Yields are seriously diminished. Tiny mites migrate to newly developing buds before old buds fall in the spring. **Where:** Widespread.	■ Plant resistant cultivars. This is the best control. ■ Early spring aphid foliar sprays may help. ■ You might try pruning out infested buds in early winter.

Macropest Plants Affected	Description of Symptoms and Pest Monitoring Its Presence/Where It Occurs	Organic Remedies

Filbert Weevil
(also known as:
Hazelnut Weevil)
   Filbert
   Western Oak
	Deformed green shells. Hollowed out kernels and shells.
	
	Small (¼"–⅜") adult beetle is light brownish-yellow with a long snout about half the length of its body. It emerges May to June and lays eggs in late June or early July in the green shell.
	
	White larvae feed first on the green shell then on the kernel. They exit through small holes and drop to the ground where they overwinter 2"–8" below the soil surface.
	
	Where: Throughout United States.
		▪ Similar to chestnut weevil and plum curculio.

Filbertworm
   Almond
   Chestnut
   Filbert
   Oak
   Persian Walnut
	Small holes in the chestnut.
	
	Small (½"-long) adult moth varies in appearance. Its forewings are reddish-brown, with a broad coppery band down the center.
	
	Larvae (½") are white with yellowish heads. They feed on nut kernels. Larvae overwinter in cocoons on the ground and pupate in spring.
	
	Where: Throughout the United States.
		▪ Early harvest of nuts and immediate destruction of infested nuts.
		▪ See your extension agent for further help.

Flathead Borer
(also known as:
Flathead Appletree
Borer)
   Apple
   Ash
   Beech
   Boxelder
   Dogwood
   Fruit trees
   Hickory
   Maple
   Oak
   Pecan
   Many trees
	Sunken areas in the bark, which indicate feeding tunnels, are filled with a dry powdery substance known as frass, a mixture of droppings and sawdust. Minor foliage damage. The bark turns dark and may exude sap. Sunny sides of the tree are attacked most.
	
	Adults (½") are dark bronze beetles with a metallic sheen, and are usually found on the warm side of trees where they lay yellow, wrinkled eggs in cracks in the bark of unhealthy or injured trees. May and June are the worst times.
	
	Eggs develop into long (1½") yellow-white, U-shaped larvae that have swollen areas just in back of their heads. They bore tunnels into the tree.
	
	Where: Widespread, but particularly in the South and Midwest. Oak is a prime target in the West; maple and fruit trees are prime targets in the East. Produces 1 generation per year.
		▪ Shade the trunks of young trees with some kind of shield.
		▪ Protect newly transplanted trees by wrapping trunks with burlap or cardboard from the soil level up to the lower branches. Or, cover with a thick coat of white exterior latex paint.
		▪ Keep young trees pruned to a low profile.
		▪ Seal wounds with tree paint.
		▪ Encourage predators such as crows, wasps, woodpeckers, predatory beetles, and vireos.

Flea Beetle
(many species)
(also known as:
Corn Flea Beetle,
Potato Flea Beetle)
   Bean
   Brassicas
   Corn
continued
	Numerous small holes in leaves in early summer. Worst after mild winters and cool, wet springs. Adults transmit Stewart's Wilt to sweet corn and Early Blight to potatoes.
	
	These tiny (⅛") dark brown or black beetles jump when disturbed. They can have white or yellow markings. Adults lay eggs in the soil and enjoy the sun.
		▪ Use row covers. (Pantyhose can be used over small cabbages.)
		▪ Plant as late as possible.
		▪ Seed thickly until the danger of infestation is past.
		▪ Attach sticky bands around the base of wintering plants.

Macropest Plants Affected	Description of Symptoms and Pest Monitoring Its Presence/Where It Occurs	Organic Remedies
Flea Beetle, *continued* *Eggplant* *Lettuce* *Muskmelon* *Pepper* *Potato* *Radish* *Spinach* *Sweet Potato* *Tomato* *Watermelon*	The larvae feed on plant roots and can also damage tubers. Flea beetles stop feeding and hide in wet weather. **To Monitor:** Use white sticky traps for an early warning device. **Where:** Widespread. Usually produces 2 generations per year.	■ Use yellow sticky traps for control. ■ Frequent fall and spring cultivation will expose eggs to predators. ■ Sprinkle wood ashes (moistened to prevent blowing) around the plant base; or, mix equal parts of wood ashes and lime in small containers and place around the plants.** ■ A dusting of diatomaceous earth dries up beetles. ■ Vacuum with hand-held vacuum. Empty immediately into plastic bag. ■ Plant after a trap crop of radish or pak choi.** ■ Sprinkle crushed elderberry or tomato leaves on vulnerable plants.** ■ Mulch with chopped clover.** ■ Companion plant with cover crops of clover or annual ryegrass to reduce populations.** ■ Interplant with shading crops.** ■ Hot pepper or garlic spray.** ■ *Biological Controls:* Apply beneficial nematodes in mulch or seed furrows. ■ *Botanical Controls:* Sabadilla, rotenone (1 percent solution), pyrethrin. ■ *Allies (see chart on pages 231–238):* Candytuft, catnip, mint, shepherd's purse, tansy, tomato.
Fruit Tree Leafroller	*See* **Leafroller**	*See* **Leafroller**
Gall Wasp *Chestnut*	Vegetative buds and shoots growth is hindered by galls. Buds are turned into ⅓"–½" rose-colored balls which often hang onto the branch for several years. Buds may have some parts of leaf or stem growth. Trees lose vigor and may die. The small (⅛") adult wasp emerges in late May-early June and lays eggs inside buds. Eggs hatch in late July and larvae begin to grow. Larvae overwinter inside the bud. **Where:** Prevalent in the Southeast, particularly Georgia. Produces 1 generation per year.	■ Prune and destroy infested shoots.
Garden Symphylan or Centipede *Asparagus* *Cucumber* *Lettuce* *Radish* *Tomato*	Stunted plants that slowly die. Destroyed root hairs. This pest is not a true centipede, which is beneficial and grows to 3" long. Small (½"), white worm-like creature with twelve pairs of legs thrives in damp soil, leaf mold, and manure piles. It feeds on root hairs. After harvest, it burrows down 12" into the soil where it lays clusters of white spherical eggs. **Where:** Warm climates and greenhouses. Particularly damaging to asparagus in California.	■ Inspect soil. Two or more of these pests per shovel means you can expect damage. Avoid planting where you find damaging populations. ■ Pasteurize potting soil. ■ Solarize outdoor growing beds, where possible. ■ In California, flood asparagus field for 3 weeks in late December to early January, to a depth of 1–3 feet.

| Macropest
Plants Affected | Description of Symptoms and Pest
Monitoring Its Presence/Where It Occurs | Organic Remedies |
| --- | --- | --- |
| **Garden Webworm**
Bean *
Beet
Corn (sweet) *
Pea *
Strawberry * | Holes in leaves and stems. Folded leaves held together with fine webs. Defoliation.

Tan-brown moths (1"), with gray markings, appear in spring and lay clusters of eggs on the leaves of host plants.

Caterpillars (1") are greenish with small dark spots and hairy. They hatch, feed, and spin webs for shelter. When disturbed they drop to the ground or hide inside silken tubular shelters on the ground. They feed for about 1 month before pupating. The last generation overwinters in the soil in the pupal phase.

Where: Widespread, but only serious in parts of the South and Midwest. Produces several generations per year. | ■ Cut off and destroy webbed branches.
■ Handpick caterpillars.
■ Remove infested leaves and stems.
■ Crush worms inside silken tubes on the ground.
■ *Botanical Controls:* Dust with rotenone as a last resort, or use a rotenone/pyrethrin mix. |
| **Gopher and Groundhog**
Flowers
Fruit trees
Vegetables | Burrows and chewed vegetation. Fan or crescent-shaped mounds of dirt next to holes.

Gophers eat the roots of vegetables, fruit trees, and grasses. They also dine on bulbs and tubers. Unlike groundhogs, gophers can't climb fences and — unlike the solitary mole — they invade in numbers.

Where: Widespread. | ■ Trapping or shooting are the only sure controls. Determine all openings to the tunnel system, then fumigate.
■ For gophers, place ¼" hardware cloth 2' down into the soil and extending above ground 1'.
■ Gophers don't like scilla bulbs (also known as squills).** These spring flowering bulbs are minimal care and are best for borders or rock gardens.
■ Plant the animal's favorite foods (e.g., alfalfa and clover) at a distance.**
■ Place empty narrow-mouth bottles in hole; wind vibrating in bottles repels gophers, groundhogs, and moles.**
■ Dog manure placed in animals' holes is reported to drive them away.**
■ The product named Hinder is reputed to repel groundhogs. Spray on foliage, borders, and animal paths.
■ Sprinkle human hair throughout the garden (you can get a huge supply from your local hairdresser).** This is unsightly, but found to be effective by some. |
| **Grape Berry Moth**
Grape | Young grapes are webbed together, fail to mature, brown, and fall to the ground.

Adult moths emerge in late spring and lay flat round eggs on stems, flowers, and grapes. Larvae pupate in cocoons attached to bark, in debris, or in fallen leaves.

Where: Prevalent in northeastern states, west to Wisconsin and Nebraska, south to Louisiana and Alabama. Produces 2 generations per year. | ■ One month before harvest (late summer), hoe around grape vines. Create a wide, flat ridge to seed with a winter cover crop.
■ Turn under any cocoons on the soil surface. Water well to compact the soil and seal in the cocoons where they'll be smothered. |

Macropest Plants Affected	Description of Symptoms and Pest Monitoring Its Presence/Where It Occurs	Organic Remedies
Grasshopper (also known as: Locust) *All plants*	Chewed leaves and stems. Defoliation. The large (1"–2") brown, gray, yellow, or green heavy-shelled adult has large hind legs, big jaws, and antennae. It lays eggs in weeds or soil. Grasshoppers can pollute well water and reservoirs. Larvae overwinter in the soil. **Where:** Live primarily in grassland areas, particularly in dry seasons.	■ Repeated fall cultivation. ■ Use row covers. ■ Encourage natural predators like birds, cats, chickens, field mice, skunks, snakes, spiders, squirrels, and toads. Also, blister beetle larvae prey on grasshopper eggs, so unless they're a pest themselves, leave these alone. If numerous, the larvae can eat up to 40–60 percent of the area's grasshopper eggs. ■ Fill a jar with a mixture of molasses and water. Bury it up to its mouth in the soil; clean and refresh as needed.** ■ Spray insecticidal soap, mixed with beneficial nematodes, directly on the grasshopper. Apply in evening hours. Soap alone is not very effective against hard-bodied insects — you can also try mixing in hot peppers. ■ *Biological Controls:* Preying mantis. *Nosema locustae,* a beneficial protozoan often sold as Grasshopper Attack, controls most grasshopper species. It must be applied in early spring — before grasshoppers grow to more than ¾" — or they won't eat enough for it to be effective. It lasts several years, and its effects are greatest the summer following its application.
Greenhouse Leaftier	*See* **Celery Leaftier**	*See* **Celery Leaftier**
Gypsy Moth *Apple* *Apricot* *Basswood* *Birch* *Linden* *Oak* *Peach* *Pear* *Willow*	Rapid defoliation. Masses of worms feeding. Large holes in leaves. No tents. Defoliation in 2 successive years may kill deciduous trees. This hairy gray or brown caterpillar (¹⁄₁₆"–2") has five pairs of blue and six pairs of red spots. Larvae crawl to top of trees and dangle on silky threads to be blown to another tree. When more mature (2½") they hide in daylight and feed at night. The adult female white moth doesn't fly, but lays tan eggs in 1"-long masses on trunks, branches, and under rocks. The adult male moth is large (1½") and brown. Adults live less than 2 weeks. Larvae pupate and overwinter in dark cocoons or tie themselves to a branch with silken threads. **Where:** Prevalent primarily in the east, but moving south and west. Produces 1 generation per year. Worst attacks follow a dry fall and warm spring.	■ *August to April:* To destroy egg masses, paint with creosote or drop into water laced with insecticidal soap. (Don't use kerosene — it is toxic to the soil and difficult to dispose of safely.) ■ *Late April to early June:* Attach a 12"-wide burlap strip to tree, about chest height, by draping it over a string. Caterpillars will hide under the cloth during the day. Every afternoon, using gloves, sweep worms into soapy water. ■ *Late April to early June:* Apply sticky bands; remove in mid-July. ■ *Fall:* Check lawn furniture, wood piles, walls, and outbuildings for egg masses. Also check all vehicles for egg masses to avoid transporting eggs to new areas. Destroy all egg masses. ■ Use gypsy moth pheromone traps to monitor populations and to control. ■ *Biological Controls:* Bt is effective when applied every 10-14 days starting in April and continuing through mid-June until the caterpillars are 1" long. Trichogramma and chalcid wasps provide limited control. Lacewings, tachinid flies, predaceous ground beetles, white-footed mice can all help. Also try *Glyptapanteles flavicoxis* and *Cotesia melanoscelus.* Use beneficial nematodes at the tree base to prevent migration. ■ *Botanical Controls:* Ryania, pyrethrin.

Macropest / Plants Affected	Description of Symptoms and Pest / Monitoring Its Presence/Where It Occurs	Organic Remedies
Harlequin Bug (also known as: Cabbage Bug, Calicoback, Terrapin Fire Bug) *Brassicas** *Eggplant* *Radish*	Wilting plants, especially seedlings. Yellowish or black spots on leaves. White blotches. Very destructive. This small (¼"), flat and shield-shaped bug has a shiny black and red-orange back. It sucks leaf juices and smells bad. The adult female lays two neat rows of black-ringed white eggs on leaf undersides. Eggs hatch in 4–7 days. Nymphs suck leaf juices, causing leaf blotches. The adult overwinters in cabbage stalks. **Where:** Appears in southern half of the United States, from coast to coast. Produces several generations per year.	■ Handpick adults and eggs and destroy. ■ Insecticidal soap. Lace the spray with isopropyl alcohol, which helps it penetrate the shells of hard-bodied insects. Soap alone is not very effective against hard-bodied insects. ■ Fall cultivation. ■ Mustard greens or turnips can be used as trap crops.** ■ In spring, place old cabbage leaves in the garden to attract the bugs; destroy them when collected.** ■ *Biological Controls:* Praying mantis might help. ■ *Botanical Controls:* Sabadilla, rotenone (5 percent solution), pyrethrin.
Hickory Shuckworm *Hickory* *Pecan*	Premature nut drop, poor quality kernels, dark-stained spots on shells. Very damaging. Large (⅔") caterpillars are cream-colored with brownish heads. They overwinter in shucks on the ground or in the tree. Small (½") dark brown-black adult moths emerge when nuts begin to develop and continue emerging throughout the summer. They lay eggs on foliage and nuts. **Where:** Prevalent in eastern Canada and United States, south to Florida, west to Missouri, Oklahoma, and Texas. Produces 1–4 generations per year.	■ Blacklight traps can reduce populations (one per three trees). ■ Collect all prematurely dropped nuts; at harvest, collect all shucks. If legal, burn. Otherwise, destroy larvae by dropping shucks and nuts in water laced with insecticidal soap or boiling water. (Don't use kerosene — it is toxic to the soil and difficult to dispose of.) ■ *Biological Controls:* Trichogramma wasp — release 2–3 times per season (mid-April; 2 weeks later; and again 2 weeks following).
Imported Cabbage Worm, Moth and Butterfly *Brassicas** *Radish*	Huge ragged holes in leaves with bits of green excrement. Tunnels inside broccoli, cabbage, and cauliflower heads. This large (1¼"), velvety smooth worm, light to bright green, has one yellow stripe down its back. It feeds on foliage and pupates by suspending itself by silken threads from plants or objects. The adult (2") is a day-flying, white to pale yellow butterfly, with grayish tips and 3–4 black spots on each wing. Butterflies drop hundreds of single, light yellow-green eggs on leaf undersides, which hatch in 4–8 days. **Where:** Widespread. Produce 3–6 generations per year.	■ Use row covers all season. Also try nylon stockings over cabbage heads. Nylon stretches, allowing sun, air, and water through but keeping the butterfly out. ■ Sprinkle damp leaves with rye flour; worms eat it, bloat, and die.** ■ Handpick worms in early morning. Handpick eggs off the undersides of leaves every few days. ■ Fall cultivation, repeated again in the spring. ■ Any green mulch deters this moth. ■ Make a viral insecticide (*see* directions under Organic Remedies for **Cabbage Looper**). ■ Use butterfly nets to catch moths; each one caught means 200–300 worms destroyed. ■ Encourage bluebirds, chickadees, English sparrows. ■ *Biological Controls:* Bt, applied every 10–14 days until heads form, is effective. Lacewings. Trichogramma and braconid wasps. ■ *Botanical Controls:* Sabadilla. ■ *Allies (see chart on pages 231–238)* Celery, dill, garlic, hyssop, mint, onion, rosemary, sage, tansy, thyme, tomato, and more.

Macropest Plants Affected	Description of Symptoms and Pest Monitoring Its Presence/Where It Occurs	Organic Remedies
Inchworm	*See* **Cankerworm**	*See* **Cankerworm**

Japanese Beetle

Plants Affected:
Asparagus
Basil
Bean *
Corn (sweet) *
Grape *
Grasses
Okra
Onion
Peach
Potato
Raspberry
Rhubarb
Rose *
Tomato
Most fruit trees *

Description:

Lacy, skeletonized leaves. Beetles also feed on fruit and corn silk. Grubs feed on grass roots.

This medium-large (½") beetle is shiny metallic green with copper-brown wings. The adult lays eggs in the soil, and eats and flies only during daylight, often up to 5 miles.

The grub, similar to our native white grub, is gray-white with a dark brown head and two rows of spines. It's smaller, about 1", and lies curled in the soil. It overwinters deep in the soil.

Where: Mostly in the eastern United States, but this beetle is slowly moving further west. Eradication near Sacramento, California was attempted in the early 60s. Produces 1 generation per year.

Organic Remedies:

■ Handpick in early morning by shaking tree limbs or branches. Catch them on a sheet spread on ground. Drop bugs into water laced with insecticidal soap. (Don't use kerosene — it is toxic to the soil and difficult to dispose of.)

■ High soil pH discourages grubs.

■ Make a bait of water, sugar, mashed fruit, and yeast. Place on the periphery, not middle, of the garden in sunny spots at least 1' off ground. Strain out beetles every evening.**

■ Use commercially available yellow pheromone traps. Place at a distance from the crop so that existing beetles won't be attracted to the crop, and new beetles from other areas won't be drawn in.

■ Encourage starlings, the only bird that eats adult beetles. Other birds eat the grubs.

■ Time plantings to avoid beetle peak.

■ Four o'clocks *(Mirabilis),* larkspur, and geraniums all poison the beetle. These are good interplantings.

■ Try trap crops of African marigold, borage, evening primrose, *mirabilis* (four o'clocks), soybeans, white roses, white and pastel zinnias.**

■ *Biological Controls:* Apply beneficial nematodes at a rate of 50,000 per square foot of lawn to prevent chewing damage. *Bacillus popilliae,* or milky spore disease, can be applied to lawns and orchard grasses. It attacks grubs and is effective for 15–20 years after just one application.

■ *Botanical Controls:* Rotenone (5 percent solution), pyrethrin.

■ *Allies (see chart on pages 231–238):* Catnip, chives, garlic, rue, and tansy.

June Beetle
(also known as:
May Beetle)
Corn (sweet)
Potato
Strawberry

Description:

Damaged leaves of berry plants (adult feeding). Sudden wilting, especially in May or June, and roots and underground stems are chewed or severed (grub feeding).

Night flying adults are large brown beetles. They emerge in May or June. They lay eggs in midsummer (*see* **White Grub**). White grubs, slightly larger than the Japanese beetle grub, feed for 2 years before pupating.

Where: Causes serious damage in the midwestern and southern United States. Has 1 emergence per year.

Organic Remedies:

■ *See* Organic Remedies for **White Grub**.

■ Handpick beetles and drop into water laced with insecticidal soap. (Don't use kerosene — it is toxic to the soil and difficult to dispose of.)

■ Shake beetles from the tree or shrub early in the morning while they're sluggish, and let fall onto a sheet beneath; collect and destroy beetles.

■ Encourage birds.

■ *Botanical Controls:* Rotenone (5 percent solution).

Macropest / Plants Affected	Description of Symptoms and Pest / Monitoring Its Presence/Where It Occurs	Organic Remedies
Lace Bug (many species) (also known as Eggplant Lace Bug) *Eggplant* *Potato* *Tomato*	Pale, discolored (bronzed) and curled leaves. Plants may die. Leaves may be dotted with dark, shiny droppings. Nymphs and adults suck plant juices from leaves and stems. They feed in groups on leaf undersides. Small adults lay black eggs on leaf undersides in either fall or spring. Eggs hatch in spring. Brown-black nymphs start feeding immediately. Adults overwinter in garden trash. **Where:** Prevalent in the southern half of the United States, from coast to coast.	▪ Check for eggs every 7–10 days, and destroy all egg clusters. ▪ Insecticidal soap spray.
Leaf Beetle	*See* **Bean Leaf Beetle**	*See* **Bean Leaf Beetle**
Leaf-footed Bug *Almond* *Bean** *Nuts* *Potato** *Tomato**	Chewed leaves in vegetables. In almond there may be poorly developed misshapen nuts or premature nut drop. This large (¾") bug resembles the squash bug, but its hind legs are expanded and look like leaves. It is dark brown with a yellow band across its body. When handled it emits a distinctive odor. Adults lay barrel-shaped eggs on leaves of host plants. Nymphs look like adults. Adults hibernate in winter, especially in thistle, and emerge in early summer. **Where:** Widespread, but primarily a problem in the South and westward to Arizona. Produces 1 generation per year.	▪ Handpick and destroy bugs. ▪ Handpick and destroy eggs. ▪ *Botanical Control:* Sabadilla.
Leafhopper (many species) (Beet Leafhopper is also known as Whitefly in the West) *Aster* *Bean* *Beet* *Carrot* *Celery* *Chard* *Citrus* *Corn* *Eggplant* *Fruit trees* *Grape* *Lettuce* *Potato* *continued*	White or yellow mottled, curled leaves die and drop. Excreted honeydew attracts ants and supports black sooty mold. Leafhoppers transmit Curly Top, where mature leaves roll upward, turn yellow with purple veins, and become stiff and brittle. Especially damaging in potatoes due to decreased yields. Nymphs suck plant juices. Small (¼"–⅓"), green, brown, or yellow slender bugs suck juices from leaves, stems, and buds. Nymphs move sideways. The beet leafhopper (⅓") is yellow-green, jumps quickly into the air, and looks like a whitefly. The potato leafhopper (⅓") is green with white spots. The six-spotted leafhopper (⅛") is yellowish with six black spots. Adults lay eggs in early spring on leaf undersides. The second generation of eggs, 2 weeks later, may be laid in plant stems. Adults overwinter in garden trash and weeds.	▪ Use row covers in early spring. ▪ Avoid planting, if possible, in wide open space. ▪ Insecticidal soap spray. If the infestation is bad, add isopropyl alcohol to the spray. ▪ Sprinkle diatomaceous earth or wood ashes, moistened to prevent blowing, around the plant base. Both will dry out leafhoppers. ▪ Remove weeds and afflicted plants. ▪ Fall cultivation. ▪ A reflective mulch such as aluminum foil will repel them. ▪ Keep beets and spinach far from tomatoes. Also avoid planting carrots, asters, and lettuce together if your garden has a problem with the six-spotted leafhopper. ▪ Plant resistant varieties. ▪ Black-lights trap adults.** ▪ Boil 1 pound tobacco in 1 gallon of water; strain; and use as a spray.**

Macropest Plants Affected	Description of Symptoms and Pest Monitoring Its Presence/Where It Occurs	Organic Remedies
Leafhopper, *continued* *Raspberry* *Rhubarb* *Rose* *Spinach* *Squash* *Tomato*	**Where:** Widespread. For specific regions, *see* entries **Beet** and **Potato Leafhoppers.** Produces 1–5 generations per year.	■ Encourage song birds. ■ *Biological Controls:* Lacewings eat the eggs. ■ *Botanical controls:* Sabadilla, rotenone (5 percent solution), pyrethrin. ■ *Allies (see chart on pages 231–238):* Bean, blackberry, clover, goosegrass, red sprangletop, rye, and vetch. Geraniums and petunias allegedly repel leafhoppers.
Leaf Miner (many species; the one whose symptoms are described here is the Spinach species.) *Bean* *Beet greens* *Blackberry* *Cabbage* *Chard* *Chestnut* *Lamb's quarters* *Lettuce* *Oregano* *Pepper* *Radish* *Spinach* *Swiss chard* *Turnip*	White-brown tunnels or blotches on leaves. Yellowed, blistered, or curled leaves. Stem damage below the soil surface. Leafminers are disease vectors for black leg and soft rot. Larvae (⅓") are pale green or whitish. They mine between the upper and lower edges of leaves, causing a scorched, blotched, and blistered appearance. Adults are tiny (⅛"–¼") black or gray flies that lay eggs on leaf undersides. Eggs are tiny, white, and lined up in groups of four to five. If hatched, the leaf will have a grayish blister. **Where:** Widespread. Produces several generations per year.	■ Use row covers. ■ Cut out the infested parts of leaves with grayish blisters. ■ Remove all lamb's quarters unless used as trap crop. ■ Handpick and destroy eggs. ■ Plant fall crops to avoid the insect. ■ Rotate crops. ■ Apply superior horticultural oil. ■ Encourage the chickadee, purple finch, robin. ■ Controls are usually not warranted on the chestnut. ■ *Biological Controls:* Beneficial nematodes give some control. Ladybugs and lacewings may eat leafminer eggs.
Leafroller (also known as: Fruit Tree Leafroller) *Apple* *Other fruit trees*	Rolled leaves with fine webbing that holds the leaves shut. Chewed fruit, leaves, and buds. Small (¾") green caterpillars usually have dark heads. They feed for about 4 weeks then spin webs around leaves and sometimes around the fruit. They pupate in these rolled leaves. The adult is a light brown moth that lays eggs with a camouflage coating in clusters of 30–100 in midsummer on twigs and bark. Eggs overwinter and hatch into caterpillars in spring. **To Monitor:** Use pheromone traps to monitor moth populations and to know when to spray to prevent egg-laying. **Where:** Widespread, but most damage occurs in northern United States and southern Canada. Produces 1 generation per year.	■ Handpick eggs in the winter. ■ Spray light or superior horticultural oil in early spring before buds appear. ■ *Predators:* Trichogramma wasps will eat the caterpillars. ■ *Biological Controls:* Dipel Bt is an effective control; be sure to spray inside the rolled leaf. ■ *Botanical Control:* Rotenone (5 percent solution).
Locust	*See* **Grasshopper**	*See* **Grasshopper**

Macropest Plants Affected	**Description of Symptoms and Pest** Monitoring Its Presence/Where It Occurs	**Organic Remedies**
Mealy Bug *Fruit trees* *Greenhouses* *Houseplants* *Rosemary* *Vegetables*	Cotton tufts on the leaf underside. Honeydew excretions attract ants and support black sooty mold. Dwarfed plants. Wilt. Premature fruit drop. These minuscule bugs suck plant sap. They lay tiny, yellow, smooth eggs where leaves join the stem. **Where:** Widespread, but particularly a problem in warm climates. Produces numerous generations (each cycle takes 1 month).	■ Strong water jets directed at the undersides of leaves. ■ Destroy mealybugs with cotton swabs dipped in alcohol. ■ Spray light or superior horticultural oil before buds appear, to smother eggs. ■ Insecticidal soap spray, especially in the early spring dormant stage. ■ Use sticky bands to trap ants. ■ *Biological Controls:* Green lacewings. *Crytolaemus* ladybug (Australian and uncommon) is a predator and also works in the greenhouse. *Pauridia* parasites prey on bugs.
Measuring Worm	*See* **Cankerworm**	*See* **Cankerworm**
Mexican Bean Beetle *Bean* * *Kale* *Squash*	Lacy, skeletonized leaves. Pods and stems are eaten in bad infestations. Orange-yellow fuzzy larvae (⅓") are longer than the adult, and attach themselves to leaves, usually on the underside, or inside a curled leaf. The small (¼") copper, round-backed adult beetle, with sixteen black spots in three horizontal rows on its back, looks like an orange ladybug. The female adult lays orange-yellow eggs in groups of 40–60 on leaves. Eggs hatch in 5–14 days. Most beans can tolerate 10–20 percent defoliation (more prior to bloom) without loss in yields. **Where:** Widespread, but particularly a problem in the East and Southwest. Produces 2 generations per year in cold climates, and 3–5 in warmer regions.	■ Handpick and destroy beetles, larvae, and egg clusters. ■ Use row covers. ■ A reflective mulch like aluminum foil will repel them. ■ A spray of crushed turnips with corn oil.** ■ Spray cedar sawdust or chips boiled in water.** ■ *Fall:* Pull up infested plants as soon as the main harvest is over but while pests are still present. Stuff vines in a plastic bag, tie, and leave in sun for 10–14 days to kill the bugs. ■ Fall cultivation. ■ Early planting. ■ Encourage insect-eating birds. ■ *Biological Controls:* Spined soldier bug is excellent control. Predatory mites. *Pediobius foveolatus* wasps parasitize larvae; they are excellent controls, but expensive. ■ *Botanical Controls:* Rotenone (1 percent solution), pyrethrins. ■ *Allies (see chart on pages 231–238):* Garlic, marigold, nasturtium, petunia, potatoes, rosemary, and savory.
Millipede *Lettuce* *Root vegetables* *Rose* *Seeds*	Ragged holes in stems and roots, especially seedlings. Fungal disease may be present. This is a caterpillar-like worm (½"–1"), with a hard-shelled body divided into multiple segments and with 30–400 pairs of legs. It moves slowly by contracting and stretching, feeds at night on decaying vegetation, and sometimes transmits diseases. It lays sticky sacs of hundreds of eggs on or in the soil in summer. Adults live 1 to 7 years. **Where:** Widespread, but most damaging in the South and West. Produces 1 generation per year.	■ Peat compost is more hostile to millipedes than other types such as leaf or manure compost. ■ Place window-screen wire under plants.

Mite

(many species)

Apple
Apricot
Asparagus
Bean
Blackberry
Blueberry
Brassicas
Celery
Chestnut
Cucumber
Eggplant
Grape
Herbs
Muskmelon
Peach
Peanut
Pepper
Raspberry
Strawberry

Yellowed, dry leaves, with yellow or red spots or blotches and small white dots. Veins yellow or turn reddish-brown first. Fine webbing between leaves and across undersides. Poorly developed fruit that drops early.

Mites suck chlorophyll out of plants and inject toxins. They can lower chlorophyll by as much as 35 percent. They are worst in hot, dry conditions.

Mites are very tiny red, green, yellow, black, or brown arachnids that are difficult to see without a magnifying lens. Some are beneficial. Females lay numerous eggs on webbing under leaves. Mites overwinter in the soil.

To detect, hold a white paper underneath and tap the leaves to see if mites, the size of salt grains, are dislodged.

Where: Widespread. Many types exist only in specific locales, but general characteristics remain the same. Produce up to 17 generations per year. Each life cycle takes 7–14 days.

■ Spray forceful jets of water in early morning, 3 days in a row, or every other day (three times).

■ Spray insecticidal soap at least three times, every 5–7 days.

■ Mix ¼ pound of glue in a gallon of water; let stand overnight. Spray on twigs and leaves.** When dried it will flake off, taking trapped mites with it. Spray three times, every 7–10 days.

■ Vacuum plants with hand-held vacuum. Empty bag immediately into plastic bag or mites will crawl back out.

■ Fruit trees — high nitrogen fertilizers can increase mite populations, so avoid them.

■ Spray fruit trees with horticultural oil late in the dormant period, right at bud break, when mite eggs are most vulnerable.

■ Cooking oil spray mix, as recommended by USDA.

■ Ensure adequate water.

■ *Biological Controls:* Predatory mites are good outdoors and in greenhouses. Green lacewings and ladybugs feed on the mites.

■ *Botanical Controls:* Sabadilla, pyrethrins (apply twice, 3–4 days apart).

■ *Allies (see chart on pages 231–238):* Alder, bramble berries, coriander, dill, rye mulch, sorghum mulch, wheat mulch.

Mole

Many vegetables

Extensive tunnels. Main runways are usually 6"–10" below ground with frequent mounds of soil heaped above ground.

Moles are solitary, unlike gophers. They tunnel extensively, often using each tunnel only once. They eat grubs and beetles, which isn't bad, but also feed on earthworms — their favorite food. Their tunnels can harm the root systems of young plants.

Where: Appear throughout the United States, but are a major problem in the West.

■ The best control is traps. Set traps at the first sign of tunnels. This can be anytime in most western states. In cooler climates, this will be in spring. Determine which runs are active before setting traps by stepping lightly on them, mark the spots, and check again in 2 days. If spots are raised, the tunnel is active. Spear or harpoon-type traps are considered the easiest to use.

■ Plant 4 or 5 poisonous castor bean plants (*Euphobia lathyris*), also known as "mole plants", nearby.** (*Note:* This plant can become a pest itself in areas of the West and South. It is also poisonous to humans.)

■ Scatter red pepper or tobacco dust to repel moles.**

■ Wearing gloves to prevent human scent, place Juicy Fruit gum in tunnels. Moles are alleged to love it, eat it, and die from it.**

■ Control grubs, food for moles.

■ Plant favorite foods (e.g., alfalfa and clover) at a distance.

Macropest Plants Affected	Description of Symptoms and Pest Monitoring Its Presence/Where It Occurs	Organic Remedies
Mouse (many species) *Apple* *Fruit trees* *Greenhouses* *Onion (storage)* *Strawberry*	Chewed tree trunks at ground level. Gnawed roots (by pine mice). In strawberry beds, you may find nests in mulch and destroyed roots. The house mouse is uniformly gray. The vole, or field mouse, is white-bellied with gray-brown fur on top. The deer mouse, or white-footed mouse, resembles the vole but has white feet. Mice will move into mole tunnels and feed on crop roots. **Where:** Widespread.	▪ At planting, install hardware cloth girdles 6" in diameter and 18" high around tree trunks. Set them at least 6" into the soil, preferably in coarse gravel. ▪ Remove protective cover for mice by removing all vegetation within a 3' radius of trunk. In winter, pull mulch at least 6" away from tree trunks. Keep grass mowed. ▪ For strawberries, wait to mulch until mice have made winter homes elsewhere, when the ground has developed a frosty crust. ▪ Make gravel barriers around garden plots, at least 6"–8" deep and 12" or more wide. This prevents rodents from tunneling and, if kept free of weeds, from crossing the area. ▪ Encourage owls and snakes. ▪ Don't mulch perennials until a few frosts have occurred. ▪ Sprinkle mint leaves in garden.** ▪ *Allies (see chart on pages 231–238)* wormwood.
Navel Orangeworm *Almond* *Citrus** *Walnut*	Worms burrow into fruit and nuts on the tree and in storage. Worms are yellow or dark gray with dark heads. They pupate in cocoons within the fruit. The gray adult moth has crescent-shaped dots along its outer margins. **Where:** Prevalent in Southwestern United States and California.	▪ Clean orchard sanitation. ▪ Early harvest. ▪ Nuts can be fumigated before storage with methyl bromide. ▪ Remove and destroy nuts left on the tree in winter. ▪ *Biological Controls: Goniozus legneri* and *Pentalitomastix plethoricus* both parasitize the pupae. Release them in early spring or after harvest.
Nematode (many species) (also known as: Roundworm, Eelworm) *Apple* *Bean* *Carrot* *Celery* *Cucumber* *Dill* *Eggplant* *(in South)* *Garlic* *Mustard* *Okra* *Onion*	Malformed flowers, leaves, stems, and roots. Stunted, yellowing leaves. Leaves may wilt during the day. Dwarfed plants, with poorly developed roots, leaves, and flowers. Dieback. Root-knot nematodes cause galls, knots, or branched root crops. Lesion nematodes cause root fungal infections and lesions on roots. Nematodes are blind and usually microscopic. Not all are harmful; some are beneficial (*see* page 165).	▪ Plant resistant varieties. ▪ Solarize soil. ▪ Increase soil organic matter. Heavy mulch or compost is one of the best deterrents. Compost is host to saprophytic nematodes and predacious fungi that destroy harmful nematodes. Compost also releases fatty acids toxic to nematodes. Leaf mold compost is especially effective — particularly pine needles, rye, and timothy grasses. ▪ Disinfect tools used in infected soil. ▪ Long crop rotation. ▪ A fertilizer mixture of 70 percent fish emulsion and 30 percent yucca extract (Pent-A-Vane) reduces nematodes. ▪ Kelp meal and crab shell meal (chitin) stimulate beneficial fungi that prey on nematodes. Dig these into the soil 1 month before planting to reduce populations.

continued

Macropest Plants Affected	Description of Symptoms and Pest Monitoring Its Presence/Where It Occurs	Organic Remedies
Nematode, *continued* *Parsley* *Pea* *Potato* *Raspberry* *Strawberry* *Sweet Potato* *Tomato* *Many others*	**Where:** Widespread, especially in warm areas and areas with sandy or loamy soils. Not very common in clay soils. The eggs of some nematode species remain viable in the soil for years.	▪ Sprinkle an emulsion of 1 part corn oil/10 parts water.** ▪ White and black mustard exude oil hostile to nematodes. ▪ Cover crops of barley, castor bean, corn, cotton, joint vetch, millet, rye, sesame, or wheat reduce populations. All plants must be turned under to be effective. Winter rye, when tilled under in spring, produces an organic acid toxic to nematodes. (*Note:* The only rye that can control nematodes is cereal rye *(Secale cereale)*.) ▪ Plant tomatoes near asparagus; asparagus roots are toxic to tomato nematodes. ▪ A solution of water hyacinth leaves or flowers macerated in water (1:3 on a weight basis) has been shown to kill nematodes (1989 study by botanists in India). Also, tomato and eggplant roots soaked in this solution for 80 minutes prior to plantings grew three times faster than unsoaked controls. ▪ *Allies (see chart on pages 231–238):* Asparagus, barley, corn, garlic, hairy indigo, marigold (*Tagetes* sp.), mustard (white or black). (*Note:* Research shows that marigolds suppress root lesion nematodes for 3 years when planted in the entire infested area for a full season. Spot plantings are not as effective, and may reduce yields of nearby crops.)
Nut Curculio *Chestnut* *Oak*	Premature nut drop. Circular cavities in nuts and shells. The small (³⁄₁₆") adult is black with reddish-brown blotches, and a long, curved snout of curculios. It emerges in May and June, occasionally feeds on foliage, and deposits eggs when the bur cracks to expose the nut. Larvae feed on nut kernels for about 3 weeks then emerge through small (³⁄₁₆") holes. **Where:** Present in the Southeast. Produces 1 generation per year.	▪ Same controls as for the **Plum Curculio.** ▪ Drop infected nuts into water to kill larvae.
Onion Eelworm	*See* **Nematodes**	*See* **Nematodes**
Onion Fly Maggot (also known as: Onion Maggot) *Onion *** *Radish* *continued*	Rotting bulbs in storage. Destroyed seedlings. Faded and wilted leaves. Lower stems of onion near the bulb are damaged or destroyed. Worse damage than that caused by the cabbage maggot. This is a small (⅓"), legless, white worm that tapers to a point at the head. It feeds on stems and bulbs.	▪ Avoid planting in rows and close spacing: This discourages maggot movement between plants. ▪ Red onions are the least vulnerable, followed by yellow, and then white varieties. ▪ Sprinkle diatomaceous earth around the plant base, and work slightly into the soil. If this isn't available, then sprinkle wood ashes (moistened to prevent blowing) near the base of the plants.

Macropest Plants Affected	Description of Symptoms and Pest Monitoring Its Presence/Where It Occurs	Organic Remedies
Onion Fly Maggot, *continued*	The adult fly resembles a hairy housefly. It lays eggs at the base of plants, near the bulb or neck, or in the bulb. **Where:** Particularly prevalent in northern and coastal regions, where cool, wet weather abounds. Produces 3 generations per year. The last generation attacks harvest and storage onions.	■ Don't store damaged bulbs. ■ Encourage robins and starlings. ■ *Biological Controls:* Beneficial nematodes.
Oriental Fruit Moth *Apple* * *Peach* * *Pear* *Plum* *Quince*	Wormy fruit. Terminals of rapidly growing shoots wilt, turn brown in a few days, and die. Gummy exudate; holes in fruit and in fruit stems. These small larvae (½") are yellow-pink with brown heads, and are very active. When small, they tunnel into tender shoots and later enter fruit through the stem end. They don't tunnel to the core of apples, but in peaches feed close to the pit. On the outside fruit may not look damaged. Larvae emerge from fruit and pupate in silken cocoons attached to tree trunks, weeds, or garden debris. The adult moth (½") is gray, and lays white eggs on leaves and twigs. **To Monitor:** Pheromone traps are available for early detection. Captures exceeding five to ten moths per trap per week warrants control action. **Where:** Prevalent east of the Mississippi and in the upper Northwest. Several generations per year.	■ If this is a consistent pest, plant early-ripening cultivars to starve the last generation. ■ Prune trees annually to avoid dense growth. ■ Plant early maturing varieties of peach and apricot. ■ Inspect tree trunks and destroy all cocoons. ■ Pheromone-based mating disruption lures are commercially available but may not be effective in small orchards. ■ *Biological Controls:* Import the Braconid wasp *Macrocentrus ancylivorus* and release according to instructions from supplier. ■ *Botanical Controls:* Ryania, rotenone, pyrethrins. ■ *Allies (see chart on pages 231–238):* Goldenrod, lamb's quarters, strawberries.
Parsleyworm (also known as: Carrotworm, Celeryworm, Black Swallowtail) *Carrot* * *Celery* *Celeriac* *Dill* *Parsley* * *Parsnip*	Chewed leaves, often down to bare stems. Damage is usually minor because of low populations. This long (2"), stunning green worm has a yellow-dotted black band across each segment. It emits a sweet odor and projects two orange horns when disturbed. The adult is the familiar black swallowtail butterfly. Its large black forewings (3"–4" across) have two rows of parallel yellow spots. Its rear wings have a blue row of spots with one orange spot. Adults lay white eggs on leaves which hatch in 10 days. **Where:** Occurs east of the Rockies, and a similar species west of the Rockies. Produces several generations per year.	■ Handpick in early morning. ■ Encourage song birds. ■ *Biological Controls:* Lacewing larvae; parasitic wasps.
Peach Tree Borer (Greater) *Apricot* *Cherry* *Nectarine* *continued*	Brown gummy sawdust (frass) on the bark, usually near the ground. Very damaging. Trees can die. Large (1¼"), yellow-white larvae have dark brown heads. They feed under the bark at or below the soil surface all winter. The highest they'll usually go is about 12" above the soil.	■ Insert stiff wires into holes to kill larvae. **Do not** remove gummy exudate, which helps to seal wounds. ■ Use sticky bands, from 2" below the soil line to 6" above. Destroy and replace the bands each week.

Macropest Plants Affected	Description of Symptoms and Pest Monitoring Its Presence/Where It Occurs	Organic Remedies
Peach Tree Borer (Greater), *continued* *Peach ** *Plum*	Adult moths (1") are blue, clear-winged, and look like wasps. They emerge in the North in July and August, and in the South in August and September. They lay brown-gray eggs at the trunk base in late summer to fall. **Where:** Appear where vulnerable plants are grown, particularly in eastern states and the lower half of the United States from coast to coast. Produces 1 generation per year.	■ *Tobacco dust ring:* Encircle the trunk with a piece of tin, 2" away from the bark. In mid-May fill with tobacco dust. Repeat every year. ■ Tie soft soap around the trunk from the soil line up to the crotch; soap drips repel moths and larvae.** ■ In the near future, pheromone dispensers should be available. These confuse males and stop mating, but may not be effective in small orchards. ■ Encourage birds. ■ *Biological Controls:* Spray or inject beneficial nematodes into the holes. Spray Bt every 10 days or syringe it into the holes. ■ *Allies (see chart on pages 231–238):* Garlic.
Peach Tree Borer (Lesser) *Apricot* *Cherry* *Nectarine* *Peach ** *Plum*	Same symptoms as Greater Peach Tree Borer, but damage is in upper limbs. They invade through wounds created by such things as winter injury, pruning, and cankers. **Where:** Appears in same areas as the Greater Peach Tree Borer, but produces 2–3 generations per year.	■ *See* first and last three Organic remedies listed for the **Greater Peach Tree Borer.** ■ Take measures to minimize winter injury (*see* **Sunscald** on page 181), pruning wounds, or other entry sites. ■ Use sticky bands on affected limbs; destroy and replace bands each week.
Peach Twig Borer *Almond* *Apricot* *Peach ** *Plum*	Red-brown masses of chewed bark in twig crotches. Infested fruit late in the season. Small (less than ½") red-brown larvae construct cocoons under curled edges of bark. The adult is a small (½"), steel-gray moth. **Where:** Widespread, but very damaging on the West Coast. Produces 3–4 generations per year.	■ Increase organic matter in soil. ■ Take measures to minimize winter injury (*see* **Sunscald** on page 181), pruning wounds, or other entry sites. ■ Insert stiff wires into holes to kill larvae. **Do not** remove gummy exudate, which helps to seal wounds. ■ Tie soft soap around the trunk from the soil line up to the crotch; soap drips repel moths and larvae.** ■ In the near future, pheromone dispensers should be available. These confuse males and stop mating, but may not be effective in small orchards. ■ Encourage birds. ■ Pheromone traps are available that catch males (not the same as mating-disruption lures). These can be used to monitor population levels and, in small areas, to help control populations. ■ Spray dormant lime-sulfur spray (diluted 1:15) before the pink stage and after petal fall.
Pear Psylla *Pear* *continued*	Yellow leaves. Leaf drop. Low vigor. Honeydew excretion attracts yellow jackets and ants and supports black soot mold. Blackened leaves and fruit. Scarred and malformed fruit. Nymphs and adults suck plant juices, and can transmit fire blight and pear decline. Very damaging.	■ Spray insecticidal soap, in high pressure, as soon as females emerge and when leaf buds are just beginning to turn green. Continue through season as needed. ■ Dust tree and leaves with limestone.

| Macropest
Plants Affected | Description of Symptoms and Pest
Monitoring Its Presence/Where It Occurs | Organic Remedies |
|---|---|---|
| **Pear Psylla,**
continued | Nymphs are very tiny and yellow, green or light brown. They feed on the top sides of leaves until only the veins remain.

Adults are tiny (1/10"), light brown to dark orange-red, and have clear wings. Before buds open, adults lay tiny yellowish-orange eggs in cracks and crevices, in the base of terminal buds, and in old leaf scars. Also check tender growing tips of the highest shoots. Nymphs hatch in 2–4 weeks. Most hatch by petal fall.

Where: Present in the eastern (east of Mississippi) and northwestern states. There are 3–5 generations per year. | ■ Destroy all debris, which harbors the eggs. Adults and eggs spend winter on or near tree.

■ Spray light horticultural oil in the fall, and again in spring at the green tip stage; continue to spray every 7 days until larvae emerge.

■ Plant tolerant varieties. (Bartlett and D'Anjou are the most susceptible).

■ *Botanical Controls:* Rotenone (5 percent solution). |
| **Pearslug**
(also known as:
Cherryslug)
*Apple
Cherry
Pear *
Plum* | Pink-brown patches on upper surface of leaves. Lacy skeletonized leaves. Defoliation. Streaks of chocolate-covered sawdust on apples.

Larvae (1/2") are dark green-orange, covered with slime, tadpole-shaped, and look like small slugs with large heads. Larvae feed for 2–3 weeks on upper leaf surfaces. Larvae in apples feed just under fruit skin until about one-third grown, then bore through the fruit. After feeding they drop to the ground to pupate.

The adult is a small black-and-yellow sawfly, little larger than a housefly, with two sets of transparent wings hooked together. At bloom time, the adult emerges from a cocoon in the soil. The sawfly inserts its eggs into leaves or into the skin of fruit.

Where: Widespread. Produces 2 generations per year. | ■ Shallow cultivation, no more than 2" deep, at the tree base right before full bloom. This exposes cocoons to predators.

■ Dust trees with wood ashes — slightly moistened to prevent blowing — which will dry out larvae and kill them.** Wash trees with water after 5 days.

■ Pick up fallen fruit every day.

■ *Botanical Controls:* A pyrethrin/rotenone/ryania blend. |
| **Pecan Casebearer**
Pecan | Small cocoons at the base of the bud indicate overwintering larvae. Tunneled shoots. Signs of eaten nuts in the early maturation phase. Trees will experience little damage, but nut yields are reduced.

This small (1/2") caterpillar is olive gray to jade green with a yellow-brown head. When buds open, caterpillars feed on buds and shoots.

Adult moths emerge when the nut forms. They lay single, light-colored eggs on the blossom end of the nut. Larvae then feed on developing nuts.

Where: Present wherever pecans are grown. Produces 2 generations in northern climates, 4 generations in southern climates. | ■ Blacklight traps (one for every three trees) will reduce populations.

■ Collect all prematurely dropped nuts; at harvest time, collect all shucks. If legal, burn. Otherwise, destroy in hot water or water laced with insecticidal soap. (Don't use kerosene — it is toxic to the soil and difficult to dispose of.)

■ *Biological Controls:* Trichogramma wasps — release 2–3 times per season (once in mid-April; again 2 weeks later; and a third time 2 weeks following). |

Macropest Plants Affected	Description of Symptoms and Pest Monitoring Its Presence/Where It Occurs	Organic Remedies
Pecan Weevil *Hickory* *Pecan*	Premature nut drop and hollowed kernels. Similar to the Chestnut Weevil. The adult (¾") is light brown and, as it ages, may become dark brown. Its snout is needle-thin and can be as long as its body. Adults feed on husks and young nuts. Grubs are white with reddish-brown heads. They feed on kernels, emerge, and pupate in "cells" as much as 12" below the soil surface. Adults may not emerge for 2–3 years. **Where:** Present wherever pecan and hickory are grown. Has 1 emergence per year.	■ Use same controls as for **Chestnut Weevil** and **Plum Curculio.** ■ Burlap bands wrapped around trees. (*See* **Sticky Bands** on page 171.)
Phylloxera Aphid	*See* **Aphid**	*See* **Aphid**
Pickleworm *Cucumber* *Melon* *Squash*	Holes in buds, blossoms, and fruits of most *cucurbits.* Masses of rotting green excrement. This medium (¾") caterpillar is green or copperish. The first generation emerges midsummer. Damage is worst late in the season when the broods are largest. The adult nocturnal moth is yellowish. It lays eggs that develop into small caterpillars that are pale yellow with black dots. These change color as they mature. **Where:** Prevalent primarily in the Southeast and the Gulf states, particularly Florida and Louisiana. Produces 3–4 generations per year.	■ Plant susceptible crops as early as possible to avoid pest. ■ Destroy all plant debris after harvest. ■ Cultivate the soil deeply in early fall, after harvest. ■ Plant resistant varieties. ■ *Botanical Controls:* Apply Rotenone (5 percent solution) at petal fall, and every 10–14 days through September.
Pill Bug (also known as: Roly-poly)	*See* **Sow Bug.** (Unlike sow bugs, pill bugs roll up into tight balls about the size of a pea.)	*See* **Sow Bug**
Plum Curculio *Apple* *Apricot* *Blueberry* *Cherry* *Peach* *Pear* *Plum* *	Eaten leaves and petals. Crescent-shaped cavities in fruits. Sap exudate from apple fruit dries to a white crust. Misshapen fruit. Premature fruit drop. Brown rot disease. This small (¼") dark brown beetle, has a long down-curving snout and 4 humps on its back. It emerges at blossom time when temperatures climb above 70°F. When disturbed, it folds its legs and drops to the ground. It lays eggs in crescent shape fruit wound. Grubs are gray-white with brown heads and curled bodies. They feed at the fruit center for 2 weeks and emerge only after fruit falls to ground. They pupate in the ground. Adults take about 1 month to emerge. **Where:** Appears east of the Rockies. Produces 1–2 generations per year.	■ Hang white sticky traps (8"x10") in trees at chest height for both monitoring and control. Use several per tree. Remove after 3 to 4 weeks. ■ Starting at blossom time, every day in the early morning spread a sheet or tarp under the tree and knock branches with a padded board or pole. Shake collected beetles into a bucket of water laced with insecticidal soap. (Don't use kerosene — it is toxic to the soil and difficult to dispose of.) ■ Remove all diseased and fallen fruit immediately. Destroy larvae by burning fruit or burying in the middle of a hot compost pile. ■ Keep trees pruned: Curculios dislike direct sun. ■ Encourage the chickadee, bluebird, and purple martin. Domestic fowl will also eat these insects.

Macropest Plants Affected	Description of Symptoms and Pest Monitoring Its Presence/Where It Occurs	Organic Remedies
Plume Moth *Artichoke*	Irregular holes in stems, foliage, and bud scales. Small worms are on bud scales and new foliage. Damage is year-round, but worst in the spring. Larvae bore into the fruit, blemish the scales, and tunnel into the heart. Nocturnal adult brown moths (1") have plumed wings and fly near the plant. They lay eggs on leaf undersides. **Where:** Lives on the Pacific and Texas coasts.	▪ Pick and destroy all wormy buds. ▪ Remove and destroy all plant debris in the fall. ▪ Remove all nearby thistles. ▪ *Biological Controls:* Bt is effective.
Potato Bug	*See* **Colorado Potato Beetle**	*See* **Colorado Potato Beetle**
Potato Flea Beetle	*See* **Flea Beetle**	*See* **Flea Beetle**
Potato Leafhopper (also known as: Bean Jassid) *Apple* * *Bean (South)* *Peanut* *Potato (East and South)* *	*See* **Leafhopper.** This leafhopper causes "hopperburn:" a triangular brown spot appears at leaf tips, leaf tips curl, yellow, and become brittle. Reduced yields in potatoes. **Where:** Lives primarily in eastern and southern United States. It migrates south for winter, and returns north in spring to feed first on apples, then on potatoes. Produces 2 generations in Mid-Atlantic states.	▪ *See* **Leafhopper.** ▪ Potato leafhoppers are said to be trapped by black fluorescent lamps.**
Potato Tuberworm (also known as: Tuber Moth) *Eggplant* *Potato* * *Tomato*	Wilted shoots and stems. Dieback. The gray-brown adult moth is small with narrow wings. It lays eggs on the leaf undersides or in tubers. Larvae (¾") are pink-white with brown heads. They tunnel into stems and leaves. They pupate on the ground in cocoons covered with soil, and can emerge in storage to pupate. **Where:** Present in the South from coast to coast, and northward to Washington, Colorado, Virginia, and Maryland. Worst in hot, dry years. Produces 5–6 generations per year.	▪ Plant as early as possible. ▪ Keep soil well cultivated and deeply tilled. ▪ Cut and destroy infested vines before harvesting. ▪ Destroy all infested potatoes. ▪ Screen storage areas and keep storage area cool and dark. (Darkness discourages moth activity.)
Rabbit *Bean* *Carrot* *Lettuce* *Pea* *Strawberry* *Tulip shoots* *Bark of fruit trees*	A small white or gray mammal with long ears and short tail that travels primarily by hopping. Rabbits eat vegetables, herbs, flowers, and chew on young fruit trees. **Where:** Widespread.	▪ Sprinkle any of the following around plants: Blood meal, moistened wood ashes, ground hot peppers, chili or garlic powder, crushed mint leaves, talcum powder.** Replenish frequently, especially after rain. You can also sprinkle black pepper right on the plants, which gives rabbits sneezing fits and keeps them away. ▪ Cover seedlings with plastic milk jugs that have the bottoms cut out. Anchor them well in the soil, and keep the cap off for ventilation. This can also be used as a season extender in the spring. ▪ Place old smelly leather shoes on the garden periphery.**

continued

Macropest Plants Affected	Description of Symptoms and Pest Monitoring Its Presence/Where It Occurs	Organic Remedies
Rabbit, *continued*		■ Place fake snakes near garden.** ■ Wrap base of fruit trees with hardware cloth. ■ Set rabbit traps. ■ Encourage owls and sparrow hawks with nest boxes. ■ The product named Hinder is reputed to be an effective repellant. Spray on foliage, borders, and animal paths. When painted on bark it is also supposed to prevent tree girdling by rabbits. ■ Fine-woven fences are effective deterrents. ■ Garlic, marigold, and onion are said to deter rabbits.**
Raspberry Caneborer *Blackberry* *Raspberry*	Sudden wilting of tips. Two rows of punctures about 1" apart. Medium-sized (½") adult is a long-horned black-and-yellow beetle. It lays one egg between a double row of punctures on the stem near the cane tip. A small worm hatches and burrows 1"–2" deep near the base of the cane to hibernate. This is a major cane pest. **Where:** Present in Kansas and eastward. Produces 1 generation per year.	■ Cut off cane tips 6" below the puncture marks, and burn or destroy. ■ **Botanical controls:** Rotenone (1 percent solution). Apply two treatments 7 days apart, timed to coincide with adult emergence during June. Consult your County Extension Agent for the local adult activity period.
Raspberry Root Borer (also known as: Raspberry Crown Borer) *Blackberry* *Raspberry*	Wilting and dying canes in early summer, usually when berries are ripening. Stunted plants. Larvae are small, white, and hibernate at the soil level near canes. They tunnel into cane crowns and bases. The adult moth has clear-wings and a black body with four yellow bands. **Where:** Prevalent in eastern United States. Produces 1 generation.	■ Cut out infected canes below the soil line.
Raspberry Sawfly	*See* **Blackberry Sawfly**	*See* **Blackberry Sawfly**
Rednecked Cane Borer	*See* **Caneborer**	*See* **Caneborer**
Root Fly and Root Maggot	*See* **Corn Maggot** and **Cabbage Maggot**	*See* **Corn Maggot** and **Cabbage Maggot**
Rose Chafer (also known as: Rose Bug) *Grape ** *Peony* *Rose ** *Other fruits and* *flowers* *continued*	Chewed foliage. Destroyed grass roots. This slender, adult beetle (⅓"–½") is tan, with a reddish-brown head and long spiny, slightly hairy, legs. It emerges in late May to early June and feeds for 3–4 weeks, attacking flowers first, then fruit blossoms and newly set fruit. It lays eggs in the soil which hatch in 1–2 weeks. Larvae (¾") feed on grass roots, then pupate 10"–16" deep in the soil.	■ Handpick adults. ■ Cheesecloth fences, stretched higher than the plants, will deter the beetle as it doesn't fly over barriers. ■ Do not allow chickens to clean garden because these beetles are poisonous to chickens.

Macropest Plants Affected	Description of Symptoms and Pest Monitoring Its Presence/Where It Occurs	Organic Remedies
Rose Chafer, *continued*	**Where:** Prevalent east of the Rockies; primarily a pest in sandy soils and north of New York City. Produces 1 generation annually.	■ Ohio State University research shows commercially available white traps are most effective with this pest (and no chemical attractants are necessary).
Roundworm	*See* **Nematode**	*See* **Nematode**
Sap Beetle (many species) (also known as: Corn Sap Beetle, Strawberry Sap Beetle) *Corn* *Strawberry* *Raspberry*	Brown hollowed-out kernels at the corn ear tip. Sometimes individual damaged kernels are scattered throughout. Round cavities eaten straight into ripe strawberries. Feeding injury between the raspberry and stem. Injury predisposes small fruit to secondary rot organisms. This small (³⁄₁₆"), black, oblong beetle invades ears through the silk channel or via holes in the husk caused by other pests. This is often associated with corn borer or corn earworm damage. A smaller, brown, oval beetle attacks small fruit. White, maggot-like larvae eat inside kernels and infested fruit. They scatter when exposed to light. **Where:** Widespread.	■ Clean and complete harvesting of small fruit and removal of damaged, diseased, and overripe berries helps to reduce populations. ■ Deep plowing in fall or early spring reduces overwintering populations of the corn sap beetle. ■ Destroy alternate food sources, such as old vegetable crops beyond harvest. ■ Mineral oil, applied just inside the tip of each ear, suffocates the worms. Apply only after silk has wilted and started to brown at the tip, or pollination will be incomplete. Use ½ of a medicine dropper per small ear, ¾ of a dropper per large ear. You might add red pepper to the oil to see if it increases the effectiveness. Apply two or more applications of oil, spaced at 2 week intervals. ■ Fall cultivation. In the spring, cultivate the top 2 inches of soil. ■ Plant resistant varieties with tight husks. Or clip husks tightly with clothespins. You can also try covering ears with pantyhose. ■ *Biological Controls:* Minute pirate bugs. Lacewings. Trichogramma wasps and Tachinid flies lay eggs in the moth eggs and prevent hatching. Inject beneficial nematodes into infested ears; they seek out and kill worms in 24 hours. Bt can be applied to borers before they move into the stalks. Then wettable Bt, applied every 10–14 days, is effective. ■ *Botanical Controls:* Ryania, rotenone (1 percent solution), pyrethrin. Use pheromone traps to identify moth flight paths before spraying. Spray moths before they lay eggs. ■ *Allies (see chart on pages 231–238):* Corn, marigold, and soybean.
Scale (many species) *Fruit trees* *Nut trees* *Shrubs* *continued*	Small spots of reddened tissue on leaves or branches. Fine dusty ash. Hard bumps on fruit. Dead twigs or branches. Limbs lose vigor, leaves yellow, and the plant dies, usually from the top down. Honeydew excretions support black fungus and attract ants. Scales are extremely small, and suck plant nutrients from bark, leaves, and fruit. You may see the insect's "armor," which is either a part of its body or — in some species — is made up of old skeletons and a waxy coating that shields them from attacks. This armor may look like flaky, crusty parts of the bark.	■ Spray insecticidal soap. ■ Apply horticultural oil spray late in the spring, right at bud break. One spray should be sufficient. ■ Mix ¼ pound of glue in a gallon of water; let stand overnight. Spray on twigs and leaves.** When dried it will flake off, taking trapped mites with it. Spray three times, every 7–10 days. ■ Scrape scale off plants or touch them with a an alcohol-soaked cotton swab. Repeat every 3 or 4 days until scale falls off.

Macropest Plants Affected	Description of Symptoms and Pest Monitoring Its Presence/Where It Occurs	Organic Remedies
Scale, *continued*	The immature insect (¹⁄₁₆") crawls to a feeding spot where it stays for the remainder of its life. Ants carry scales from plant to plant. **Where:** Different species occur throughout United States. Produces 1–3 or more generations per year.	■ *Biological Controls:* Use *Comperiella bifasciata* for yellow scale; the Chalcid wasp *A. luteolus* for soft scale in California; *A. melinus* for red scale; the *Metaphycus helvolus* wasp for softscale or black scale; the *Vedalia* ladybug for cottony cushion scale; and the *Chilococorus nigritis* ladybug for all scales.
Seedcorn Maggot	*See* **Corn Maggot**	*See* **Corn Maggot**
Skipjack	*See* **Wireworm**	*See* **Wireworm**
Slug (many species) **and Snail** *Artichoke* *Asparagus* *Basil* *Bean* *Brassicas* *Celeriac* *Chard* *Celery* *Cucumber* *Eggplant* *Greens* *Lettuce* *Onion* *Pea* *Pepper* *(seedling)* *Sage* *Squash* *Strawberry* *Most fruit trees*	Large, ragged holes in leaves, fruits, and stems, starting at plant bottom. Trails of slime on leaves and soil. Slugs are large (½"–10" long), slimy wormlike creatures that resemble snails without shells. They are mollusks but have no outer protective shells. Their eyes are at the tips of 2 tentacles. They come in all colors — brown, gray, purple, black, white, and yellow — and can be spotted. They feed mainly from 2 hours after sundown to 2 hours before sunrise. Females lay clusters of twenty-five oval white eggs in damp soil, which hatch in about 1 month. Snails — also in the mollusk family — have hard shells and scrape small holes in foliage as they feed and lay masses of eggs. Eggs are large (⅛") and look like clusters of white pearls. Snails can go dormant in periods of drought or low food supply. **Where:** Widespread, but they rank as one of the top pests,(if not *the* top one) in the western United States. They thrive in temperatures below 75°F.	■ Remove all garden debris. ■ Cultivation or spading in spring or times of drought will help destroy dormant slugs and eggs. ■ Place stale beer in shallow pans, the lip of which must be at ground level.** Replace every day and after rain, and dispose of dead slugs. Because slugs are attracted to the yeast, an even more effective solution is made by dissolving 1 teaspoon of dry yeast in about ¼ cup of water. Where slugs are too numerous for this solution (e.g., in the West), try the following other traps. ■ *Board trap:* Set a wide board about 1" off the ground in an infested area. This provides day-time shelter for them and easy collection for you. ■ *Gutter trap:* Set aluminum gutter around the garden beds and coat them with Ivory soap. The slugs will get trapped in this. Empty and kill them regularly. ■ *Seedlings:* Keep seedlings covered until they're 6" high, particularly pea seedlings. Try plastic jugs with the bottoms cut out, anchored firmly in the soil, with the caps off for ventilation. Make sure no slugs are inside. ■ *Asparagus:* Plant crowns in wire baskets anchored several inches down in the ground. ■ *Barriers for raised beds:* (A) strips of aluminum screening about 3" high, pushed about 1" into the soil. Bend top of the screen outward, away from bed, and remove two strands from the edge so it's rough. (B) A 2" strip of copper flashing tacked around the outside of beds, 1" from top of bed. This carries a minor electric charge that repels slugs. Copper bands around tree trunks works similarly. Snail Barr is available commercially. (C) Crushed eggshells around plants. (D) Strips of hardware cloth tacked onto top edges of bed, extending 2" above edge. Make sure there are sharp points along the top edge. ■ Sprinkle diatomaceous earth around the plant base and work slightly into the soil. If not available, sprinkle wood ashes around the plant base. Avoid getting on plants.

Macropest **Plants Affected**	Description of Symptoms and Pest **Monitoring Its Presence/Where It Occurs**	**Organic Remedies**
Slug and Snail, *continued*		■ Don't apply mulch until soil has warmed to 75°F, which is warmer than slugs like. ■ Destroy all eggs. Find them under rocks, pots, and boards. ■ Use the weed Plantain as a trap crop, but first be sure it doesn't itself become a pest in your area.** ■ Spray with wormwood tea.** ■ Encourage predators such as birds, ducks, lightening bug larvae, ground beetles, turtles, salamanders, grass, and garter snakes. Ducks have a voracious appetite for these pests. ■ *Biological Controls:* Predatory snail, *Ruminia decollata,* will feed on brown garden snails. They can't be shipped to most places — like northern California or the Northwest because they kill native snails. ■ *Allies (see chart on pages 231–238):* Fennel, garlic, and rosemary.
Southern Corn Rootworm	*See* **Cucumber Beetle**	*See* **Cucumber Beetle**
Sow Bug (also known as: Dooryard Sow Bug) *Seedlings*	Chewed seedlings, stems, and roots. *See* also Description of Symptoms for **Pill Bug.** These bugs are crustaceans. They are small (¼"–½") oval, hump-backed bugs with fourteen legs. Sow bugs scurry when disturbed and generally hide under leaves and debris. The Pill Bug will roll itself into a ball for protection. **Where:** Widespread. Common in gardens, but not usually a severe problem. Produces 1 generation per year.	■ Apply wood ashes or an oak leaf mulch. ■ Water plants with a very weak lime solution. Mix 2 pounds per 5 gallons, and let sit for 24 hours before using. ■ Bait with one-half potato placed cut-side down on the soil surface. In the morning collect and kill bugs.** ■ *Botanical Controls:* If the problem is severe, rotenone (1 percent solution).
Spider Mite	*See* **Mite**	*See* **Mite**
Spinach Flea Beetle	*See* **Flea Beetle**	*See* **Flea Beetle**
Spittlebug (many species) (also known as: Froghopper) *Corn* *Many others*	Foamy masses ("frog spit"), usually at stem joints. Faded, wilted, curled, or discolored leaves. Stunted, weakened, and sometimes distorted plants. Adults (⅓") are dull brown, gray, or black, sometimes with yellow markings. They hop and look like short, fat leafhoppers. They lay eggs in plant stems, and in grasses between the stem and leaf sheath. The foam covers the eggs, which overwinter. In spring when nymphs hatch, they produce even more froth for protection. Adults and nymphs suck plant juices from leaves and stems. **Where:** Widespread, but worst in the Northeast, Oregon, and high humidity regions. Produces 1 or more generations.	■ Many species are not a serious problem, so you may want to leave them alone. ■ If seriously damaging, cut out plant parts with "spittle" or simply remove the foamy mass. Destroy egg masses or nymphs contained inside.

Macropest Plants Affected	Description of Symptoms and Pest Monitoring Its Presence/Where It Occurs	Organic Remedies
Spotted Asparagus Beetle *Asparagus* * *Aster* *Cucurbits* * *Zinnia*	Defoliation and misshapen fruit. It usually appears in July. This slender reddish brown-orange beetle has six black spots on each side of its back. It lays single greenish eggs on leaves, which develop into orange larvae in 1–2 weeks. Larvae bore into the berry and eat seeds and pulp, then pupate in the soil. **Where:** Present east of the Mississippi. Produces 1 generation per year.	■ Handpick in the morning when the beetle can't fly, due to cool temperatures. ■ *See* Organic Remedies for **Asparagus Beetle.**
Squash Bug *Cucumber* *Muskmelon* *Pumpkin* * *Squash* * *Watermelon*	Rapidly wilting leaves dry up and then turn black. No fruit development. These medium (⅝"), brown-black bugs feed by sucking plant sap and injecting toxins. When crushed at any age they emit a foul odor. They like moist, protected areas and hide in deep, loose mulch like hay or straw, as well as in debris or under boards. They lay clusters of yellow, red, or brown eggs on the undersides of leaves along the central vein. Eggs hatch in 7–14 days. Young bugs have red heads and bright green bodies that turn to gray as they mature. Bugs overwinter under vines, in boards and buildings, and under dead leaves. **Where:** Widespread. Produces 1 generation per year.	■ Use row covers. When female blossoms (fruit blooms) open, lift edges of covers for only 2 hours in the early morning — twice a week — until blossoms drop. This permits pollination. ■ Handpick bugs. ■ Sprinkle a barrier of wood ashes — moistened to prevent blowing — around the plant base.** Don't get ashes on the plant. Renew periodically. ■ In the fall, leave a few immature squash on the ground to attract the remaining bugs. Destroy squash covered with bugs. ■ Trellised plants are less susceptible to this bug. ■ Pull vulnerable plants as soon as they finish bearing, place in a large plastic bag, tie securely, and place in direct sun for 1 to 2 weeks. This destroys all eggs. ■ Spray insecticidal soap, laced with isopropyl alcohol to help it penetrate the shell. Soap, however, is not very effective against hard-bodied insects. ■ Time plantings to avoid bug. ■ Rotate crops. ■ Use heavy mulch materials. Avoid aluminum and white or black plastic mulch, which increase squash bug populations (according to Oklahoma State University studies). ■ Place boards in garden where they will hide and be easy to catch.** ■ Plant resistant varieties. ■ Encourage birds. ■ *Biological Controls:* Praying mantises eat eggs and nymphs. Tachinid flies are natural predators. ■ *Botanical Controls:* Sabadilla, rotenone (1 percent solution). ■ *Allies (see chart on pages 231–238):* Borage, catnip, marigold, mint, nasturtium, radish, and tansy.

Macropest Plants Affected	**Description of Symptoms and Pest** Monitoring Its Presence/Where It Occurs	**Organic Remedies**
Squash Vine Borer *Cucumber* *Gourd* *Muskmelon* *Pumpkin* *Squash*	Sudden wilting of plant parts. Moist yellow sawdustlike material (frass) outside small holes near the plant base. This long (1") dirty-white worm, with brown head and legs, bores into stems where it feeds for 4–6 weeks. It overwinters 1"–2" below the soil surface. The adult wasplike moth (1½") has clear copper-green forewings, transparent rear wings, and rings on its abdomen colored red, copper, and black. It lays rows or clusters of individual tiny, longish, brown or red eggs near the plant base on the main stem. **Where:** Lives east of the Rockies. Produces 1 generation per year in the North, and 2 generations per year in the southern and Gulf states.	▪ Use row covers. When female blossoms (fruit blooms) open, lift cover edges twice a week — for just 2 hours in early morning — until blossoms drop. This permits pollination. ▪ Reflective mulch such as aluminum foil will repel them.** ▪ Stem collars can prevent egg-laying. ▪ If not grown on a trellis, pinch off the young plant's growing tip to cause multistemming. For trailing squash stems, bury every fifth leaf node to encourage rooting. When one part becomes infested, cut it off and remove. Leave other sections to grow. Mound soil over vines up to blossoms. ▪ Slit stem vertically to remove and destroy borers. Mound soil around the slit stem to encourage new rooting. Remove and destroy damaged stems. ▪ Handpick the eggs. ▪ Sprinkle wood ashes, crushed black pepper, or real camphor around plants to deter borer.** ▪ Time planting to avoid borer. In the North, plant a second crop in midsummer to avoid borer feeding. ▪ Plant resistant varieties. ▪ Remove plants as soon as they finish bearing, place in a plastic bag, tie securely, and place in direct sun for 1–2 weeks to destroy borers and eggs. ▪ *Biological Controls:* Inject beneficial nematodes into infected vines at 4" intervals over bottom 3' of vine, using 5,000 nematodes per injection; use them in mulch around vines as well. Bt is another effective control; inject it into the vine after the first blossoms and again 10 days following. Clean syringe between injections. Trichogramma wasps attack borer eggs. Lacewings are also predators. ▪ *Allies (see chart on pages 231–238):* Borage, nasturtium, radish (plant radishes around the plant base).
Squirrel *Fruit* *Nuts* *Seeds*	The symptoms of squirrels are obvious — you'll see the squirrel digging in your garden, or scurrying in and around the bottom of your fruit and nut trees. They steal seeds, fruit, and nuts. **Where:** Widespread.	▪ Before planting corn try mixing 1 teaspoon of pepper with 1 pound of the corn seed.** ▪ Gather fruits and nuts every day. You may need to harvest fruit slightly underripe, for they can clean out every single ripe fruit in one night.

Macropest Plants Affected	Description of Symptoms and Pest Monitoring Its Presence/Where It Occurs	Organic Remedies
Stink Bug (many species) *Bean** *Cabbage* *Cucumber** *Mustard* *Okra* *Pepper** *Snapdragon* *Tomato**	Tiny holes in leaves and stems, particularly in new growth. Holes are surrounded by milky spots. Stunted, distorted, and weak plants. Adults and nymphs suck sap. The medium-sized (⅓"–¾") adult is an ugly gray, brown, green, or black. Its back is shaped like a shield. It emits a very unpleasant odor when touched or frightened. Adults lay eggs on plants in mid-spring, and hibernate in debris. Some Stink Bugs prey on the Colorado Potato Beetle. **Where:** Widespread, many different species. Produces 1–4 generations per year.	▪ Main control is to keep the garden well weeded. ▪ Insecticidal soap sprays must be laced with isopropyl alcohol to help penetrate the bug's outer shell: Soap alone is not very effective against hard-bodied insects. ▪ Hand pick and destroy. ▪ *Botanical Controls:* Sabadilla, rotenone (1 percent solution), pyrethrins.
Strawberry Clipper	*See* **Strawberry Weevil**	*See* **Strawberry Weevil**
Strawberry Crown Borer *Strawberry*	Stunted or weakened plants. Chewed leaves and stems. Small yellow grubs bore into strawberry roots and crowns, and turn pink the longer they feed. The small (⅕") adult brown, snout-nosed beetle has reddish patches on its wings. It feeds on stems and leaves. Adults overwinter just below soil surface, and lay eggs in spring in shallow holes in the crown at the base of leaf stalks. **Where:** Present east of the Rockies, particularly in Kentucky, Tennessee, and Arkansas. Produces 1 generation per year.	▪ If a patch is infested with crown borer, plant new strawberries at least 300 yards away from the area. Beetles can't fly and won't migrate. ▪ Pull and destroy plants that show damage. Replacement plants can be established immediately. ▪ Make sure plants are healthy and fed with compost — Healthy plants can usually tolerate these beetles. ▪ *Allies (see chart on pages 231–238):* Borage.
Strawberry Leaf Roller *Strawberry*	Rolled-up leaves. Skeletonized leaves that turn brown. Withered and deformed fruit. Yellow-green-brown larvae (½") feed inside rolled leaves. Small (½") adult moths, gray to reddish-brown, emerge in May to lay eggs on leaf undersides. **Where:** Northern United States, Louisiana and Arkansas. Produces 2 or more generations per year.	▪ For minor infestations, remove and burn leaves. ▪ For larger infestations, mow or cut plants off 1" above the crowns. Burn or destroy plants. ▪ *See* Organic Remedies for **Leaf Roller.**
Strawberry Weevil or Clipper *Brambles* *Strawberry*	Holes in blossom buds and severed stems. These small (¹⁄₁₀") reddish-brown beetles, with black snouts, feed at night and hide in daylight. Females lay eggs in buds, then sever them. Small white grubs feed inside severed buds and emerge after fruit is picked in July. **Where:** Live in northern United States. Produces 1 generation per year.	▪ Remove and destroy all stems hanging by threads. These carry the eggs. ▪ Remove mulch, maintain open-canopy beds, and renovate immediately after harvest to discourage new adults. ▪ Plant late-bearing strawberries. ▪ *Biological Controls:* Beneficial nematodes are effective, especially the new Hh strain. ▪ *Botanical Controls:* Sabadilla, rotenone (5 percent solution), and pyrethrins (apply 2 treatments 7–10 days apart, starting at early bud development). ▪ *Allies (see chart on pages 231–238):* Borage.

Macropest Plants Affected	Description of Symptoms and Pest Monitoring Its Presence/Where It Occurs	Organic Remedies
Strawberry Root Weevil (many species) *Strawberry*	Adults eat notches into leaves. Larvae eat roots and crown, which weaken, stunt, and eventually kills the plants. Beetles are small to large (½₂"–1"), shiny brown, gray to black. Females lay eggs on the soil surface in spring. Small, white to pinkish, thick-bodied, legless curved grubs feed on roots and then hibernate in soil. **Where:** Prevalent in northern United States. Produce 1 generation annually.	▪ Remove and destroy plants showing damage. ▪ Planting annual crops can, in some areas, help avoid weevil damage. ▪ *Botanical Controls:* Generally ineffective because of the difficulty in timing sprays to coincide with adult emergence.
Striped Blister Beetle *All vegetables*	Eaten blossoms, chewed foliage, eaten fruit. Human skin that contacts a crushed beetle will blister. Slender adult beetles (½") are black with a yellow stripe. They swarm in huge numbers and can destroy everything in sight. They lay eggs in the soil which hatch midsummer. Other blister beetles may be less damaging. Larvae are heavy-jawed, burrow in the soil, and eat grasshopper eggs. They become hard-shelled as pseudopupa, and remain dormant for under 1 year up to 2 years. **Where:** Present east of the Rockies. Produce 1 generation per year.	▪ Handpick with gloves to protect skin. ▪ Use row covers or netting. ▪ *Botanical Controls:* Rotenone dust.
Striped Flea Beetle	*See* **Flea Beetle**	*See* **Flea Beetle**
Tarnished Plant Bug *Bean* *Celery* *Most vegetables* *Peach* *Pear* *Raspberry* *Strawberry*	This bug attacks more plants than any other insect — 328 hosts have been recorded. Deformed, dwarfed flowers, beans, strawberry, and peaches. Wilted and discolored celery stems. Deformed roots. Black terminal shoots. Pitting and black spots on buds, tips, and fruit. Fireblight. Small (¼") highly mobile adults suck juice from young shoots and buds. They inject a poisonous substance into plant tissue and can spread fireblight. Generally brownish and oval, this insect can have mottled yellow, brown, and black triangles on each side of its back. It lays light yellow, long, curved eggs inside stems, tips, and leaves. Adults hibernate through winter under stones, tree bark, garden trash, or in clover and alfalfa. Nymphs are green-yellow with black dots on the abdomen and thorax. **Where:** Widespread. Several generations per year.	▪ Remove all sites of hibernation. ▪ Use row covers. ▪ Use white sticky traps. ▪ Spray insecticidal soap weekly in the early morning, though this is not very effective against hard-bodied insects. ▪ *Biological Controls:* Try beneficial nematodes in the fall to kill overwintering forms. ▪ *Botanical Controls:* Sabadilla, rotenone (5 percent solution), pyrethrins (in 3 applications 2–3 days apart). Spray in the early morning when bugs are sluggish.

Macropest Plants Affected	Description of Symptoms and Pest Monitoring Its Presence/Where It Occurs	Organic Remedies
Tent Caterpillar (also known as: Eastern Tent Caterpillar, Apple Tree Caterpillar) *Apple** *Cherry* *Peach* *Pear*	Woven tent-like nests, full of caterpillars, in tree forks. Defoliation. Large (2") caterpillars are black, hairy, with white and blue markings and a white stripe down the back. They feed in daylight on leaves outside the tent. Adults (1¼") are red-brown moths. Females lay egg masses in a band around twigs, and cover them with a foamy substance that dries to a dark shiny brown, hard finish. Eggs hatch the following spring. **Where:** Prevalent east of the Rockies; a similar species exists in California. Produces 1 generation per year. Worst infestations come in 10-year cycles.	■ Destroy nests by hand. Wearing gloves, in early morning pull down nests and kill caterpillars by crushing or dropping into a bucket of water laced with insecticidal soap. (Don't use kerosene — it is toxic to the soil and difficult to dispose of.) ■ Use sticky burlap bands. Remove pests daily. ■ In winter, cut off twigs with egg masses and burn. Check fences and buildings for eggs as well. ■ Remove nearby wild cherry trees. ■ Attract Baltimore orioles, bluebirds, digger wasps, and chickadees. ■ *Biological Controls:* Bt, sprayed every 10–14 days. ■ *Botanical Controls:* Pyrethrins. ■ *Allies (see chart on pages 231–238):* Dill.
Thrips (many species) *Bean* *Corn* *Onion* *Peanut* *Pear* *Squash* *Tomato*	Damaged blossoms, especially those colored white and yellow. Buds turn brown. Whitened, scarred, desiccated leaves and fruit. Pale, silvery leaves eventually die. Dark fecal pellets. Tiny (½₅") straw-colored or black slender insects with two pairs of slender wings edged with hairs. Nymphs and adults both suck plant juices and scrape and sting the plant. They transmit spotted wilt to tomatoes. Adults insert eggs inside leaves, stems and fruit. Eggs hatch in 1 week. **Where:** Widespread. Have 5–8 generations per year.	■ Immediately remove infested buds and flowers. ■ A reflective mulch like aluminum foil is reported to repel them.** ■ Control weeds. ■ Spray insecticidal soap. ■ Spray a hard jet of water in early morning, 3 days in a row. ■ Dust with diatomaceous earth. ■ Garlic or onion sprays.** ■ Spray light horticultural oil twice on mornings, 3–4 days apart. ■ Ensure sufficient water supply. ■ Rotate crops. ■ *Biological Controls:* Predatory mites (*Amblyseiulus mackenseii* and *Euseius tularensis*). Green lacewing larvae, ladybugs, and predatory thrips, prey on thrips. Beneficial nematodes may work in soil control in the greenhouse. ■ *Botanical Controls:* Rotenone (5 percent solution), pyrethrins. A mix might work best. Sulfur and tobacco dusts also work. ■ *Allies (see chart on pages 231–238):* Carrots, corn.
Tobacco Hornworm (also known as: Southern Hornworm) *Eggplant* *Pepper* *Tomato*	Description is virtually the same as the **Tomato Hornworm,** except this worm has a red horn. **Where:** Worst in the Gulf states and on ornamentals in California.	■ Use same Organic Remedies as for **Tomato Hornworm.**

Macropest Plants Affected	Description of Symptoms and Pest Monitoring Its Presence/Where It Occurs	Organic Remedies
Tomato Fruitworm	*See* **Corn Earworm**	*See* **Corn Earworm**
Tomato Hornworm *Dill* *Eggplant** *Pepper** *Potato** *Tomato**	Holes in leaves and fruit. Dark droppings on leaves. Defoliation. This very large (3"–4") green worm has white bars down both sides and a black or green horn at its tail end. The large (4"–5") adult moth emerges in May and June, and is sometimes called the Hawk or Hummingbird Moth. It has long narrow gray wings, yellow spots on its abdomen, flies at dusk, and feeds like a hummingbird. It lays single, green-yellow eggs on leaf undersides. Pupae (2") emerge and overwinter 3"–4" under the soil in a hard-shelled cocoon. **Where:** Widespread. There is 1 generation per year in the North, and 2 per year in South.	■ Handpick larvae and eggs. Look for green droppings under the plant. ■ Do not pick worms with cocoons on their backs. Eggs of the Braconid wasp, a predator, are in the cocoons. If you see these, make the NPV control spray described under the Organic Remedies for Corn Earworm. Also, do not pick eggs with dark streaks, which means they're parasitized by the Trichogramma wasp. ■ Apply hot pepper or soap and lime sprays directly on worms.** ■ Encourage birds. ■ Blacklight traps and bug zappers are effective against the adult, as well. But these kill beneficial insects.** ■ Fall cultivation. ■ *Biological Controls:* Lacewings, braconid and trichogramma wasps, and ladybugs attack the eggs. Release at first sign of adults laying eggs. Bt (berliner/kurstake strain), sprayed every 10–14 days, is very effective. ■ *Botanical Controls:* Rotenone (1 percent solution), pyrethrins. ■ *Allies (see chart on pages 231–238):* Borage and dill (both used as trap crops), and opal basil and marigold.
Vine Borer	*See* **Squash Vine Borer**	*See* **Squash Vine Borer**
Vole (Field Mouse)	*See* **Mouse**	*See* **Mouse**
Walnut Caterpillar *Hickory* *Pecan* *Walnut*	Defoliation, usually in large branches first. Black walnuts are prime targets. This black caterpillar (2"), with long white hairs, lifts its head and tail when disturbed. At night they gather at branch bases. Pupae overwinter 1"–3" below the soil surface. Adult moths emerge in spring. They are dark tan with four brown transverse lines on their forewings. They lay clusters of eggs on leaf undersides. **Where:** Prevalent in eastern United States south to Florida, and west to Texas and Wisconsin. Produces 1 generation per year in northern climates, 2 generations in southern climates.	■ In late evening, brush congregating caterpillars into water laced with insecticidal soap. (Don't use kerosene — it is toxic to the soil and difficult to dispose of.) ■ Spray with dormant horticultural oil. Make sure all parts of the tree are covered.
Walnut Husk Fly and Maggot *Peach (in West)* *Walnut* *continued*	Dark liquid stain over the walnut shell, and sometimes the kernels. This is a by-product of larvae feeding. Kernels may have an off-taste.	■ Destroy worms in infested nuts by dropping husks into a pail of water. Remove dead maggots when removing the husk. ■ Fall cultivation.

Macropest Plants Affected	Description of Symptoms and Pest Monitoring Its Presence/Where It Occurs	Organic Remedies
Walnut Husk Fly and Maggot, *continued*	Small larvae feed on the outer husk, then drop to the ground. Pupae hibernate under the trees in the ground in hard brown cases. Adult flies, the size of houseflies, emerge in midsummer. They are brown with yellow stripes across their backs, and have transparent wings. Females lay eggs inside husks. **Where:** Various species occurs throughout the United States. Produce 1 generation per year.	■ Plant late-maturing cultivars in eastern United States. ■ For large orchard sprays, consult your extension agent or *Nut Tree Culture in North America* (*see* Bibliography on page 263.)
Webworm (Garden)	*See* **Garden Webworm**	*See* **Garden Webworm**

Weevil
(many species)
  Apple
  Bean
  Blueberry
  Brassicas
  Carrot
  Celeriac
  Cherry
  Peach
  Pear
  Pea
  Pepper
  Plum
  Raspberry
  Strawberry
  Sweet Potato
	Zigzag paths in roots, fruit, stems.
	
	This is a family of hard-shelled, snout-nosed, tear-shaped small beetles. Usually brown or black, they feed at night and hide during the day.
	
	Small, white larvae feed inside fruit, stems, or roots. Adults usually lay eggs on the plant, sometimes inside.
	
	Bean and pea weevil larvae feed in young seed, and emerge when beans are in storage. They can do extensive damage in storage.
	
	Where: Widespread. Usually have 1 generation per year.
		■ Heat beans and peas before storing: Beans at 135°F for 3–4 hours, peas at 120°–130° for 5–6 hours. Store in a cool, dry place.
		■ Clean cultivation is essential.
		■ Deep cultivation exposes larvae.
		■ *Pea weevil:* Plant crops early.
		■ *Sweet potato weevil:* Rotate crops, and use certified disease-free slips.
		■ *Brassicas:* Rotate crops.
		■ Try dusting with lime when the leaves are wet or dew-covered.
		■ Encourage song birds.
		■ *See* Organic Remedies under **Carrot Weevil, Plum Curculio, Strawberry Clipper** and **Root Weevil** for additional controls.
		■ *Biological Controls:* Beneficial nematodes are helpful when applied in early spring near planting time.
		■ *Botanical Controls:* Sabadilla, rotenone (5 percent solution), pyrethrins.
		■ *Allies (see chart on pages 231–238):* Radish, summer savory and tansy.

Whitefly
  Greenhouses
  Most fruits
  Most vegetables
  Rosemary
	Leaves yellow and die. Black fungus. Honeydew excretions coat leaves and support black fungus.
	
	Tiny (¹⁄₁₆") insects with white wings suck plant juices from the undersides of leaves, stems, and buds. They lay groups of yellow, conical eggs on leaf undersides. Nymphs hatch in 4–12 days and are legless white crawlers.
	
	Where: Widespread. Produce several generations per year.
		■ Spray insecticidal soap, every 2–3 days for 2 weeks.
		■ Use sticky yellow traps. In greenhouses place them at plant canopy height and shake plants.
		■ Mix 1 cup alcohol, ½ teaspoon Volck oil or insecticidal soap, and 1 quart water. Spray twice, at 1 week intervals, to the point of runoff. This suffocates whiteflies but doesn't harm plants.
		■ Use forceful water jet sprays, in early morning, at least 3 days in a row.
		■ Hot pepper and garlic sprays.**
		■ Cooking oil spray mix, as recommended by USDA.

continued

Macropest Plants Affected	Description of Symptoms and Pest Monitoring Its Presence/Where It Occurs	Organic Remedies
Whitefly, *continued*		■ Check phosphorus and magnesium levels — whitefly may be a sign of a deficiency. Magnesium may be applied by mixing ½ cup Epsom salts in 1 gallon water, and thoroughly soaking soil with solution. ■ Increase air circulation. ■ Marigold root secretion is alleged to be absorbed by nearby vegetables and repel whiteflies.** ■ *Biological Controls:* Ladybugs and green lacewings. Trichogramma and chalcid parasitic wasps. Whitefly parasites, *Encarsia formosa,* can be used in greenhouses. ■ *Botanical Controls:* Ryania, pyrethrins. ■ *Allies (see chart on pages 231–238):* Mint, nasturtium, thyme, and wormwood.
White-fringed Beetle *Virtually all* *vegetation*	Severed roots. Chewed lower stems, root tissue, tubers. Plants yellow, wilt, and die. Extremely damaging. Larvae (½") are yellow-white, curved, legless, and emerge in May, with the greatest numbers in June and July. They feed for 2–5 months, and may travel ¼ to ¾ mile. They overwinter in the top 9" of the soil, and pupate in spring. Adult beetles (½") are brownish-gray with broad, short snouts, have short pale hairs all over, and non-functional wings banded with white. They feed in large numbers. **Where:** Appear in the Southeast (Florida, Alabama, Arkansas, Georgia, Kentucky, Louisiana, Missouri, South Carolina, North Carolina, Tennessee, Virginia), but are moving north and have been seen in New Jersey. Produce 1–4 generations per year.	■ Large-scale government quarantine and eradication measures have eliminated this in some areas, but home gardeners have limited methods of dealing with the beetle. If you experience this pest, notify your extension agent. They should be alerted to the movement of this pest and may be able to help you with control measures. ■ Deep spading in spring can help destroy overwintering grubs. ■ Dig very steep-sided ditches, 1' deep, to trap crawling beetles. Capture and destroy.
White Grub (larvae of June and Japanese Beetles) *Apple* (young) *Blackberry* *Corn* * *Grain roots* * *Lawns* * *Onion* *Potato* * *Strawberry* *	Sudden wilting, especially in early summer. *See Description of Symptoms for* **June Beetle.** Medium to large (¾" to 1½") plump, white, curved worms have brown heads and several legs near the head. They feed on plant roots. The adult is usually either the May or June beetle. **Where:** Widespread. It takes them 10 months to several years to complete one life cycle. Has 1 emergence per year.	■ Fall and spring cultivation. ■ Don't plant susceptible crops on areas just converted from untilled sod, as grubs will come up through the grass. ■ Allow chickens to pick over garden following fall and spring cultivations. ■ Encourage birds. ■ *Biological Controls:* Beneficial nematodes in spring or early summer, as mulch or dressing. Milky spore disease, which takes a few years to spread enough to be effective.

Macropest Plants Affected	Description of Symptoms and Pest Monitoring Its Presence/Where It Occurs	Organic Remedies
Wireworm (many species) *Bean** *Cabbage* *Carrot** *Celeriac* *Corn** *Lettuce** *Melon* *Onion** *Pea* *Potato** *Strawberry** *Sweet Potato* *Turnip*	Plants wilt and die. Damaged roots. Thin and patchy crops. Large (1½"), slender, fairly hard-shelled worms, with only three pairs of legs near the head; they feed underground. They do not curl up when disturbed. They core into roots, bulbs, and germinating seeds. Corn, grasses, and potatoes may be badly damaged. The adult beetle is also known as the Click beetle or Skipjack. It flips into the air with a clicking sound when placed on its back. It can't fly well or long. The egg-adult cycle takes 3 years — 2 of which are in the larvae feeding phase. **Where:** Widespread, but particularly a problem in poorly drained soil or recently sod soil. Overlapping generations are present at all times.	▪ Frequent fall and spring cultivation to expose worms to predators, at least once a week. ▪ Don't grow a garden over grass sod. Plow or till soil once every week for 4–6 weeks in the fall before beginning your garden. ▪ Alfalfa is said to repel wireworms; white mustard and buckwheat are alleged to repel wireworms; clover and timothy (and other grass hays) are said by some to repel worms — others say they attract them.** You might try it as a trap crop, away from your garden. ▪ Potato trap: Cut potato in half, spear with a stick, and bury 1" to 4" in soil, with stick as a handle above ground.** Set 3' to 10' apart. Pull potatoes in 2 to 5 days. Destroy potato and all worms. Some gardeners reported capturing 15–20 worms in one potato. ▪ Put milkweed juice on the soil around affected plants; this supposedly repels worms.** ▪ *Biological Controls:* Apply beneficial nematodes 2 months before planting. ▪ *Allies (see chart on pages 231–238):* Alfalfa, clover. (*Note: see* preceding tip on alfalfa and clover.)
Woolley Aphid	*See* **Aphid**	*See* **Aphid**

PART 5

Allies and
Companions

What They Might Do — How and Where They Do It

Allies are supposed to actively repel insects, or enhance the growth or flavor of the plant they help — the target plant. Companions, by contrast, are supposed to share space and growing habits well, but do not necessarily play an active role in pest protection or growth for each other. Allies can be and are considered companions, but companions are not necessarily allies.

The following chart tells what plants each ally is supposed to help, what it does (e.g., repels insects, aids growth), how it does it (e.g., visual masking), and where, if available, the data on its effects was gathered. Some sources claim to have evidence for an ally working, but fail to mention the nature of the evidence. Evidence to some people may constitute a one-time occurrence, whereas others may have a more rigorous, scientific standard, requiring multiple occurences. Unfortunately, we don't know which is true for each of these claims, so in all such cases we have listed the evidence as "uncertain." For cross-reference, most target plants are listed as companions in the individual listing of the ally plant.

Be aware of the controversy over allies and companions. Efforts to test these claims scientifically with proper controls are few, and results are often difficult to interpret. For example, a particular species of marigolds was shown in field trials to repel nematodes, but only in mass plantings. In small quantities planted next to the target crop they actually decreased yields. As a result, we've tried to include references to as many of the scientific trials as possible, including those where a putative ally carried with it some negative effects. Also, it is important to realize that an ally may effectively deter one insect pest but at the same time may attract other insect pests.

Companion planting should be approached with skepticism, a healthy experimental attitude, and curiosity. Conduct your own trials, as the success of allies and companions depends greatly on your microclimate, soil conditions, and cropping history, to name just a few variables. All references to specific mechanisms of action, when associated with a specific testing site, are from Robert Kourik's book, *Designing and Maintaining Your Edible Landscape Naturally* (*see* Bibliography). For further information on the original research articles, consult his book.

KEY

AH = **provides alternate host plant**

VM = **visual masking**

AW = **provides alternate host for parasitic wasps**

TR = **roots excrete toxic substances**

CM = **masking by chemical repellant confuses pest**

* = **control method is best described in original article (as per Kourik's book)**

P = **attracts beneficial parasites**

TC = **temperate climate**

PI = **physical interference so pest can't reach target**

Some Evidence = **some scientific trials conducted, with specific place of trial identified**

BP = **attracts beneficial predators**

PW = **attracts beneficial parasitic wasps**

Uncertain = **no scientific evidence for effectiveness (or source of claim unidentified)**

Plant Ally	Plant Enhanced by Ally (Target)	Pest Controlled/Other Benefits	Method of Control (test site)
Alder	Fruit Trees	Red Spider Mite	BP (UK)
Alfalfa	Barley Corn	Aphid Wireworm	BP (Czechoslovakia) Uncertain
Anise	Most Vegetables	Aphid	Uncertain
Asparagus	Some Vegetables	Nematodes: Asparagus roots contain a toxin in the roots	Uncertain
Barley (as a cover crop)	Many Vegetables Soybean	Reduces Nematode populations Soybean pests	Uncertain BP (Virginia)
Basil	Asparagus Most Vegetables Tomato Tomato	Asparagus beetle/*improves growth* Flies/*improves growth and flavor* *Improves growth and flavor* Tomato Hornworm (with Opal Basil)	Uncertain Uncertain Uncertain Uncertain
Beans French beans All beans Green beans All beans Snap beans	 Brussels Sprouts Corn Cucumber Eggplant Potato Potato	 Aphid Leaf Beetle, Leafhopper, Fall Armyworm *Adds nutrients* Colorado Potato Beetle *Repels insects* Colorado Potato Beetle, Leafhopper (*may also reduce potato yield*)	 PI (England) BP/PI (Tropics) Uncertain Uncertain Uncertain Uncertain Uncertain
Bee Balm (Monarda didyma)	Tomato	*Improves growth and flavor*	Uncertain
Beet	Onion	*Improves growth*	AW (TC)
Blackberry	Grape	Leafhopper (Pierces disease)	Uncertain
Black Salsify (Oyster Plant)	Various vegetables	Carrot Rust Fly	Uncertain
Borage (as a trap crop)	Squash Strawberry Tomato	Squash Vine borer/*improves growth and flavor* Strawberry Crown borer/*improves growth and flavor* Tomato Hornworm/*improves growth and flavor*	Uncertain Uncertain
Bramble Berries (e.g., Raspberry)	Fruit trees	Red Spider Mite	BP (England)
Brassicas	Peas	Root Rot (Rhizoctonia)	Uncertain
Broccoli	Cucumber Beet (sugar)	Striped Cucumber Beetle Green Peach Aphid	PI (Michigan) PW (Washington)
Buckwheat (as a cover crop)	Fruit trees	Codling Moth	P
Cabbage	Celery Tomato Tomato	*Repels insects* Flea Beetle Diamondback Moth	Uncertain CM (TC) CM (tropics)

Plant Ally	Plant Enhanced by Ally (Target)	Pest Controlled/Other Benefits	Method of Control (test site)
Candytuft	*Brassicas*	Flea Beetle	CM (New York)
Caraway	Fruit trees	*Attracts beneficial insects*	Uncertain
	Gardens	*Loosens soils*	Uncertain
	Onion	Thrips/*improves growth*	VM (Africa)
	Peas	*Improves growth*	Uncertain
	Pepper	*Improves growth*	Uncertain
Catnip	Beans	Flea Beetle (plant in borders) (may also increase whiteflies on snap beans)	Uncertain
	Broccoli	Cabbageworm, Flea Beetle (some evidence catnip increases Cabbageworms and lowers cabbage yield)	Uncertain
	Cucumber	Cucumber Beetles	Uncertain
	Pepper	Green Peach Aphid (catnip may compete with pepper)	Uncertain
	Potato	Colorado Potato Beetle	Uncertain
	Squash	Squash Bug (squash may not grow as large)	Uncertain
	All vegetables	Aphid, Flea Beetle, Japanese Beetle	Uncertain
Celery	*Brassicas*	Cabbageworm	Uncertain
	Beans	*Improves growth*	Uncertain
Chamomile	*Brassicas*	*Improves growth and flavor*	Uncertain
	Onion	*Improves growth and flavor*	Uncertain
Chervil	Radish	*Improves growth and flavor*	Uncertain
Chive	Carrot	*Improves growth and flavor*	Uncertain
	Celery	Aphid	Uncertain
	Lettuce	Aphid	Uncertain
	Peas	Aphid	Uncertain
	All vegetables	Japanese Beetle	Uncertain
Clover			
Red	Barley	Aphid	BP (Czechoslovakia)
White	Brussels Sprouts	Aphid; Cabbage Butterfly and Root Fly	VM (England)
Unspecified	Brussels Sprouts	Aphid	PI (England)
Red and white	Cabbage and Cauliflower	Aphid, Imported Cabbage Butterfly	PI; BP
Unspecified	Cabbage	Cabbage Root Fly	BP (Ireland)
Unspecified	Corn	Corn Borer	PI (England)
Unspecified	Fruit trees	Aphid, Codling Moth	P
Unspecified	Fruit trees	Reduces Leafhopper population	Uncertain
New Zealand white	Oats	Fruit Fly	PI (England)
Dutch white	Turnip	Cabbage Root Maggot	CM (Pennsylvania)
Unspecified	Many vegetables	Repels Wireworm	Uncertain

Note: Clover can also attract leafhoppers which will then damage susceptible crops.

Coriander	All fruit trees	*Attracts beneficial insects*	Uncertain
	Eggplant	Colorado Potato Beetle	Uncertain
	Potato	Colorado Potato Beetle	Uncertain
	Tomato	Colorado Potato Beetle	Uncertain
	Many vegetables	Aphid, Spider Mite	Uncertain
	Various vegetables	Carrot Rust Fly	Uncertain

Plant Ally	Plant Enhanced by Ally (Target)	Pest Controlled/Other Benefits	Method of Control (test site)
Corn	Beans	*Improves growth*	Uncertain
	Cucumber	Striped Cucumber Beetle	PI (Michigan)
	Cucurbits	*Improves growth*	Uncertain
	Peanut	Corn Borer	VM (TC)
	Pumpkin	*Improves growth*	Uncertain
	Soybean	Corn Earworm	PW (Georgia)
	Squash	Cucumber Beetle	PI (tropics)
	Squash	Western Flower Thrips	BP (California)
	Many vegetables	Nematode (plant corn as cover crop)	Uncertain
Corn spurry (*Spergula arvensis*)	Cauliflower	Aphid, Flea Beetle, Cabbage Looper	BP (California)
Cover grass	Brussels Sprouts	Aphid	PI (England)
Cucumber	Radish	*Repels insects*	Uncertain
Dead Nettle (*Lamium* genus)	Potato	Colorado Potato Beetle	Uncertain
		Improves growth and flavor	Uncertain
Dill	*Brassicas*	Cabbage Looper, Imported Cabbageworm	Uncertain
	Brassicas	*Improves growth and vigor*	Uncertain
	Cabbage	Spider Mite, Caterpillars	Uncertain
	Fruit trees	Codling Moth, Tent Caterpillar	Uncertain
	Tomato	Tomato Hornworm (use dill as trap crop)	Uncertain
Eggplant	Potato	Colorado Potato Beetle (as trap crop)	Uncertain
Fennel	Most vegetables	Aphid	Uncertain
Flax	Carrot	*Improves growth and flavor*	Uncertain
	Onion	Colorado Potato Beetle	Uncertain
	Onion	*Improves growth and flavor*	Uncertain
Garlic	Beet	*Improves growth and flavor*	Uncertain
	Brassicas	Cabbage Looper, Maggot, Worm	Uncertain
	Brassicas	*Improves growth and flavor*	Uncertain
	Celery	Aphid	Uncertain
	Fruit trees	Codling Moth	Uncertain
	Lettuce	Aphid	Uncertain
	Peach tree	Peach Borer	Uncertain
	Raspberry	*Improves growth and health*	Uncertain
	Rose	*Improves growth and health*	Uncertain
	Many vegetables	Japanese Beetle, Mexican Bean Beetle, Nematodes, Slug, and Snail	Uncertain
Goldenrod	Peach tree	Oriental Fruit Moth	* (TC)
	Various vegetables	Cucumber Beetles	Uncertain
Goosegrass (*Eleusine indica*)	Beans	Leafhopper	CM (tropics)
Hairy Indigo	Various vegetables	Nematodes	Uncertain
Horseradish	Potato	Potato Bug (planted in patch corner)	Uncertain

Plant Ally	Plant Enhanced by Ally (Target)	Pest Controlled/Other Benefits	Method of Control (test site)
Hyssop	Cabbage	Cabbage Looper, Moth, Worm	Uncertain
	Grape	*Increases yields*	Uncertain
Johnson Grass (*Sorghum halepense*)	Grape	Pacific Mite	BP (TC)
	Grape	Williamette Mite	BP (California)

Caution: While this grass may help with these mites, one Arkansas grower noted that it killed his vines. So you may want to make sure the grass is not allowed close to the vines.

Lamb's Quarters	Collards	Green Peach Aphid	BP (Ohio)
	Cauliflower	Imported Cabbage Butterfly	BP (California)
	Peach tree	Oriental Fruit Moth	* (TC)
Lettuce	Carrot	Carrot Rust Fly	Uncertain
	Radish	*Improves growth*	Uncertain
Marigold (*Tagetes* sp.)	Asparagus	Asparagus Beetle	Uncertain
	Beans	Mexican Bean Beetle	Uncertain
	Eggplant	Nematode	TR (Connecticut)
	Lima Bean	Mexican Bean Beetle	Uncertain
	Lima Bean	Nematode	TR (Connecticut)
	Rose	Aphid	Uncertain
	Squash	Beetles, Nematode	Uncertain
	Tomato	Aphid, Tomato Hornworm	Uncertain
	Many vegetables	Cabbage Maggot	Uncertain

Note: Research at the Connecticut Agricultural Experiment Sation has shown that small French (*Tagetes patula* L.) marigolds suppress meadow, or root lesion, nematodes for up to 3 years and one or more other nematodes for 1 or more years. Marigolds are effective when rotated, or grown in the entire infested area for a full season. Interplanting is not as effective, and can reduce crop yields, but some beneficial nematicide effects may be seen the following year. To reduce competition, interplant marigolds 2 or more weeks after other plants. Two theories exist on how marigolds work: (1) they produce a chemical from their roots that kills nematodes, and (2) they do not serve as a host to nematodes and, in the absence of a host, the nematode population dies.

Marjoram	Vegetables	*Improves flavor*	Uncertain
Mint	*Brassicas*	Cabbage Looper, Moth, and Worm	Uncertain
	Brassicas	*Improves growth and flavor*	Uncertain
	Broccoli	Ants	Uncertain
	Peas	*Improves growth and flavor*	Uncertain
	Squash	Squash Bug	Uncertain
	Tomato	*Improves growth and flavor*	Uncertain
	Many vegetables	Whitefly	Uncertain
Mirabilis (Four O'Clocks)		*Acts as trap crop for Japanese beetles*	Uncertain
Mustard (white or black)	Many vegetables	Nematodes	Uncertain
	Broccoli	Aphids	* (CA)
Nasturtium	Asparagus	Carrot Rust Fly	Uncertain
	Beans	Mexican Bean Beetle	Uncertain
	Brassicas	Aphid, Beetles	Uncertain
	Brassicas	Cabbage Looper and Worm	Uncertain
	Celery	Aphid	Uncertain
	Cucumber	Aphid, Cucumber Beetles	Uncertain
	Fruit trees	*Provides general protection (under tree)*	Uncertain
	Pepper	Green Peach Aphid	Uncertain
	Potato	Colorado Potato Beetle	Uncertain
Continued	Radish	*Provides general protection*	Uncertain

Plant Ally	Plant Enhanced by Ally (Target)	Pest Controlled/Other Benefits	Method of Control (test site)
Nasturtium, *continued*	Squash	Beetles, Squash Bug	Uncertain
	Many vegetables	Whitefly	Uncertain
Onion family	Beet	Insects	Uncertain
	Brassicas	Cabbage Looper, Maggot Worm	Uncertain
	Carrot	Carrot Rust Fly	CM (UK/Africa)
	Potato	Colorado Potato Beetle	Uncertain
	Swiss Chard	*Improves growth*	Uncertain
	Many vegetables	Aphid	Uncertain
Oregano	Beans	*Improves flavor and growth*	Uncertain
	Cucumber	*Deters pests*	Uncertain
	Squash	*General pest protection*	Uncertain
Parsley	Asparagus	Asparagus Beetle/*helps growth*	Uncertain
	Tomato	*Improves growth*	Uncertain
Peas	Carrot, Corn	*Improves growth and flavor by adding nutrients to the soil*	Uncertain
	Turnip	*Improves growth*	Uncertain
Pennyroyal	Various vegetables	Carrot Rust Fly	PW (USSR)
***Phacelia* sp.** (herbs)	Apple	Aphid, San Jose Scale	BP (Ohio)
Pigweed (*Amaranthus* sp.)	Collards	Green Peach Aphid (*A. retroflexus*)	BP (Ohio)
	Corn	Fall Armyworm (*A. hybridus*)	BP, PW (Florida)
	Corn, Onion, and Potato	*Brings nutrients to soil surface where available to plants*	Uncertain
Potato	Beans	Mexican Bean Beetle	Uncertain
	Corn	*Repels insects*	Uncertain
	Eggplant	*Useful as trap plant*	Uncertain
Radish	*Brassicas*	Cabbage Maggot	Uncertain
	Cucumber	Striped Cucumber Beetle	Uncertain
	Lettuce	*Improves growth*	Uncertain
	Squash	Squash Bug and Vine Borer (use radish as a trap crop)	Uncertain
	Sweet Potato	Sweet Potato Weevil	Uncertain
Ragweed Giant Normal	Collards	Flea Beetle	CM (New York)
	Corn	Corn Borer	AH (Canada)
	Peach tree	Oriental Fruit Moth	AW (Virginia)
	Peach tree	Oriental Fruit Moth	* (TC)
Red Sprangletop (*Leptochioa filliformis*)	Beans	Leafhopper	CM (tropics)
Rosemary	*Brassicas*	Cabbage Moth/*repels insects*	Uncertain
	Carrot	Carrot Rust Fly/*repels insects*	Uncertain
	Many vegetables	Slug, Snail	Uncertain
	Beans	Mexican Bean Beetle	Uncertain

Plant Ally	Plant Enhanced by Ally (Target)	Pest Controlled/Other Benefits	Method of Control (test site)
Rue	Cucumber	Cucumber Beetles	Uncertain
	Rose	Japanese Beetle	Uncertain
	Raspberry	Japanese Beetle	Uncertain
	Many vegetables	Flea Beetle	Uncertain
Rye (as cover crop)	Fruit trees	Aphid	BP
	Fruit trees	Leafhopper	Uncertain
	Many vegetables	Nematode (turn cover crop under)	TR
	Soybean	Seedcorn Maggot	PI (Ohio)
Rye (mulch)	Fruit trees	European Red Mite	BP (Michigan)
Sage	*Brassicas*	Cabbage Looper, Maggot, Moth, and Worm	Uncertain
	Carrot	Carrot Rust Fly/*improves growth*	Uncertain
	Marjoram	*Improves growth*	Uncertain
	Strawberry	*Improves growth*	Uncertain
	Tomato	*Improves growth*	Uncertain
Savory (Summer)	Beans	Mexican Bean Beetle/*improves growth and flavor*	Uncertain
	Onion	*Improves growth and flavor*	Uncertain
	Sweet Potato	Sweet Potato Weevil	Uncertain
Shepherd's Purse	*Brassicas*	Flea Beetle	CM (New York)
	Corn	Black Cutworm	PW (Illinois)
Smartweed	Peach tree	Oriental Fruit Moth	* (TC)
Sorghum (cover crop mulch)	Cow pea	Leaf Beetle	CM (TC)
	Fruit trees	European Red Mite	BP (Michigan)
Southern Wood	Cabbage	Cabbage Moth	Uncertain
Soybeans	Corn	Corn Earworm	BP (Florida)
	Corn	Cinch Bug	Uncertain
Strawberry	Peach tree	Oriental Fruit Moth	BP (TC)
	Spinach	*Improves growth*	Uncertain
Sudan Grass	Grape	Williamette Mite	BP (California)
Sweet Potato	Corn	Leaf Beetle	PW (tropics)
Tansy	*Brassicas*	Cabbageworm, Cutworm (There is some evidence tansy increases Cabbageworms)	Uncertain
	Cucumber	Ants, Cucumber Beetles, Squash Bug	Uncertain
	Fruit Trees	Ants, Aphid, Japanese Beetle	Uncertain
	Potato	Colorado Potato Beetle	Uncertain
	Raspberry	Ants, Japanese Beetle	Uncertain
	Squash	Squash Bug (May make squash plants smaller) Sweet Potato Weevil	Uncertain
	Sweet Potato	Flea Beetle, Japanese Beetle	Uncertain
	All vegetables		Uncertain

Plant Ally	Plant Enhanced by Ally (Target)	Pest Controlled/*Other Benefits*	Method of Control (test site)
Thyme	*Brassicas*	Cabbage Looper and Worm, insects (May lower cabbage yields)	Uncertain
	Strawberry	Worms	Uncertain
	Many vegetables	Whitefly (In beans, may cause higher Whitefly population)	Uncertain
Tomato	Asparagus	Asparagus Beetle	Uncertain
	Brassicas	Imported Cabbage Butterfly	Uncertain
	Cabbage	Diamondback Moth	* (tropics)
	Collards	Flea Beetle	CM (New York)
Turnip	Peas	*Improves growth*	Uncertain
Vetch	Fruit trees	Aphid	Uncertain
Weedy Ground Cover	Apple	Tent Caterpillars	PW (Canada)
	Apple	Codling Moth	PW (Canada)
	Brussels Sprouts	Cabbage Butterfly and Worm	BP (England)
	Collards	Flea Beetle	VM (New York)
	Collards	Cabbage Aphid	PW (California)
	Mung Bean	Beanfly	PI (TC)
	Walnut	Walnut Aphid	AW (California)
Wheat (as a cover crop)	Soybean	Soybean pests	BP (Virginia)
	Many vegetables	Nematode	Uncertain
Wheat (mulch)	Fruit trees	European Spider Mite	BP (Michigan)
Wildflowers	Fruit trees	*Attracts beneficial insects*	Uncertain
Wormseed mustard	*Brassicas*	Flea Beetle	CM (New York)
Wormwood (pulverized)	*Brassicas*	Cabbage Maggot	Uncertain
	Fruit trees	Codling Moth	Uncertain
	Many vegetables	Mice, Whitefly	Uncertain
	Carrot	Carrot Rust Fly	Uncertain

Appendices and Bibliography

What Makes Your Garden "Organic"?

Organic Foods Production Association of America Draft Guidelines

How do you or I, the small backyard gardener, know whether our garden is really organic? As of this writing, general national standards for certifiable organic growing conditions are clearly delineated by the 1990 Organic Foods Production Act. More detailed standards will be in place by the time this book is released and will be based on recommendations by the National Organic Standards Board (NOSB). As of October 1993, anyone selling on an annual basis more than $5,000 worth of organic produce must be certified annually by an approved program in order to label their products organic. Many of the state associations listed in Appendix D offer programs to certify farms as organic. State guidelines may be more restrictive than the Federal standards, but cannot discriminate against products that meet federal standards.

In 1985, the Organic Foods Production Association of North America (OFPANA) took the lead in generating draft national guidelines. OFPANA's draft guidelines are based on suggestions and reviews by state organizations, and are still in the process of evolving. The guidelines have provided a solid foundation for federal standards, and are being reviewed and further refined by the NOSB.

It is important to understand that even the Federal standard of approved and prohibited substances in place as of October 1993, by law must be reviewed and updated at least every five years. This mandated review reflects an understanding that what is organic will necessarily evolve as field and laboratory research provide new information about the effects substances have on soil and food crops. So, we backyard gardeners should not treat the following lists as the final word on what we should or should not use. We need to stay open to new information as it becomes available. Perhaps most important to remember, organic growing is an approach that treats the garden or farm as a living system. Just as human medicine continues to evolve in its philosophy, technology, and methods, so will organic growing continue to evolve.

Organic farming is not merely a list of acceptable and prohibited materials.
It is a management-intensive technology designed to achieve a balance in the
agricultural system similar to that found in natural systems. Such balance produces
healthy soils and high-quality crops and livestock.

From Crops Standards Committee of the National Organic Standards Board, Position Paper No. 1

With OFPANA's generous permission, I am pleased to share excerpts from the draft guidelines with you here. This gives us *something,* even if not final or absolute, by which we can measure — or at least approximate — our organic temperature.

If you would like a complete copy of the draft guidelines, please send $30 to cover the cost of printing and postage to: Katherine DiMatteo, Director, OFPANA, P.O. Box 1078, Greenfield, MA 01302. To get on the mailing list of the National Organic Standards Board, you may write to: National Organic Standards Program, USDA/AMS/TMD, Room 2510-South, P.O. Box 96456, Washington, DC 20090-64560. Please indicate whether you would like press releases, full board and committee meeting summaries, or committee position papers.

What is Prohibited in Organic Growing?

The 1990 Organic Foods Production Act prohibits the use of synthetic chemicals, unless the synthetic substance is specifically named — along with its specific use — in the National List of approved synthetic substances. To be approved, the synthetic substance must not harm human health and the environment, must be necessary because of the unavailability of a wholly natural alternative, and must be consistent with organic farming and handling.

Prohibited Substances

The following substances are being *recommended* for prohibition by OFPANA. All synthetically derived fertilizers and pesticides not specifically mentioned by name will be prohibited.

Ammonia products
Anhydrous ammonia
Anti-coagulant rodent baits (synthetic)
Bird baits and poisons (synthetic)
Calcium nitrate
Carbamates
Carrot oil
Chlorinated hydrocarbons
Creosote
Cryolite (synthetic)
Diammonium phosphate (DAP)
Dimethyl sulfoxide
Drip irrigation cleaners (synthetic)
Exhaust fumes
Formaldehyde
Fumigants in packaging materials
Fumigants (synthetic)
Fungicides and bactericides (synthetic)
Growth regulators (synthetic)
Gypsum by-product
Herbicides (synthetic)
Ionizing radiation
Leather meal, leather tankage, and leather dust
Magnesium nitrate
Malathion
Methyl bromide
Methyl sulfoxide

Mono ammonium phosphate (MAP)
Moth balls and moth crystals
Muriate of potash (Potassium chloride)
Nematicides
Nicotine concentrates
Nitric acid
Organophosphates
Parathion
Pentachlorophenol
Petroleum solvents (aromatic)
Phosphoric acid
Piperonyl butoxide
Plant Protectants (synthetic)
Potassium sulfate (synthetic)
Pyrethroids
Sewage sludge
Sodium hydroxide
Soil fumigants
Spray adjuvants (synthetic)
Super phosphate
Transpiration blockers (synthetic)
Triple phosphate
Urea
Vitamin B1 — plant growth hormone
Weed oils
Wetting agents (synthetic)

What is Allowed?

Allowed Cultural and Mechanical Devices *(Recommended for approval)*

The following substances or practices are currently *recommended* to be included on the allowed list, on the condition that they not be used in conjunction with synthetic inputs.

Balloons
Barriers
Bird traps and netting
Cover crops
Crop rotation
Explosive devices
Flaming
Grazing
Green manures
Guns
Hand removal of insects
Intercropping

Mechanical and cultural controls
Mowing
Nitrogen fixing crops
Predators
Resistant varieties
Rodent traps
Sanitary practices
Sound devices
Thermal weed control
Tillage
Vacuums
Weeder geese

Allowed Plant and Soil Inputs *(Recommended for approval)*

The following substances are recommended to be allowed if they are obtained from natural sources, do not contain prohibited synthetic additives, and are not created with synthetic processes of extraction or refinement.

Animal manures. *See manures.*

Blood meal.

Bone meal.

Borate.

Boron products (soluble). Use restricted to documented field deficiency.

Composts. See OFPANA standards for definition and guidelines for composts. No prohibited materials may be used in composting, including no synthetically "fortified" compost starters.

Cottonseed meal. *See Plant products* (regulated).

Epsom salts. Mined source only. Regulated by all groups because of high salt content and/or need for justification of use by soil testing.

Feather meal.

Feldspar. Mined source only.

Fish emulsions. Forms containing synthetic preservatives or which are "fortified" with synthetic plant nutrients are prohibited. "Stabilized" products are acceptable. Stabilizers in fish emulsion cannot exceed 1 percent by weight of P_2O_5. (A-12, R-5)

Fish meal.

Fish solubles.

Granite dust. Mined source only.

Grape and other pomaces.

Greensand. Mined source only.

Guano (bat or bird).

Gypsum (mined).

Herbal preparations.

Hoof and horn meal.

Humates.

Humic acid derivatives.

Kelp extracts.

Kelp Meal.

Kieserite. Mined source only.

Langbeinite

Leaves.

■ **Leaf mold**

Limestone. Mined source only.

■ **Aragonite**

■ **Calcium carbonate**

■ **Dolomite**

Manures (composted).

Manures (raw). See OFPANA Guidelines for more information. Restrictions include prohibiting the application of raw manures within 60 days before harvest, and also when the application in any way can significantly contribute to water contamination by nitrates or bacteria. Composting is strongly recommended to stabilize the nitrogen content, kill weed seeds, and help neutralize pesticide residues. Fresh and "sheet composted" manures are regulated for use only in moderate amounts and as a supplement to other soil building practices. Apply when soil is sufficiently warm (about 50°F) and moist to ensure active microbial digestion. Regulated use on perennials, green manures, crops not for human consumption, and crops not to be harvested for 4 months. *On nitrate accumulators, manure must be applied more than 4 months before planting with warm soil.* Manure sources and handling must be documented.

Marl. Mined source only.

Microbial inoculants for soil, plants, compost, and seed. Must not contain any prohibited additives.

Micronutrient sprays. Materials derived from natural sources.

Mined minerals. (*See* specific names.)

Mulches (organic).

Oystershell.

Peat moss.

Perlite.

Phosphate rock. Mined source only.

- ■ **Colloidal phosphate** (soft rock phosphate).

Plant products. All those not listed under **Plant products restricted** are allowed, including:

- ■ **Alfalfa meal**

- ■ **Peanut meal**

- ■ **Rice residues**

- ■ **Sawdust**

- ■ **Soybean meal**

- ■ **Straw**

- ■ **Vegetable cuttings and cannery waste**

Plant products (restricted).

- ■ **Cocoa bean hulls.** Must be documented residue-free because may contain pesticides banned in United States.

- ■ **Cotton gin trash.** Composting is required to break down pesticide residues.

- ■ **Mushroom compost.** Must be documented residue-free or from a recomposted source.

- ■ **Sugar beet lime.** Must be documented residue-free because may contain herbicide residue seeds.

- ■ **Tobacco dust.** May use only as a fertilizer.

Potassium sulfate. Mined source only.

Pumice.

Rock dust. Mined source only.

Sand.

Sea animal wastes.

Seaweed and seaweed products.

Sulfur. Includes elemental sulfur and sulfur flowers. Restricted to use on soils due to negative effects on soil life. Prohibited for post-harvest treatment.

Sulfate of potash magnesia.

Trace minerals (natural source). (*See* following section on **Allowed Compatible Synthetics**).

Vermiculite.

Wood ash. Allowed if from a naturally occurring material *except manure (due to environmental concerns). Wood stove ashes must be free of contaminants from colored paper, plastic, etc.* Caution: it is easy to toxify soil with too much ash. Use with moderation.

Worm Castings.

Zeolite. Mined source only.

Allowed Pest Controls *(Recommended for Approval)*

Bacillus thuringiensis (Bt).

Beneficial organisms. Including but not limited to:

- ■ **Algae**

- ■ **Animals**

- ■ **Bacteria**

- ■ **Fungi**

- ■ **Insects**

- Milky spore disease

- Nematodes

- *Nosema locustae*

- Protozoa

- Viruses

Botanicals. All are restricted to localized and cautious use because of the nonselective action of botanicals. Botanicals include, but are not limited to:

- **Neem and Neem Extracts.**

- **Pyrethrums.** Restricted to naturally occurring forms without synthetic additives.

- **Quassia.**

- **Rotenone.** Do not use within 5 days of harvest. Restricted to use on fields where toxicity to fish is not a problem.

- **Ryania.** Do not use within 5 days of harvest.

- **Sabadilla.**

- **Strychnine** (botanical extract from *Nox vomica).* Restricted to use as a rodent control only. Highly toxic.

Deer and rabbit repellents. Natural sources only.

Diatomaceous earth.

Garlic.

Herbal preparations.

Insect extracts. ("Bug juice").

Sodium floualuminate (Cryolite). Mined source only. Restricted use. Residues can be toxic and persistent, but are easily washed off. It is recommended to wash off all residues before marketing.

Sticky barriers.

Suffocating oils (vegetable and animal-derived). Petroleum-based suffocating oils are allowed only on woody plants for pest control purposes. Vegetable and animal-derived oils are allowed on all plants and are preferred for all uses.

Sulfur. Includes elemental sulfur dust, liquid sulfur, and sulfur flowers. Allowed for foliar use as an insecticide and fungicide. Prohibited for post-harvest treatment of crops.

Tobacco dust. Restricted to use on crops where there is a documented pest problem without a biological alternative for resolution. Restricted to localized and cautious use because of nonselective action of botanicals.

Virus sprays.

Allowed Production Aids *(Recommended for Approval)*

Alcohol (natural sources). Includes ethanol and methanol.

Biodynamic preparations.

Carbon dioxide gas.

Chelates (natural sources).

Citric acid.

Citrus oil.

Enzymes. Restricted to microbiologically-derived sources.

Fruit waxes. Restricted to sources such as carnuba or wood-extracted wax which do not contain any prohibited synthetic substances.

Gibberellic acid. Restricted to fermentation process sources. Gibberellic acid fortified with prohibited synthetic substances is prohibited.

Inoculant. See microbial inoculant.

Nitrogen gas, N_2. Restricted to post-harvest use.

Oxalic acid. Restricted to use as a greenhouse disinfectant.

Plant extracts. Restricted to use as plant protectant or adjuvants.

Soda ash. Restricted to post-harvest use in floating tree fruits.

Tree seals. Plant or milk-based paints are recommended.

Vegetable oil spray adjuvants. Includes spreader stickers, surfactants, and carriers. Restricted to adjuvants comprised of at least 90 percent plant oil. May not contain synthetic pesticides.

Vitamins (natural).

Allowed Compatible Synthetics *(Recommended for Approval)*

Materials listed here may be synthetic analogs of natural substances, materials which are exempted under the Organic Foods Production Act, or materials considered to be compatible with organic farming.

Allowed Compatible Synthetic Plant and Soil Inputs

Fish emulsions. Restricted to forms that do not contain synthetic preservatives and which are not "fortified" with synthetic plant nutrients. Stabilizers in fish emulsion cannot exceed 1 percent by weight of P_2O_5.

Micronutrient sprays. Restricted to cases where deficiencies are documented by soil or plant tissue tests.

Sodium molybdate. Restricted to use as a last resort for documented deficiency.

Sulfates of zinc or iron. Restricted to cases where deficiencies are documented by soil or plant tissue testing.

Sulfur (the synthetic analog of the natural element). Restricted use on soils due to its negative effects on soil life.

Trace minerals (synthetic). Restricted to cases where deficiencies are documented.

Allowed Compatible, Synthetic Pest Controls

Boric acid. Restricted to use on inedible plant parts.

Bordeaux mixes (copper sulfate mixed with hydrated lime). Mined ingredients preferred. Restricted use on soils and crops due to potential build-up of copper in soil. Accumulation can be especially toxic in acid soils.

Copper. Includes fixed copper groups which do not require a tolerance level set by federal agencies, such as hydroxides, basic sulfates, oxychlorides and oxides. These are considered as Bordeaux Mixes. *See* **Bordeaux Mixes.**

Copper sulfate. *See* **Bordeaux** and **Copper.**

Dormant oils. Restricted to use as a dormant spray on woody plants.

Hydrated lime. Restricted to foliar application as a fungicide only. *See* also **Controlled Atmosphere Lime.**

Lime sulfur (includes calcium polysulphide). Regulated to foliar application as a fungicide.

Pheromones.

Soap-based herbicides. Restricted to use on non-food crops.

Soaps.

Sodium bicarbonate (baking soda). Allowed uses include disease control.

Suffocating oils (petroleum-based). Restricted to use on woody and perennial plants. Allowed for both dormant and summer use.

Sulfur (the synthetic analog of the natural element). Foliar use as an insecticide or fungicide is allowed. Prohibited for post-harvest treatment of crops.

Summer oils. See suffocating oils.

Allowed Compatible Synthetic Production Aids

Alcohol. Includes ethanol and methanol from synthetic sources. Alcohols are allowed as solvents and carriers in brand-name products. Isopropyl alcohol is prohibited.

Arsenic ("pressure-treated" lumber). Can be allowed for existing installations, but not for new plantings. There is a strong concern about uptake of arsenic compounds from pressure-treated lumber used for trellising vines, and other field applications.

Chelates. Restricted use in combination with micronutrients in cases of documented deficiencies.

Controlled atmosphere lime (as hydrated lime from controlled atmosphere storage which has removed CO_2 from the air). Restricted to post-harvest use in controlled atmosphere storage. Prohibited for use as a fertilizer.

Hydrogen peroxide (synthetic analog of a natural molecule). Allowed for use as a root dip, foliar feed, disinfectant, disease inhibitor, and substitute for chlorine as an irrigation system cleaner.

Newspaper mulch.

Petroleum spray adjuvants. Includes spreader stickers and carriers. Dormant oils are allowed for use as spray adjuvants on woody perennials only. Petroleum oil adjuvants may not contain any synthetic pesticides. See suffocating oils.

Plastics for mulch, row covers, and solarization. Restricted to use only during growing or harvest season. Plastic must be removed at the end of each growing or harvest season. It must not be incorporated into soil or left in field to decompose.

Sodium silicate. Restricted to post-harvest use in floating tree fruits.

Tree seals. Plant or milk-based paints are recommended. Lime-based or interior latex are allowed. Other petroleum materials may be used if it is documented that there are no available alternatives. Restricted to substances not combined with fungicides or other synthetic chemicals.

OFPANA Crop Production Guidelines — Excerpted from the Second Draft: May 1992

1. Introduction

...OFPANA's guidelines were envisioned as a fluid document, which would evolve as new information and understanding came to light. There still exist many conflicts and inconsistencies among certification programs: such diversity is welcome and necessary....

2. General Principles of Organic Production

2.1 Basic Precepts of Organic Agriculture

The fundamental reference point for determining organic production standards should be the following "Statement of Principles of Organic Agriculture," as drafted by the Organic Farmers Associations Council (OFAC) in February 1990:

Organic farming practices are based on a common set of principles that aim to encourage stewardship of the earth. Organic procedures work in harmony with natural ecosystems to develop stability through diversity, complexity, and the recycling of energy and nutrients. They:

- Seek to provide food of the highest quality, using practices and materials that protect the environment and promote human health.

- Use renewable resources and recycled materials to the greatest extent possible, within agricultural systems that are regionally organized.

- Maintain diversity within the farming system and in its surroundings, including the protection of plant and wildlife habitat.

- Replenish and maintain long-term soil fertility by providing optimal conditions for soil biological activity.

- Provide livestock and poultry with conditions which meet both health and behavioral requirements.

- Seek an adequate return from their labor, while providing a safe working environment and maintaining concern for the long range social and ecological impact of their work....

Section 4 Standards For Organic Farm Management

Section 4.1 Criteria for Soil Qualification

...The Organic Foods Production Act clearly states that prohibited materials cannot have been applied to certified fields within 3 years prior to harvest of organic products....

Section 4.3 Soil Management Criteria

The most important element of an organic farm management plan is the approach taken to improving soil quality and maintaining fertility levels...

The fertility of the soil is based on the harmonious interaction of physical, chemical, and biological factors. It is the proper cyclic interplay of these factors that creates a healthy soil. Of critical significance is the maintenance of active humification, whereby not only nutrients but a broad array of plant growth promoting substances and pathogen suppressants are supplied. In an ecologically managed system, fertilization consists of fostering this biological activity, with the proper management of organic matter being the key task. This is accomplished through judicious tillage, crop rotations, and the addition to the soil of manure and other organic wastes. Soil mineral balance, which is also essential for soil health and the production of quality organic food, may require the application of mineral fertilizers.

4.3.1 Rotations

The rotation plan constitutes a core document around which any organic farm plan must be constructed. Producers of perennials are a possible exception, although advances in the sciences of permaculture and polyculture create new possibilities for successions, intercropping, alley cropping, and other diversity-enhancing measures within perennial systems.

The rotation of crops is a key component of organic weed, pest and disease prevention systems. It also has beneficial effects on soil nutrient levels, tilth, and organic matter content. Every organic farm plan must include some provision for rotation of annual crops, depending on principal crops being produced, topography, suitability of soils to various uses, alternative sources of fertility, and presence of livestock on the farm. Access to markets for alternative crops in rotation is an important consideration requiring assistance at the public policy level.

Elements to consider in developing rotation plans include:

- alternation of sod crops with crops requiring tillage
- nitrogen fixing crops
- green manure crops
- cover, nurse, and "catch" crops
- smother crops
- deep rooting crops
- alternation of heavy and light feeders
- plants with allelopathic or mineral accumulation properties
- plants which provide habitat for beneficial insects

4.3.2 Tillage and Soil Erosion Prevention

The primary purposes of tillage are to establish seedbeds that are conducive to crop growth, to control weeds, and to incorporate organic matter (crop residues, fertilizers, etc.) into the soil. Tillage also creates a soil environment that promotes the free movement of air (carbon dioxide, oxygen, and nitrogen) and water through soil, and in the presence of aerobic bacteria and other soil life forms, the decay or "digestion" of organic matter within the soil.

Damage done to agricultural soils by careless tillage probably surpasses that caused by inappropriate chemical use. Organic producers must use tillage systems which minimize erosion, compaction, and organic matter oxidation. Regular monitoring of soil physical qualities, such as aggregation, oxygen diffusion rate (ODR) and water infiltration rate, is recommended. Farming practices that minimize or eliminate tillage, such as mowing, grazing, or permaculture systems, are excellent alternatives....

4.3.3 Manure Management and Compost

Animal manure is one of the most beneficial inputs in organic food production. There is general consensus that a farm with livestock can be self-sustaining far more readily than one without.

However, many of the beneficial effects of manure can be wasted by improper management. Soil bacteria can be disrupted by a sudden influx of soluble nutrients from raw manure, and manure runoff is a common source of nonpoint surface water pollution.

Properly managed, raw manure can be used in a manner that benefits the soil and protects water. Acceptable application of raw manure depends on its origin, soil temperature, soil organic matter content, soil type, moisture, quantity and quality of soil organisms, and provision for a sufficient "digestion" period. The best time to use raw manure is in a rotation, when seeding or incorporating a green manure crop.

The full potential of manure as a biological activator can be achieved by aerobic digestion (high heat) or controlled fermentation (low heat). Both procedures, called composting, stabilize the nutrients in the manure by blending it with other organic materials in a controlled humification process. It is the assured production of humus that makes the composting process cost-effective to farmers. Composting is particularly important for manures and other organic wastes brought in from off-farm, especially from industrial sources which might contain residues of pesticides or animal drugs....

4.3.3.1 Raw Manure Application

...For example, longer waiting periods should be required after application of raw poultry manure, and on land to be planted to known nitrate accumulator crops such as leafy greens, radishes and beets.

Rules aimed at preventing contamination of groundwater by manure runoff should also be specified. Maximum application rates, prohibition against spreading manure on snow or frozen ground, or within a certain distance of waterways, should all be included in standards governing use of raw manure in organic production systems.

Allowed:

Application of raw manure to land from which crops intended for human consumption will be harvested in more than 60 days.

Prohibited:

Application of raw manure to land from which crops intended for human consumption will be harvested within 60 days.

4.3.3.2 Sewage Sludge and Industrial Organic Wastes

Sewage sludge, whether composted or uncomposted, should be treated with caution because of its possible content of pathogens and heavy metals. It can be a rich source of organic matter and soil nutrients, however, and so can be allowed in a rotation on green manure crops if shown to fall within Federal or State guidelines (whichever are stricter) for permissible levels of toxic contaminants....

4.4 General Crop Management

A sound ecological soil management program is essential to the prevention of many crop management problems. It is scientifically accepted that well nourished plants are more resistant to pests and diseases, both pre- and post-harvest. The careful selection of crops and plant varieties complement sound ecological soil management practices. Choices should be appropriate to the soil and regional climate to insure optimum crop success....

4.4.2 Irrigation

In many areas, there is legitimate concern about the source and possible contamination of irrigation water. High levels of nitrates, chlorides, selenium, and boron can be carried in such water, and its excessive use can salinize the soil. Water conserving methods of irrigation should be expected of organic producers; depletion of groundwater reserves in some areas calls into serious question the ongoing production of irrigated crops in those regions. Where irrigation is essential to crop production, routine analysis of water quality and soil salinization must occur....

Seed Companies and Nurseries

Abundant Life Seed Foundation, P.O. Box 772, Port Townsend, WA 98368, (206) 385-5660

Good selection of vegetables, small grains, herbs, and flowers. Organic, untreated, open-pollinated seeds.

Adams County Nursery, P.O. Box 108, Aspers, PA 17304, (717) 677-8105

A large selection of fruit varieties for commercial and home growers, on a number of different rootstocks.

Bountiful Gardens, Ecology Action, 19550 Walker Road, Willits, CA 95490

A nonprofit organization that sponsors educational programs, and offers a good selection of untreated, open-pollinated seeds for vegetables, herbs, flowers, green manures, and grains.

W. Atlee Burpee Seed Co., Warminster, PA 18974, (215) 674-9633, Fax: (215) 674-4170

Conventional vegetables, fruits, herbs, and flowers.

Casa Yerba, 3459 Days Creek Rd., Days Creek, OR 97429

Organically grown herb plants and seeds.

Companion Plants, 7247 N. Coolville Ridge Rd., Athens, OH 45701, (614) 592-4643

$2 for catalog. Huge selection of herbs for culinary, medicinal, and other purposes.

The Cook's Garden, P.O. Box 65, Londonderry, VT 05148, (802) 824-3400, Fax: (802) 824-3027

Large selection of vegetable seeds for outdoor, coldframe and greenhouse culture, especially lettuce. Untreated, organic, open-pollinated seeds.

Cumberland Valley Nurseries, Inc., P.O. Box 471, McMinnville, TN 37110, (800) 492-0022, Local (615) 668-4153

Fruit trees, with an unusually extensive collection of peach trees.

Dabney Herbs, P.O. Box 22061, Louisville, KY 40222, (502) 893-5198

$2 for catalog. Herbs for all purposes.

Fedco Seeds, 275 Upper Bellsqueeze, Clinton, ME 04927, (207) 872-9093

Large selection of vegetable seeds and seedlings. Also have large selection of trees.

Henry Field's Seed & Nursery Co., Shenandoah, IA 51602, (605) 665-9391

Conventional vegetables and fruits.

Fowler Nurseries, Inc., 525 Fowler Rd., Newcastle, CA 95658, (916) 645-8191

$3 for catalog. Selection of fruits, especially for West Coast climate.

Fox Hill Farm, 444 W. Michigan Ave, Box 9, Parma, MI 49269-0009, (517) 531-3179

Good selection of herbs.

Garden City Seeds, 1324 Red Crow Road, Victor, MT 59875-9713, (406) 961-4837

Good selection of northern vegetable varieties. Open-pollinated seeds. Some are certified organic.

Grimo Nut Nursery, R.R. 3, Lakeshore Rd., Niagara-on-the-Lake, Ontario L0S 1J0, (416) 935-9773

$1 for catalog. One of the best nut nurseries around for high quality seedlings.

Gurney's Seed & Nursery Co., Yankton, SD 57079, (605) 665-1930

Good selection of vegetables.

Harris Seeds, 60 Saginaw Drive, P.O. Box 22960, Rochester, NY 14692-2260, Orders: (800) 544-7938, Other: (716) 442-0410

Good vegetable selection.

Hartmann's Plantation, Inc., Box E, 310 60th Street, Grand Junction, MI 49056, (616) 253-4281, Fax: 616-253-4457

The largest blueberry nursery in the nation. Huge selection.

High Altitude Gardens, P.O. Box 4619, Ketchum, ID 83340, (208) 788-4363

A nice selection of seeds for short season vegetables, wildflowers, grasses, and herbs — which all grow at 6,000 feet! Many open-pollinated varieties.

Horticultural Enterprises, Box 810082, Dallas, TX 75381-0082

Huge selection of peppers.

American Forestry Technology, Inc., 1001 North 500 West, West Lafayette, IN 47906, (317) 583-3311

The only source of the patented "Purdue Number 1" seedling.

Johnny's Selected Seeds, Foss Hill Road, Albion, ME 04910, (207) 437-9294, Fax: (207) 437-2165

Good selection of vegetables — especially carrots and greenhouse varieties. Most are untreated seeds.

J.W. Jung Seed Co., Randolph, WI 53956, (414) 326-4100

Selection of vegetables, flowers, herbs, berries, and fruit trees.

Kelly Bros. Nurseries, Inc., 1700 Morrissey Drive, Bloomingdale, IL 61704, (309) 663-9551

Selection of fruits, berries, and ornamentals.

Krohne Plant Farms, Rt. 6, Box 586, Dowagiac, MI 49047, (616) 424-5423

Large selection of strawberries, and some asparagus.

Henry Leuthardt Nurseries, Montauk Highway, Box 666, East Moriches, Long Island, NY 11940, (516) 878-1387

Nice selection of fruits. Noted for its selection of espalier trees.

Miller Nurseries, Inc., West Lake Road, Canandaigua, NY 14424, (800) 836-9630

Fruit and nut tree and berry selection.

Native Seeds/SEARCH, 2509 N. Campbell Ave, #325, Tuscon, AZ 85719, Public Ed. Office Phone (No Orders) 602-327-9123

A nonprofit seed conservation organization. They are working to preserve the traditional crops and their wild relatives of the U.S. Southwest and Northwest Mexico. Grains, vegetables, herbs, fruit, cotton, tobacco, books, food, baskets, and dye for wool.

NYFT — New York Fruit Testing Cooperative Association, Inc., Box 462, Geneva, NY 14456, (315) 787-2205

$5 for catalog and membership. Selection of fruit trees and berries, with a number of experimental new crosses for trial gardeners.

Nichols Garden Nursery & Rare Seeds, 1190 North Pacific Highway, Albany, OR 97321, (503) 928-9280, Fax: (503) 967-8406

Good selection of vegetables and herbs, often rare and unusual.

Nolin River Nut Tree Nursery, 797 Port Wooden Road, Upton, KY 42784, (502) 369-8551

One of the few nut tree nurseries. Offers specific varieties.

Northwoods Nursery, 28696 S. Cramer Road, Molalla, OR 97038, (503) 651-3737

Fruits and fruit trees.

Nourse Farms, Inc., Box 485, RFD, South Deerfield, MA 01373, (413) 665-2658 , Fax: (413) 665-7888

Good selections of strawberries, raspberries, and asparagus. Most everything propagated by tissue culture.

Park Seed Co., Cokesbury Road, Greenwood, SC 29647-0001, (803) 223-7333

Vegetables, especially hybrids, flowers, shrubs, and ornamentals.

Pinetree Garden Seeds, Box 300, New Gloucester, ME 04260, (207) 926-3400

Extensive selection of vegetable seeds. Also have large book section in catalog.

Plants of the Southwest, 930 Baca Street, Santa Fe, NM 87501, (505) 983-1548

Good selection of plants native to the Southwest, and for Western mountains and high plains.

Raintree Nursery, 391 Butts Rd., Morton, WA 98356, (206) 496-6400

Good selection of fruit trees and berries for the Northwest. An informative catalog.

Rayner Bros., Inc., Box 1617, Salisbury, MD 21801, (301) 742-1594

Huge selection of strawberries.

Redwood City Seed, P.O. Box 361, Redwood City, CA 94064, (415) 325-7333

$1 for catalog. Large selection of unusual varieties, especially from the Orient, Mexico, and Europe.

Richters Herb Catalogue, Goodwood, Ontario, Canada L0C 1A0, (416) 640-6677 , Fax: (416) 640-6641

Cadillac catalog of herbs for all purposes.

Rocky Meadow Orchard & Nursery, Rt.2 Box 2104, New Salisbury, IN 47161, (812) 347-2213

Nice selection of fruit trees on various rootstocks.

Ronniger's Seeds, Star Route 73, Moyie Springs, ID 83845, (208) 267-7938

$2 for catalog. Large selection of potato varities.

Saginaw Valley Nut Nursery, 8285 Dixie Highway, Rte #3, Birch Run, MI 48415

One of the few nut tree nurseries. Offers specific varieties.

Sandy Mush Herb Nursery, Rt.2 Surret Cove Road, Leicester, NC 28748, (704) 683-2014

$4 for catalog. Large selection of culinary, ornamental, medicinal, and other purpose herbs.

Seeds Blum, Idaho City Stage, Boise, ID 83706

$2 for catalog. Good selection of heirloom and open-pollinated seeds. A fun and informative catalog.

Shepherd's Garden Seeds, Shipping Office, 30 Irene St., Torrington, CT 06790, (203) 482-3638

$2 for catalog. Gourmet vegetables, with some flowers and herbs.

Sonoma Antique Apple Nursery, 4395 Westside Rd., Healdsburg, CA 95448, (707) 433-6420

$1 for catalog. Organically grown antique apple and other fruit trees. Espaliered trees.

South Carolina Foundation Seeds, Clemson University, Clemson, SC 29634, (803) 656-2520

Sweet potato varieties.

Southern Exposure Seed Exchange, Box 158, North Garden, VA 22959

$3 for catalog. Open-pollinated and heirloom vegetable varieties. Special varieties for solar greenhouses. Untreated seeds. Very informative catalog.

Southmeadow Fruit Gardens, Lakeside, MI 49116, (616) 469-2865

$6 for catalog, 112 pages illustrated, with a free listing update. Huge selection of antique and some newer fruit trees.

St. Lawrence Nurseries, R.D. 2, Potsdam, NY 13676, (315) 265-6739

$1 for catalog. Very hardy berries and fruit trees for the North.

Stark Bro's Nurseries, Louisiana, MO 63353-0010, (800) 325-0611 , Fax: (314) 754-5290

Fruit trees, berries, and nuts. Many common and some unusual varieties. Some varieties listed in this book are offered in their catalog for professional growers.

Stokes Seeds, Inc., P.O. Box 548, Buffalo, NY 14240-0548, (416) 688-4300

Good selection of vegetables and flowers. Good greenhouse varieties. Some open-pollinated and untreated seeds.

Territorial Seed Company, P.O. Box 27, Lorane, OR 97451

Nice selection of vegetable seeds for the Northwest. Many open-pollinated varieties.

Thompson & Morgan Seedsmen, Box 1308, Jackson, NJ 08527, (201) 363-2225 , Fax: (201) 363-9356

Cadillac catalog of flowers and also some vegetables. Many unusual and interesting varieties.

Tomato Growers Supply Co., Box 2237, Fort Myers, FL 33902, (813) 768-1119

Huge selection of tomatoes, most hybrids.

Van Well Nursery, Box 1339, Wenatchee, WA 98801, (509) 663-8189, Washington: (800) 572-1553

Retail and wholesale selection of conventional fruit trees and berries.

William Dam Seeds Ltd., Box 8400, Dundas, Ontario, Canada L9H 6M1, (416) 628-6641

Good selection of vegetables, especially cold-tolerant varieties, and some cover crops and herbs. Untreated seeds.

Windmill Point Farm & Nursery, 2103 Perrot Blvd., N.D. Ile Perrot, Quebec, J7V 5V6 Canada, (514) 453-9757

$2.50 for catalog. Good selection of fruits on a variety of rootstocks and some specific nut varieties.

Equipment and Pest Control Suppliers

Ag Life, 6012 River Road, Sharpsburg, MD 21782, (301) 416-2666

Botanical and mineral controls, fungicides, soaps, oils, fencing, pet products, more.

Ag Biochem Inc., 3 Fleetwood Ct., Orinda, CA 94563

Beneficial insects and other biocontrol agents.

Alsto's Handy Helpers, P.O. Box 1267, Galesburg, IL 61401-1267, (800) 447-0048

Selection of garden tools, supplies, and accessories.

A.M. Leonard, Inc., 6665 Spiker Road, Piqua, OH 45356, (800) 543-8955

Extensive offering of garden tools, light and heavy.

Arbico Inc., P.O. Box 42470-CRB, Tucson, AZ 85738, (800) 767-2847

Beneficial insects and organisms, traps, soil test kits, compost, fertilizers, more.

Biofac, Inc., P.O. Box 87, Mathis, TX 78368

Beneficial insects.

Bozeman Bio-Tech, 1612 Gold Avenue, P.O. Box 3146, Bozeman, MT 59772, (800) 289-6656

Environmentally safe controls for grasshoppers, including "Semaspore" which contains *Nosema locustae* to stop them feeding.

Clyde Robin Seed Co., 3670 Enterprise Avenue, Hayward, CA 94545, (415) 785-0425

Pest control supplies, beneficial insects, and seed mixes to attract beneficials.

Diggers, P.O. Box 1551, Soquel, CA 95073, (408) 462-6095

Wire gopher baskets: 20-gauge galvanized root guard (¾-inch mesh in 1- to 5-foot widths), and 15 gallon containers.

Gage Industries, Lake Oswego, OR 97035

Write for your nearest distributor of Dura pots, which are made from recycled plastic.

Gardens Alive!, Natural Gardening Research Center, Hwy 48, P.O. Box 149, Sunman, IN 47041, (812) 623-3800

Row covers, sprayers, beneficial insects, different Bt's, beneficial nematodes, botanical and mineral products, traps, composting and irrigation supplies, pet products, more.

Gardener's Supply, 128 Intervale Road, Burlington, VT 05401, (802) 863-1700

Tools, seed starting kits, row covers, organic fertilizers, greenhouses, drip irrigation, composting supplies, sprayers, bird houses, botanical and mineral products, soaps.

Growing Naturally, P.O. Box 54, 149 Pine Lane, Pineville, PA 18946, (215) 598-7025

Traps, composters, beneficial insects, biological controls, fences, soil conditioners and fertilizers, watering devices, row covers, chipper/shredders, more.

IFM (Integrated-Fertility-Management), 333 Ohme Gardens Road, Wenatchee, WA 98801, (800) 332-3179, (509) 662-3179

Promotes ecologically sound orchard, farm and garden practices. Garden equipment, nutrient analysis, soil amendments, foliar sprays, green manures, pest controls, botanical and biological controls, beneficial predators, and parasites.

Mellinger's, 2310 W. South Range Rd., North Lima, OH 44452, (800) 321-7444

Besides a wide range of plants, offers lots of drip irrigation equipment, greenhouses, pots, planters, sprayers, organic fertilizers, fungicides, insecticides, rooting hormones, traps, tools, beneficial insects. More. Often wholesale prices.

Natural Insect Control, P.O. Box 1020, Buffalo, NY 14213-1020, (416) 382-2904

Environmentally-safe pest controls and beneficial insects.

Necessary Trading Co., P.O. Box 305, New Castle, VA 24127, (703) 864-5103, Fax: (703) 864-5186

Traps, beneficial insects, biological controls, oils, soaps, pheromone traps (mating disruption), fungicides, disease controls, organic fertilizers, green manure crops, soil testing kits, composting supplies, sprayers, more.

Nematode Farm, Inc., 2617 San Pable Avenue, Berkeley, CA 94702

Sells beneficial nematodes.

The Nitron Formula: Natural Products For Organic Growing, 100 W. Rock, P.O. Box 400, Fayetteville, AR 72702

Unusual agricultural enzymes to condition, rebuild, loosen, and detoxify soil. Irrigation equipment, organic fertilizers and amendments. More.

NPI Nutri-link, 417 Wakara Way, Salt Lake City, UT 84108

Mycorrhizal fungi inoculum for blueberries and greenhouse plants.

Peaceful Valley Farm Supply, P.O. Box 2209, Grass Valley, CA 95945, (916) 272-GROW

Catalog $2.00. Tools, composting supplies, row covers, many cover crops and mixes, sprayers, soil amendments, greenhouse covering, seed thresher, and also bulbs.

Plow and Hearth, P.O. Box 830, Orange, VA 22960, (800) 627-1712

Fine selection of garden tools, supplies, and accessories.

Ringer, 9959 Valley View Road, Eden Prairie, MN 55344, (800) 654-1047

Pest control supplies, garden tools, sprayers, compost supplies.

Reuter Laboratories, P.O. Box 346, Haymarket, VA 22069

Various pest and disease biocontrols.

Safer's Inc., 189 Wells Avenue, Newton, MA 02159, (617) 964-2990

Pest control supplies, beneficial insects, predators, and parasites.

Smith & Hawken, 25 Corte Madera, Mill Valley, CA 94941, (415) 383-8070

A cadillac selection of garden tools. Also offer irrigation supplies, composting equipment, clothing, books, and furniture.

Vertical Veggies, 728 Fourth Avenue, Salt Lake City, UT 84103

Collapsible 4-sided tomato square cages, 6 feet high, 18 inches on a side. Unlike most cages, these store flat.

State Gardening Associations

Biodynamic, Biological, Ecological, and Organic — as of April 1993

We urge you to contact your local growers association for a list of locally recommended insect and disease controls. Issues of disease and insect control vary widely from region to region. Pests in the Northeast may never be seen on the West Coast, in the Southwest or Florida, and vice-versa. Many of the following state associations have compiled lists of substances that are permitted, regulated, or prohibited in organic growing. Some states may be more strict than the federal guidelines. The organizations listed below should be able to provide guidance on safe pest control for your region. For growers seeking help in producing and marketing, these associations may also be able to connect you with various types of cooperatives.

As a sign of the explosive growth occurring in this field, since the 1990 edition of this book I have had to add to this list over 75 new organizations! For the backyard gardener, joining your local organization could be a way to learn more as well as to network and make new friends.

For further information at the national level, contact The Organic Foods Production Association of North America (OFPANA), P.O. Box 1078, Greenfield, MA, 01301 (FAX: (413) 774-6432). The following list of organizations was kindly provided by OFPANA.

CODES

CCOF = Certified California Organic Growers
NOFA = National Organic Farmers Association
OCIA = Organic Crop Improvement Association

Arizona
Arizona Organic Advisory
    Board
(602) 662-4365
Fax: (602) 662-4528
Contact: Ron Powers

OCIA – Arizona
Sunset Route, Box 6
Willcox, AZ 85643
(602) 8288-3370
Contact: Craig Bull

Arkansas
Ozark Organic Growers
    Association
HCR 72, Box 34
Parthenon, AR 72666
(501) 446-5783

Arkansas Organic Small
    Farm Viability Project
Route 2, Box 76
West Fork, AR 72774
(501) 545-3658
Contact: Tim Snell

Ozark Organic Growers
    Association
South Central Chapter
Route 4, Box 158
Huntsville, AR 72740
(501) 545-3658
Contact: Mark Cain

Ozark Small Farm
    Viability Project
P.O. Box 501
Jasper, AR 72641
Contact: Peggy Bonds

Ozark Small Farm
    Viability Project
P.O. Box 378
Jasper, AR 72641
(501) 434-5594
Contact: David Hahn

California
Demeter Association for
    Biodynamic Agricul-
    ture
10535 Lindley Avenue
Northridge, CA 91326
(818) 558-6637
Fax: (818) 558-6637
Contact: Deborah
    Hawkins

California Organic
    Certification
    Committee
P.O. Box 545
Nogales, AZ 85628
(602) 761-1838
Fax: (602) 287-2345
Contact: Andrew G.
    Watson

California Organic Field
    Crops Association
P.O. Box 401
Davis, CA 95617
(916) 756-2508
Contact: Daniel Cohen

Wes Pak Organic
4572 Avenue 400
Dinuba, CA 93618
(209) 591-4424
Fax: (209) 591-7055
Contact: Jim Stewart

CCOF – Central Office
P.O. Box 8136
Santa Cruz, CA 95061
(408) 423-2263
Fax: (408) 423-4528
Contact: Mark Lipson

CCOF – Big Valley
6901 Hultberg Road
Hilmar, CA 95324
(209) 667-7494
Contact: Glen Anderson

CCOF – Central Coast
    Chapter
P.O. Box 372
Santa Cruz, CA 95063
(408) 335-9364
Contact: Wendy
    Krupnick

CCOF – Desert Valley
    Chapter
P.O. Box 908
Indio, CA 92202
(609) 345-6171
Contact: Brad Milliken

CCOF – Fresno-Tulare
    Chapter
5587 E. National
Fresno, CA 93727
(209) 291-0963
Contact: Tom Willey

CCOF – Kern Chapter
Route 2, Box 291
Delano, CA 93215
(805) 725-1046
Contact: Tom Pavich

CCOF – Mendocino
    Chapter
18501 Greenwood Road
Philo, CA 95466
(707) 895-2333
Contact: Tim Bates

CCOF – North Coast
    Chapter
P.O. Box 2406
Sebastopol, CA 95473
(707) 874-1357
Contact: David Letourneau

CCOF – North Valley
    Chapter
5034 Larkin Road
Oroville, CA 95965
(916) 589-0695
Contact: Leon Lowrey

CCOF – OFAC Contact
2190 Sprowl Creek Rd
Garberville, CA 95440-
    9609
Contact: Patti
    Laboyteaux

CCOF – Pacific SW
    Chapter
32929 Lilac Road
Valley Center, CA 92082
(619) 728-9664
Contact: Rich Taylor

CCOF – San Luis Obispo
    Chapter
6080 Parkhill Road
Santa Margarita, CA
    93453
Contact: Don Woods

CCOF – Sierra Gold
    Chapter
7740 Fairplay Road
Somerset, CA 95684
(209) 245-3248
Contact: Brian Fitzpatrick

CCOF – Siskyou-
    Humboldt Chapter
13611 Meamber Creek
    Road
Ft. Jones, CA 96032
(916) 468-5297
Contact: Myrna Stafford

CCOF – South Coast
    Chapter
P.O. Box 40144
Santa Barbara, CA 93140
(805) 687-7109
Contact: Marshall
    Chrostowski

CCOF – Yolo Chapter
Star Route, Box 3
Capay, CA 95679
Contact: Kathy Barsotte

OCIA – California
P.O. Box 200
Ballico, CA 95303
(209) 632-6424
Contact: Bill Reichle

Colorado
Colorado Department of
    Agriculture
Plant Ind. Div.
700 Kipling Street, Suite
    4000
Lakewood, CO 80215

---

(303) 239-4140
Fax: (303) 239-4125
Contact: Dan Gallegos
and Jim Rubingh

Colorado Organic
Producers Association
1020 WCR 72
Wellington, CO 80549
(303) 568-7654

Colorado Organic
Producers Association
Route 2, 3889 75th
Boulder, CO 80301
Contact: John Ellis

OCIA – Colorado
5140 Race Ct #4
Denver, CO 80216
(303) 297-9393
Contact: Mel Coleman

Connecticut
NOFA – Connecticut
Meetinghouse Hill Road
Durham, CT 06422
(203) 349-1417
Contact: Barbara Baffa

NOFA – Connecticut
86 Fleming Road
Meridan, CT 06450
Contact: Wayne Young

NOFA – Connecticut
153 Bowers Hill Road
Oxford, CT 06483
Contact: Bill Deusing

Florida
Florida Department of
Agriculture
Room 429, Mayo Bldg
Tallahassee, FL 32399-
0800
(904) 488-9682
Fax: (904) 488-7127
Contact: Michael
Matthews

Florida Certified Growers
& Consumers
Route 1, Box 1250
Melrose, FL 32666
(904) 475-2037
Contact: Robin Lauriault

Florida Certified Growers
& Consumers
Route 1, Box 116
Jennings, FL 32052
(904) 938-2045
Contact: Wade Howell

OCIA – Florida & Sunbelt
Organic Growers
Association
Route 3, Box 32G
Alachua, FL 32615

(904) 462-1302
Contact: Marc Ketchel

OCIA – Florida
P.O. Box 2344
Ft. Pierce, FL 34954-2344
(407) 461-4066
Contact: Steve Rosslow

Sunbelt Organic
Producers Association
Route 1, Box 31-K
Alachua, FL 32615
Contact: Harry Kalajian

Georgia
Georgia Organic Grow
Association
General Delivery
Madras, GA 30254
(404) 621-4642
Contact: Larry Conklin

Idaho
Idaho Department of
Agriculture
P.O. Box 790
Boise, ID 83701
(208) 334-2623
Fax: (208) 334-2170
Contact: James Boatman

Idaho Organic Producers
Association
1741 Bullock Lane
Middleton, ID 83644
(208) 585-6140
Contact: Tim Sommer

Illinois
Land of Lincoln Organic
Growers Association
2400 Spring Creek Road
Barrington Hills, IL 60010
(312) 658-7400
Contact: Barbara
MacArthur

OCIA – Illinois
Route 2, Box 73
Lawrenceville, IL 62429
(618) 884-9001
Contact: Sheryl Ring-
Laakman

Indiana
Indiana Organic Growers
Association
P.O. Box 208
Patricksburg, IN 47455
(812) 859-4195
Contact: Sophia
Hauserman

OCIA – Indiana
RR 2, Box 182
Clayton, IN 46118
(317) 539-6579
Contact: Cissy Bowman

Iowa
OCIA – Iowa
Rt 1, Box 176
Harlan, IA 51537
(712) 627-4217
Contact: Ken Rosmann

Iowa Organic Growers &
Buyers Association
22 East Court Street
Iowa City, IA 52240
(319) 351-7888
Contact: Hilary Strayer

Iowa Organic Growers &
Buyers Association
ISU Extension
2517 Park Avenue
Muscatine, IA 52761
Contact: Denise
Chevalier

Kansas
Northeast Kansas
Organic Food
Producers
P.O. Box 153
Beattie, KS 66406
(913) 353-2414
Contact: Judy Nickelson

OCIA – Kansas
P.O. Box 83
Oakley, KS 67748
(913) 672-4328
Contact: Kevin Stoppel

OCIA – Kansas
P.O. Box 133
Whiting, KS 66552
(913) 873-3431
Contact: Diane Dysart

OCIA – Kansas
Route 3, Box 170
Colby, KS 67701
(913) 462-6045
Contact: Dan Bourquin

Kansas Organic Producers
RR 1
Home, KS 66438
Contact: Joe Vogelsberg

Kentucky
Kentucky Certification
Program
KY Department of
Agriculture
63 Wilkinson Blvd
Frankfort, KY 40601
(502) 549-3039
Contact: Kathy Aman

Kentucky New Farm
Coalition
104 Hanson Street
Berea, KY 40403
(606) 986-8640
Contact: Bill Riley

Maine
Maine Organic Farmers
& Gardeners
P.O. Box 2176
283 Water Street
Augusta, ME 04330
(207) 622-3118
Fax: (207) 626-5820
Contact: Nancy Ross

Maryland
Maryland Department of
Agriculture
50 Harry S. Truman
Highway
Annapolis, MD 21401
(301) 841-5770
Fax: (301) 841-5987
Contact: Suzie Harrison

MD Organic Food &
Farm Production
6201 Harley Road
Middletown, MD 21769
Contact: Eric Rice

Massachusetts
NOFA – Massachusetts
P.O. Box 31
Belchertown, MA 01007
Contact: Judy Gillan

NOFA – Massachusetts
P.O. Box 1021
Belchertown, MA 01007
Contact: Alex Stone

NOFA – Massachusetts
Route 137, Hyde Hill Road
Williamsburg, MA 01096
Contact: Margaret
Christie

NOFA – Massachusetts
Farm Center, c/o
Hampshire College
Amherst, MA 01002
Contact: David Holm

Michigan
Organic Growers of
Michigan
State Chairman
135 East 120 Street
Grant, MI 49377
(616) 834-5481
Contact: Gary Larison

Organic Growers of
Michigan, Thumb
Chapter
3928 South Sheridan
Lennon, MI 72641
(313) 621-4977
Contact: Lee Purdy

Organic Growers of
Michigan, SW Chapter
26041 County Road 681
Bangor, MI 49013

(616) 427-8986
Contact: Maynard
Kaufman

Organic Growers of
Michigan
3rd Coast Chapter
6677 Twelve Mile Road
Rockford, MI 49341
(616) 866-1679
Contact: Fred Reusch

OCIA – Michigan
3915 Dearing Road
Parma, MI 49269
(517) 788-7728
Contact: Tom Summers

Minnesota
Minnesota – Full Circle
Organic Growers
Cooperative
Route 1, Box 52-BB
Lake City, MN 55041

Organic Growers &
Buyers Association
1405 Silver Lake Road
New Brighton, MN 55112
(612) 636-7933
Fax: (612) 636-4135
Contact: Yvonne Buckley

Minnesota – IKWE
Marketing Collective
Route 1, Box 286
Ponsford, MN 56575

OCIA – Minnesota
Route 1, Box 203B
Mazeppa, MN 55956
(507) 843-5863
Contact: Roger and
Vickie McDonough

Mississippi
Mississippi Organic
Growers Association
Route 1, Box 442
Lumberton, MS 39455
(601) 796-4406
Contact: Tom Dana

Missouri
Ozark Organic Growers
Association
NE Chapter
Route 5, Box 1026
Ava, MO 65608
(417) 683-5109
Contact: Gregg Thorsen

Ozark Organic Growers
Association, Spring-
field Chapter
1510 South Jameston
Road
Springfield, MO 65809
(417) 865-0593
Contact: Gary Jensen

Montana

Organic Certifiers
Association of Montana
105 Mount
Missoula, MT 59801

Organic Certifiers
Association of Montana
P.O. Box 871
Helena, MT 59624
(406) 848-7381

OCIA – MT Southwest &
Organic Certification
Association of MT
Baker Ranch, Box 94
Shawmont, MT 59078
(406) 632-4528
Contact: Terry Lechner

OCIA – MT Northeast
Box 5035
Wolf Point, MT 59210
(406) 653-2492
Contact: Kathy Forsness

OCIA – MT North Central
Box 678
Big Sandy, MT 59520
Contact: Bob Boettcher

Nebraska

Nebraska Sustainable
Agriculture Society
P.O.Box 736
Hartington, NE 68739

OCIA – Nebraska
4914 Ft Kearney Road
Grand Island, NE 68801
(308) 382-2707
Contact: George Myers

OCIA – Nebraska
HC 54 Box 8A
Kimball, NE 69145
(308) 235-2840
Contact: Bernard Culek, Jr.

New Hampshire

New Hampshire Depart-
ment of Agriculture
10 Ferry Street
Caller, Box 2042
Concord, NH 03301
(603) 271-2753
Fax: (603) 271-1109
Contact: Vickie Smith

NOFA – New Hampshire
Route 1, Box 516
Andover, NH 03216
(603) 648-2521
Contact: Richard Estes

NOFA – New Hampshire
Route 152
S. Nottingham, NH 03291
Contact: Bill Kiser

New Mexico

New Mexico Organic Com-
modity Commission
106 Nambe Avenue
Santa Fe, NM 87501
(505) 984-1441
Contact: Sarah Grant

Organic Growers
Association of New
Mexico
1312 Lobo Place, NE
Albuquerque, NM 87106
(505) 268-5504
Contact: Sarah McDonald

OCIA – New Mexico
Route 3, Box 770
Portales, NM 88130
(505) 356-8701
Contact: Alba Carter, Jr.

New Jersey

NOFA – New Jersey
Route 2, Box 263A
Pennington, NJ 08504
(609) 737-6848
Contact: Jennifer Morgan

NOFA – New Jersey
171 North Union Street
Lambertville Natural
Lambertville, NJ 08530
Contact: David Sharp

NOFA – New Jersey
14 Princeton Road
Hopewell, NJ 08525
Contact: Al Johnson

New York

NOFA – New York
Route 1, Box 134A
Port Crane, NY 13833
(607) 648-3696
Contact: Pat Kane

NOFA – New York
P.O. Box 21
South Butler, NY 13154

NOFA – New York
108 Crest Lane
Ithaca, NY 14850
Contact: Veet Deha

NOFA – New York
Rose Valley Farm
Rose, NY 14542
(315) 587-9787
Contact: Elizabeth
Henderson

NOFA – New York
P.O. Box 68
Alpine, NY 14805
Contact: Abby Scaman

Finger Lakes OG Coop
P.O. Box 549

Trumansburg, NY 14886

North Carolina

Carolina Farm Steward-
ship Association
Route 3, Box 494
Silver City, NC 27344
(919) 663-2429
Contact: Kate Havel

OCIA – North Carolina
Route 5, Box 262
Washington, NC 27889
(919) 946-7402
Contact: Brownie Van
Dorp

North Dakota

Farm Verified Organic
P.O. Box 40A, RR 1
Medina, ND 58467
(701) 486-3579
Fax: (701) 486-3580
Contact: Hugo Skoppek

Northern Plains
Sustainable
Agriculture Society
RR 1, Box 129
Kulm, ND 58456
Contact: Tom Stadler

OCIA – North Dakota
RR 2, Box 80
Motts, ND 58646
(701) 563-4455
Contact: Charles E.
Wallace, Jr.

OCIA – North Dakota
HC 2, Box 38
Garrison, ND 58540
(701) 337-5813
Contact: Tom and Jim
Krzmarzick

Ohio

OCIA – Ohio
2688 E. Smithville Wester
Wooster, OH 44691
(216) 345-5080
Contact: Dean McIlvaine

OCIA – Federation
3185 Township Road 179
Bellefontaine, OH 43311
(513) 592-4983
Contact: Betty Kananen

OCIA – Ohio
3185 Township Road 1
Bellefontaine, OH 43311
(513) 592-4983
Fax: (513) 593-3831
Contact: Betty Kananen

Ohio Ecological Food &
Farm Association
2315 Sawbury Blvd
Columbus, OH 43235

(614) 766-1966
Contact: Mary Failey

Ohio Ecological Food &
Farm Association
9665 Kline Road
West Salem, OH 44287-
9562
Contact: Sylvia Upp

Ohio Ecological Food &
Farm Association
86663 Fife Road
Cadiz, OH 43907
Contact: Mick Lubek

Oregon

Oregon Tilth Provender
P.O.Box 218
Tualatin, OR 97062
(503) 692-4877
Fax: (503) 691-2514
Contact: Yvonne Frost

Organically Grown Coop
2545 Prairie Road, ST
Eugene, OR 97402

Pennsylvania

Biodynamic Farming &
Garden Association
P.O.Box 550
Kimberton, PA 19442
(215) 935-7797
Contact: Rod Shouldice

NOFA – Pennsylvania
RR#2, Box 116A
Volant, PA 16156
(412) 530-7220
Contact: Ron Gargasz

OCIA – Pennsylvania
P.O. Box 158
Port Clinton, PA 19549
(215) 562-5502
Contact: Jodi Snyder

OCIA – Pennsylvania
318 Love Road
Valencia, PA 16059
(412) 898-2242
Contact: T. Lyle Ferderber

Pennsylvania Tuscarora
Organic Growers
HCR 71, Box 168B
Hustontown, PA 17229

Rhode Island

Rhode Island Organic
Certification
Div of Agriculture, Roger
Williams Bldg
Providence, RI 02908-
5025
(401) 277-2781
Fax: (401) 277-6047
Contact: Robert Relli

NOFA – Rhode Island
P.O. Box 83
Peace Dale, RI 02883
Contact: Su Rubinoff

NOFA – Rhode Island
P.O. Box 512
Carolina, RI 02812
Contact: Polly Williams

NOFA – Rhode Island
358 South Road
Wakefield, RI 02879
Contact: Jeanne Wetlaufer

South Carolina

South Carolina Organic
Association
129 Organic Lane
W. Columbia, SC 29169
(803) 791-5733
Contact: Margaret
Locklear

South Dakota

OCIA – South Dakota
Box 573
Frederick, SD 57441
(605) 329-2029
Contact: Lonny Mikkonen

Tennessee

Tennessee Alternative
Growers Association
Rt 10, Box 66B
Lookville, TN 38501
Contact: Shannon Stoney

Mid-South Organic
Network
7750 Macon Road
Cordova, TN 38018
(901) 756-8586
Contact: Jeff Restuccio

Tennessee Land
Stewardship Association
Sunshine Ridge, Route 1
Liberty, TN 37095
(615) 563-2353
Contact: Jim Joyner

Tennessee Land Steward-
ship Association
P.O. Box 4123
Murfreesboro, TN 37133
Contact: Steve Mills

Tennessee Organic
Harvesters
Route 2, Box 305
Mosheim, TN 37818

Texas

Texas Department of
Agriculture
Consumer Service Division
P.O. Box 12847
Austin, TX 78711
(512) 475-1641

Fax: (512) 453-7643
Contact: Brent Wiseman

Texas Organic Growers
 Resident Committee
Route 2, Box 840
Lorena, TX 76655
(817) 881-2053
Contact: Dossie Raines

Centro 16 De Septiembre
Farmworker Coop
P.O. Box 27
San Juan, TX 78589

Texas Organic Growers
 Association
207 South Elerson
DeSoto, TX 75115
Contact: Jim Smalley

Utah
OCIA – Utah
P.O. Box 247
Tremonton, UT 84337
(801) 872-8191
Contact: Martha Franks

Vermont
Deep Root Organic
 Cooperative
RFD #1
Bellows Falls, VT 05101
(802) 722-3546
Contact: Paul Harlow

Deep Root Organic
 Truckfarmers
P.O. Box 100
Westminster Stn, VT
 05159
Contact: Dan Cheetam

NOFA – Vermont
Route 1, Box 177
Richmond, VT 05477
(802) 434-4435
Fax: (802) 223-0269
Contact: Enid Wonnacott

NOFA – Vermont
RFD Box 299
Danby, VT 05739
Contact: Ray Pratt

NOFA – Vermont
Route 1, Box 329N
Pownal, VT 05261
Contact: John Primmer

Vermont Northern
 Growers
Box 125
East Hardwick, VT 05836
(802) 533-7175
Contact: Lou Pulver

Virginia
Virginia Department of
 Agriculture

1100 Bank Street
Richmond, VA 23219
(804) 786-3568
Fax: (804) 371-7679
Contact: Mark Tubbs

Virginia Biological
 Farmers Association
Box 252
Flint Hill, VA 22627
(703) 675-3982
Fax: (703) 675-1149
Contact: John Burns

Virginia Biological
 Farmers Association
HCR 2, Box 530
Madison, VA 22727
(703) 675-1149
Contact: Tom Scot

Virginia Biological
 Farmers Association
P.O. Box 3024
Charlotttesville, VA 22747
Contact: Jeanne Nye

Washington
Washington Department
 of Agriculture
406 General Administra-
 tion Building
Olympia, WA 98504
(206) 664-0351
Fax: (206) 902-2087
Contact: Miles McEvoy

Washington Tilth
P.O. Box 10813
Bainbridge Island, WA
 98110-0813
(206) 842-5612

Tilth Producers
 Cooperative
1219 Sauk Road
Concrete, WA 98237
(206) 853-8449
Fax: (206) 853-8353
Contact: Anne Schwartz

Farmers Wholesale Coop
P.O. Box 7446
Olympia, WA 98507

West Virginia
Mountain State OGBA
212-C E. Main Street
Spencer, WV 25276
Contact: Bill Quick

Mountain State OGBA
HCR01, Box 68
Moyers, WV 26813
Contact: Kip Mortenson

Mountain State OGBA
Route 10, Box 30
Morgantown, WV 26505
(304) 296-3978

Contact: Keith Dix

Wisconsin
Wisonsin Natural Foods
 Associates
6616 CTH I
Waunakee, WI 53597
(608) 846-3287
Contact: Paul White

CROPP
Route 1, Box 77A
Chaseburg, WI 54621
(608) 483-2604
Contact: Spark Burmaster

OCIA – Wisconsin
RR 1, 1198
Soldiers Grove, WI 54655
(608) 734-3711
Contact: Marta and
 David Engel

Wisconsin Organic
 Growers
Route 1, Box 160
Spring Valley, WI 54767
(715) 772-3104
Contact: Faye Jones

**Regional and
International
Associations**
OCIA – International
30 Route 214
Milan, Québec GOY 1EO,
 Canada
(819) 657-4674
Fax: (819) 657-4674
Contact: Robert
 Beachemin

Quality Assurance
 International
Suite 300
12526 High Bluff Drive
San Diego, CA 92130
(619) 792-3531
Fax: (619) 755-8348
Contact: Griffith McLellan

OCIA – Alberta
RR1
Westlock, ALB TOG 2LO
 CAN
(403) 349-2294
Contact: Judy Larsen

OCIA – Alberta #2
Box 30
Vulcan, ALB TOL 2BO
 CAN
(403) 485-2808
Contact: Dwayne and
 Doreen Smith

OCIA – Alberta #3
Box 876
Vulcan, ALB CAN
(403) 485-6493

Contact: Allan Graff

OCIA – Argentina
Casilla de Correo 1017
8400 Can Carlos, de Bar,
 ARG

OCIA – Guatemala
7264 NW 25 Street
Miama, FL 33122
(305) 592-1771
Contact: Roberto Caceres
 Estrada

OCIA – Manitoba
Box 368
Riverton, MAN ROC 2RO
 CAN
(204) 378-2459
Contact: Stefan Bjornson

OCIA – Mexico
Nicolas Bravo S/N
Ometepec, GRO, 41700
 MEX
Contact: Adolfo Bautista
 Santiago

OCIA – New Brunswick
RR3
Mouth of Keswick, NB
 EOH 1NO CAN
(506) 363-3744
Contact: Karen and
 Brock Davidge

OCIA – Nicaragua
Cenzontle-Las Segovias, A
 Esteli, NIC
(505) 71-2618
Contact: Paul Rice

OCIA – Nova Scotia
RR3
Wolfville, NS BOP 1XO
 CAN
(902) 542-2349
Contact: Dave and Alan
 Stewart

OCIA – Ontario
P.O. Box 16
Wabigoon, ONT POV
 2WO CAN
(807) 938-2380
Contact: Lorne Mitchell

OCIA – Ontario #2
RR2
Milford, ONT KOK 2PO
 CAN
(613) 476-3750
Contact: Phil and
 Catherine Mathews

OCIA – Peru
Ways Mills
Ayers Cliff, QUE JOB 1CO
 CAN
Contact: Ashanikas

OCIA – Peru #2
Bagua Grade
Utcubamba, PER
51-74-231400
Contact: Guadalupe
 Copia Hurtado

OCIA – Peru #3
Leoncio Prado S/N La
 Coip
San Ignacio, Cajamarca,
 PER
51-74-231400
Contact: Carlos
 Yajahuanca Martine

OCIA – Peru #4
Jose Olaya S/N Chirinos
San Ignacio, Cajamarca,
 PER
51-74-231400
Contact: Hipoloto
 Fuentes Quinonez

OCIA – Prince Edward
 Island
Box 299
Cornwall, PEI COA 1HOA
 CAN
(902) 675-3501
Contact: Daphne Harker

OCIA – Québec Estrie
259 Rang 11
Ste Edwidge, QUE JOB
 2RO CAN
(819) 849-3169
Contact: Chantal Blain

OCIA – Québec
90 rg Audette
Farnham, QUE J2N 2P9
 CAN
(514) 293-5107
Contact: Real Samson

OCIA – Québec
966 Petite Montagne
St-JOS-Beauce, QUE GOS
 2VO CAN
(418) 253-5806
Contact: Serge Lessard

OCIA – Saskatchewan
Box 128
Macoun, SASK SOC 1PO
 CAN
(306) 634-9327
Contact: George and
 Curtis Kuchinka

OCIA – Saskatchewan #2
Box 63
Ernfold, SASK SOH 1KO
 CAN
(306) 629-3303
Contact: Kevin and
 Warren Beach

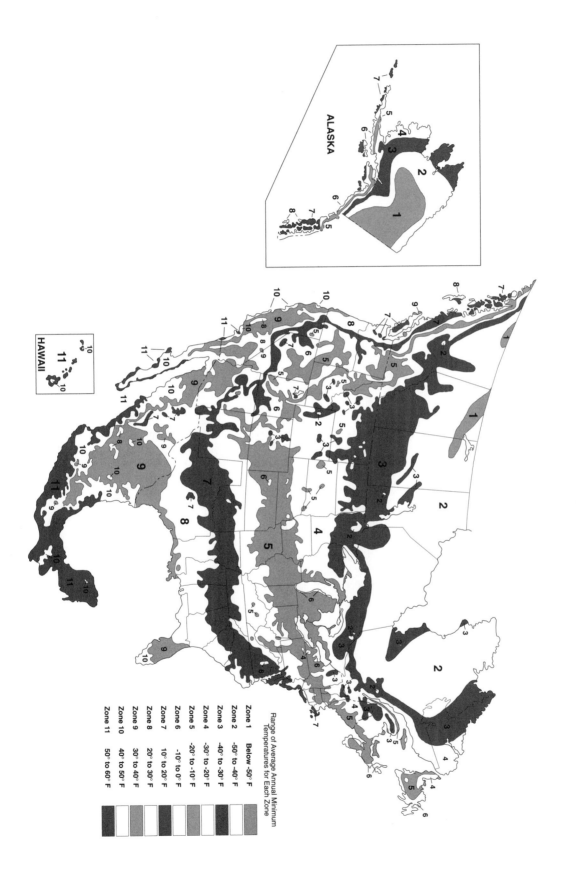

USDA Hardiness Zone Map

ALASKA

HAWAII

Range of Average Annual Minimum
Temperatures for Each Zone

Zone 1   Below -50° F
Zone 2   -50° to -40° F
Zone 3   -40° to -30° F
Zone 4   -30° to -20° F
Zone 5   -20° to -10° F
Zone 6   -10° to 0° F
Zone 7   0° to 10° F
Zone 8   10° to 20° F
Zone 9   20° to 30° F
Zone 10   30° to 40° F
Zone 11   40° to 50° F

Suggested Reading:
Magazines, Journals, and Newsletters

■ *American Vegetable Grower.* Meister Publishing Co., 37841 Euclid Avenue, Willoughby, OH 44094.

A monthly magazine covering new trends in commercial growing. One section covers greenhouse production.

■ *Common Sense Pest Control,* Bio-Integral Resource Center, P.O. Box 7414, Berkeley, CA 94707, or call (415) 524-2567.

Less technical than the *IPM Practitioner,* this quarterly provides practical and in-depth recommendations for managing specific pests. By becoming a member of BIRC you can receive technical advice about specific pest problems, troubleshooting, access to workshops and training, and subscriptions to this quarterly and to *IPM Practitioner.*

■ *Fine Gardening.* Taunton Press, Inc., Newtown, CT 06470.

A relatively new bimonthly magazine that stands out as a star. This is a collector's magazine to be savored, like all other Taunton Press publications. At least one or two articles per issue on edibles (vegetables, fruits, or herbs) are balanced with articles on landscaping, ornamentals, insects, diseases, and gardening methods. These are among the best researched and informative articles in popular journals. The photographs are superb.

■ *Harrowsmith Country Living.* Camden House Publishing, Inc., Ferry Road, Charlotte, VT 05445.

A bimonthly magazine of Canadian origin that covers country gardening, home building, and current issues with a clear bent toward ecological responsibility. Good photography and excellent articles.

■ *The Herb, Spice, and Medicinal Plant Digest,* Department of Plant & Soil Sciences, University of Massachusetts, Amherst, MA 01003. Quarterly.

■ *HortIdeas.* Gregory and Patricia Y. Williams, Route 1, Box 302, Black Lick Road, Gravel Switch, KY 40328.

A great monthly newsletter that abstracts the best and latest gardening research from both popular and technical journals. An excellent way of keeping up on the latest advances, cultivars, tools, methods, and much more.

■ *The IPM Practitioner,* Bio-Integral Resource Center, P.O. Box 7414, Berkeley, CA 94707, or call (415) 524-2567.

This monthly journal surveys current developments in least-toxic pest management. By becoming a member of BIRC you can receive technical advice about specific pest problems, troubleshooting, access to workshops and training, and subscriptions to this monthly as well as *Common Sense Pest Control.*

■ *Mother Earth News.* Sussex Publishers, 24 East 23rd Street, New York, NY 10010.

A bimonthly magazine that covers different aspects of country living, including one section on gardening. One of the oldest "homesteading" magazines, it has evolved greatly over the years from a "how-to," semi-technical magazine to a more slick, general interest periodical.

■ *National Gardening.* National Gardening Association, 180 Flynn Avenue, Burlington, VT 05401.

A monthly magazine that covers all aspects of gardening, and provides up-to-date information on NGA projects as well as how to participate in them. Good explanatory photographs accompany informative articles.

■ *The New Farm, Magazine of Regenerative Agriculture.* Regenerative Agriculture Association, 222 Main Street, Emmaus, PA 18098.

Seven issues per year cover growing techniques and issues oriented primarily to the larger scale farmer, but which also may be of interest to the backyard gardener. Great for future-thinking growers.

■ *Rodale's Organic Gardening.* Rodale Press Inc., 33 East Minor Street, Emmaus, PA 18049.

A monthly magazine covering all aspects of organic gardening as well as the results of gardening trials and experiments conducted by the Rodale Research Center. This has long been the most popular monthly, and with its new glossy and slick format it promises to draw in even larger readership. There is still at least one good article on food crops in each issue, balanced with others on ornamentals, machine tools, and methodology.

■ *Sunset: The Magazine of Western Living.* Lane Publishing Co., Menlo Park, CA 94025.

This hefty monthly features a regular section on western U.S. gardening and landscaping, which includes the coastal areas, eastward to Colorado and southward through the desert areas. Highly recommended for western gardeners.

Books

General Gardening and Vegetable Growing

■ Appelhof, Mary. *Worms Eat My Garbage: How to Set Up and Maintain a Worm Composting System.* Kalamazoo, MI: Flower Press, 1982.

A small, very easy-to-read paperback. Appelhof tells you all you need to know about how to grow earthworms without much effort. Not as complete as Minnich's book, but most people don't need the detail that Minnich offers.

■ Arms, Karen. *Environmental Gardening.* Savannah, Georgia: Halfmoon Publishing, 1992.

A fun and informative new resource for all gardeners. A biologist by training, Arms covers general principles and numerous specifics such as water gardening, trees, attracting wildlife, saving water and energy, annuals, shrubs, trees, lawns, and edible plants. She accomplishes her goal of providing a guide for which gardening practices are environmentally sound and which are dangerous or unethical.

■ *Backyard Composting.* Ojai, California: Harmonious Press, 1992.

A great little handbook that makes composting super simple and easy. This is all you need to get your backyard compost pile started. It also provides a bunch of other information for those trying to be more environmentally sensitive. Don't miss this gem.

■ Ball, Jeff. *The Self-Sufficient Suburban Garden: A step-by-step planning and management guide to backyard food production.* Emmaus, PA: Rodale Press, 1983.

An excellent book for novice gardeners, enjoyable, practical, and informative.

Useful Charts: (1) How Much To Plant; (2) Seed-Starting Tips; (3) Planting Guide; (4) Interplanting Guide; (5) Companion Planting; (6) Succession Planting; (7) Growing Guide; (8) Food Storage Options; and more.

■ Ball, Jeff. *Jeff Ball's 60-Minute Garden: One hour a week is all it takes to garden successfully.* Emmaus, PA: Rodale Press, 1985.

One of our favorite books, not only because its goal of low-time gardening matches ours, but because it is so well written and fun to read. Practical, informative, and easy to follow. Diagrams of useful garden tools, such as a compost sifter, with shopping lists and instructions.

Useful Diagrams and Construction Plans: (1) Boxed Bed With PVC Foundations; (2) Tunnels; (3) Trellis and Orchard Fence; (4) Compost Bin and Sifter; (5) Seedling Box; (6) Garden Sink; (7) Birdhouse Design.

■ Bartholomew, Mel. *Square Foot Gardening.* Emmaus, PA: Rodale Press, 1981.

Another fun book, good for both novice and experienced gardeners, based on the PBS television series. The square foot method is an interesting, practical method of intensive gardening, in some ways more formulaic (and therefore easier) than French intensive. The back of the book contains cultural notes on vegetables and, of course, square foot spacing rules for each vegetable.

■ Barton, Barbara. *Gardening By Mail: a source book, 3rd Edition.* Boston, MA: Houghton Mifflin Co., 1990.

A unique and important resource for gardeners that provides the most complete listing anywhere of plant and seed sources, garden suppliers, professional societies and associations, magazines, newsletters, horticultural libraries, and books.

■ *Best Ways To Improve Your Soil.* Emmaus, PA: Rodale Press, 1987.

A small, inexpensive booklet packed with information. Very useful.

Useful Charts: (1) Soil Types; (2) Cover Crop Planting Guide; (3) Composting Materials; (4) Nutrient Profiles of Common Organic Amendments.

■ Bubel, Nancy. *The New Seed-Starters Handbook.* Emmaus, PA: Rodale Press, 1988.

For the person who wants an in-depth discussion of how to get your plants off to a good start, Bubel covers everything from germinating to transplanting. Also one of the few books that tells you how to save your own seeds. The last third of the book is devoted to cultural briefs on how to start from seed vegetables, fruits, herbs, and — more unusual — flowers, wildflowers, trees, and shrubs.

Useful Charts: Soil Deficiency: Symptoms and Treatment. Many more.

■ Campbell, Stu. *Let It Rot!: The Gardener's Guide to Composting.* Pownal, VT: Garden Way Publishing, (updated and revised edition) 1990.

The author explains the technical aspects of composting in simple, easy-to-understand terms, provides detailed information on selecting the right materials, and covers the mechanics clearly and comprehensively.

■ Campbell, Stu. *The Mulch Book: A Complete Guide for Gardeners.* Pownal, VT: Garden Way Publishing, (revised and updated edition) 1991.

Explains the labor-saving way to maintain a healthy garden. Nothing beats mulch for controlling weeds, retaining moisture, and fertilizing and insulating soil, with a minimum of effort. The author explains how to make your own mulch, when to mulch, and which ones to use in various types of gardens.

■ Carr, Anna. *Good Neighbors: Companion Planting for Gardeners.* Emmaus, PA: Rodale Press, 1985.

This book is a great resource for learning more about companion planting, and learning to separate fact from lore. I especially like the appendix that suggests possible companion planting experiments for backyard gardens, and introduces ways to assess your results.

Useful Charts: (1) Read your weeds; (2) Recipes for botanical pesticides and repellants; (3) Legumes for companion planting; (4) Weeds to watch out for. More!

HOUGHALL COLLEGE LIBRARY

■ Coleman, Eliot. *The New Organic Grower: a master's manual of tools and techniques for the home and market gardener.* Chelsea, VT: Chelsea Green Publishing, 1989.

I love this book, not just because one reviewer called it the perfect companion to my book *Gardening At A Glance* (the first version of this book), but because it really **is** the perfect companion: While *The Organic Gardener's Home Reference* is strong on information for individual crops and pest control, Coleman's book is strong on understanding, approach, and techniques. Coleman is a joy to read and learn from. I find his book especially useful for the sections on green manure rotations and crop rotations.

Useful Charts: Many are useful, but I especially like the rotation charts for green manure and vegetable crops.

■ Creasy, Rosalind. *The Complete Book of Edible Landscaping: Home Landscaping with Food-Fearing Plants and Resource-Saving Techniques.* San Francisco, CA: Sierra Club, 1982.

An excellent book on how to make your garden an attractive landscape, and your landscape into an attractive garden. Useful to all gardeners. Major principles of edible landscaping are covered in this timely book. Creasy also covers gardening techniques, culture, hygiene, diseases, and insects.

Useful Charts: The last half of the book is a very useful "encyclopedia" of fruit, vegetable, herb, and nut culture. Includes varieties and sources.

■ Creasy, Rosalind. *Cooking From the Garden.* San Francisco, CA: Sierra Club, 1988.

A true gem that is filled with valuable growing information and visual beauty. Creasy creates and explores specialty gardens of different nationalities, traditions, colors, and flavors. In the process she shares a wealth of information on varieties known for such things as color, flavor, and heirloom history. Mouth-watering recipes accompany every section, including such wonders as violet vichyssoise and lavender ice cream. To top it off, she includes an encyclopedia at the end on how to grow each type of vegetable.

■ Editors of Garden Way Publishing. *Herbs, Fruits and Vegetables.* Pownal, VT: Garden Way Publishing, 1990.

Two of a series of gardening books, each subtitled *1001 Gardening Questions Answered*, that offer information about propagation, planting, maintenance, cultivation harvesting, and potential pests and predators.

■ *Encyclopedia of Organic Gardening* (revised edition). Emmaus, PA: Rodale Press, 1978.

A good general reference book to supplement or be supplemented by others, this covers to a greater or lesser degree every plant one might be curious about. It also covers general topics such as fertilizer, fruit cultivation, landscaping, and much more.

Useful Charts: (1) Planting Dates (gives dates based on average LFD); (2) Shrubs: Recommended Shrubs For The Home Grounds; (3) Straw: Mineral Value of Straws; (4) Trace Elements: Chart On Signs Of Deficiency and Accumulator Plants; (5) Wild Plants, Edible; more.

■ Editors of Garden Way Publishing. *The Big Book of Gardening Skills.* Pownal, VT: Garden Way Publishing, 1993.

Comprehensive, illustrated guide to growing flowers, fruits, herbs, and vegetables, on a small or large scale. Numerous charts on planting, garden design, organic pest and disease control, succession planting, and more.

■ Foster, Catharine Osgood. *Building Healthy Gardens: A Safe and Natural Approach.* Pownal, VT: Garden Way Publishing, 1989.

The author presents new techniques and discoveries for reaping abundant harvests without chemical fertilizers, pesticides, or herbicides.

■ Faeth, Paul, Robert Repetto, Kim Kroll, Qi Dai, and Glenn Helmers. *Paying The Farm Bill: U.S. Agricultural Policy and the Transition to Sustainable Agriculture.* Washington, D.C.: World Resources Institute (WRI), March 1991. Write to: 1709 New York Avenue, NW, Washington, DC 20006.

An important study that offers perhaps the first comprehensive comparison of conventional farming with sustainable agriculture techniques. If all environmental costs are factored in, WRI shows sustainable farming techniques not only save the environment but save money as well. A Pennsylvania farm using conventional crop rotation of corn and soybeans resulted in a loss of $61 per acre over 10 years, while a rotation of several crops of corn, soybean, wheat, and clover **saved** $325 per acre.

■ Fukuoka, Masanobu. *The One-Straw Revolution: An Introduction to Natural Farming.* Emmaus, PA: Rodale Press, 1978.

Now considered a classic on the subject, this book discusses the importance and methods of no-till cultivation. Some of the methods may not be generally applicable, however, because they're designed for a mild Japanese climate.

■ *Gardening: The Complete Guide to Growing America's Favorite Fruits and Vegetables.* National Gardening Association, Addison-Wesley Publishing Company, Inc., 1986.

For novice and advanced gardeners, this book discusses how to plan and prepare the garden site. It also provides cultural information for individual vegetables and fruits.

■ Hamilton, Geoff. *The Organic Garden Book: The Complete Guide To Growing Flowers, Fruit and Vegetables Naturally.* New York: Crown Publishers, 1987.

Excellent color photographs, some of the best we've seen, and diagrams, are what make this book special. The photographs cover everything from different soil types to how to harvest different vegetables. This book also contains excellent pictures of the different methods of training fruit trees and provides good cultural notes.

Useful Charts: At the back of the book, a good list of gardening activities is broken down by season and type of garden (ornamental, fruit, vegetable, greenhouse).

■ Hart, Rhonda Massingham. *Trellising: How to Grow Climbing Vegetables, Fruits, Flowers, Vines, and Trees.* Pownal, VT: Storey Publishing, 1992.

This book explains the benefits of using trellises and ways to improve and increase yields, cut time output, and use less space. Also shows how to design and construct different types of garden supports and to plant and grow more than two dozen varieties of vegetables, fruits, and flowering vines on trellises.

■ Hart, Rhonda Massingham. *Bugs, Slugs, and Other Thugs.* Pownal, VT: Storey Communications, 1991.

Explains how to stop pests without risk to the environment. Chapters are organized by predator, and each is illustrated with descriptions of their habitats, life cycles, habits, favorite garden targets and damage caused.

■ Hill, Lewis. *Secrets of Plant Propagation: Starting Your Own Flowers, Fruits, Berries, Shrubs, Trees, and Houseplants.* Pownal, VT: Garden Way Publishing, 1985.

A complete guide to starting new plants.

■ Hirshberg, Gary and Tracy Calvan, editors. *Gardening For All Seasons: A Complete Guide to Producing Food at Home 12 Months of the Year.* Andover, MA: The New Alchemy Institute, Brick House Publishing, 1983.

We've found this book useful for its charts, tables, and cultural notes on vegetables.

Useful Charts: (1) Varieties Of Vegetables For Greenhouse Growing; (2) pH Preference Of Vegetables, Fruits, Flowers and Grains; (3) Disease-Resistant Plant Varieties; (4) Insect-Resistant Plant Varieties; (5) Insect-Repellant Plant Varieties; (6) Companion Planting Guide; (7) Planting Table; (8) Chart Of Nitrogen, Phosphorous and Potassium Components Of Organic Materials; (9) Plants That Attract Birds.

■ Hunt, Marjorie B. and Brenda Bortz. *High-Yield Gardening: How to get more from your garden space and more from your gardening season.* Emmaus, PA: Rodale Press, 1986.

Chock full of useful suggestions for increasing your garden yield, this is a good general book for both beginning and experienced gardeners.

Useful Charts: (1) Cultural Notes, presented alphabetically by plant; (2) Soil Type; (3) Cover Crop Planting Guide; (4) Composting Materials; (5) Nutrient Profiles of Common Organic Materials; (6) Survey of Raised Beds; (7) High-Yield Low-Space Versions of Popular Vegetables; (8) High-Yielding Varieties for Vertical Growing; (9) Garden Time-Savers; (10) Critical Times For Watering; (11) Succession Plant-

ing; (12) Traditional Companions; (13) Space-Efficient Root Patterns; more.

■ Jeavons, John. *How To Grow More Vegetables.* Berkeley, CA: Ten Speed Press, 1982.

An excellent discussion on the importance and methods of French intensive raised-bed gardening. Jeavons is well known for advocating high-yield, intensive techniques. Here's a good, detailed description on how to double-dig.

Useful Charts: (1) 4-Year Garden Plan; (2) Companion Plants; (3) Growing Data on Vegetables, Fruits, Grains; (4) Fertilizers and Their Components.

■ Jacobs, Betty E.M. *Growing and Using Herbs Successfully.* Pownal, VT: Garden Way Publishing, 1981.

Complete information about herbs.

■ Knott, James Edward, Lorenz, Oscar A., and Donald N. Maynard, editors. *Knott's Handbook for Vegetable Growers, 3rd Edition.* New York: John Wiley & Sons, 1988.

A professional's resource book and authority on all aspects of vegetable growing. Just when you thought you had a handle on the issues involved in vegetable growing, this book can be both a humbling and stimulating experience. Covers everything from hydroponic solutions to irrigation rates. A small ringbinder, it's easy to carry around and fun to browse through for both trivia and essentials. Since this book's purpose is useful charts, we can list only a few of the ones that might be appropriate for the nonprofessional. Page numbers for the charts are given because they're a bit hard to find.

Useful Charts: (1) Composition of Fresh Raw Vegetables, 23-28; (2) Diagnosis and Correction of Transplant Disorders, 46; (3) Soil Temperature Conditions for Germination, 71; (4) Days Required for Seedling Emergence, 74; (5) Composition of Organic Material, 101; (6) A Key to Nutrient-Deficiency Symptoms, 162; (7) Practical Soil Moisture Interpretation Chart, 170; (8) Disease Control for Vegetables, 257; (9) Insect Control for Vegetables, 272.

■ Kourik, Robert. *Designing and Maintaining Your Edible Landscape Naturally.* Santa Rosa, CA: Metamorphic Press, 1986.

For the novice and experienced gardener, this is must reading on edible landscaping, the gardening wave of the future. Unusual, informative, and fun, Kourik's book discusses everything from aesthetics to specific gardening techniques — how to plan gardens, the pros and cons of tillage, how to prune, and much more.

Useful Charts: (1) Companion Planting Research Summaries; (2) Intercropping for Pest Reduction; (3) Green Manure Plants; (4) Dynamic Accumulators; (5) Seven-Step Rotation for Fertility; (6) Multi-Purpose Edibles; (7) Soil Indicators (plants); (8) Ripening Dates for Fruit & Nut Varieties; (9) Series of Charts on Fruit Tree Rootstocks; (10) Disease-Resistant Trees; and more.

■ Kourik, Robert. *Drip Irrigation For Every Landscape and All Climates.* Santa Rosa, CA: Metamorphic Press, 1992.

A step-by-step guide to easy and simple drip irrigation. No need to be mystified any longer when this book is available. Illustrations, charts, and sources.

■ Larkcom, Joy. *The Salad Garden.* New York: Viking Press, 1984.

A fun book for those interested in salad greens and cooking.

■ McClure, Susan. *The Harvest Gardener.* Pownal, VT: Garden Way Publishing, 1992.

A compilation of tips and advice by the author and several other gardeners about choosing cultivars, scheduling plantings, organizing garden space, coping with the vagaries of weather and pests, harvesting and storing the crop. Also includes an encyclopedia of culture, harvest, and storage of fruits, herbs, and vegetables.

■ Minnich, Jerry. *The Earthworm Book.* Emmaus, PA: Rodale Press, 1977.

The best book we've found on the subject, this covers everything you might want or need to know about earthworm cultivation. It explains the important benefits of earthworms in your garden and how to grow them easily on a small scale.

■ *Organic Gardening's Soil First Aid Manual.* Emmaus, PA: Rodale Press, 1982.

A small paperback, this is a useful collection of short articles by different people on ways to improve your soil. Interesting and good background material.

■ Pleasant, Barbara. *Warm-Climate Gardening*. Pownal, VT: Garden Way Publishing, 1993.

The author offers advice about how to recognize and exploit the cool seasons within a warm-climate gardening year. Also includes information on drought-resistant plants, summer hardiness, and scheduling maintenance chores when it's too hot to garden.

■ O'Keefe, John M. *Water-Conserving Gardens and Landscapes*. Pownal, VT: Storey Publishing, 1992.

Explains how to meet the challenges of dwindling and overused water supplies, drought conditions, high water costs, and pollution by groundwater. Includes information on drip irrigation systems, alternative gardening techniques such as raised beds, containers, and hardscapes.

■ Poincelot, Raymond P. *No-Dig, No-Weed Gardening*. Emmaus, PA: Rodale Press, 1986.

An excellent discussion of the benefits of not tilling the soil and how to maintain such a garden. Useful cultural notes on vegetables and flowers.

■ Raymond, Dick. *Down-to-Earth Gardening Know-How for the '90s: Vegetables and Herbs*. Pownal, VT: Storey Publishing, (revised and updated version) 1991.

A book full of useful charts and graphs. Page numbers for the charts are given because of the potential difficulty of locating them.
Useful Charts: (1) Green Manures; (2) Plant Diseases; (3) Herbs; (4) Garden Planning Charts and Plans; (5) Planning Chart, including Amounts To Plant.

■ Raymond, Dick. *Joy of Gardening*. Pownal, VT: Garden Way Inc., 1982.

A good book on garden preparation, maintenance, and culture of vegetables and fruits. Good photographs. Good discussion of cover crops.
Useful Charts: (1) Vegetable Planting Guide, useful to use especially for planning amounts to plant; (2) Detailed First Frost Date In The Fall Map of the U.S.; (3) Mulching Guide,

comparing advantages and disadvantages of different mulch types.

■ Reilly, Ann. *Park's Success With Seeds*. Greenwood, S.C.: Park Seed Co., 1978.

A guide to how to start most species from seed.

■ Riotte, Louise. *Carrots Love Tomatoes: Secrets of Companion Planting for Successful Gardening*. Pownal, VT: Garden Way Publishing, 1975.

Vegetables and fruits have natural preferences; this book shows you how to arrange your garden to take advantage of these productive relationships.

■ Riotte, Louise. *Roses Love Garlic: Secrets of Companion Planting With Flowers*. Pownal, VT: Garden Way Publishing, 1983.

The author explores companion planting with flowers and shows how to combine flower and vegetable gardens for striking display of color, form, and productivity.

■ Riotte, Louise. *Successful Small Food Gardens: Vegetables, Herbs, Flowers, Fruits, Nuts, Berries*. Pownal, VT: Garden Way Publishing, 1993.

This newly revised and updated edition of Riotte's classic intensive-gardening book addresses the needs of the small-space garden. Included is information on companion plants, succession planting, raised beds, container growing, watering and drainage techniques, increasing soil quality, edible flowers, herbs, and shrubs.

■ Restuccio, Jeffrey P. *Fitness the Dynamic Gardening Way: A Health and Wellness Lifestyle*. Cordova, Tennessee: Balance of Nature Publishing, 1992.

A marvelous one-of-a-kind book that shows gardeners how normal gardening tasks can be part of a fitness program. It can be quite helpful to pro gardeners because it shows the correct postures gardeners should use to avoid injuries. For fitness people, it provides a new way to get an outside workout while doing something creative like growing a garden. The fitness information is detailed and replete with charts and diagrams.

■ Rogers, Marc. *Saving Seeds: The Gardener's Guide to Growing and Storing Vegetable and Flower Seeds*. Pownal, VT: Storey Publishing, 1990.

A small paperback, this is an easy guidebook to saving seeds. It presents general principles and specifics for each vegetable.

■ Sunset Books and Sunset magazine editors. *Sunset Western Garden Book*. Menlo Park, CA: Lane Publishing, 1988.

Often considered the Western gardener's bible, this book covers all growing areas west of the Rockies. Among other goodies it includes a plant selection guide for different growing conditions, and a huge encyclopedia of over 6,000 plants. A great book.

■ Thomson, Bob. *The New Victory Garden*. Little, Brown & Co, 1987.

Based on the popular PBS television series, this book emphasizes how to achieve the maximum yield per unit of effort. Perhaps the most unique aspect of this book is its monthly guide on what to do for each vegetable. There is also a short but good section on fruit cultivation, as well as interesting chapters on cider-making and bird feeders.
Useful Charts: Sample page of a gardening journal.

■ Tilgner, Linda. *Tips for the Lazy Gardener*. Pownal, VT: Garden Way Publishing, 1985.

This book shows that it is possible to produce better vegetables with less work and more pleasure. The author says that the secret to successful lazy gardening is effective planning: layout of the garden, choice of plants, schedule of seasonal jobs, and maintenance.

■ Van Patten, George F. *Organic Garden Vegetables*. Portland, Oregon: Van Patten Publishing, 1991.

A well-researched and inexpensive guide on how to grow over 50 vegetables, from soil preparation to harvesting. Designed for easy, quick reference.

■ Whealy, Kent, ed. *The Garden Seed Inventory*. Decorah, Iowa: Seed Saver Publications, 1992.

As the Director of the Seed Savers Exchange, Whealy compiles a complete listing of all (over 5,000) nonhybrid varieties offered by over 200 seed companies. Each entry describes the variety, provides synonyms, provides a range of maturity dates and lists all known sources. Known by some as the seed savers bible.

■ Yeomans, Kathleen, RN. *The Able Gardener.* Pownal, VT: Garden Way Publishing, 1992.

Tips, techniques, and inspiration to make gardening easier and more enjoyable no matter what your ability. Included are practical techniques like raised beds and automatic watering systems, and imaginative suggestions like fragrance and indoor gardens.

Other books with information on General Gardening and Vegetable Growing:

■ Smith, see under *Greenhouses.*

■ Wolfe, see under *Greenhouses.*

Fruits and Nuts

■ *Best Methods For Growing Fruits and Berries.* Emmaus, PA: Rodale Press, 1981.

A small booklet, this provides good discussions of individual fruit cultures.

■ Bilderback, Diane E. and Dorothy Hinshaw Patent. *Backyard Fruits & Berries: How To Grow Them Better Than Ever.* Emmaus, PA: Rodale Press, 1984.

A good, very thorough book on fruit culture. Fun and informative.

■ Hill, Lewis. *Fruits and Berries For The Home Garden.* Pownal, VT: Garden Way Publishing, Storey Communications, Inc., 1977.

A good book on all aspects of fruit culture. Both entertaining and informative, Lewis goes the extra mile to explain the whys and hows behind so many orchard practices.

■ Hill, Lewis. *Pruning Simplified, Updated Edition.* Pownal, VT: Garden Way Publishing, Storey Communications, Inc., 1986.

A great guide on how to prune everything from evergreens and ornamentals to fruit and nut trees. Useful illustrations of before-and-after proper pruning.

■ James, Jr., Theodore. *How To Grow Fruit, Berries, and Nuts in the Midwest and East.* Tucson, AZ: HP Books, Fisher Publishing Co, 1983. (Also available for other regions.)

A very good thin paperback on fruit and nut culture, with excellent pictures on planting, pruning, and grafting.

■ Jaynes, Richard A., editor. *Nut Tree Culture in North America.* Hamden, CT: Northern Nut Growers Association, Inc., 1979.

The only current standard reference on nut culture, this book is essential for anyone interested in growing nut trees. Jaynes has the experts cover all aspects of growing nut trees in detail.

■ Otto, Stella. *The Backyard Orchardist: A Complete Guide to Growing Fruit Trees in the Home Garden.* Maple City, Michigan: OttoGraphics, 1993.

A super resource and excellent guide for the fruit hobbyist. While not strictly organic in approach, Otto provides the information you would need to take an organic approach if you so choose. She covers everything from site preparation to pest control, harvest, and storage.

Useful Charts: Many charts and tables fill the book. I especially like (1) Best fruit choices for U.S. regions; (2) Common tree fruit insect pests in various regions of the U.S.; (3) Periods of Active Insect Pressure; (4) Appendix One, a question and answer format for troubleshooting seasonal problems; and (5) Appendix Two, a monthly almanac of things to do and watch for in the orchard.

■ Page, Stephen and Joe Smillie. *The Orchard Almanac: A Spraysaver Guide.* Rockport, ME: Spraysaver Publications, 1986.

An excellent small handbook on fruit culture with a special emphasis on how to control insects and diseases organically. An excellent presentation of what to do on a monthly basis.

Useful Charts: Good charts at the end of the book on rootstocks, fertilizers, and sprays.

■ Southwick, Lawrence. *Planting Your Dwarf Fruit Orchard.* Pownal, VT: Garden Way Publishing, 1979.

A good introduction to planting and pruning fruit trees, this booklet also has a nice glossary of pruning terms.

Other books with information on Fruits, Nuts, and Pruning:

■ Baumgardt, John Philip. *How To Prune Almost Everything.* New York: Quill, 1982.

■ Creasy, see under *Landscaping.*

■ *Encyclopedia of Organic Gardening,* see under *General.*

■ Hamilton, see under *General.*

■ Kourik, see under *General.* Note his charts on rootstocks, disease resistant fruits, ripening dates, and excellent section on pruning.

■ Thomson, see under *General.*

Herbs

■ Jacobs, Betty E.M. *Growing and Using Herbs Successfully.* Pownal, VT: Garden Way Publishing, 1981.

Complete information about herbs.

■ Garland, Sarah. *The Herb Garden.* New York: Penguin Books, 1985.

Comprehensive coverage of how to grow fragrant herbs for culinary and other purposes.

■ Hutson, Lucinda. *The Herb Garden Cookbook.* Texas Monthly Press, 1987.

A good book on how to grow and how to cook with herbs, including many recipes. Particularly useful information for Southwestern gardeners.

■ Kowalchik, Claire and William H. Hylton, editors. *Rodale's Illustrated Encyclopedia of Herbs.* Emmaus, PA: Rodale Press, 1987.

Hands down the best and most complete book we've seen on herbs, covering everything from herb culture to how to use herbs for healing.

Useful Charts: (1) Companion Planting; (2) A Sampling of Dangerous Herbs; (3) A Sampling of Herbs for Dyeing; (4) Herb Pests; (5) Herb Diseases; and more.

■ *Magic and Medicine of Plants.* Pleasantville, New York: Reader's Digest, 1986.

A wonderful resource for learning about the medicinal purposes of almost 300 plants, including herbs. Illustrated with art as well as excellent color photographs, this book features excellent chapters on the history of plants in magic and medicine, an exceptionally clear and illustrated chapter on the anatomy of plants, and plant entries that differentiate between folk medicine and scientifically proven medicinal purposes. The herb gardener will also enjoy the chapter offering designs for herb gardens and recipes for both culinary and medicinal purposes.

■ Phillips, Roger and Nicky Foy. *The Random House Book of Herbs.* New York: Random House, 1990.

One of the best books I've seen for identifying and learning about the historical and modern uses for over 400 herbs. Extensive, complete, with over 400 excellent color photographs.

■ Shaudys, Phyllis V. *Herbal Treasures: Inspiring Month by Month Projects for Gardening, Cooking, and Crafts.* Pownal, VT: Garden Way Publishing, 1990.

A month-by-month collection of herb crafts, recipes, and gardening ideas. Also included are projects with herbs, reference materials, and suppliers.

■ Shaudys, Phyllis V. *The Pleasure of Herbs: A Month-by-Month Guide to Growing, Using and Enjoying Herbs.* Charlotte, VT: Garden Way Publishing, 1986.

Each month presents a new set of fun projects, from seed-starting, herbal gifts, to creating culinary herbal delights. Cultural information, gardening techniques, and multiple ideas on how to store and use herbs, all are covered. Also included is a brief encyclopedia of herbs.

Other books with information on Herbs:

■ Bubel, see under *General.*

■ Creasy, see under *Landscaping.*

■ *Encyclopedia of Organic Gardening,* see under *General.*

Insects and Diseases

■ Ball, Jeff. *Rodale's Garden Problem Solver: Vegetables, Fruits, Herbs.* Emmaus, PA: Rodale Press, 1988.

A good book specifically on organic disease and insect control for major plants. Very easy to use. You can problem solve by plants, or by the specific insect or disease.

■ Carr, Anna, compiler. *A Gardener's Guide to Common Insect Pests.* Emmaus, PA: Rodale Press, reprint 1989.

An excellent small, inexpensive booklet with great color photos of insects, and short descriptions of their habits and natural controls.

■ Cravens, Richard H. and the Editors of Time-Life Books. *The Time-Life Encyclopedia of Gardening: Pests and Diseases.* Alexandria, VA: Time-Life Books, 1977.

A good background book on pests, identification, habits, and regions affected. Nice illustrations.

■ *Healthy Garden Handbook.* Mother Earth News. New York, NY: Simon & Schuster, Inc., 1989.

A good guide on organic insect and disease control, this book discusses general methods of maintaining a healthy garden, and specific pest remedies. It offers excellent color photographs of plant allies, diseases, and all developmental phases of pests. A garden remedy section troubleshoots problems you may encounter with each vegetable.
Useful Charts: Insect peak emergence times.

■ MacNab, A.A., and A.F. Sherf, and J.K. Springer. *Identifying Diseases of Vegetables.* University Park, PA: Pennsylvania State University, 1983.

Over 200 top-notch photographs of the most common diseases in vegetables. Excellent for field identification of vegetable crop diseases.

■ Olkowski, William, Sheila Daar, and Helga Olkowski. *Common-Sense Pest Control: Least Toxic Solutions for Your Home, Garden, Pets and Community.* Newtown, CT: Taunton Press, 1991.

The definitive reference on Integrated Pest Management, this hefty reference makes scientific advancements accessible to the non-professional. The authors — one horticulturist and two entomologists — have been leaders in reporting on advancements through the nonprofit Bio-Integral Resource Center (BIRC) in Berkeley, California. You will discover ways to control garden, household, and community pests. You can learn about just about anything relating to pest control, from pesticide toxicity

levels and effects on different organs, to different garden mulches for weed control.

Become a member of BIRC by calling (415) 524-2567 for further information. Members can receive technical advice about specific pest problems, troubleshooting, access to workshops and trainings, and subscriptions to the quarterly *Common Sense Pest Control* as well as the monthly *IPM Practitioner.*
Useful Charts: Too numerous to list! One that might be especially helpful to organic gardeners is the chart on "Plants That Attract Beneficial Insects."

■ Pleasant, Barbara. *The Gardener's Bug Book: Earth-Safe Insect Control.* Pownal, VT: Storey Publishing, 1994.

An easy-to-use guide to identifying both the beneficial and harmful insects in your garden. Includes instructions for homemade pest control remedies that are safe for you and your garden.

■ *Shepherd's Purse Organic Pest Control Handbook.* Summertown, TN: Pest Publications, Book Publishing Co., 1987.

A small useful booklet with good color drawings of insects, and notes on their biological, cultural, and acute control. Suppliers of beneficial insects are listed.

■ Sherf, Arden F. and Alan A. MacNab. *Vegetable Diseases and Their Control, 2nd Edition.* New York: John Wiley & Sons, Inc., 1986.

A professional's textbook on vegetable diseases. Each disease is covered by a detailed description of symptoms, cause, disease cycle, and control. Controls are not limited to organic methods.

■ Smith, Miranda and Ana Carr. *Rodale's Garden Insect, Disease & Weed Identification Guide.* Emmaus, Pa: Rodale Press, 1988.

An excellent field guide to insects and diseases, with ninety-seven photos for identification.

■ Steiner, M.Y. and D.P. Elliot. *Biological Pest Management For Interior Plantscapes, 2nd Edition.* Vegreville, AB. Alberta Environmental Centre, 1987.

A excellent short booklet on major greenhouse insects and their cultural, biological, and chemical control. Describes for each insect the damage, occurrence, appearance, and life history.

Useful Charts: (1) Minor Pest Problems and Their Control; (2) Summary of Primary Predators and Parasites of Major Plant Pests; (3) Reported Toxicity of Common Greenhouse Pesticides to Various Biological Control Agents; (4) Suppliers of Biological Control Agents.

■ Yepsen, Jr., Roger, editor. *The Encyclopedia of Natural Insect & Disease Control.* Emmaus, PA: Rodale Press, 1984.

An excellent reference covering major insects and diseases. Excellent color photos. Page numbers for the charts are given because of the potential difficulty of locating them.

Useful Charts: (1) Insect & Disease Resistant Vegetable Varieties, 346; (2) Insect Emergence Times, divided into 16 zones, 399.

Other books with information on Pest and Disease Control:

■ *Encyclopedia of Organic Gardening,* see under *General.*

■ Hirshberg, see under *General.*

■ Kourik, see under *General.*

■ Lorenz, see under *General.*

■ Raymond, both books, see under *General.*

Harvest and Storage

■ Bubel, Mike and Nancy. *Root Cellaring: Natural Cold Storage of Fruits and Vegetables.* Pownal, VT: Garden Way Publishing, 1991.

The only reference book we know on root cellars that is thoroughly researched by investigating what has and hasn't worked over the years. Many other books are pure theory; this one isn't. Many useful diagrams.

■ McClure, Susan. *The Harvest Gardener.* Pownal, VT: Garden Way Publishing, 1992.

A compilation of tips and advice by the author and several other gardeners about choosing cultivars, scheduling plantings, organizing garden space, coping with the vagaries of weather and pests, harvesting and storing the crop. Also includes an encyclopedia of culture, harvest, and storage of fruits,

herbs, and vegetables.

■ *Organic Gardening Harvest Book.* Emmaus, PA: Rodale Press, 1975.

A small, inexpensive booklet with good information on different methods of harvesting vegetables and fruits.

Useful Charts: (1) Guide for Drying Vegetables (Times and Temps); (2) Selection and Preparation of Vegetables for Freezing.

■ Stoner, Carol Hupping, editor. *Stocking Up: How To Preserve the Foods You Grow, Naturally.* Emmaus, PA: Rodale Press, 1977 and 1988.

An excellent guide to freezing, canning, drying, and other methods of saving the harvest.

Useful Charts: Timetable for Processing Fruits, Tomatoes, and Pickled Vegetables in Boiling-Water Bath.

Greenhouses

■ Ball, Vic, ed. *Ball Red Book: Greenhouse Growing, 14th edition.* Reston, VA: Prentice Hall, Reston Publishing Co., 1985.

A reference book on greenhouse structures, tools, methods, insect control, mechanization, and computerization. Half the book is devoted to greenhouse culture of flowers, shrubs, and a few vegetables. Essential for all commercial greenhouse growers.

■ Smith, Miranda. *Greenhouse Gardening.* Emmaus, PA: Rodale Press, 1985.

This book covers everything from greenhouse design, soils, fertilizers, insects and diseases, to vegetable varieties.

■ Wolfe, Delores. *Growing Food In Solar Greenhouses: A month by month guide to raising vegetables, fruits and herbs under glass.* Garden City, NJ: Doubleday & Company, Inc., 1981.

The monthly schedule covers such things as micro-climates, raising animals in the greenhouse, container growing, propagation, diseases, and insects. Fun and informative.

Other books on Greenhouses:

■ See Hamilton, under *General.*

■ See Hirshberg, under *General.*

■ See Steiner and Elliot, under *Insects and Diseases.*

Landscaping

■ Allen, Oliver E. *Gardening with the New Small Plants: A Complete Guide to Growing Dwarf and Miniature Shrubs, Flowers, Trees and Vegetables.* Boston, MA: Houghton Mifflin Co, 1987.

An excellent introduction to and discussion of small plants — whether in or out of rock gardens. The author suggests specific species and varieties of shrubs, flowers, trees and vegetables, as well as sources of availability.

■ Franklin, Stuart. *Building a Healthy Lawn: A Safe and Natural Approach.* Pownal, Vermont: Garden Way Publishing, 1988.

Written by a professional landscaper, this book offers clear directions for growing and maintaining a healthy lawn without the use of heavy chemicals. Includes chapters on mowing, watering, fertilizing, weed control, diseases, and insects, and a useful month-by-month guide to lawn care.

■ Leighton, Phebe and Calvin Simonds. *The New American Landscape Gardener: A Guide to Beautiful Backyards and Sensational Surroundings.* Emmaus, PA: Rodale Press, 1987.

The many charts of both edible and non-edible plants for different scapes makes this a helpful aide in landscaping. General design principles and design flaws are discussed in-depth. Very readable.

Useful Charts: (1) Plants For Meadows; (2) Plants For a Sunspot; (3) Plants For a Rock Garden; (4) Plants For a Winter Landscape; (5) Plants For a Water Garden; (6) Plants For a Wildlife Garden; (7) Plants For a Woodswalk.

■ Raymond, Dick. *Down-to-Earth Natural Lawn Care.* Pownal, Vermont: Storey Publishing, 1993.

A guide to installing and maintaining a healthy lawn using natural methods.

Useful Charts: (1) Types of Grasses; (2) Lawn Maintenance Schedules for All Areas of the Country.

■ Smyser, Carol A. *Nature's Design: A Practical Guide To Natural Landscaping.* Emmaus, PA: Rodale Press, 1982.

How to make a contour map, how to assess the impact of water on your property, how to analyze your soil, climate conditions, and natural plant and wildlife habitats. A very interesting and thought-provoking book, bursting with useful diagrams and pictures. A large section of the book is devoted to landscape construction, including how to find native plants, and propagation techniques.

Useful Charts: (1) How To Evaluate Your Landscape in Terms of Energy Efficiency and Environmental Impact; (2) Plant Selection Charts for 10 Ecoregions, listing the appropriate trees, shrubs, and forbs with their habitat, growth characteristics and any notable qualities; (3) Functional Uses of Plants; (4) Aesthetic Uses of Plants; (5) Landscape Pest Primer; (6) Plant Associations That Attract Wildlife, divided into regions; (7) Build A Better Birdhouse, includes all pertinent information that might be needed for 12 different birds; (8) A Gardener's Avian Friends, covering pests they eat and plants for food and shelter, broken down by region.

■ Wirth, Thomas. *Victory Garden Landscape Guide.* Little, Brown & Co., 1984.

A fun and useful month-by-month guide on landscaping. Wirth offers interesting and useful ideas and charts on everything concerning landscaping, from terraces and patios to fruit trees. He divides each month into four categories: (1) Landscaping Opportunities; (2) Plants For a Purpose; (3) Materials and Construction; (4) Plants By Design.

Other Books With Information on Landscaping:

■ Creasy, see under *General.*

■ *Encyclopedia of Organic Gardening,* see under *General.*

■ Kourik, see under *General.*

Index

Page references in italics refer to diagrams.

Gardening Notes

Gardening Notes

Gardening Notes

Gardening Notes

Gardening Notes